Dictionary of Quotations in Sociology

Dictionary of Quotations in Sociology

PANOS D. BARDIS

Greenwood Press
Westport, Connecticut • London, England

Library of Congress Cataloging in Publication Data

Bardis, Panos Demetrios.
Dictionary of quotations in sociology.

Bibliography: p.
Includes index.
1. Sociology—Dictionaries. 2. Sociology—Quotations, maxims, etc.—History—Sources.
3. Sociology—Bibliography. I. Title.
HM17.B37 1985 301′.03′21 85-943
ISBN 0-313-23778-6 (lib. bdg.)

Library of Congress Catalog Card Number: 85-943
ISBN: 0-313-23778-6

First published in 1985

Greenwood Press
A division of Congressional Information Service, Inc.
88 Post Road West
Westport, Connecticut 06881

Printed in the United States of America

10 9 8 7 6 5 4 3 2 1

Copyright Acknowledgments

To Donna Jean, Byron Galen, Jason Dante

CONTENTS

PREFACE

Let us assume that a man hears about Dante Alighieri and his *Divine Comedy* for the first time. He is so impressed that he is anxious to secure a copy of this immortal masterpiece and read it. Unfortunately, he finds none. This forces him to read books *about* Dante and thus enjoy at least the verses that their authors have quoted. But he soon realizes that each of these authors merely states that Dante was a sublime genius, without ever reproducing even one of his verses as an illustration, although he often quotes what other authors say *about* the Homer of Florence.

We can easily imagine this man's frustration.

Well, this is exactly how I often felt when, as a student, I read sociology books; for each author would compose long and almost dithyrambic encomia about an important concept introduced by a great and famous sociologist, but would not quote even a single sentence from the original. Quite frequently, however, I did find long quotations from other secondary sources that, again, said something *about* the same concept and its originator.

While working on the present dictionary, I soon realized that this situation has not changed. Indeed, the authors of introductory and even specialized volumes in sociology will often discuss a momentous concept from a well-known classic, define it in *their own words*, praise it enthusiastically, but never quote even a few words from the original. Once more, secondary sources dealing with the same concept are cited generously.

Also frustrating is a tendency to give exclusively, both in the text and in the bibliography, the year in which a classic was reprinted. Thus, the uninitiated could conclude, for instance, that Marx and Engels first published their *Communist Manifesto* in 1964.

Accordingly, one can imagine my enthusiasm when Greenwood Press suggested that I prepare a dictionary of quotations in sociology and related fields. How exciting, I thought, to hear famous, and even less famous, authors telling us about their own contributions, in their own words. And how revealing to know, not only *what* was said, and *how* it was said, but also *when* it was said.

Of course, we already have several valuable dictionaries in sociology, but these provide definitions rather than quotations. We also have a few useful anthologies. Of necessity, however, these include only a few authors, only a limited list of concepts, and extremely long passages—even entire articles or chapters.

Since sociology has often been accused of temporocentrism, it was decided to make the present reference volume somewhat sociohistorical. That approach enables the reader to explore the continuity prevailing in concepts, theories, and society. Thus, all quotations appear in chronological order under the appropriate entry heading, and except for those from the books of the Bible and a few other sources, they are followed by dates.

Another weakness of sociology, ethnocentrism, has been reduced in this book by emphasizing the crosscultural approach. Since sociology is the science of society, it should study all societies, both past and present. Accordingly, non-American cultures and authors have been included as frequently as possible. The value of such knowledge cannot be overstressed.

A more common intellectual sin nowadays is overspecialization. This explains why we have finally begun to pursue interdisciplinary research, although such pursuit is still rudimentary. For this reason, the present book contains, not only sociological quotations, but also related statements from other disciplines. Again, this approach can be quite productive.

In brief, then, the purpose of this book is to present the nature, origin, development, and current status of general sociological concepts through direct quotations. About 75 percent of these quotations come from modern sociology, the remaining 25 percent representing other social sciences, philosophy, religion, the belles-lettres, and so on. Both Oriental and Western authors are included, covering ancient, medieval, and modern times.

The process of selecting the general concepts to be covered in this dictionary was quite complex. Suffice it to say, the main sources consulted were as follows:

1. The tables of contents and indices of reference works in sociology and of basic textbooks in general sociology and all sociological subfields.

2. Sociological and related journals (but no quotations were taken from such sources; only books have been quoted in this dictionary).

3. Regional, national, and international sociological and related conferences, whose programs proved to be very useful.

My research indicated that sociological encyclopedias and dictionaries do not agree on terms, the relative importance of each concept, and so on. They also tend to be somewhat inconsistent within themselves. Thus, some subjectivity in my selection of topics was inevitable.

The quotations themselves derived from primary sources located in American and foreign libraries, as well as from book displays at various scientific conferences. My correspondence with scholars that I know in other countries, with new contacts made for the purpose of expanding this dictionary crossculturally, and with the sociology departments of more than 500 colleges and universities all over the world enabled me to secure additional sources.

The following explanations are also necessary:

1. Each entry heading represents a general concept. Quotations pertaining to

important subconcepts or subtopics appear under the relevant general heading. Alphabetization of the entry headings is according to the key word ("MARRIAGE, MIXED," not "MIXED MARRIAGE"), the number form always being the singular ("FOLKWAY," not "FOLKWAYS"; "MOS," not "MORES").

2. The author's name, if English, is limited to the first name or initial and the last name. Foreign names, however, are complete (Johann Christoph Friedrich von Schiller), although a few exceptions have been unavoidable. Moreover, when the authorship of a book is uncertain, the following explanations are given: "Plato, *Epinomis*, perhaps spurious," or "Plato, *Eryxias*, spurious"; but "Plato, *Republic*."

3. For the sake of readability and consistency, all book titles are given in English, with the exception of works that are well known by their original title such as *I Ching*, *Summa Theologica*, *Principia*, *Les Misérables*, and *Mein Kampf*.

4. To indicate origin, development, and continuity, whenever possible, the date of first publication is given. Posthumous publications are presented as such. For obvious reasons, no dates are included for the Bible, the Talmud, the Koran, and other such sources. Approximate dates are preceded by "c." (circa); "A.D." is always omitted, but not "B.C."

5. Perhaps the most difficult problem was the need to limit length—length of the list of entries, length of the list of authors, length of each entry, and length of each quotation. Needless to say, despite my constant and intense pursuit of objectivity and fairness, some degree of subjectivity was absolutely unavoidable. A few comments seem necessary at this point.

a. Going to an original source to select a quotation was preceded by careful examination of a concept's importance, timeliness, and the amount of empirical research dealing with it. The importance of the author and of his or her book was also taken into consideration. Still, countless authors, sources, and quotations that are as important as those included were ineluctably omitted—as were even additional brilliant statements found in the sources quoted. Once more, I apologize for such selectivity, but there is no perfect solution to such problems.

b. Since the emphasis has been on general concepts, "DIVORCE," "FAMILY," and "MARRIAGE" are included, but not "MATRIARCHY" or "PATRIARCHY"—family sociology alone, especially when multidisciplinary, encompasses thousands of terms and concepts.

c. Emphasis was also placed on ideas mentioned frequently in the relevant literature.

d. For obvious reasons, nonsociological quotations are usually brief and aphoristic.

Although quotations dealing with important sociological concepts are both interesting and useful, they provide only a beginning for those who want additional information regarding such concepts. Accordingly, I have included a carefully selected and rather complete and representative bibliography on the same concepts. Generally, these are not the sources that I consulted for quotations (a few exceptions include a general textbook in medical sociology, which I did quote, and which would also be useful to the reader who needs details about this field). The reader, if interested, can generally pursue those sources in the library. What I considered much more useful was a substantial bibliography—general and multidisciplinary—consisting of basic and historical sources that supplement the text. Thus, the supplementary bibliography should enable the reader who has read the original quotations on a given concept to secure additional information on its definition and history, on recent research dealing with it, and so on.

In closing, I would like to state that I would never have written this dictionary if I had not been encouraged by editors Cynthia Harris and Mary Sive of Greenwood Press, as well as by Don Martindale, who emphasized repeatedly the originality and importance of such a reference work. I am exceedingly grateful to all three.

I also appreciate the boundless support and understanding received from my wife Donna Jean and our sons Byron Galen and Jason Dante.

P.D.B.

Dictionary of Quotations in Sociology

A

ABORTION

"If men strive, and hurt a woman with child, so that her fruit depart from her, and yet no mischief follow: he shall be surely punished, according as the woman's husband will lay upon him; and he shall pay as the judges determine. And if any mischief follow, then thou shalt give life for life" (Exodus 21:22–23).

"I will not give a pessary to a woman to cause abortion" (Hippocrates, *Oath*, c. 400 B.C.).

"When the men and women have passed the age of legal reproduction . . . we must admonish them preferably not even to bring to light what is conceived in this way, but to dispose of it, if they cannot prevent the birth" (Plato, *Republic*, c. 400 B.C.).

"There should be a law forbidding the rearing of misshapen children . . . there should be a limit fixed to the production of children, and if, through coitus and despite these regulations, any people have a child, abortion must be procured before the child develops sensation and life; for the distinction between legal and criminal abortion will be based on having sensation and being alive" (Aristotle, *Politics*, c. 350 B.C.).

"For destroying the embryo . . . he must perform . . . penance" (*The Laws of Manu*, c. 200 B.C.).

"When a woman giving birth to a child is in danger, the unborn child may be cut to pieces and removed, for her life takes precedence over the life of the unborn child" (Talmud: Tents 7:6).

"No pretext can alter the fact that the whole circle of those concerned is in the strict sense engaged in the killing of human life. For the unborn child is from the very first a child. It is still developing and has no independent life. But it is a man and not a thing, nor a mere part of the mother's body" (Karl Barth, *Christian Dogmatics*, 1927).

"There are hundreds of working mothers [in Chile] who, because of anxiety about the inadequacy of their wages, induce abortion in order to prevent a new child from shrinking their already insignificant resources" (Salvador Allende, *The Medical-Social Reality of Chile*, 1939).

"[Among the Trukese, Caroline Islands, western Pacific] abortions are said to be performed by the mother of the girl, who presses on the girl's abdomen until the fetus is expelled" (Ann Fischer in Victor Christopherson, ed., *Readings in Comparative Marriage and the Family*, 1967).

"It might be said that in all essential respects the individual is whoever he is going to become from the moment of impregnation. . . . Subsequent development cannot be described as becoming something he is not now. It can only be described as a process of achieving, a process of becoming what he already is. Genetics teaches us that we were from the beginning what we essentially still are in every cell and in every generally human attribute and in every individual attribute" (Paul Ramsey in John Noonan, ed., *The Morality of Abortion*, 1970).

"The problems associated with abortion practices are complicated and interwoven . . . they are categorized under various headings—moral, legal, social, medical . . . all of them are basically moral problems" (John Rockefeller in Robert Hall, ed., *Abortion in a Changing World*, 1970).

"Abortion may be defined as the loss of a pregnancy before the fetus or fetuses are potentially capable of life independent of the mother. In most mammals this period extends roughly over the first two-thirds of the pregnancy. Loss subsequent to this is regarded as premature birth" (Malcolm Potts et al., *Abortion*, 1977).

"Abortion policy as a public question has produced unyielding positions at either extreme and ambivalence in the middle. The United States is far from any consensus on the ethical and theological issues involved in this complex and depressing problem. But since the Supreme Court's 1973 decision in *Roe v. Wade*, national abortion policy has been explicit, as have efforts to change it by several states and localities. The seemingly unending and fierce battle over abortion policy is either fought or reflected in each branch of the national government as well as in electoral campaigns" (Bruce MacLaury in Gilbert Steiner, ed., *The Abortion Dispute and the American System*, 1983).

ACCULTURATION

"[Acculturation is] the process by which one group of people learns from another, whether the culture or civilization be gotten by imitation or by inculcation" (Robert Park and Ernest Burgess, *Introduction to the Science of Sociology*, 1921).

"The term 'acculturation' is an ethnocentric term with a moral significance . . . by the preposition *ad* which begins it [it implies] the concept of *terminus ad quem*. The uncultured man must receive the benefits of our culture; it is he who must change, and be converted into one of us" (Bronislaw Malinowski in F. Ortiz, *Cuban Counterpoint of Tobacco and Sugar*, 1940).

"Acculturation comprises those changes produced in a culture by the influence of another culture which result in an increased similarity to the two. The influencing may be reciprocal or overwhelmingly one-way" (Alfred Kroeber, *Anthropology*, 1948).

''When a group or society is in contact with a more powerful society, the weaker group is often obliged to acquire cultural elements from the dominant group. The process of extensive borrowing in the context of superordinate-subordinate relations between societies is usually called *acculturation*'' (Carol and Melvin Ember, *Cultural Anthropology*, 1977).

''[Acculturation is] the process whereby a group assumes many of the major sociocultural characteristics of a different group with which it is in contact'' (Frank Vivelo, *Cultural Anthropology Handbook*, 1978).

''The acculturation of the famine Irish [in the United States] was seriously retarded because their sheer numbers were bound to disrupt the earlier, settled pattern of social relationships in their adopted communities. The Irish neighborhood groupings which developed out of necessity in shantytowns and city slums and which presented a glaring contrast with the culture of established Anglo-Americans, nevertheless came to provide social satisfactions that were hard to abandon'' (Marjorie Fallows, *Irish Americans*, 1979).

''[Acculturation is the] process by which people adopt traits of a culture not their own. The term is also used to refer to the results of this process'' (Melvin DeFleur, *Sociology*, 1981).

''Historically, ethnic awareness and ethnic enclaves in the United States were an acknowledged part of a group's distinct history and were viewed by the host culture as stepping-stones in the process of acculturation'' (Alice Scourby in Harry Psomiades and Alice Scourby, eds., *The Greek American Community in Transition*, 1982).

ACTION, SOCIAL

''Action which is transient, passing to some extrinsic thing, is really mediate between the agent and the subject receiving the action. The action which remains in the agent is not really a medium between the agent and its object, but only according to the manner of signification'' (Thomas Aquinas, *Summa Theologica*, 1273).

''Every one, I think, finds in himself a power to begin or forbear, continue or put an end to several actions in himself. From the consideration of the extent of this power of the mind over the actions of the man, which every one finds in himself, arise the ideas of liberty and necessity'' (John Locke, *Essay Concerning Human Understanding*, 1690).

''The application of the same term to the agencies on which human actions depend as is used to express those agencies of nature which are really uncontrollable . . . is a mere illusion. There are physical sequences which we call necessary . . . human actions are [never] ruled by any one such motive with such sway that there is no room for the influence of any other. The causes, therefore, on which action depends are never uncontrollable'' (John S. Mill, *A System of Logic*, 1843).

''Desire is the essential basis of all actions'' (Lester Ward, *Dynamic Sociology*, 1883).

''Activity in whatever form is the [attitude-value] bond. . . . It is these meanings [the definition of the situation] which determine the individual's behavior'' (William Thomas and Florian Znaniecki, *The Polish Peasant in Europe and America*, 1920).

''A motive does not exist prior to an act and produces it. It is an act *plus* a judgment upon some element of it, the judgment being made in the light of the consequences of the act'' (John Dewey, *Human Nature and Conduct*, 1922).

'' 'Classes' are not communities; they merely represent, and frequent, bases for social action . . . the direction of interests may vary according to whether or not social action of a larger or smaller portion of those commonly affected by the class situation . . . has grown out of the class situation, from which the individual may expect promising results for himself. The emergence of . . . mere social action from a common class situation is by no means a universal phenomenon . . . class situations emerge only on the basis of social action. However, social action that brings forth class situations is not basically action among members of the identical class; it is an action among members of different classes'' (Max Weber, *Economy and Society*, 1922, posthumously).

''Not every kind of action, even of overt action, is 'social.' . . . Overt action is non-social if it is oriented solely to the behavior of inanimate objects. Subjective attitudes constitute social action only so far as they are oriented to the behavior of others. For example, religious behavior is not social if it is simply a matter of contemplation or of solitary prayer. The economic activity of an individual is only social if, and then only in so far as, it takes account of the behavior of someone else. . . . Social action, which includes both failure to act and passive acquiescence, may be oriented to the past, present, or expected future behavior of others. Thus it may be motivated by revenge for a past attack, defense against present, or measures of defense against future aggression . . . mere 'imitation' of the action of others, such as that on which Tarde has rightly laid emphasis, will not be considered a case of specifically social action if it is purely reactive so that there is no meaningful orientation to the actor imitated. . . . A social action is not identical either with the similar actions of many persons or with action influenced by other persons. Thus, if at the beginning of a shower a number of people on the street put up their umbrellas at the same time, this would not ordinarily be a case of action mutually oriented to that of each other, but rather of all reacting in the same way to the like need of protection from the rain'' (Max Weber, *The Theory of Social and Economic Organization*, 1922, posthumously).

''Preliminary to any self-determined act of behavior there is always a stage of examination and deliberation which we may call the definition of the situation. And actually not only concrete acts are dependent on the definition of the situation, but gradually a whole life-policy and the personality of the individual himself follow from a series of such definitions'' (William Thomas, *The Unadjusted Girl*, 1923).

''Behavior, then, consists of a series of experiences which are distinguished from all other experiences by a primordial intentionality of spontaneous activity which remains the same in all intentional modifications . . . behavior is merely experiences looked at in a certain light, that is, referred back to the activity which originally produced them'' (Alfred Schutz, *The Phenomenology of the Social World*, 1932).

''Social actions are the simplest kind of social data: they constitute the background of mores and laws, of personal roles and of group organization; they may be said to be the stuff out of which all the more complex and elaborate social realities are made. Consequently, their study must precede other sociological studies and condition them. . . . Social actions . . . are actions which have as objects conscious beings, individually or collectively, and which purpose to influence those beings. While thus distinguishing social actions, we have intentionally neglected to define actions in general, relying on the popular understanding of the term. . . . The primary empirical evidence about any cultural human action is the experience of the agent himself, supplemented by the experience of those who react to his action, reproduce it, or participate in it. The action of speaking a sentence, writing a poem . . . as empirical datum, is what it is in the experience of the speaker and his listeners, the poet and his readers. . . . The scientist who wants to study these actions inductively must take them as they are in the human experience. . . . I have expressed this elsewhere by saying that such data possess for the student a *humanistic coefficient*. The humanistic coefficient distinguishes cultural data from natural data, which the student assumes to be independent of the experience of human agents'' (Florian Znaniecki, *Social Actions*, 1936).

''Actions must always be thought of as involving a state of tension between two different orders of elements, the normative and the conditional. . . . Elimination of the normative aspect of action altogether eliminates the concept of action itself. . . . Elimination of conditions, of the tension from that side, equally eliminates action and results in idealistic emanationism . . . 'utilitarian dilemma': . . . either the active agency of the actor in the choice of ends is an independent factor in action, and the end element must be random; or the objectionable implication of the randomness of ends is denied, but their independence disappears and they are assimilated to the conditions of the situation'' (Talcott Parsons, *The Structure of Social Action*, 1937).

''In the process of making a decision, some desire, some valuation, simple or complex, has become dominant for the time being, as a determinant of action within the individual's scheme of values, [which is] *his dynamic assessment of a situation*. . . . In all conscious behavior there is thus a twofold process of selective organization. On the one hand the value-system of the individual, his active cultural complex, his personality, is focussed in a particular direction, towards a particular objective. . . . On the other hand certain aspects of external reality are selectively related to the controlling valuation, are distinguished from the rest of the external world, are in a sense withdrawn from it, since they now become themselves value factors, the means, obstacles, or conditions relevant to the value quest'' (Robert MacIver, *Social Causation*, 1942).

''The five [cathectic-evaluative mechanisms] are reinforcement-extinction, inhibition, substitution, imitation and identification'' (Talcott Parsons, *The Social System*, 1951).

''One does not necessarily 'merely rationalize' behavior already enacted but acts because he has rationalized. The rationalization is his motive'' (Donald Cressey in Arnold Rose, *Human Behavior and Social Processes*, 1962).

''Action can be coerced, but a coerced show of feeling is only a show'' (Erving Goffman, *Asylums*, 1962).

''Social action theory treated social reality as consisting of particular interhuman acts. Comparable to the pluralistic behavioral insistence that interhuman behaviors have beliefs and desires at their core was the concern of social action theory with the meaningful dimensions of interhuman behavior. For social action theory, too, only individuals innovate, though they often do so in the name of the groups in which they operate'' (Don Martindale, *Social Life and Cultural Change*, 1962).

''Each term in a scientific model of human action must be constructed in such a way that a human act performed within the life-world by an individual actor in the way indicated by the typical construct would be understandable for the actor himself as well as for his fellow-men in terms of common-sense interpretation of everyday life'' (Alfred Schutz, *Collected Papers*, 1962, posthumously).

''The 'direction' of organized social action which sustains specific values conditions what constitutes a problem. The value-interest implications of a social structure are the guiding threads along which problems emerge. Problems are relative to an ethos'' (C. W. Mills in Irving Horowitz, ed., *Power, Politics and People*, 1963).

''The main task of the theoretical human sciences . . . consists in identifying the non-intentional social repercussions of intentional human actions'' (Karl Popper, *Conjectures and Refutations*, 1963).

''Most human pleasures have their roots in social life. Whether we think of love or power, professional recognition or sociable companionship, the comforts of family life or the challenge of competitive sports, the gratifications experienced by individuals are contingent on actions of others. . . . Much of human suffering as well as much of human happiness has its source in the actions of other human beings. One follows from the other, given the facts of group life, where pairs do not exist in complete isolation from other relations. The same human acts that cause pleasure to some typically cause displeasure to others'' (Peter Blau, *Exchange and Power in Social Life*, 1964).

''By 'cultural dope' I refer to the man-in-the-sociologist's-society who produces the stable features of the society by acting in compliance with pre-established and legitimate alternatives of action that the common culture provides'' (Harold Garfinkel, *Studies in Ethnomethodology*, 1967).

''Action is built up in coping with the world instead of merely being released from a pre-existing psychological structure by factors playing on that structure. By making indications to himself and by interpreting what he indicates, the human being has to forge to piece together a line of action. In order to act the individual has to identify what he wants, establish an objective or goal, map out a prospective line of behavior, note and interpret the actions of others, size up his situation, check himself at this or that point, figure out what to do at other points, and frequently spur himself on in the fact of dragging dispositions or discouraging settings'' (Herbert Blumer, *Symbolic Interactionism*, 1969).

''Parsons, however, does not speak of 'human nature' but instead moves toward more behavioristic distinctions between types of social action. Insofar as these entail *imputed* states of mind they are not, of course, any more behavioristic or 'empirical' than attributes of human nature'' (Alvin Gouldner, *The Coming Crisis of Western Sociology*, 1970).

''[Man possesses] some irreducible measure of freedom to act as he chooses'' (Ralf Dahrendorf, *Homo Sociologicus*, 1973).

''Max Weber had forged the tools he needed for his concrete research but . . . his main problem, understanding the subjective meaning a social action has for the actor, needed further philosophical foundation'' (Alfred Schutz in Don Ihde and Richard Zaner, eds., *Interdisciplinary Phenomenology*, 1977, posthumously).

''My reasons for being an indeterminist [do] not include . . . the intuitive idea of free will: as a rational argument in favor of indeterminism it is useless'' (Karl Popper, *The Open Universe*, 1982).

ADAPTATION

''Among the wild I am very wild, but among the righteous I am the most righteous of all men'' (Theognis, Fragment, c. 550 B.C.).

''The degree of adaptation of species to the climates under which they live is often overrated'' (Charles Darwin, *The Origin of Species*, 1859).

''[Adaptation is] the felicitous interference of two imitations, occurring first in one single mind'' (Gabriel Tarde, *Social Laws*, 1898).

''Another serious mistake which must be avoided in characterizing the practical organization of objects in actuality is stating the problem in terms of an ideal or real *adaptation* between the active being and the pre-existing reality. The conception of ideal adaptation is inherent in the current belief that the active subject consciously selects in advance, from among pre-existing objects, those which, by their nature as determined independently of the present activity, are apt in themselves to be the *means* for the realization of the *end* which, though set freely, must be set so as to be attainable with such means as reality puts at the subject's disposal'' (Florian Znaniecki, *Cultural Reality*, 1919).

''A process of active adaptation on the part of individuals and groups, carried on by the human brain as an active adaptive organ and by means of intercommunication among the members of human groups [leads to cultural evolution]'' (Charles Ellwood, *Cultural Evolution*, 1927).

''An adjustive effort of any kind is preceded by a decision to act or not act along a given line . . . [such decisions are preceded by a definition of the situation, namely] an interpretation or point of view, and eventually a policy and behavior pattern. . . . [Man's basic problem is] one of adjustment, and the forms of adjustive effort are 'behavior' '' (William Thomas, *Primitive Behavior*, 1937).

''We find five logically possible, alternative modes of adjustment or adaptation *by individuals* within the culture-bearing society or group. These are schematically presented in the following table, where (+) signifies 'acceptance,' (−) signifies 'elimination' and (±) signifies 'rejection and substitution of new goals and standards.'

		Culture Goals	**Institutionalized Means**
I.	Conformity	+	+
II.	Innovation	+	−
III.	Ritualism	−	+
IV.	Retreatism	−	−
V.	Rebellion	±	±''

(Robert Merton, ''Social Structure and Anomie,'' 1938, in Robert Brown, ed., *Mental Hygiene*, 1969).

''[The region is] a complex pattern of adaptations between the environmental factors and the plant and animal communities including human societies'' (Radhakamal Mukerjee, *The Regional Balance of Man*, 1938).

''[The modes of adaptation are] conformity . . . innovation . . . ritualism . . . retreatism . . . rebellion'' (Robert Merton, *Social Theory and Social Structure*, 1957).

''Every culture is a special case of the adaptive process, of the complex ways in which people make effective use of their energy potentials. . . . Every culture can be conceptualized as a strategy of adaptation, and each represents a unique social design for extracting energy from the habitat. Every energy system requires appropriate organization of social relations; no energy system can be effective in human society without groups that are designed for using it'' (Y. Cohen, *Man in Adaptation*, 1968).

''All organisms live and must adapt to a 'temporally programmed world' '' (Eliot Chapple, *Culture and Biological Man*, 1970).

''The societal form of organization is a mode of adaptation whereby certain types of organisms have increased their chance of surviving and multiplying'' (Gerhard Lenski, *Human Societies*, 1970).

''First steps toward culture provided a new environment in which some individuals were more fit, in the Darwinian sense, than others; their offspring were better adapted to culture and capable of further innovations; and so on. The argument can be made that, far from removing mankind from the process of evolution, culture has provided the most salient natural selection pressure to which man has been subject in his recent evolutionary past'' (G. McClearn in L. Ehrman et al., eds., *Genetics, Environment, and Behavior*, 1972).

''A peculiar irony accompanied the evolution of human beings . . . their system of biological, preprogrammed (in older terminology, instinctive) responses weakened as their individual intelligence and adaptability increased'' (Don Martindale, *The Nature and Types of Sociological Theory*, 1981).

''An adaptation can be considered as any characteristic of an organism that increases its fitness'' (David Barash, *Sociobiology and Behavior*, 1982).

''The essence of man's history on earth and in the sky is the sequence of our combined adaptations to climate and to culture'' (Carleton Coon, *Racial Adaptations*, 1982).

ADOLESCENCE

''There are three things which the superior man guards against. In youth, when the physical powers are not yet settled, he guards against lust'' (Confucius, *Analects*, c. 500 B.C.).

''Good youths often seem simple, and are easily victimized by evil people'' (Plato, *Republic*, c. 400 B.C.).

''The friendship of young people is based on pleasure, since they live by emotion and tend to pursue what is especially pleasant to them at the present time'' (Aristotle, *Nicomachean Ethics*, c. 350 B.C.).

''Youth is hot and bold, age is weak and cold'' (William Shakespeare, *The Passionate Pilgrim*, 1599).

''Only time can cure a person of childhood and youth, which are truly ages of imperfection in every respect'' (Baltasar Gracián y Morales, *The Discreet One*, 1646).

''When one is young, one venerates and despises without that art of nuances which constitutes the best gain of life'' (Friedrich Wilhelm Nietzsche, *Beyond Good and Evil*, 1886).

''All the eligible [Tswana] boys were initiated simultaneously in groups . . . the boys were first circumcized in order of tribal precedence. They were then systematically taught a number of secret formulae and songs, admonishing them to honour, obey, and support the Chief; to be ready to endure hardships and even death for the sake of the tribe . . . to value cattle as the principal source of livelihood . . . to honour and ungrudgingly obey old people; and to abandon all boyish practices. Much of this instruction dealt also with the important topic of sex, the boys being taught the physiology of sex relations, the duty of procreation and other rules of conduct in married life, and the dangers of promiscuous intercourse with ritually 'unclean' women. They were further taught tribal traditions and religious beliefs . . . subjected to starvation and blows, discomfort and actual torture . . . all with the object of hardening them'' (I. Schapera, *A Handbook of Tswana Law and Custom*, 1938).

''[Youth] makes the only proper bridge between the bourgeois and the state of nature; it is a pre-bourgeois state from which all student romance derives, that truly romantic period of life'' (Thomas Mann, *Doctor Faustus*, 1947).

''With the establishment of a good initial relationship to the world of skills and tools, and with the advent of puberty, childhood proper comes to an end. Youth begins. But in puberty and adolescence all samenesses and continuities relied on earlier are more or less questioned again, because of a rapidity of body growth which equals that of early childhood and because of the new addition of genital maturity'' (Erik Erikson, *Childhood and Society*, 1950).

''For boys, not only is the athletic star's image more attractive at the beginning of the school year; the boys move even slightly further in that direction—at the expense of the popularity image—over the period of the school year. The girls are somewhat similar: at the beginning of the school year, the activities leader and most popular are about equally attractive images, both more often mentioned than the brilliant student. By spring, the activities leader image has gained slightly in attractiveness, at the expense of both the brilliant student and the most popular . . . the image of athletic star is most attractive for boys; the images of activities leader and most popular are more attractive to girls than brilliant student'' (James Coleman, *The Adolescent Society*, 1961).

''[In England] the picture which adults had of teenagers was widely different from the picture that adolescents had of themselves. The adults' picture was overwhelmingly negative, with scarcely any reference to teenagers' increasing social and technical competence. . . . Although in some respects this study suggests important differences from American conditions, it is in line with those American investigations which have shown adolescents belittled by their elders'' (F. Musgrove, *Youth and the Social Order*, 1964).

''He [adolescent with poor self-image] is more vulnerable in interpersonal relations (deeply hurt by criticism, blame, or scolding); he is relatively awkward with others (finds it hard to make talk, does not initiate contacts, etc.); he assumes others think poorly of him or do not particularly like him; he has low faith in human nature; he tends to put up a 'front' to people; and he feels relatively isolated and lonely'' (Morris Rosenberg, *Society and the Adolescent Self-Image*, 1965).

''The emergence of distinct youth cultures is related to the emergence of industrialization'' (David Gottlieb et al., *The Emergence of Youth Societies*, 1966).

''When maturing in his physical capacity for procreation, the human youth is as yet unable either to love in that binding manner which only two persons with reasonably formed identities can offer each other, or to care consistently enough to sustain parenthood'' (Erik Erikson, *Identity*, 1968).

''After the age of eleven or twelve, nascent formal thought restructures the concrete operations by subordinating them to new structures whose development will continue throughout adolescence and all later life'' (Jean Piaget and B. Inhelder, *The Psychology of the Child*, 1969).

''Compared to their predecessors in 1800 or 1900, young people in the 1970s spend much more time in school, much less at work. They are essentially consumers rather than producers'' (Joseph Kett, *Rites of Passage*, 1977).

''Our age has exploded with youthful unrest. This may well be the distinguishing mark that future historians of Western civilization will assign to the last decades of the twentieth century'' (Hans Sebald, *Adolescence*, 1977).

''Treating mental disorders in . . . adolescence serves a dual purpose. Its main aim is to alleviate the suffering of . . . adolescents and help them to overcome their handicaps and shortcomings, thus enabling them to lead a normal life. The second task is of preventive nature'' (Benjamin Wolman, ed., *Handbook of Treatment of Mental Disorders in Childhood and Adolescence*, 1978).

''American children far from becoming overly dependent on their mothers, form strong attachments to neither parent. . . . Adolescence, formerly the tumultuous transition from childhood dependence to the responsibilities of adulthood, has become almost obsolete'' (Christopher Lasch, *Haven in a Heartless World*, 1979).

''Adolescence is intimately linked to matters historical: the evolution of social age categories, the emergence of youth-related institutions, the impact of social change in lives'' (Glen Elder in Joseph Adelson, ed., *Handbook of Adolescent Psychology*, 1980).

ADOPTION

''And the child grew, and she brought him unto Pharaoh's daughter, and he became her son. And she called his name Moses'' (Exodus 2: 10).

''If a citizen wishes to adopt a son who is put away, no law shall prevent him'' (Plato, *Laws*, c. 400 B.C.).

''An adopted son shall never take the family name and the estate of his natural father'' (*The Laws of Manu*, c. 200 B.C.).

''[In adopting an illegitimate child] instead of considering objectively what is best for the child and for the mother, workers of all kinds have too often been influenced by punitive and sentimental attitudes towards the errant mother. At one time the punitive attitude took the form of removing the baby from the mother as a punishment for her sins. Nowadays this punitive attitude seems to lead in the opposite direction and to insist that she should take full responsibility for caring for what she has so irresponsibly produced'' (John Bowlby, *Maternal Care and Child Health*, 1952).

''[In the Islamic family] a marriage between an adoptive parent and an adopted child is legal, though such unions are frowned upon in most areas'' (Arthur Jeffery in Ruth Anshen, ed., *The Family*, 1959).

''The Trukese [Caroline Islands, western Pacific] say that the use of a woman is to bear children. If she cannot bear them herself, she may enhance her status somewhat by adopting a child or by assisting substantially in the care of someone else's child.'' (Ann Fisher in Victor Christopherson, ed., *Readings in Comparative Marriage and the Family*, 1967).

''Adoptive parents will encounter many pitfalls as they rear their child. . . . An increasing number of adoptive parents are those who have had natural children who are all of the same sex. Rather than take a chance of having a child of the same sex, they adopt a child of the opposite sex. . . . A rarer breed of adopting parents are single people. They are usually women, and even though this practice has been legally permitted for many years, only in recent years has it actually been done. . . . Many unwed mothers who give their child up for adoption . . . go through a great deal of emotional turmoil'' (Joseph Ansfield, *The Adopted Child*, 1971).

''Adoptees in their hundreds stress over and over again that the desire to know their mother and discover the truth about their origins is a perfectly normal human need and is, in fact, a basic human right which has hitherto been denied them. This need to know is not a passing fad. It is not a rebellious teenager's defiance or attempt to 'get back at' adoptive parents. It is a lifelong need. . . . To be curious about one's biological mother and father is perfectly natural and in no way implies criticism of, or ingratitude to, adoptive parents'' (Angela Hamblin, ed., *The Other Side of Adoption*, 1977).

''There is a broad range of feelings and attitudes among adoptees—depending on the temperament and personal situation of each child and family. . . . Adoption is certainly more openly acknowledged and discussed today than in the past. Most children now know they're adopted, whereas fifty years ago many were not told. However, many adoptees still have little information about their birthparents, and exactly how much adoptees should know about their backgrounds is a major issue'' (Jill Krementz, *How It Feels to Be Adopted*, 1982).

ALIENATION

''The loss or sacrifice of . . . private property signifies the *alienation of the man* as much as of the *property* itself. . . . If I cede my private property to another it ceases to be mine; it becomes independent of me, something outside my domain, something external to me. I thus externalize, alienate my private property. I defined it as *alienated* private property so far as I myself am concerned. But I only define it as something *alienated* in general; I renounce only my *personal* connection with it, I return it to the *elemental* powers of nature when I alienate it only from myself . . . if the product of labor is alienation, production itself must be active alienation, the alienation of activity, the activity of alienation. The estrangement of the object of labor merely summarizes the estrangement, the alienation in the activity of labor itself. . . . [Man] does not fulfill himself in his work but denies himself, has a feeling of misery rather than well-being, does not develop freely his spiritual and physical powers but is physically exhausted and spiritually debased'' (Karl Marx, *Early Writings*, 1844).

''Hegel grasps the self-creation of man as a process, objectification as loss of the object, as alienation and transcendence of this alienation. . . . Hegel's standpoint is that of modern political economy. He conceives *labour* as the *essence*, the self-confirming essence of man; he observes only the positive side of labour, not its negative side. Labour is *man's coming to be for himself* within *alienation*, or as an *alienated* man . . . the object produced by labour, its product, now stands opposed to it as an *alien being*, as a *power independent* of the producer. The product of labour is labour which has been embodied in an object and turned into a physical thing; this product is an *objectification* of labour. The performance of work is at the same time its objectification. The performance of work appears in the sphere of political economy as a *vitiation* of the worker, objectification as a *loss* and as *servitude to the object*, and appropriation as *alienation*. So much does the performance of work appear as vitiation that the worker is vitiated to the point of starvation. . . . The alienation of the worker in his object is expressed as follows in the laws of political economy: the more the worker produces the less he has to consume; the more value he creates the more worthless he becomes; the more refined his product the more crude and misshapen the worker; the more civilized the product the more barbarous the worker; the more powerful the work the more feeble the worker; the more the work manifests intelligence the more the worker declines in intelligence and becomes a slave of nature . . . the relationship of the worker to his own activity as something alien and not belonging to him, activity as suffering (passivity), strength as powerlessness, creation as emasculation, the *personal* physical and mental energy of the worker, his personal life (for what is life but activity?), as an activity which is directed against himself, independent of him and not belonging to him. This is *self-alienation*. . . . Human alienation, and above all the relation of man to himself, is first realized and expressed in the relationship between each man and other men. . . . Every self-alienation of man, from himself and from nature, appears in the relation which he postulates between other men and himself and nature'' (Karl Marx, *Economic and Philosophic Manuscripts*, 1844).

''When Dasein, tranquillized, and 'understanding' everything, thus compares itself with everything, it drifts along towards an *Entfremdung* [alienation] in which its ownmost potentiality-for-Being is hidden from it. Falling Being-in-the-world is not only tempting and tranquillizing; it is at the same time *alienating*. Yet this alienation cannot mean that Dasein gets factically torn away from itself. On the contrary, this alienation drives it into a kind of Being which borders on the most exaggerated 'self-dissection,' tempting itself with all possibilities of explanation, so that the very 'characterologies' and 'typologies' which it has brought about are themselves already becoming something that cannot be surveyed at a glance. This alienation *closes off* from Dasein its authenticity and possibility, even if only the possibility of genuinely foundering'' (Martin Heidegger, *Being and Time*, 1927).

''He who regards his own life and that of his fellow-creatures as meaningless is not only unfortunate but almost disqualified for life'' (Albert Einstein, *The World as I See It*, 1934).

''The For-itself is like a tiny nihilation which has its origin at the heart of Being; and this nihilation is sufficient to cause a total upheaval to happen to the In-itself. This upheaval is the world . . . for the For-itself there appears a new danger, a threatening mode of being which must be avoided, a concrete category which it will discover everywhere. The slimy . . . manifests a certain relation of being with itself and this relation has originally a psychic quality because I have discovered it in a plan of appropriation and because the sliminess has returned my image to me. . . . For Leibniz we are free since our acts derive from our essence. Yet the single fact that our essence has not been chosen by us shows that all this freedom in particulars actually covers over a total slavery. God chose Adam's essence. Conversely if it is the closing of the account which gives our life its meaning and its value, then it is of little importance that all the acts of which the web of our life is made have been free; the very meaning of them escapes us if we do not ourselves choose the moment at which the account will be closed. . . . Two brothers appeared at the divine tribunal on the Day of Judgment. The first said to God, 'Why did you make me die so young?' And God said, 'In order to save you. If you had lived longer, you would have committed a crime as your brother did.' Then the brother in turn asked, 'Why did you make me die so old?' . . . the meaning of my life escapes me'' (Jean-Paul Sartre, *Being and Nothingness*, 1943).

''The very same society that produces this sense of alienation and estrangement generates in many a craving for reassurance, an acute need to believe, a flight into faith'' (Robert Merton, *Mass Persuasion*, 1946).

''We are also reproached for leaving out of account the solidarity of mankind and considering man in isolation. And this, say the Communists, is because we base our doctrine upon pure subjectivity—upon the Cartesian 'I think': which is the moment in which solitary man attains to himself; a position from which it is impossible to regain solidarity with other men who exist outside of the self. The *ego* cannot reach them through the *cogito*. . . . The existentialist frankly states that man is in anguish. . . . There are many, indeed, who show no such anxiety. But we affirm that they are merely disguising their anguish or are in flight from it. . . . And when we speak of 'abandonment'—a favorite word of Heidegger—we only mean to say that God does not exist, and that it is necessary to draw the consequences of his absence right to the end. . . . Dostoievsky once wrote 'if God did not exist, everything would be permitted'; and that, for existentialism, is the starting point. Everything is indeed permitted if God does not exist, and man is in consequence forlorn, for he cannot find anything to depend upon either within or outside himself'' (Jean-Paul Sartre, *Existentialism and Humanism*, 1946).

''Men are estranged from one another as each secretly tries to make an instrument of the other, and in time a full circle is made: One makes an instrument of himself and is estranged from it also'' (C. W. Mills, *White Collar*, 1951).

"The facts to which the term alienation refers are objectively the different kinds of disassociation, break, or rupture between human beings and their objects, whether the latter be other persons, or the natural world, or their own creations of art, science, and society; and subjectively the corresponding states of disequilibrium, disturbance, strangeness, and anxiety" (F. Heinemann, *Existentialism and the Modern Predicament*, 1953).

"In all the social sciences, the various synonyms of alienation have a foremost place in studies of human relations. Investigations of the 'unattached,' the 'marginal,' the 'obsessive,' the 'normless,' and the 'isolated' individual all testify to the central place occupied by the hypothesis of alienation in contemporary social science" (Robert Nisbet, *The Quest for Community*, 1953).

"The neurotic person is an alienated person. His actions are not his own; while he is under the illusion of doing what *he* wants, he is driven by forces which are separated from his self, which work behind his back; he is a stranger to himself, just as his fellow man is a stranger to him. . . . The insane person is the *absolutely alienated* person. He has completely lost himself as the center of his own experience; he has lost the sense of self. . . . By alienation is meant a mode of experience in which the person experiences himself as an alien. He has become, one might say, estranged from himself" (Erich Fromm, *The Sane Society*, 1955).

"The history of man could well be written as a history of the alienation of man" (Erich Kahler, *The Tower and the Abyss*, 1957).

"Alienation exists when workers are unable to control their immediate work processes, to develop a sense of purpose and function which connects their jobs to the overall organization of production, to belong to integrated industrial communities, and when they fail to become involved in the activity of work as a mode of personal self-expression" (Robert Blauner, *Alienation and Freedom*, 1964).

"The constant exercise of impersonal labor has resulted in the total depersonalization of the laborer. He has been shaped by his work, used by it, mechanized, and assimilated" (Jacques Ellul, *The Technological Society*, 1964).

"The [Korean] student, in particular, becomes exposed to the modern world and to the advanced nations of the West. In his mind two great gaps exist, one between the principles of modernity—equality, justice, community, economic well-being—and their realization in his own society, and a second between the actual conditions which exist in the advanced nations of the world and those prevailing in his own society. . . . The student thus becomes ashamed and alienated from his own society" (Samuel Huntington, *Political Order in Changing Societies*, 1968).

"Virtually everything about American cities today . . . drives men apart, alienating them from each other. The recent and shocking instances in which people have been beaten and even murdered while their neighbors looked on without even picking up the phone indicates how far this trend toward alienation has progressed" (Edward Hull, *The Hidden Dimension*, 1969).

''New productive processes and equipment inevitably affect *the network of social relations* among workers engaged in production. . . . Management may thus nourish *the job insecurities and anxieties of workers*'' (Robert Merton in Simon Marcson, ed., *Automation, Alienation, and Anomie*, 1970).

''Obscenity is traditionally among the armoury of weapons employed by the alienated'' (Richard Neville, *Play Power*, 1970).

''In conceiving of . . . alienation in terms of a separation *through surrender to another*, however, Marx obscures its basic character, and encounters problems of both over- and under-inclusiveness. It would seem more fruitful to drop all reference to the mediation of an 'alien will' in the explication of the concept of such alienation itself, and to focus solely upon the relation of labor to the individual. It might of course turn out to be the case that this alienation very frequently *does* involve the surrender of labor to the direction of another man; but this would be a factual correlation rather than a matter of definition'' (R. Schacht, *Alienation*, 1971).

''Any reification of men's objects, and transcendence of men's products over men so that they do not see their interests, powers, and abilities affirmed and expressed therein, is evidence of the alienation of man from his self-activity, his objects, and himself. The whole notion of social alienation presupposes this immanent conception of human nature. Alienation is an historical state which will ultimately be overcome as man approaches freedom'' (John Horton in John Glass and John Staude, eds., *Humanistic Society*, 1972).

''Alienation consists of an inability to participate in collective decisions. . . . Alienation from a coherent structure of values makes collective action difficult'' (Benjamin Zablocki, *Alienation and Charisma*, 1980).

''[The alienated are] politically suspicious, resentful, disillusioned; given the right chance, they will translate their feelings into actions, and sometimes violent ones'' (Paul Sniderman, *A Question of Loyalty*, 1981).

''The first factor [that influences alienation] is found in the realization that to be alienated from something presupposes the existence of an opposite state of nonalienation. . . . The second factor . . . is that it [alienation] implies the presence of a potential dialogue between the individual and the context from which he is alienated. . . . A third factor that influences alienation is the nature and level of the individual's awareness of this particular context'' (Brian Baxter, *Alienation and Authenticity*, 1982).

ANOMIE

''[Anomie is] a situation in which the social norms regulating individual conduct have broken down or are no longer effective as rules for behavior. . . . The state of *anomie* is impossible wherever solidary organs are sufficiently in contact or sufficiently prolonged'' (Émile Durkheim, *The Division of Labor in Society*, 1893).

''[Anomie is] a social disorder . . . in which common values have been submerged in the welter of private interests seeking satisfaction by virtually any means which are effective. Drawn from a highly competitive, segmented urban society, our informants live in a climate of reciprocal distrust which, to say the least, is not conducive to stable human relationships'' (Robert Merton, *Mass Persuasion*, 1946).

''Whatever the sentiments of the reader concerning the moral desirability of coordinating the goals-and-means phases of the social structure, it is clear that imperfect coordination of the two leads to anomie. Insofar as one of the most general functions of the social structure is to provide a basis for predictability and regularity of social behavior, it becomes increasingly limited in effectiveness as these elements of the social structure become dissociated'' (Robert Merton, *Social Theory and Social Structure*, 1949).

''[Anomie is manifested in] the retreat of the individual into his own ego, the skeptical rejection of all social bonds. . . . It signifies the state of mind of one who has been pulled up from his moral roots, who no longer has any standards but only disconnected urges, who no longer has any sense of continuity, of folk, of obligations'' (Robert MacIver, *The Ramparts We Guard*, 1950).

''The nature of the value system determines the form anomie takes''(Ephraim Mizruchi, *Success and Opportunity*, 1964).

''[Anomie is] conflict of socially accepted norms in an individual'' (Robert Nisbet, *The Social Bond*, 1970).

''An *anomic* or *normless* situation [is one] in which people disagree on the rules, or refuse to accept the official rules, or evade the rules'' (R. Denisoff and Ralph Wahrman, *An Introduction to Sociology*, 1979).

ANTHROPOLOGY

''Whoever considers the past and the present will readily observe that all cities and all peoples are and ever have been animated by the same desires and the same passions'' (Niccolò Machiavelli, *Commentary*, 1519).

''The people of the South are of a contrary humor and disposition to them of the North: these are great and strong, they are little and weak'' (Jean Bodin, *The Six Books of the Republic*, 1576).

''For of many colors are the species of men, and the black race of the Ethiopians, and the yellow offspring of America . . . one species flourishes in one place, another in another'' (Giordano Bruno, *On the Immense and Innumerable*, 1590).

''The agreement of so many genera of animals in a certain common schema, which appears to be fundamental not only in the structure of their bones, but also in the disposition of their remaining parts—so that with an admirable simplicity of original outline, a great variety of species has been produced by the shortening of one member and the lengthening of another, the involution of this part and the evolution of that—allows a ray of hope, however faint, to penetrate into our minds, that here something may be accomplished by the aid of the principle of the mechanism of nature (without which there can be no natural science in general). This analogy of forms, which with all their differences seem to have been produced according to a common original type, strengthens our suspicions of an actual relationship between them in their production from a common parent, through the gradual approximation of one animal-genus to another—from those in which the principle of purposes seems to be best authenticated, that is, from man, down to the polype, and again from this down to mosses and lichens, and finally to the lowest stage of nature noticeable by us'' (Immanuel Kant, *Critique of Judgment*, 1790).

''A state of Peace among men who live side by side with each other, is not the natural state. The state of nature is rather a state of War; for although it may not always present the outbreak of hostilities, it is nevertheless continually threatened with them. The state of Peace must, therefore, be established; for the mere cessation of hostilities furnished no security against their recurrence'' (Immanuel Kant, *Perpetual Peace*, 1795).

''Biological theory finds 'facts and reasons' to justify this primary variation of the hierarchy of values. . . . Yet biological theory reduces them all to the criterion of utility. . . . These biological views, whose fundamental falsity cannot be demonstrated here, are also applied to the problem of the origin of *civilization* and *culture*. Here again, considerations of utility are supposed to have brought about the formation of tools, science, the origin of language, and the development of art and religion. Thus the practice of life is closely connected with theory. The theory seems to justify the practice, but in reality it is determined by the same shift in values. This view of life has more or less conquered the civilized world and has come to be dominant chiefly in England'' (Max Scheler, *Ressentiment*, 1912).

''All positive investigations into the origins of man in a biological sense—the morphological and physiological comparisons of races in connection with the comparison of races and primates, as well as paleontology—vacillate between the polyphyletic hypothesis on the one hand, i.e., the theory that man does *not* represent a *closed unity* of consanguinity, and the monophyletic theory on the other. Thus the unity of the definition of man as a biological species is itself questionable. And hence there is less justification for the ethical presupposition of a unitary moral disposition in 'man' (when this concept is taken naturalistically)'' (Max Scheler, *Formalism in Ethics and Non-Formal Ethics of Values*, 1916).

''Those uniform manners and institutions, those spiritual currents which we call *culture* certainly do not follow unerringly the path of political forms and institutions. From these they frequently part company and go their separate way—often they take the opposite path, as happened when Rome, having conquered Greece politically, was Hellenized in the process'' (Max Scheler, *The Reconstruction of European Culture*, 1917).

''Because every species, including the human species as a whole, is subject, according to the insights of modern biology, to birth, aging, and death (natural death of a species), it is becoming impossible to ignore the fact that mankind, within its natural life-span, has reached an age where only a *fundamental overturning of its ethos* promises prosperous development and potential progress—as measured by the eternal hierarchy of values'' (Max Scheler, *Problems of a Sociology of Knowledge*, 1924).

''It would be the task of a philosophical anthropology to show in detail how all the specific achievements and works of man—language, conscience, tools, weapons, ideas of right and wrong, the state, leadership, the representational function of art, myths, religion, science, history and social life—arise from the basic structure of the human nature. . . . As soon as man has separated himself from the rest of nature and looks upon nature as an 'object'—this belongs to his essence and constitutes the very act of becoming man—he must, then, turn around with a sense of awe and ask: 'Where do I stand? What is my place in the universe?' '' (Max Scheler, *Man's Place in Nature*, 1927).

''It [the term 'pre-literate'] is neutral, connoting no reflection of inferiority'' (Ellsworth Faris, *The Nature of Human Nature*, 1937).

''In practice, anthropology is mostly classified as being both a biological science and a social science'' (Alfred Kroeber, *Anthropology* 1948).

''The history of culture probably knows only two truly decisive watersheds: the prehistoric transition from a hunting to a settled culture, and the modern transition to industrialism. In both cases we are confronted with a total intellectual and moral revolution. The transition from hunting to cattle raising and agriculture must have required many centuries, and the associated stresses must have been of the greatest magnitude. For it by no means involved only a transformation of economic life, but rather a total restructuring of all attitudes, a restructuring that left nothing unaffected. . . . Fast-growing agrarian societies become dependent upon atmospheric, climatic, and vegetative elements whose laws they have not yet mastered; and this chronic and unavoidable dependency reaches into the very core of the sense of existence. . . . In our social capacities we often act 'schematically,' that is, we enact habitualized, well-worn behavior patterns which unfold 'by themselves.' . . . The common view that mass culture threatens the personality is only half correct . . . there has never been in the world as much differentiated and articulated *subjectivity* as today. Evidence for this is offered for instance by the contemporary arts as a whole; by the public's inexhaustible willingness to lend benevolent attention to the most extravagant displays of subjectivity'' (Arnold Gehlen, *Man in the Age of Technology*, 1957).

''[Physical anthropology consists] of human paleontology and human biology. Two factors have contributed to the development of human paleontology. One is inductive—the finding of hominid fossils. The other is deductive, based upon a consideration of the relation between man and other organisms'' (J. Slotkin, *Readings in Early Anthropology*, 1965).

''[The six regions and the number of clusters of societies are] Africa 85, Circum-Mediterranean 55, East Eurasia 66, Insular Pacific 70, North America 69, South America 67'' (George Murdock, *Ethnographic Atlas*, 1967).

''Even though projective techniques continue to be used in cross-cultural research, they no longer exercise the dominance over psychological anthropology that they once did. There are many reasons for their loss of popularity. Their dubious validity is but one, their expense to administer is another, and their association with theories of 'depth' psychology is yet another. Still another, perhaps equally important reason, is that most of the projectives have been associated with the study of typical personality, and psychological anthropology is no longer centrally concerned with typical personality. Other interests, and thus other methods, have grown up alongside the projectives, and have begun to take over center stage'' (R. Edgerton in R. Naroll and R. Cohen, eds., *A Handbook of Method in Cultural Anthropology*, 1970).

''This history of anthropology is the history of ideas about man—his physical and cultural origins, development, and nature. Men have always provided themselves with anthropological ideas. Thus in the broadest sense the study of the history of anthropology embraces the anthropologies of all peoples, past and present'' (Gerald Broce, *History of Anthropology*, 1973).

''Anthropology is a product of scientific developments that took place in the Western world. . . . The Greeks and Romans may be said to have laid the foundations for anthropology as they did for ethics, aesthetics, metaphysics, logic, history, and other intellectual pursuits'' (Fred Voget in John Honigmann, ed., *Handbook of Social and Cultural Anthropology*, 1973).

''Anthropologists not only study all varieties of people, they also study many aspects of human experience'' (Carol and Melvin Ember, *Cultural Anthropology*, 1977).

''The two major characteristics of anthropology are that it is *comparative* and *holistic*. . . . It attempts to see human beings in the broad view, not just in isolated societies. . . . The other major characteristic . . . is the insistence that societies be treated as wholes, as functional units, or—in the terms of cybernetics—as systems'' (Frank Vivelo, *Cultural Anthropology Handbook*, 1978).

''Anthropology . . . accepts the human being as the product of about four million years of evolution as a hominid who lives in organized social groups in accordance with biologically *and* culturally determined modes of behavior'' (E. Hoebel and Thomas Weaver, *Anthropology and the Human Experience*, 1979).

''Paleoanthropology has the paradoxical distinction of being both a very new scientific discipline and a rather old one. Its roots extend into the mid-nineteenth century when anatomists, medical doctors, and 'natural historians,' stimulated by the discovery of 'Neanderthal man' in 1856, were first confronting the implications of extinct human types'' (G. Kennedy, *Paleoanthropology*, 1980).

''It is difficult to decide where, from a pedagogical standpoint, to begin an account of what today might be considered to be social anthropological thought. One can go back to Plato and Aristotle, or yet further back; and I used to give a course of lectures of Ibn Khaldun'' (Edward Evans-Pritchard, *A History of Anthropological Thought*, 1981).

''The peoples of the world can be conveniently divided into six large geographical regions which cover approximately equal areas and contain comparable numbers of distinct peoples and cultures'' (George Murdock, *Atlas of World Cultures*, 1981).

''Anthropology . . . is a *holistic* science with the entire gamut of humankind as the focus of study. Other disciplines that deal with people—sociology, psychology, economics, political science, history, for example—tend to specialize in single aspects of human activity'' (Harry Nelson and Robert Jurmain, *Introduction to Physical Anthropology*, 1982).

''Anthropology in America is a schizophrenic system: you have cultural anthropologists and physical anthropologists, and they have nothing to do with one another'' (Derek Freeman, *Margaret Mead and Samoa*, 1983).

ARCHEOLOGY

''That the country of Denmark was once cultivated and worked by giants is attested by the enormous stones attached to the barrows and caves of the ancients'' (Saxo Grammaticus, *History of Denmark*, c. 1200).

''On the North part of this Fort [in Oldbury, Britain] have been found, by plowing, divers Flint stones, about four inches and a half in length, curiously wrought by grinding, or some such way'' (William Dugdale, *The Antiquities of Warwickshire*, 1656).

''[The first humans] began with sharpening into the figures of axes those hard flints, those *thunder-stones*, which their descendents imagined to have been produced by thunder, and to have fallen from the clouds'' (Georges Louis Leclerc de Buffon, *Natural History*, c. 1780).

''The DANES have contributed to the peopling of AMERICA . . . the TOLTECAS, or whatever nation it may have been, that constructed the eminences and fortifications in that continent [Central America], were their descendents'' (Benjamin Barton, *Observations on Some Parts of Natural History*, 1787).

''It has been hitherto thought that the occurrence of stone implements indicates the 'Age of Stone.' My excavations here in Troy, however, prove this opinion to be completely erroneous; for I very frequently find implements of stone even immediately below the debris belonging to the Greek colony'' (Henry Schliemann, *Troy and Its Remains*, 1875).

''The integrity of Dr. Schliemann in the whole matter—of which his self-sacrificing spirit might surely have been a sufficient pledge—and the genuineness of his discoveries, are beyond all suspicion. We have, indeed, never seen them called in question, except in what appears to be an effusion of spite from a Greek, who seems to envy a German his discoveries on the Greek ground which Greeks have neglected for fifteen centuries'' (Philip Smith in Henry Schliemann, *Troy and Its Remains*, 1875).

''Because the study of the past by means of ancient manuscripts has almost reached its limits, archaeology now has an important place in the reconstruction of history. Although called an 'auxiliary science,' archaeology makes use of many other branches of learning, and requires the knowledge of numerous disciplines and complex techniques'' (Henri-Paul Eydoux, *The Buried Past*, 1962).

''It was from America . . . that the two most significant aids to modern archaeology came: contributions from atomic physics and biology respectively. They brought the fulfillment of archaeology's oldest dream, the possibility of exact dating'' (C. Ceram, *Gods, Graves, and Scholars*, 1967).

''In American usage the term 'archaeology' is applied to both the discipline itself and to the subject matter. That is, archaeology and prehistory are employed interchangeably. In Europe archaeology is more apt to be reserved for the discipline while prehistory refers to the substance'' (Gordon Willey and Jeremy Sabloff, *A History of American Archaelogy*, 1974).

''The history of archaeological method as we understand it today is less than a century old. Site excavation around the Mediterranean earlier in the nineteenth century tended to resemble treasure hunts. . . . Systematic attempts to construct links between early civilizations began with the work of Oskar Montelius in 1903'' (Stuart Fleming, *Dating in Archaeology*, 1976).

''Rational enquiry into the origins of man as opposed to romantic nostalgia or mythological thinking was initiated by the Greeks, who were the founders of so many intellectual disciplines. . . . There are records . . . of enterprises which fall well within the modern definition of archaeology. The historian Thucydides tells how the Athenians formed deductions about the inhabitants of Delos from the burial methods and grave goods they found in tombs'' (Anne Ward, *Adventures in Archaeology*, 1977).

''All archaeologists, no matter where they happen to be at work, have the same goal: They are trying to reconstruct man's life and culture in past ages through the systematic study of what they find'' (George Sullivan, *Discover Archaeology*, 1980).

ART, SOCIOLOGY OF

''All great arts demand discussion and high speculation about nature; for this loftiness of mind and effectiveness in all directions seem somehow to come from such pursuits. This was in Pericles added to his great natural abilities; for it was, I think, his falling in with Anaxagoras, who was just such a man, that filled him with high thoughts and taught him the nature of mind'' (Plato, *Phaedrus*, c. 400 B.C.).

''But of all arts there are, speaking generally, two kinds . . . acquisitive and productive art comprise all the arts'' (Plato, *The Sophist*, c. 400 B.C.).

''Experience is a knowledge of particulars, but art is knowledge of universals'' (Aristotle, *Metaphysics*, c. 350 B.C.).

''If you would have me weep, you must first of all feel grief yourself'' (Horace, *The Art of Poetry*, 8 B.C.).

''Wherever art displays itself, there would seem to be an absence of truth'' (Quintilian, *Principles of Oratory*, c. 90).

''The arts imitate nature'' (Marcus Aurelius, *Meditations*, c. 170).

''There is no art that can be learned without a master'' (Saint Jerome, *Letter to Rusticus*, c. 400).

''How innumerable are those things made by every art and workmanship in garments, shoes, vessels, and the like, in paintings as well as in every kind of statue—far beyond necessity and moderate use and any meaning of devotion—which men have made for the delight of their eyes'' (Saint Augustine, *Confessions*, 401).

''Art is a virtue on the same footing as speculative habits'' (Thomas Aquinas, *Summa Theologica*, 1274).

''Nature scarcely ever gives us the very best; for that we must have recourse to art'' (Baltasar Gracián y Morales, *The Art of Worldly Wisdom*, 1642).

''Experience, as Polus rightly remarks, begets art, inexperience is waited on by accident'' (William Harvey, *Generation of Animals*, 1651).

''*Art* is distinguished from *nature* as making is from acting or operating in general, and the product or the result of the former is distinguished from that of the latter as *work* from *operation* . . . although we are pleased to call what bees produce (their regularly constituted cells) a work of art, we only do so on the strength of an analogy with art; that is to say, as soon as we call to mind that no rational deliberation forms the basis of their labor, we say at once that it is a product of their nature (of instinct), and it is only to their Creator that we ascribe it as art'' (Immanuel Kant, *Critique of Judgment*, 1790).

''The artist is the child of his time; but woe to him if he is also its disciple, or even its favorite'' (Johann Christoph Friedrich von Schiller, *On the Esthetic Education of Man*, 1795).

''There is no better deliverance from the world than through art; and a man can form no surer bond with it than through art'' (Johann Wolfgang von Goethe, *Elective Affinities*, 1809).

''It depends little on the object, much on the mood, in art'' (Ralph Waldo Emerson, *Journals*, 1836).

''Fine art is that in which the hand, the head, and the heart of man go together'' (John Ruskin, *The Two Paths*, 1859).

''Nobody, I think, ought to read poetry, or look at pictures or statues, who cannot find a great deal more in them than the poet or artist has actually expressed'' (Nathaniel Hawthorne, *The Marble Faun*, 1860).

''Art is essentially the affirmation, the blessing, and the apotheosis of existence'' (Friedrich Wilhelm Nietzsche, *The Will to Power*, 1888).

''Every artist writes his own autobiography'' (Havelock Ellis, *The New Spirit*, 1890).

''No great artist ever sees things as they really are. If he did he would cease to be an artist'' (Oscar Wilde, *Intentions*, 1891).

''In art, as in love, instinct is sufficient'' (Anatole France, *The Garden of Epicurus*, 1894).

''Art is the response to the demand for entertainment, for the stimulation of our senses and imagination, and truth enters into it only as it subserves these ends'' (George Santayana, *The Sense of Beauty*, 1896).

''[If a person] puts his room to rights as a matter of routine he is anesthetic. But if the original emotion of impatient irritation has been ordered and tranquilized by what he has done, the orderly room reflects back to him the change that has taken place in himself. . . . His emotion as thus 'objectified' is esthetic'' (John Dewey, *Art as Experience*, 1934).

''[The arts present] the enduring essence of society that transcends the barriers of class, race, or epoch . . . the perfectibility of man . . . [the arts] immortalize the collective visions and values of historical cultures and the essential oneness of mankind'' (Radha-Kamal Mukerjee, *The Dynamics of Morals*, 1950).

''Art is to be thought of as any embellishment of ordinary living that is achieved with competence and has describable form . . . the student of culture must regard as art whatever a people recognizes as manifestations of the impulse to make more beautiful and thus to heighten the pleasure of any phase of living'' (Melville Herskovits, *Cultural Anthropology*, 1952).

''The audience for which a primitive artist works is composed of members of his own community steeped in the same mythological tradition as himself and familiar with the same environment of material fact and ritual activity; the primitive artist can therefore afford to communicate in shorthand; symbols have the same basic significance and the same range of ambiguity for artist and audience alike'' (Edmund Leach in Edward Evans-Pritchard, *The Institutions of Primitive Society*, 1954).

''The increasing abstractness of the arts and sciences has the effect of strengthening religion'' (Arnold Gehlen, *Man in the Age of Technology*, 1957).

''For many people art, displacing religion, has become the justification of life'' (Jacques Barzun, *The House of Intellect*, 1959).

''Literature, painting, music, and the dance have something vital to say to the social scientist . . . social scientists have themselves a contribution to make . . . a sociologist or psychologist brings to the arts a trained intelligence and a point of view'' (Robert Wilson, ed., *The Arts in Society*, 1964).

''Although a concern with the arts and their practical effects on society has a long history in Western civilization, sociological approaches to the arts are relatively recent, outgrowths of two major intellectual trends in the eighteenth century. One was the further differentiation of the arts from crafts and from science. . . . The second trend occurred in conceptions of history'' (Milton Albrecht et al., eds., *The Sociology of Art and Literature*, 1970).

''We cannot validly equate the arts of nonliterate peoples with those of late civilizations in which writing has permeated the culture as the ordinary medium of communication and information storage. . . . In pre-literate or proto-literate culture, the art symbol becomes the fact; that is it simultaneously represents, defines, and manifests its referent. In such cultures, art objects and events serve as media for information storage'' (Charlotte Otten, ed., *Anthropology and Art*, 1971).

"Even the briefest review of the relations between art and community indicates that most of the theories of art have fastened upon significant elements of aesthetic activity. To be sure, art does not imitate either activity or nature, but it works with the materials of both. In various ways the theory of art as catharsis and as self-expression calls attention to forms of satisfaction that the art affords to man" (Don Martindale, *American Society*, 1972).

"The problems, insights, ideas and forms which come to the artist and to the scientist seem to come as often from the unconscious as the conscious mind, from wide, eclectic, and unorganized reading, observing, or experiencing, from musing, browsing, and dreaming, from buried experiences, as from anything immediately and consciously in view" (Robert Nisbet, *Sociology as an Art Form*, 1976).

"Life, art, esthetics. In flux. Changing. All evolutionary, sometimes revolutionary. Sometimes art strikes out ahead of life. Sometimes life—society—gets there first. There is a reciprocating push-me, pull-you, with art and society held to each other by an elastic of communcation. This elastic is a foundation of shared visual experiences. In these shared visual experiences is preserved the sense of history and cultural evolution" (Lawrence Jeppson, *The Neo-Iconography of Tsing-fang Chen*, 1978).

"Folk art is mainly a copy of high art" (Arnold Hauser, *The Sociology of Art*, 1981).

"The social history of the arts has some serious consequences for the philosophy of art. By relativising their apparently supra-historical status, it puts into question those very works of art which aesthetics generally takes as its unproblematic subject-matter" (Janet Wolff, *Aesthetics and the Sociology of Art*, 1983).

ASSIMILATION

"The concept of assimilation, so far as it has been defined in popular usage, gets its meaning from its relation to the problem of immigration" (Robert Park and Ernest Burgess, *Introduction to the Science of Sociology*, 1924).

"Intermarriage may be considered the most rigid test of assimilation. When the descendants of immigrants may marry into the dominant group without opposition, it may be assumed that they are accepted and are permitted to participate freely in the life of the older population. So long as relations are restricted solely to economic activities, there is little or no intermarriage" (William Smith, *Americans in the Making*, 1939).

"The immigrants' children experienced pressure toward assimilation and Americanization that led them to ignore or despise Old World cultures. The effect was to alienate them from their parents. . . . They rejected much of the old culture as through public schools and mass media, they rapidly learned the new" (John and Mavis Biesanz, *Introduction to Sociology*, 1961).

"The greater the religious divergence of the minority from the majority, the less its structural assimilation. The greater the racial divergence . . . the less its structural assimilation. The greater the class divergence . . . the less its structural assimilation'' (Edward Murguia, *Chicano Intermarriage*, 1982).

ATTITUDE

''[An attitude is] a process of individual consciousness which determines the real or possible activity of the individual in the social world . . . the more generally an attitude is shared by the members of a given social group and the greater the part which it plays in the life of every member [the more important it is] . . . [attitudes may be manifested in] a set of rules for definite situations which may be even expressed in abstract formulas . . . the more or less clear conception of the conditions and consciousness of attitudes [is the definition of the situation]'' (William Thomas and Florian Znaniecki, *The Polish Peasant in Europe and America*, 1920).

''[The] concept of social attitudes has been so significant in the contemporary analyses of human behavior'' (Kimball Young, ed., *Social Attitudes*, 1931).

''Officer candidates are subject to intensive training, a great part of which is directed toward molding a man's attitudes to conform to the traditional stereotypes'' (Samuel Stouffer, *The American Soldier*, 1949).

''Attitude research continues to occupy a central position in social psychology . . . yet we cannot avoid the impression that much effort has been wasted and that the contributions might have been even greater if research had been more cumulative'' (Marvin Shaw and Jack Wright, *Scales for the Measurement of Attitudes*, 1967).

''The public's attitudes on different aspects of the civil rights question have varied considerably over the years, although a moderate trend sympathetic to the Negro has been observed in the last few years'' (Alfred Hero in John Robinson et al., *Measures of Political Attitudes*, 1968).

''Today all of us, whether dealing with people in a business, political, or academic setting, are faced with rebellious attitudes toward the accepted standards and values of our society. Coping with these attitudes is often called 'dealing with problems' '' (Elizabeth Gane in G. Hallen and Rajeshwar Prasad, eds., *Towards Global Sociology*, 1970).

''Attitudes have been studied almost exclusively by using self-reported beliefs, feelings and action tendencies. Treating self-reports as virtually the only window onto the psychological world of the individual is most unfortunate . . . it is only one way'' (Gene Summers, ed., *Attitude Measurement*, 1970).

''Attitudes and behaviors are related to an extent that ranges from small to moderate in degree'' (Howard Schuman and Michael Johnson in Alex Inkeles, ed., *Annual Review of Sociology*, 1976).

''The similar or identical *mentality* (to paraphrase the term *attitude*) is transmitted to the individual during this enculturation process, and that is why an attitude can be thought of as a *learned* predisposition. Attitudes thus serve several functions with regard to the individual in his group . . . adopting the group's attitudes helps the individual gain access or remain within the group or society'' (Horst Arndt in Harald Niemeyer, ed., *Social Relations Network*, 1980).

''Where a strong, relevant attitude is closely related to the behavior under study, where few other attitudes are relevant, and where few facts contradict the attitude, behavior does in fact closely match the attitude'' (Charles Morris, *Psychology*, 1982).

AUTOMATION

''Owing to the extensive use of machinery and to division of labour, the work of the proletarians has lost all individual character, and, consequently, all charm for the workman. He becomes an appendage of the machine, and it is only the most simple, most monotonous, and most easily acquired knack, that is required of him . . . in proportion as the use of machinery and division of labour increases, in the same proportion the burden of toil also increases, whether by prolongation of the working hours, by increase of the work exacted in a given time or by increased speed of the machinery, etc.'' (Karl Marx and Friedrich Engels, *Communist Manifesto*, 1847).

''By means of electricity, the world of matter has become a great nerve, vibrating thousands of miles in a breathless point of time'' (Nathaniel Hawthorne, *The House of the Seven Gables*, 1851).

''You cannot endow even the best machine with initiative'' (Walter Lippmann, *A Preface to Politics*, 1914).

''A world technology means either a world government or world suicide'' (Max Lerner, *Actions and Passions*, 1949).

''It is critical vision alone which can mitigate the unimpeded operation of the automatic'' (Marshall McLuhan, *The Mechanical Bride*, 1951).

''The most important question that the industrial wage earner faces with respect to increasing mechanization is how it is going to affect his means of livelihood. . . . The most obvious and troublesome fear of the workman is that of outright loss of employment'' (Wilbert Moore, *Industrial Relations and the Social Order*, 1951).

''By his very success in inventing labor-saving devices, modern man has manufactured an abyss of boredom'' (Lewis Mumford, *The Conduct of Life*, 1951).

''Where there is the necessary technical skill to move mountains, there is no need for the faith that moves mountains'' (Eric Hoffer, *The Passionate State of Mind*, 1954).

''The computing machine represents the center of the automatic factory, but it will never be the whole factory . . . it is all one to the machine whether it performs overall work or white collar work . . . the automatic machine, whatever we think of any feelings it may have or may not have, is the precise economic equivalent of the slave. Any labor which competes with slave labor must accept the economic conditions of slave labor'' (Friedrich Klemm, *Technology*, 1954).

''The danger of the past was that men became slaves. The danger of the future is that men may become robots'' (Erich Fromm, *The Sane Society*, 1955).

''Applied Science is a conjuror, whose bottomless hat yields impartially the softest of Angora rabbits and the most petrifying of Medusas'' (Aldous Huxley, *Tomorrow and Tomorrow and Tomorrow*, 1956).

''The industrial regime tends to make the unorganized or unorganizable individual, the pauper, into the victim of a kind of human sacrifice offered to the gods of civilization'' (Jacques Maritain, *Reflections on America*, 1958).

''The technology of automation differs from the much earlier one of 'individual production,' since there, skill was an important principle. Neither does it focus on the 'product,' as did the Henry Ford concept of 'mass' production. 'Automation' focuses on the *process*, which it sees as an integrated and harmonious whole'' (Edward Shils, *Automation and Industrial Relations*, 1963).

''The word 'automation' was coined in 1947 by Del Harder, vice-president of Ford Motor Company, to apply to 'automatic handling of parts between progressive production processes.' At about the same time, John Diebold, a management engineer, shortened the word 'automatization' into 'automation.' Diebold stressed the use of control devices that operate by means of 'feedback' '' (Paul Samuelson, *Economics*, 1976).

''In a manufacturing plant, technology is typically tangible in that the process of assembling the elements results in a concrete product be it clothing, automobiles, or toothpaste. This kind of technology is generally characterized by a high degree of routinization. Once the operational system is in place, the tasks are clear, the causative relationships apparent, the process highly repetitive, the product standardized. Some technologies are so perfected that human input becomes marginal'' (Marc Miringoff, *Management in Human Service Organizations*, 1980).

''Until now, automation has been largely restricted to factories that turn out thousands of identical products, because it has been too costly to retool machines at frequent intervals to perform new tasks. But the development of reprogrammable machinery makes it economically feasible to automate production processes that involve short production-runs and frequent changes in machine settings'' (Colin Norman, *The God That Limps*, 1981).

''Full automation will largely eliminate *work* in production and services, but will not put an end to human *activity* and, in this sense, to human *occupation*. It will lead to the replacement of what was previously 'work' by creative, entertaining occupation'' (Adam Schaff in Günter Friedrichs and Adam Schaff, eds., *Microelectronics and Society*, 1982).

B

BEHAVIOR, COLLECTIVE

"The individual forming part of a crowd acquires . . . a sentiment of invincible power which allows him to yield to instincts . . . a crowd being anonymous, and in consequence irresponsible, the sentiment of responsibility which always controls individuals disappears entirely" (Gustave Le Bon, *The Crowd*, 1895).

"[Collective behavior is] the result of interaction, or of impulses that are common to a number of people" (Robert Park and Ernest Burgess, *Introduction to the Science of Sociology*, 1921).

"The student of collective behavior seeks to understand the way in which a new social order arises, for the appearance of a new social order is equivalent to the emergence of new forms of collective behavior" (Herbert Blumer in A. Lee, ed., *Principles of Sociology*, 1951).

"Collective behavior, as a clearly delimited field of sociology, is still relatively new. Gustave Le Bon [*The Crowd*, 1895] is often identified as the founder because of his emphasis on the crowd as the prototype of all group behavior. He did not, however, use the term *collective behavior*. . . . It was Robert E. Park and Ernest W. Burgess who, in 1921, introduced the term [in their *Introduction to the Science of Sociology*]. . . . Collective behavior refers to the action of collectivities, not to a type of individual behavior" (Ralph Turner and Lewis Killian, *Collective Behavior*, 1972).

" 'Collective behavior' is the somewhat undescriptive term sociologists use to cover a range of more or less 'noninstitutionalized' phenomena including revolutions, social movements, protests, riots, panics, mobs, crowds, fads, crazes, rumor—and more. Many of these topics are covered, at least partly, under other sociological specialties as well, for instance under the areas of social change, social conflict, political sociology, voluntary associations, social psychology, and public opinion. And such topics are also a central concern of important segments of political science, anthropology, history, psychology, criminal justice, law, and communications" (Denton Morrison and Kenneth Hornback, *Collective Behavior*, 1976).

"The crowd is a nontraditional group of people in the same place at the same time with attention focused on a common thought, activity, or other stimulus. Crowds are temporary. An audience at a concert is a crowd, but inmates at a prison are not'' (Robert Ellis and Marcia Lipetz, *Essential Sociology*, 1979).

BIOETHICS

''A full-grown horse or dog is beyond comparison a more rational, as well as a more conversable animal, than an infant of a day, or a week, or even a month, old. But suppose they were otherwise, what would it avail? The question is not, Can they reason? nor Can they *talk*? but, *Can they suffer*?'' (Jeremy Bentham, *Introduction to the Principles of Morals and Legislation*, 1789).

''Children, who cannot give a mature and informed consent, or adult incompetents, should not be the subjects of medical experimentation unless, other remedies having failed to relieve their grave illness, it is reasonable to believe that the administration of a drug as yet untested or insufficiently tested on human beings, or the performance of an untried operation, may further the *patient's own recovery*'' (Paul Ramsey, *The Patient as Person*, 1970).

''Minors or mentally incompetent persons may be used as subjects only if: (1) the nature of the investigation is such that mentally competent adults would not be suitable subjects; (2) consent, in writing, is given by a legally authorized representative of the subject under circumstances in which an informed and prudent adult would reasonably be expected to volunteer himself or his child as a subject'' (American Medical Association, *Opinions and Reports of the Judicial Council*, 1971).

''If we are to preserve the dignity of the individual, and if the human species is to survive and prosper, we need to cultivate the world of ideas and perfect the techniques for arriving at value judgments in areas where facts alone are not enough'' (Va Potter, *Bioethics*, 1971).

[Exchange during trial between Surgeon and plaintiff's Attorney] S: ''I think you should strive to do for the patient what is the best thing over a long period of time for the patient.'' A: ''Isn't that up to the patient?'' S: ''No, I don't think it should be. If they go to the doctor they should discuss it. . . . A: ''Isn't this up to the patient? . . . If I want to keep these teeth, can't I do it?'' S: ''You don't know whether they are causing you trouble.'' A: ''That is up to me, isn't it?'' S: ''Not if you came to see me it wouldn't be'' (Jay Katz, *Experimentation with Human Beings*, 1972).

''If we accord moral rights on the basis of rationality, what of the status of newly born children, 'low grade' mental patients, 'intellectual cabbages' and so on? Logically, accepting this criterion, they must have no, or diminished, moral rights'' (Andrew Linzey, *Animal Rights*, 1976).

''The emergence of bioethics as a field of study is a contemporary phenomenon traceable to several causes. First, the issues of bioethics have captured the contemporary mind because they represent major conflicts in the area of technology and basic human values, those dealing with life, death, and health. . . .

Second, there is an intense and widespread interest in bioethics because it offers a stimulating intellectual and moral challenge. . . . Third, the rapid growth of the field of bioethics has been facilitated by the openness to multidisciplinary work that characterizes many scholars and academic institutions'' (Warren Reich, ed., *Encyclopedia of Bioethics*, 1978).

''Bioethics can be defined as the systematic study of value questions which arise in the biomedical and behavioral fields. Specific bioethical issues which have recently received national and international attention include euthanasia, in vitro fertilization, human experimentation, genetic engineering, abortion, the definition of death, medical confidentiality, and the allocation of scarce medical resources'' (LeRoy Walters, ed., *Bibliography of Bioethics*, 1982).

''Bioethics is an area in which the interests of science and religion meet. New technologies and applied knowledge create dilemmas in the zone where technique and human values converge and often conflict. . . . Technology poses a moral dilemma . . . on two fronts. First, dying patients can be kept 'alive' for months (or even years), and, second, technology may help people die more quickly and without prolonged struggle'' (Paul Simmons, *Birth and Death*, 1983).

BIRTH CONTROL

''To prevent [conception] . . . crocodile's dung is sprinkled'' (*Kahun Papyrus*, c. 1850 B.C.).

''Onan knew that the seed should not be his; and it came to pass, when he went in unto his brother's wife, that he spilled it on the ground'' (Genesis 38:9).

''Effeminate movements [during coitus] help a woman prevent conception'' (Lucretius, *On the Nature of Things*, c. 60 B.C.).

''When it seems wiser to prevent conception, people should abstain from intercourse . . . directly before and after menstruation'' (Soranus, *Gynecology*, c. 120).

''A man is not allowed to drink a cup of roots in order to become sterile, but a woman is allowed to drink a cup of roots in order to become sterile'' (Talmud, Levirate Marriage 8:4).

''They do not want children, although marriages are made only for them. . . . When procreation is taken away, husbands are wicked lovers, wives are prostitutes, wedding beds are stews'' (Saint Augustine, *Against Faustus*, 398).

''Sometimes it is necessary to prevent the semen from entering the uterus, as when pregnancy is dangerous to a woman. . . . There are several methods of doing this. First, at the time of ejaculation, the man withdraws. . . . Second, ejaculation is prevented. . . . Third, before coitus, apply to the mouth of the uterus some drug that blocks this opening or expels the semen and prevents conception'' (Rhazes, *Quintessence of Experience*, c. 900).

''If a woman takes a dose of substance such as quicksilver, gadfly, and medicinal leeches, she will not conceive again'' (Chen Tzu-ming, *Complete Collection of Valuable Prescriptions for Women*, 1237).

"If a woman drinks daily for half a month a pala [about two ounces] of molasses that are three years old, then she will certainly be sterile for the rest of her life" (Kalyanamalla, *The Stage of the God of Love*, c. 1550).

"As often as a man has intercourse, he should . . . use a small linen cloth made to fit over the glans and then draw forward the prepuce over the glans" (Gabriello Fallopio, *On the French Disease*, 1564, posthumously).

"In modern Europe the positive checks to population prevail less, and the preventive checks more than in past times and in the more civilized parts of the world" (Thomas R. Malthus, *An Essay on the Principle of Population*, 1798).

"If, above all, it was once clearly understood, that it was not disreputable for married persons to avail themselves of . . . precautionary means . . . a sufficient check might at once be given to the increase of population beyond the means of subsistence" (Francis Place, *Principle of Population*, 1822).

"I found a native of Santo [Oceania] with an artificial hypospadia [slitting of urethra], performed at the age of puberty" (Jacobus X, *Untrodden Fields of Anthropology*, 1898).

"Most American Victorians were aware of contraceptive devices but, for a variety of reasons, clung to the rigid sexual mores of the day. Women authors of purity manuals were even more vocally opposed to birth-control practices. While there were, of course, feminists like Annie Besant and later Margaret Sanger who sought greater sexual freedom through birth-control techniques, most sex-in-life authors chose the route of 'marital continence,' which they hoped would lessen women's role as sex objects" (John and Robin Haller, *The Physician and Sexuality in Victorian America*, 1974).

"The importance of family planning has become increasingly evident to more Canadians during the past few years. To the individual family it can mean greater health and happiness and the ability to bring up children with love, dignity, and the capability of reaching their full potential. To a nation it may mean a stabilized and optimistic society. To the world it may mean survival" (Benjamin Schlesinger, *Family Planning in Canada*, 1974).

"In the more industrialized societies of the world, and at least in the sphere of oral contraception, women tend to be almost as liberal as, or even slightly more liberal than, men are" (Panos Bardis in T. Smith and Man Das, eds., *Sociocultural Change Since 1950*, 1978).

"[At first, the U.S. birth control movement] was associated with various reformist and often radical movements, such as the Free Thought and Free Love Movements . . . it was only in the 1920s that the movement became dominated by physicians and became separated from its radical roots" (Stephen Isaacs, *Population Law and Policy*, 1981).

BOURGEOISIE

"The proletarian, then, is, in both law and fact, the slave of the bourgeoisie, which can decide his life or death" (Friedrich Engels, *The Condition of the Working Class in England*, 1845).

"The relations of productions in which the bourgeoisie exists have not a single, a simple character, but a double character, a character of duplicity; in the same relations in which wealth is produced, poverty is produced also" (Karl Marx, *The Poverty of Philosophy*, 1847).

"The bourgeoisie has been the first to show what man's activity can bring about. It has accomplished *wonders* far surpassing Egyptian pyramids, Roman aqueducts, and Gothic cathedrals" (Karl Marx and Friedrich Engels, *Communist Manifesto*, 1847).

"State, church, etc. are only justified insofar as they are committees to superintend or administer the common interests of the productive bourgeoisie" (Karl Marx, *Das Kapital*, 1879).

"I call bourgeois any person who says no to himself, gives up struggle, and renounces love for the sake of his security" (Léon-Paul Fargue, *Under the Lamp*, 1921).

BUREAUCRACY

"The German captains of industry who came to take the discretionary management in the new era were fortunate enough not to have matriculated from the training school of a country town based on a retail business in speculative real estate and political jobbery managed under the rule of 'prehension, division and silence.' They came under the selective test for fitness in the aggressive conduct of industrial enterprise" (Thorstein Veblen, *Imperial Germany and the Industrial Revolution*, 1915).

"Bureaucratic authority is carried out in its purest form where it is most clearly dominated by the principle of appointment. There is no such thing as a hierarchy of elected officials in the same sense as there is a hierarchical organization of appointed officials. In the first place, election makes it impossible to attain a stringency of discipline even approaching that in the appointed type. For it is open to a subordinate official to compete for elective honors on the same terms as his superiors, and his prospects are not dependent on the superior's judgment" (Max Weber, *The Theory of Social and Economic Organization*, 1922, posthumously).

"[During a crisis a bureaucratic ideology attempts] to find a remedy by means of arbitrary decrees rather than to meet the political situation on its own grounds" (Karl Mannheim, *Ideology and Utopia*, 1929).

"Work is of two kinds: first, altering the position of matter at or near the earth's surface relative to other such matter; second, telling other people to do so. The first kind is unpleasant and ill paid; the second is pleasant and highly paid. The second kind is capable of infinite extension: there are not only those who give orders, but those who give advice as to what orders should be given. Usually two opposite kinds of advice are given simultaneously by two organised bodies of men; this is called politics. The skill required for this kind of work is not knowledge of the subjects as to which advice is given, but knowledge of the art of persuasive speaking and writing, i.e. advertising'' (Bertrand Russell, *In Praise of Idleness and Other Essays*, 1935).

''The development of the *money economy*, in so far as a pecuniary compensation of the officials is concerned, is a presupposition of bureaucracy. Today it not only prevails but is predominant. This fact is of very great importance for the whole bearing of bureaucracy, yet by itself it is by no means decisive for the existence of bureaucracy'' (Hans Gerth and C. W. Mills, *From Max Weber*, 1946).

''Record-making devices are not only contributory to personal insight; from a scientific point of view they improve the source materials of history and therefore of science. These methods are especially valuable in improving our knowledge of the focus of attention'' (Harold Lasswell, *Analysis of Political Behaviour*, 1948).

''Wherever there is organization, whether formally democratic or not, there is a split between the leader and the led, between the agent and the initiator. The phenomenon of abdication to bureaucratic directives in corporations, in trade unions, in parties, and in cooperatives is so widespread that it indicates a fundamental weakness of democracy'' (Philip Selznick, *TVA and the Grass Roots*, 1949).

''Need for maintaining effective lines of communication upwards from men to officers at the unit level is not unique to the Army. It has its parallel in civilian industry'' (Samuel Stouffer et al., *The American Soldier*, 1949).

''Smaller and simpler organizations are typically managed with a high degree of particularism (i.e., personal consideration) of the relations of persons in authority to their own subordinates. But when the 'distance' between points of decision and of operation increases, and the number of operating units affected by decisions with it, uniformity and coordination can be attained only by a high degree of formalization'' (Talcott Parsons, *The Social System*, 1951).

''The growth of bureaucracy, both public and private, is widely recognized as one of the major social trends of our time. Long before bureaucratization became so pronounced as to be evident to many, it had become a focus of interest to social scientists'' (Robert Merton et al., *Reader in Bureaucracy*, 1952).

''The fact that the individual is serving some group which is greater than himself blinds him to the fact that his group is only a part of the whole'' (Kenneth Boulding, *The Organizational Revolution*, 1953).

''[In the communist states] membership in the new party class or political bureaucracy is reflected in larger economic and material goods and privileges than society should normally grant for such functions. In practice the ownership privilege of the new class manifests itself as an exclusive right, as a party monopoly for the political bureaucrat to distribute the national income, to get wages, direct economic development and dispose of nationalized and other property. . . . The so-called social ownership is a disguise for real ownership by the political bureaucracy'' (Milovan Djilas, *The New Class*, 1957).

''In many public administrative departments not actually at war, the staff increase may be expected to follow this formula:

$$x = \frac{2k^m + 1}{n}$$

where *k* is the number of staff seeking promotion through the appointment of subordinates; *1* represents the difference between the ages of appointment and retirements; *m* is the number of man hours devoted to answering minutes within the department; and *n* is the number of effective units being administered, *x* will be the number of new staff required next year'' (C. Parkinson, *Parkinson's Law*, 1957).

''The concentration of capital led to the formation of giant corporations managed by hierarchically organized bureaucracies. Large conglomerations of workers and clerks work together, each individual a part of a vast organized production machine, which in order to run at all, must run smoothly and without interruption. The individual worker becomes merely a cog in this machine'' (Erich Fromm in A. Neill, *Summerhill*, 1960).

''[In the Soviet Union] to correctly implement the principle of one-man management it is of great importance that there be a clear demarcation of obligations, rights, and responsibilities. . . . Every employee must be subordinate to only one individual, from whom he receives an assignment and to whom he is accountable'' (F. Aunapu, *What Management Is*, 1967).

''One can hardly find any student of society who has not dealt directly or indirectly with [bureaucracy]'' (Nicos Mouzelis, *Organisation and Bureaucracy*, 1967).

''[The technostructure] extends from the most senior officials of the corporation to where it meets, at the outer perimeter, the white and blue collar workers whose function is to conform more or less mechanically to instruction or routine. It embraces all who bring specialized knowledge, talent or experience to group decision-making or the organization which they form. I propose to call this organization the Technostructure'' (John Galbraith, *The New Industrial State*, 1971).

''The bureaucrats form a class only by reason of the fact that their functions and their rules differentiate them collectively from the exploited classes, only because they are interlinked with a directing center which decides what is produced. . . . The bureaucratic community is not guaranteed by the mechanism of economic activities; it is established by the integration of the bureaucrats around the state, in the total discipline with regard to the directing apparatus. Without this state, without this apparatus, the bureaucracy is nothing'' (C. Lefort, *Elements of a Critique of Bureaucracy*, 1971).

''[In the Soviet Union] even yesterday's proletarian revolutionaries had to use authoritarian methods, to issue orders, i.e., adopt bureaucratic procedures. Sometimes it is said that the first generation of proletarian revolutionaries could not be bureaucrats. Just the opposite is true. In the conditions of Russia, they *had* to a considerable extent to be bureaucrats'' (Roy Medvedev, *On Soviet Democracy*, 1972).

''[In communist societies] bureaucratic property is neither individual nor collective; it is private property insofar as it exists only for the bureaucracy while the rest of society is dispossessed; it is private property managed in common by a class and collective within this class. . . . In this sense one can briefly define it as private collective property'' (Cornelius Castoriadis, *The Bureaucratic Society*, 1973).

''[In the Soviet Union] while in the past people were capable of tolerating the 'inconvenience' of rude interpersonal relations and even ignoring them—since they were under the pressure of material need—now, under changed circumstances, they are just as sensitive to rudeness, coarseness, bureaucratism as they were in the past to need and deprivation'' (D. Kaidalov and E. Suimenko, *Current Problems in the Sociology of Work*, 1974).

''As bureaucracies assume more and more functions of social service and control, they can be seen as nodes in the social fabric and as a major factor of social integration. In a society dominated by bureaucracies, many human relations lose their direct character. They are mediated by organisations which more or less have the power to regulate human behaviour'' (Klaus Lenk in Günter Friedrichs and Adam Schaff, eds., *Microelectronics and Society*, 1982).

C

CAPITALISM

"By not confining his expense within his income, he [the prodigal] encroaches upon his capital. Like him who perverts the revenues of some pious foundation to profane purposes, he pays the wages of idleness with those funds which the frugality of his forefathers had, as it were, consecrated to the maintenance of industry. . . . If the prodigality of some was not compensated by the frugality of others, the conduct of every prodigal . . . tends not only to beggar himself, but to impoverish his country. . . . Capitals are increased by parsimony and diminished by prodigality . . . parsimony, and not industry, is the immediate cause of the increase of capital" (Adam Smith, *The Wealth of Nations*, 1776).

"The bourgeoisie, historically, has played a most revolutionary part. The bourgeoisie, wherever it has got the upper hand, has put an end to all feudal, patriarchal, idyllic relations. It has pitilessly torn asunder the motley feudal ties that bound man to his 'natural superiors,' and has left remaining no other nexus between man and man than naked self-interest, than callous 'cash payment.' It has drowned the most heavenly ecstasies of religious fervour, of chivalrous enthusiasm, of philistine sentimentalism, in the icy water of egotistical calculation. It has resolved personal worth into exchange value, and in place of the numberless indefeasible chartered freedoms, has set up that single, unconscionable freedom—Free Trade. In one word, for exploitation, veiled by religious and political illusions, it has substituted naked, shameless, direct, brutal exploitation" (Karl Marx and Friedrich Engels, *Communist Manifesto*, 1847).

"The capitalist mode of production has an inherent tendency toward the absolute development of its productive forces, quite aside from the value of capital and the included social values or of the societal conditions under which capitalistic production takes place. . . . The maintenance and reproduction of the working class is, and must ever be, a necessary condition to the reproduction of capital. But the capitalist may safely leave its fulfillment to the labourer's instincts of self-preservation and of propagation. . . . If a surplus population of workers is a necessary product of accumulation or of the development of wealth on a capitalist basis, this surplus population also becomes, conversely, the lever of capitalist accumulation. . . . It forms a disposable reverse army . . . a mass of human material always ready for exploitation by capital'' (Karl Marx, *Das Kapital*, 1879).

''The negative and dark sides of capitalism . . . the profound and all-round social contradictions which are inevitably inherent in capitalism . . . reveal the historically transient character of this economic regime. The progressive historical role of capitalism may be summed up in two brief propositions: increase in the productive forces of social labour, and the socialisation of that labour. But both these facts manifest themselves in extremely diverse processes in different branches of the national economy'' (Vladimir Lenin, *The Development of Capitalism in Russia*, 1899).

''The organization of free labor and the guilds in their occidental medieval form was certainly—quite against their intention—not only a handicap but also a preliminary step to the capitalistic organization of labor which could not have been dispensed with . . . capitalism during the time of its emergence required workers who, for the sake of conscience, were available for economic exploitation. Nowadays capitalism sits in the saddle and can compel their will to work without otherworldly rewards. . . . Present day capitalism, having attained supremacy in economic life, trains and, by means of economic selection, creates the economic subjects—entrepreneurs and workers—it requires'' (Max Weber, *Collected Essays in the Sociology of Religion*, 1919).

''Capitalism is present wherever the industrial provision for the needs of a human group is carried out by the method of enterprise, irrespective of what need is involved . . . a rational capitalistic establishment is one with capital accounting, that is, an establishment which determines its income yielding power by calculation according to the methods of modern bookkeeping and the striking of a balance. The device of the balance was first insisted upon by the Dutch theorist Simon Stevin in the year 1698. . . . While capitalism of various forms is met with in all periods of history, the provision of the everyday wants by capitalistic methods is characteristic of the occident alone and even here has been the inevitable method only since the middle of the 19th century. Such capitalistic beginnings as are found in earlier centuries were merely anticipatory'' (Max Weber, *General Economic History*, 1920).

''The mode of distribution [of material property] gives to the propertied a monopoly on the possibility of transferring property from the sphere of use as 'wealth' to the sphere of 'capital' '' (Max Weber, *Economy and Society*, 1922, posthumously).

''With the advent of Great Society the habit of letting things take their own course does not represent the principle of real freedom, but simply surrenders the cultural inheritance to a few capitalist concerns, which reflect only too often the lowest denominator of democratic culture'' (Karl Mannheim, *Diagnosis of Our Time*, 1943).

''No matter how real and precious the humanism of capitalist societies may be for those who enjoy it . . . it is the privilege of the few and not the property of the many'' (Maurice Merleau-Ponty, *Humanism and Terror*, 1969).

''Economic development in the capitalist manner requires not only an immense investment of money and materials, but also a stable political situation and competent administrators'' (Park Chung Hee, *To Build a Nation*, 1971).

''The bourgeois class grows and develops as a *consequence* of the actions of individual capitalists, economically determined, whatever the conflicts among the actors'' (C. Lefort, *Elements of a Critique of Bureaucracy*, 1971).

''Marx . . . overrated the role of classes in modern capitalism, just as he underrated it in the communist society'' (Henry Spiegel, *The Growth of Economic Thought*, 1971).

''The emergence of the free labour market is the decisive factor in the appearance of capitalism'' (Ernesto Laclau, *Politics and Ideology in Marxist Theory*, 1977).

''In no other capitalist state is the intervention of the state as pervasive as in France'' (J. Freiberg, *The French Press*, 1981).

''The irony of Lenin's advocacy of Taylorism is reflected in the old joke: Q. What is capitalism, Comrade? A. The exploitation of man by man. Q. And what is communism, Comrade? A. Just the reverse'' (Barry Jones, *Sleepers, Wake!*, 1982).

CAUSATION

''There are four causes, first, the final cause, second, the formal cause, which are as it were one, third, the material cause, and fourth, the efficient cause, which is the source of motion'' (Aristotle, *Generation of Animals*, c. 350 B.C.).

''A bell never rings by itself. If someone does not pull or push it, it will remain silent'' (Plautus, *The Three Penny Day*, c. 190 B.C.).

''Nothing is created out of nothing'' (Lucretius, *On the Nature of Things*, c. 60 B.C.).

''Causality is found among all natural entities'' (Thomas Aquinas, *Summa Theologica,* 1274).

''Every why hath a wherefore'' (William Shakespeare, *The Comedy of Errors*, 1593).

''When the cause is removed, the sin ceases'' (Miguel de Cervantes Saavedra, *Don Quixote*, 1615).

''Nothing exists without a cause of its existence. . . . From causes which appear *similar* we expect similar effects. This is the sum of all our experimental conclusions'' (David Hume, *Concerning Human Understanding*, 1748).

''We are placed in this world, as in a great theatre, where the true springs and causes of every event are entirely concealed from us; nor have we either sufficient wisdom to foresee, or power to prevent, those ills with which we are continually threatened'' (David Hume, *Natural Religion*, 1779, posthumously).

''If the empirical law of causality is to conduct us to a Supreme Being, this being must belong to the chain of empirical objects—in which case it would be, like all phenomena, itself conditioned'' (Immanuel Kant, *Critique of Pure Reason*, 1781).

''In a watch, one part is the instrument by which the movement of the others is effected, but one wheel is not the efficient cause of the production of the other. One part is certainly present for the sake of another, but it does not owe its presence to the agency of that other. For this reason, also, the producing cause of the watch and its form is not contained in the nature of this material but lies outside the watch in a being that can act according to ideas of a whole which its causality makes possible. Hence one wheel in the watch does not produce the other, and, still less, does one watch produce other watches'' (Immanuel Kant, *Critique of Judgment*, 1790).

''In speaking of causation, then, I do not mean to express individual agency, but any concurrence of circumstances which constitutes a cause; for I imagine we can seldom . . . calculate upon either singleness of cause, or simplicity of effect'' (James Johnson, *The Influence of Tropical Climates*, 1821).

''Plurality of Causes exists in almost boundless excess, and effects are, for the most part, inextricably interwoven with one another. To add to the embarrassment, most of the inquiries in political science relate to the production of effects of a most comprehensive description, such as the public wealth, public security, public morality and the like: results liable to be affected directly or indirectly either in *plus* or in *minus* by nearly every fact which exists, or even which occurs in human society'' (John S. Mill, *A System of Logic*, 1843).

''*Every active force produces more than one change—every cause produces more than one effect*. . . . If the advance of Man towards greater heterogeneity is traceable to the production of many effects by one cause, still more clearly may the advance of Society towards greater heterogeneity be so explained'' (Herbert Spencer, 1857, *Essays*, 1915).

''Each process is objectively necessary for the following one. Supposing therefore the activities demanded by the scheme actually performed, supposing the schematic situation constructed and developed up to the end in accordance with the scheme, the whole series of processes is fully and exclusively determined in its actual development by the teleological system of means and ends, and each process within this series is fully and exclusively determined in its appearance by the following process for which it has to prepare the necessary status. In a word, the following process is the *final cause* of the preceding process. . . . We see that the Aristotelian concept of final cause is, like many other ancient conceptions, quite unjustly neglected by modern thought'' (Florian Znaniecki, *Cultural Reality*, 1919).

''We can only hope to determine causes which always and everywhere produce certain definite attitudes'' (William Thomas and Florian Znaniecki, *The Polish Peasant in Europe and America*, 1920).

''The interpretation of a sequence of events . . . will be called *causally* adequate insofar as . . . there is a probability that it will always occur in the same way'' (Max Weber, *Economy and Society*, 1922, posthumously).

"In all conscious behavior we relate means to ends, but the process of establishing this relationship is contingent and involves an attribution of causality that may or may not be confirmed by experience . . . the various factors we causally relate to any socio-psychological phenomenon belong to different orders of reality. Yet they must somehow get together, they must somehow become comparable and co-ordinate, since they must operate with or against one another in the determination of the phenomenon" (Robert MacIver, *Social Causation*, 1942).

"The universe is orderly: all events are caused and interrelated" (Navaho Indians in Clyde Kluckhohn in F. Northrop, ed., *Ideological Differences and World Order*, 1949).

"When we turn to such matters as the causation of behavior, it seems to me no progress has been made, that we are as much in the dark as to how to proceed as in the past, and that some fundamental insights are lacking" (Noam Chomsky, *Reflections on Language*, 1975).

"A social scientist may find that the data indicate that a number of variables are correlated or associated with the variable to be explained. The leap from this factual result to the conclusion that these variables are *causes* of the phenomenon in question cannot be made without the assistance of additional assumptions. This is because there will be many more correlates of a phenomenon than there are causes" (Ann and Hubert Blalock, *Introduction to Social Research*, 1982).

"Just as biographers and critics look for external influences to account for the traits and achievements of those they study, so science ultimately explains behavior in terms of 'causes' or conditions which lie beyond the individual. As more and more causal relations are demonstrated, a practical corollary becomes difficult to resist: It should be possible to *produce* behavior according to plan simply by arranging the proper conditions" (B. F. Skinner in Robert Epstein, ed., *Skinner for the Classroom*, 1982).

CELIBACY

"I would that all men were even as I myself. But every man hath his proper gift of God, one after this manner, and another after that. I say therefore to the unmarried and widows, it is good for them if they abide even as I. But if they cannot contain, let them marry: for it is better to marry than to burn" (I Corinthians 7:7–9).

"What has the care of infants to do with the Last Judgment? Heaving breasts, the qualms of childbirth, and whimpering brats will make a fine scene combined with the advent of the Judge and the sound of the trumpet. Ah, what good midwives the executioners of the Antichrist will be!" (Tertullian, *Exhortation to Purity*, c. 200).

"Give me chastity and continence, but not right now" (Saint Augustine, *Confessions*, 401).

"Thrice blessed they, that master so their blood, to undergo their maiden pilgrimage" (William Shakespeare, *A Midsummer Night's Dream*, 1596).

"Marriage has many pains, but celibacy has no pleasures" (Samuel Johnson, *The History of Rasselas*, 1759).

"Temporary chastity [wasl formerly understood to precede marriage . . . perhaps does precede it still in more cases than modern cynics would have us believe. This is of course celibacy in the devotional sense, for the young person who refrains from sexual intercourse before marriage does so, if not out of regard for a particular intended, at least out of respect for marriage as an institution. Thus temporary celibacy differs from the other genuine varieties only in the time element" (Juanita Tanner, *The Intelligent Man's Guide to Marriage and Celibacy*, 1929).

"Irrespective of questions of morality, the rule of celibacy in modern society is harmful to the State in proportion as it contributes to the aggrandisement of those who enforce it. A sacerdotal caste, divested of the natural ties of family and of the world, with interests in many respects antagonistic to the communities in which its members reside . . . is apt to prove a dangerous element in the body politic, and the true interests of religion as well as of humanity are almost as likely to receive injury as benefit at its hands, especially when it is armed with the measureless power of confession and absolution. . . . Such a caste would seem to be the inevitable consequence of compulsory celibacy in an ecclesiastical organization" (Henry Lea, *History of Sacerdotal Celibacy in the Christian Church*, 1966).

"The marriage of the clergy in the early centuries is seen from the first as a kind of left-over 'residue' which the early church had inherited—against its own deepest wish—from an earlier, ill-defined situation generally attributed to 'human weakness,' to the urgent needs of the moment, and to the survival of ideas about the subject which were handed on from Judaism as well as from Greco-Roman paganism, even before the advent of the still more disturbing contribution of the barbarian world. Hence, by the various stages of habit, custom, regulation, and law, the history of clerical celibacy comes to appear simply as a long and glorious 'battle' for the gradual elimination of the undesirable 'residue' inherited from early days, and at the same time for the establishment of a regime of total continence" (Jean-Paul Audet, *Structures of Christian Priesthood*, 1968).

"There is the *biological* basis of singleness, as expressed in abstention from sexual relationships. By moral tradition this characteristic has always been attributed to single women but *not*, as we well know, to their male counterparts, for whom a more generous latitude in sexual involvement is not only permitted but also implicitly expected" (Margaret Adams, *Single Blessedness*, 1976).

"Religious are another group of celibates. These people freely commit themselves to a (celibate) life that includes the vows of poverty, obedience, and chastity within the context of community living. Although these celibates are a minority in terms of numbers, their life has a unique quality. Besides witnessing to a vow and to a community, they also give witness to the value of celibate living. They explicitly proclaim to society that celibate living can have significant value. Religious commit themselves to a vowed, communal, celibate life because they believe their celibacy frees them for a life of love for others and for God'' (William Kraft, *Sexual Dimensions of the Celibate Life*, 1979).

''Most women are celibate or without sex for extensive periods of time in their lives—whether as a youngster or as a widow, as a single woman, a divorcee or even during marriage for a variety of reasons. But the tendency on the part of many women is to disregard these times and to consider only the times of sexuality to be valuable. . . . Many women, it seems, cannot see that being celibate has any redeeming social value in their lives. . . . What they fail to see is that at another level, being celibate by choice is more liberating than being sexual by demand. . . . Women find that becoming celibate enables them to experience a greater degree of self-sufficiency and freedom while at the same time offering a chance to explore new dimensions in relationships'' (Gabrielle Brown, *The New Celibacy*, 1980).

CHANGE, SOCIAL

''The successive movement of the inactive and active operations constitutes what is called the course of things'' (*I Ching*, c. 1000 B.C.).

''All things are in constant flux and nothing ever remains unchanged'' (Heraclitus, *On Nature*, c. 500 B.C.).

''Everything is change. Everything yields its place and then is gone'' (Euripides, *Heracles*, 422 B.C.).

''When something changes and quits its proper limits, its change is also the death of that which came before'' (Lucretius, *On the Nature of Things*, c. 60 B.C.).

''One change always leaves the way open for the establishment of others'' (Niccolò Machiavelli, *The Prince*, 1513).

''History may be divided into three grand epochs, or states of civilization, each possessing a distinct character, spiritual and temporal . . . the first is the Theological and Military epoch. . . . The second epoch is Metaphysical and Juridical . . . the third epoch is that of Science and Industry'' (Auguste Comte, *System of Positive Polity*, 1854).

''The changes in the economic foundation lead sooner or later to the transformation of the whole immense superstructure. In studying such transformations it is always necessary to distinguish between the material transformation of the economic conditions of production, which can be determined with the precision of natural science, and the legal, political, religious, artistic or philosophic—in short, ideological forms in which men become conscious of this conflict and fight it out'' (Karl Marx, *A Contribution to the Critique of Political Economy*, 1859).

''One of the greatest pains to human nature is the pain of a new idea'' (Walter Bagehot, *Physics and Politics*, 1869).

''The proletariat seizes state power, and then transforms the means of production into state property. But in doing this, it puts an end to itself as the proletariat, it puts an end to all class differences and class antagonisms, it puts an end also to the state as the state. Former society, moving in class antagonisms, had need of the state, that is, an organization of the exploiting class at each period for the maintenance of its external conditions of production; therefore, in particular, for the forcible holding down of the exploited class in the condition of oppression. . . . The state was the official representative . . . of that class which itself, in its epoch, represented society as a whole: in ancient times, the state of the slave-owning citizens; in the Middle Ages, of the feudal nobility; in our epoch, of the bourgeoisie. When ultimately it becomes really representative of society as a whole, it makes itself superfluous . . . the seizure of the means of production in the name of society—is at the same time its last independent act as a state. The interference of a state power in social relations becomes superfluous . . . and then becomes dormant of itself. . . . The state is not 'abolished,' *it withers away*'' (Friedrich Engels, *Anti-Dühring,* 1878).

''[We] are entering a tumultuously dynamic epoch'' (Edward Ross, *The Foundations of Sociology*, 1905).

''[We need] a scientific basis for progressive, in distinction from revolutionary or reactionary, social reconstruction'' (Charles Ellwood, *The Social Problem*, 1915).

''[In South America, changes due to] industry, democracy, and science will be delayed'' (Edward Ross, *South of Panama,* 1915).

''They [reformers] say and believe that they are solving an ojective problem: 'What is the best form for a society?' Actually they are solving a subjective problem: 'What form of society best fits my sentiments?' '' (Vilfredo Pareto, *The Mind and Society*, 1916).

''[Social change may result from] the increase of population, a new physical environment, a new cultural contact, a new discovery or a new invention'' (Charles Ellwood, *Introduction to Social Psychology*, 1917).

''The vast social changes which characterize our age raise to a plane of great importance for sociology theories of social evolution and practical programmes'' (William Ogburn, *Social Change*, 1922).

''Cultures are organisms, and world history is their collective biography. . . . Every culture, every adolescence and maturing and decay of a culture, every one of its intrinsically necessary stages and periods, has a definite duration, always the same, always recurring with the emphasis of a symbol'' (Oswald Spengler, *The Decline of the West*, 1922).

''Middletown's life exhibits at almost every point either some change or some stress arising from failure to change. A citizen has a foot on the relatively solid ground of established institutional habits and the other fast to an escalator erratically moving in several directions at a bewildering variety of speeds'' (Robert and Helen Lynd, *Middletown*, 1929).

''Knowlege of antecedents, that is, of similar phenomena preceding a given phenomenon, is interesting and instructive to historians. . . . But these 'antecedents' are not the only factors involved and perhaps not the most important'' (J. Calmette, *Feudal Society*, 1932).

''Changes are going on in the universe . . . as a consequence of these changes the universe is becoming a different universe. Intelligence is but one aspect of this change. It is a change that is part of an ongoing living process that tends to maintain itself'' (George H. Mead, *The Philosophy of the Present*, 1932).

''People who do not want to change are called conservatives. They want to bring back the Good Old Days. But we know that sort of thing is foolish. We can't bring back the Good Old Days, no matter how much the old men want them'' (William Ogburn, *Recent Social Trends*, 1934).

''The moral experience is . . . nothing but a perpetual rebellion of the spirit: a rebellion against the present in the name of the future . . . it is a spiritual revolution, always going deeper and becoming more and more moral as it is revolutionized'' (Georges Davidovitch Gurvitch, *Theoretical Ethics and the Science of the Mores*, 1937).

''As one walked Middletown's residential streets in 1935 one felt overpoweringly the continuities with 1925 that these homes represent. Whatever changes may have occurred elsewhere in the city's life—in business, education, or charity—here in these big and little, clean and cluttered houses in their green yards one gained that sense . . . of life's having gone on unaltered'' (Robert and Helen Lynd, *Middletown in Transition*, 1937).

''An enormous number of sociocultural systems and processes have a limited range of possibilities in their variation, in the creation of new fundamental forms'' (Pitirim Sorokin, *Social and Cultural Dynamics*, 1941).

'' 'Change' is scientific, 'progress' is ethical'' (Bertrand Russell, *Unpopular Essays*, 1950).

''If he is not a proper catalyst of social change, neither ought a sociologist to serve as a justifier of received patterns, legitimating them with *post factum* omniscience as a product of 'inevitability.' If the sociologist may not expatiate upon what 'ought to be,' he is still privileged to deal with another realm, 'the realm of what can be ' '' (Alvin Gouldner, *Patterns of Industrial Bureaucracy*, 1954).

''Great cultural changes begin in affectation and end in routine'' (Jacques Barzun, *The House of Intellect*, 1959).

''Historical change *is* change of social relations, of the relations among their component parts'' (C. W. Mills, *The Sociological Imagination*, 1959).

''The Mexican Revolution forced us to emerge from ourselves to confront the truths of history, and to recognize that we must invent new institutions and a new future. But the Revolution has expired without resolving our contradictions'' (Octavio Paz, *The Labyrinth of Solitude*, 1961).

''Whenever there was . . . economic change we also found corresponding changes in political and ritual roles and relations as well as in the principles of social organization. Thus we have established a positive correlation between economic, political, ritual, and organizational change, with economic change being the determining variable'' (T. Epstein, *Economic Development and Social Change in South India*, 1962).

''Theories of social change can be reduced to a few basic models . . . traditionally theories of social change have been developed in great profusion around these basic models . . . recent sociological theories have only weakly and uncertainly exploited the traditional models . . . nevertheless, one of the primary justifications for the development of sociology in the first place was its interest in social and cultural change'' (Don Martindale, *Social Life and Cultural Change*, 1962).

''A Galilean change of thought is required which makes us realize that all units of social organization are continuously changing, unless some force intervenes to arrest this change'' (Ralf Dahrendorf in L. Coser and B. Rosenberg, eds., *Sociological Theory*, 1964).

''One of the most recent trends in social science has been the stress on social change and its effects on political and other kinds of behaviour'' (Jeffrey Stanyer in Instituto de Ciencias Sociales, *The County*, 1966).

''A specter is stalking in our midst whom only a few see with clarity. . . . It is a new specter: a completely mechanized society, devoted to maximal material output and consumption, directed by computers; and in this social process, man himself is being transformed into a part of the total machine, well fed and entertained, yet passive, unalive, and with little feeling'' (Erich Fromm, *The Revolution of Hope*, 1968).

''Through research . . . the development of cultural traditions has become an institutionalized dynamic factor in social change'' (Talcott Parsons in Philip Rieff, ed., *On Intellectuals*, 1970).

''Consciousness III starts with self. In contrast to Consciousness II, which accepts society, the public interest, and institutions as the private reality, III declares that the individual self is the only true reality. Thus it returns to the earlier America: 'Myself I sing' '' (Charles Reich, *The Greening of America*, 1970).

''Western society for the past 300 years has been caught up in a fire storm of change. This storm, far from abating, now appears to be gathering force. Change sweeps through the highly industrialized countries with waves of ever accelerating speed and unprecedented impact. It spawns in its wake all sorts of curious social flora—from psychedelic churches and 'free universities' to science cities in the Arctic and wife-swap clubs in California. It breeds odd personalities, too: children who at twelve are no longer childlike; adults who at fifty are children of twelve. There are rich men who playact poverty, computer programmers who turn on with LSD. There are anarchists who, beneath their dirty denim shirts, are outrageous conformists, and conformists who, beneath their button-down collars, are outrageous anarchists. There are married priests and atheist ministers and Jewish Zen Buddhists. . . . This new disease can be called 'future shock' . . . the parallel term 'culture shock' has already begun to creep into the popular vocabulary. Culture shock is the effect that immersion in a strange culture has on the unprepared visitor. Peace Corps volunteers suffer from it in Borneo or Brazil. Marco Polo probably suffered from it in Cathay . . . culture shock is relatively mild in comparison with the much more serious malady, future shock'' (Alvin Toffler, *Future Shock*, 1970).

''The concepts and tools recently developed [theories of social change] will serve as the building stones of a new theory of change that is not only grand, but also testable, and one which when tested will be found true'' (Amitai Etzioni and Eva Etzioni-Halevy, eds., *Social Change*, 1973).

''In the types of social changes men describe as crusades and social movements the definitions of social situations are being transformed. Moreover, in these, as in other human affairs conscious intention and adaptation to unintended consequences of action occur''(Don and Edith Martindale, *Psychiatry and the Law*, 1973).

''The pace of change in general, and particularly the rate at which the world is becoming a single though highly disordered system, gives a kind of urgency to the notion that crisis is the ordinary state of social life'' (Wilbert Moore, *Social Change*, 1974).

''The goal of [East] Indian Planning is economic growth coupled with social justice. . . . Multi Level Planning enables decisions to be made closest to the area and to the people'' (Shankar Ghosh, *Changing India*, 1978).

''Change, for Middletown, is something flowing irresistibly from the outside world. Continuity is furnished locally. The outside world continuously proposes new ways of living and thinking. The local community steadfastly resists most of these suggestions and modifies those it adopts into conformity with its own customs'' (Theodore Caplow et al., *Middletown Families*, 1982).

CHILD ABUSE

''There seems to be an unbroken spectrum of parental action towards children ranging from the breaking of bones and the fracturing of skulls through severe bruising, through severe spanking and on to mild 'reminder' pats on the bottom. To be aware of this, one has only to look at the families of one's friends and neighbors. . . . The amount of yelling, scolding, slapping, punching, hitting, and yanking acted out by parents on very small children is almost shocking'' (B. Steele and C. Pollack in R. Helfer and C. Kempe, eds., *The Battered Child*, 1968).

''Public concern over the scope and significance of the problem of the battered child is a comparatively new phenomenon. Participation by counsel in any significant numbers in child abuse cases in juvenile or family courts is of even more recent origin. It is small wonder that the lawyer approaches participation in these cases with trepidation'' (J. Isaacs in R. Helfer and C. Kempe, eds., *Helping the Battered Child and His Family*, 1972).

''The parent who recreates the pattern of abusive child rearing may be doing this because this is the means of child rearing he learned while growing up. It is the way he knows of responding to stress and bringing up his child'' (Richard Gelles in Suzanne Steinmetz and Murray Straus, eds., *Violence in the Family*, 1974).

''An ordinary spanking or slap by a parent would not be counted as abuse'' (Suzanne Steinmetz and Murray Straus, eds., *Violence in the Family*, 1974).

''If the child who has been physically abused is returned to his parents without intervention, 5 per cent are killed and 35 per cent are seriously reinjured. Moreover, the untreated families tend to produce children who grow up to be juvenile delinquents and murderers, as well as the batterers of the next generation'' (B. Schmitt and C. Kempe in V. Vaughan and R. McKay, eds., *Nelson Textbook of Pediatrics*, 1975).

''Although instances of child abuse and neglect can be traced back five thousand years to the beginning of man's recorded activities, it was not until the 1870s that the first societies for the prevention of cruelty to children were founded in the United States'' (Beatrice Kalisch, *Child Abuse and Neglect*, 1978).

''Attorneys are proudly unwilling to accept conclusions or impressions lacking empirical corroboration. To lawyers, the law and legal institutions become involved in child abuse when certain facts fit a standard of review. To clinicians, the law may be seen as an instrument to achieve a particular therapeutic or dispositional objective (e.g., the triggering of services or of social welfare involvement) even if, as is often the case, the data to support such objectives legally are missing or ambiguous. The clinician's approach . . . is frequently subjective or intuitive . . . while the lawyer demands evidence'' (Richard Bourne and Eli Newberger, *Critical Perspectives on Child Abuse*, 1979).

''The poor and members of ethnic minority groups seem to be subject to many of the conditions and forces which may lead to abusive behavior toward children in other groups of the population and, in addition to this, they seem to be subject to the special environmental stresses and strains associated with socioeconomic deprivation and discrimination. This would suggest that the significantly higher reporting rates for poor and nonwhite segments of the population reflect a real underlying higher incidence rate among these groups'' (D. Gil, ed., *Child Abuse and Violence*, 1979).

''Each year mounting reports of suspected child abuse reach protective service workers in the United States; the panorama of a prison corridor interrupts evening television viewing as the announcer explains that almost all criminals suffered abuse as children'' (George Gerbner et al., eds., *Child Abuse*, 1980).

''Sexual abuse if handled supportively can result in minimal long-term effects, particularly where neither parental overreaction, nor violence nor court appearance has occurred'' (Linda Corsini-Munt in Benjamin Schlesinger, *Sexual Abuse of Children*, 1983).

CHILDHOOD

''As arrows are in the hand of a mighty man; so are children of the youth'' (Psalms 127:4).

''Lazy children will master neither reading nor music nor athletics nor that which is the foundation of virtue, namely, the feeling of shame; for the feeling of shame is born exactly of these practices'' (Democritus, Fragment 179, c. 400 B.C.).

''The life of children, like that of intemperate men, is entirely governed by their desires'' (Aristotle, *Nichomachean Ethics*, c. 350 B.C.).

''The relatives shall not offer libations to a child that has not reached the third year'' (Manu, *Laws*, c. 200 B.C.).

'' 'Tis not good that children should know any wickedness'' (William Shakespeare, *The Merry Wives of Windsor*, 1601).

''Every man must be conscious of that insipidity of childhood which disgusts the sane mind; that coarseness of youth which finds pleasure in scarcely anything but material objects and which is only a very crude sketch of the man of thought'' (Baltasar Gracián y Morales, *The Discrete One*, 1646).

''If a man from his cradle had been always used to go barefoot whilst his hands were constantly wrapt up in warm mittens and covered with handshoes, as the Dutch call gloves . . . such a custom would make taking wet in his hands as dangerous to him as now taking wet in their feet is to a great many others'' (John Locke, *Some Thoughts Concerning Education*, 1693).

''They [children of the poor] do just as they please, their parents paying no attention to them, even treating them in an idolatrous manner: what the children want, they want too'' (Jean-Baptiste de la Salle, *Conduct of the Christian Schools*, 1720, posthumously).

''Childhood has its own ways of seeing, thinking, and feeling; nothing is more foolish than to try to substitute our ways'' (Jean Jacques Rousseau, *Émile*, 1762).

''When the right order of things is inverted, the faculties of the mind are weakened and lose their steadiness. You do this when, before making children sensitive to truth and wisdom by the real knowledge of actual objects, you engage them in the thousand-fold confusion of world-learning'' (Johann Heinrich Pestalozzi, *Evening Hour of a Hermit*, 1780).

''I have known mothers whose irritation at the faults of their children was greatly enhanced by the fact that they recognized them as merely the faults of their own childhood recurring once again'' (Helen Bosanquet, *The Family*, 1902).

''The child is long before puberty a being capable of mature love, lacking only the ability for reproduction'' (Sigmund Freud, *The Sexual Enlightenment of Children*, 1907).

''The family is the smallest social unit and the primary defining agency. As soon as the child has free motion and begins to pull, tear, pry, meddle, and prowl, the parents begin to define the situation through speech and other signs and pressures: 'Be quiet,' 'Sit up straight' '' (William Thomas, *The Unadjusted Girl*, 1923).

''The Celtic boy who lived in the last years of the Bronze Age in Britain saw the ending of a vast, vague, and barbaric story, not devoid of poetry and splendour, but rough and mysterious as the stones of the British temples'' (Dorothy Stuart, *The Boy Through the Ages*, 1926).

''Apart from the tender cares dictated by nature and endorsed by custom and tradition, there enters the element of cultural education. Not only is there a need of training instinct into full development, as in the animal instruction in food-gathering and specific movements, there is also the necessity of developing a number of cultural habits as indispensable to man as instincts are to animals. Man has to teach his children manual skill and knowlege in arts and crafts; language and the traditions of moral culture; the manners and customs which make up social organization'' (Bronislaw Malinowski, *Sex and Repression in Savage Society*, 1927).

''One of the first definite steps in the socialization of the child is accomplished by means of the name. . . . The name, and the manner of its bestowal, are initial reactions of the folk to the new addition to their number'' (Nathan Miller, *The Child in Primitive Society*, 1928).

''Even from the earliest years of the child's life the former dominance of the home is challenged; the small child spends less time in the home than in the ample days of the nineties'' (Robert and Helen Lynd, *Middletown*, 1929).

''The child's behavior towards persons shows signs from the first of those sympathetic tendencies and affective reactions in which one can easily see the raw material of all subsequent moral behavior'' (Jean Piaget, *The Moral Judgment of the Child*, 1932).

''In ancient Babylonia the position of the daughter was almost equal to that of the son'' (Dorothy Stuart, *The Girl Through the Ages*, 1933).

''The infant's first social achievement . . . is his willingness to let the mother out of sight without undue anxiety or rage, because she has become an inner certainty as well as an outer predictability. Such consistency, continuity, and sameness of experience provide a rudimentary sense of ego identity'' (Erik Erikson, *Childhood and Society*, 1950).

''Every child is different, every parent is different, every illness or behavior problem is somewhat different from every other'' (Benjamin Spock, *Baby and Child Care*, 1957).

''No matter how uncouth schoolchildren may outwardly appear, they remain tradition's warmest friends. Like the savage, they are respecters, even venerators, of custom; and in their self-contained community their basic lore and language seems scarcely to alter from generation to generation'' (Iona and Peter Opie, *The Lore and Language of Schoolchildren*, 1959).

''Since the beginning of the human race men have built homes and begot children . . . within the great family types, monogamous and polygamous, historical differences are of little importance in comparison with the huge mass of what remains unchanged'' (Philippe Ariès, *The Child and Familial Life*, 1960).

''[As for child care among Zaire's Mbute pygmies] it does not matter which hut, because as far as the child is concerned, all adults are his parents or grandparents. They are all equally likely to slap him for doing wrong, or fondle him and feed him with delicacies if he is quiet and gives them no trouble'' (C. Turnbull, *The Forest People*, 1962).

''The child came to the serious attention of the modern world as an object of tender solicitude and of organized welfare endeavor. It was as such that the child was first regarded by sociologists. This was wholly natural, for the desire for social uplift was the background out of which sociology arose. With this original primary emphasis upon social amelioration, the welfare of the child became an obvious and logical objective'' (James Bossard and Eleanor Boll, *The Sociology of Child Development*, 1966).

''Except for a China now gone, I am sure Japan is the happiest spot on earth. . . . Little children are loved and indulged'' (Pearl Buck, *The People of Japan*, 1966).

''The younger the child, the more we are concerned with educational processes that are universal and of fundamental importance throughout life, and least imbued with the specific cultural differences that distinguish a Frenchman from an Egyptian, or an Eskimo from a Bushman'' (Margaret Mead in Murray Wax et al., eds., *Anthropological Perspectives on Education*, 1971).

''The history of childhood is a nightmare. . . . The further back in history one goes, the lower the level of child care, and the more likely children are to be killed, abandoned, beaten, terrorized, and sexually abused'' (Lloyd deMause, ed., *The History of Childhood*, 1974).

''Little Jane Turrell, born in 1708 to President Turrell of Harvard, knew her alphabet at two, her catechism at three, and was reading Cicero and Homer in the original at an age when modern children are wading through *Dick and Jane*'' (Mary Cable, *The Little Darlings*, 1975).

''The roots of the revolution in child raising that today is commonly attributed to Dr. Spock are to be found in this book [C. and Mary Aldrich, *Babies Are Human Beings*, 1938]'' (Daniel Beekman, *The Mechanical Baby*, 1977).

''Children have always been confronted, sooner or later, with different standards from which to choose, but today the gap is wider and more widely spread through the community'' (Scottish Education Department, *Truancy and Indiscipline in Schools in Scotland*, 1977).

''Childhood is held to be a status, a position in a society relative to other age groups older than twelve years of age. . . . Children, however, are young individuals just acquiring the ways of the persons who are older than themselves'' (Marvin Koller and Oscar Ritchie, *Sociology of Childhood*, 1978).

''From the earliest Socratic dialogues onwards social theorists have systematically endeavoured to constitute a view of the child that is compatible with their particular visions of social life. Since that initial Hellenic desire to seek out the origins of virtue in order to instil rhythm and harmony into the souls of the young, up until our contemporary pragmatic concerns with the efficacy of specific child-rearing practices, after centuries of debate, we have still not achieved any consensus over the issue of childhood'' (Chris Jenks, ed., *The Sociology of Childhood*, 1982).

''In 1784, the Austrian government passed a law forbidding young children to sleep with their parents, since a common practice of that time was for parents to 'accidentally' roll over and suffocate their sleeping child'' (Carol Flake-Hobson et al., *Child Development and Relationships*, 1983).

CINEMA, SOCIOLOGY OF

''There is only one thing that can kill the Movies, and that is education'' (Will Rogers, *Autobiography*, 1949).

''The stultifying effect of the movies is *not* that the children see them but that their parents do'' (Paul Goodman, *Growing Up Absurd*, 1960).

''Sociology must involve the study of trash. The cinema is—sociologically, at least—a mass art; and it would be silly to pretend that mass taste is very high, or that the average product reaches above mass taste to any high standard of excellence . . . occasionally it even satisfies highbrow criteria: it can be informative, well done, sophisticated'' (I. Jarvie, *Movies and Society*, 1970).

''The film in America is a collaborative professional activity, a business first and an art second'' (Charles Higham, *The Art of the American Film*, 1973).

''For the first half of the twentieth century—from 1896 to 1946, to be exact—movies were the most popular and influential medium of culture in the United States. They were the first of the modern mass media, and they rose to the surface of cultural consciousness from the bottom up, receiving their principal support from the lowest and most invisible classes in American society'' (Robert Sklar, *Movie-Made America*, 1975).

CIVILIZATION

''The passage from the state of nature to the civil state produces a very remarkable change in man by substituting justice for instinct'' (Jean Jacques Rousseau, *The Social Contract*, 1762).

''By rapidly improving the means of production and by enormously facilitating communication, the bourgeoisie drags all the nations, even the most barbarian, into the orbit of civilisation'' (Karl Marx and Friedrich Engels, *Communist Manifesto*, 1847).

''Civilization has, under every aspect, made constant progress. On the other hand . . . the practical combinations that have until now guided civilization were not always those best adapted to promote its progress and frequently tended rather to impede than to assist this . . . civilization is governed by a natural law of progress'' (Auguste Comte, *System of Positive Polity*, 1854).

''[Early civilization rests] first, on the energy and regularity with which labor is conducted, and second, on the returns made to that labor by the bounty of nature'' (Henry Buckle, *History of Civilization in England*, 1861).

''Civilization is the making of civil persons'' (John Ruskin, *The Crown of Wilde Olive*, 1866).

''Civilization, taken in its wide ethnographic sense, is that complex whole which includes knowledge, belief, art, morals, law, custom, and any other capabilities and habits acquired by man as a member of society . . . the uniformity which so largely pervades civilization may be ascribed, in great measure, to the uniform action of uniform causes; while on the other hand its various grades may be regarded as stages of development or evolution, each the outcome of previous history, and about to do its proper part in shaping the history of the future'' (Edward Tylor, *Primitive Culture*, 1871).

''Civilization is used in a number of different ways. To some it means certain finer, choicer, and more spiritual or moral achievements of mankind and is thus contrasted with barbarism or savagery'' (William Ogburn, *Social Change*, 1922).

''There is held to be no surer test of civilisation than the increase per head of the consumption of alcohol and tobacco'' (Havelock Ellis, *The Dance of Life*, 1923).

''Civilization represents the human effort to conquer the world of nature and of culture by means of intelligence in the spheres of science, technology, and planning'' (Alfred Weber, *Cultural History as Cultural Sociology*, 1935).

''Civilization is not found in a more or less high degree of sophistication, but in a conscience that is shared by an entire nation'' (Albert Camus, *Notebooks*, 1937).

''All civilizations have been generated, and are perpetuated, only by the use of symbols'' (Leslie White, *The Science of Culture*, 1949).

''As regards the growth of civilization . . . change and progress can take place through an invention without any . . . constitutional alteration of the human species'' (Alfred Kroeber, *The Nature of Culture*, 1952).

''The communities which more than any other serve as vehicles of Western civilization are nation-states. The intellectual roles standing at their core are those of humanist and scientist. At the basis of all distinctively modern developments lies a fabulously effective mastery of nature. Moreover, having displayed unparalleled powers to transform physical nature, science has been applied to ever-widening spheres of life outside the strictly material'' (Don Martindale, *Social Life and Cultural Change*, 1962).

''Civilized society [eighteenth and nineteenth centuries] on the whole is characterized by the extended family, and by strong loyalty to the kinfolk. . . . As we move to post-civilized society, we find an extension of loyalty from the kinship group to larger areas such as the national state, or even to the world as a whole'' (Kenneth Boulding, *The Meaning of the Twentieth Century*, 1964).

''Most civilizations have tended to move from a heroic age through a time of troubles, to a universal state partially integrating the civilization'' (Quincy Wright in G. Hallen and Rajeshwar Prasad, eds., *Towards Global Sociology*, 1970).

CLASS, SOCIAL

''Citizens, you are brothers, but God has made you differently. Some of you have the power of command, having been made of gold; others, of silver, to be assistants; and others, of brass and iron, to be farmers and craftsmen'' (Plato, *Republic*, c. 400 B.C.).

''In every state, the people are divided into three types: the very wealthy, the very poor, and, thirdly, those found between these two'' (Aristotle, *Politics*, c. 350 B.C.).

''I was told that the Privileged and the People formed two nations'' (Benjamin Disraeli, *Sybil*, 1845).

''The separate individuals form a class only insofar as they have to carry on a common battle against another class; otherwise they are on hostile terms with each other as competitors. On the other hand, the class in its turn achieves an independent existence over against the individuals, so that the latter find their conditions of existence predestined, and hence have their position in life and their personal development assigned to them by their class, become subsumed under it'' (Karl Marx and Friedrich Engels, *The German Ideology*, 1846).

''In the earlier epochs of history, we find almost everywhere a complicated arrangement of society into various orders, a manifold gradation of social rank. In ancient Rome we have patricians, knights, plebeians, slaves; in the Middle Ages, feudal lords, vassals, guild-masters, journeymen, apprentices, serfs; in almost all of these classes, again, subordinate gradations. . . . The modern bourgeoisie is itself the product of a long course of development, of a series of revolutions in the methods of production and the means of communication'' (Karl Marx and Friedrich Engels, *Communist Manifesto*, 1847).

''What [Ricardo] forgets to stress is the continued increase of the middle classes which stand between the workers on the one hand and the capitalists and great landowners on the other, and which feed off rent value in increasing numbers. These middle classes weigh directly on the working-class base and increase the social security and power of the ten thousand persons on top'' (Karl Marx, *Theories of Surplus Value*, 1863).

''A really human morality which transcends class antagonisms and their legacies in thought becomes possible only at a stage of society which has not only overcome class contradictions but has even forgotten them in practical life'' (Friedrich Engels, *Anti-Dühring*, 1878).

''What constitutes a class? . . . The reply to this follows naturally from the reply to another question, namely: What makes wage-labourers, capitalists and landlords constitute the three great social classes? At first glance—the identity of revenues and sources of revenue. There are three great social groups whose members, the individuals forming them, live on wages, profit and ground-rent respectively, on the realisation of their labour-power, their capital, and their landed property. However, from this standpoint, physicians and officials, e.g., would also constitute two classes, for they belong to two distinct social groups, the members of each of these groups receiving their revenue from one and the same source'' (Karl Marx, *Das Kapital*, 1879).

''A state of a society, if it be bad for one class, is bad for all . . . [Greed leads to] the exceeding indigence of the poor and the exceeding opulence of the rich'' (Lester Ward, *Dynamic Sociology*, 1883).

''[There is no corruption] where there is neither poverty to be bribed nor wealth to bribe'' (Edward Bellamy, *Looking Backward*, 1888).

''In all societies—from societies that are very meagerly developed and have barely attained the dawnings of civilization, down to the most advanced and powerful societies—two classes of people appear, a class that rules and a class that is ruled'' (Gaetano Mosca, *Elements of Political Science*, 1896).

''When a principled anti-caste sect recruits former members of various Hindu castes and tears them away from the context of their former ritualistic duties, the caste responds by excommunicating all the sect's proselytes. Unless the sect is able to abolish the caste system altogether, instead of simply tearing away some of its members, it becomes, from the standpoint of the caste system, a quasi-guest folk, a kind of confessional guest community in an ambiguous position in the prevailing Hindu order'' (Max Weber, *The Religion of India*, 1917).

''[Among the Incas the] gentry-priesthood class . . . controlled everything, ran everything, and operated the state economy as a dominant class, sitting on top of all the others'' (Nikolai Ivanovich Bukharin, *Theory of Historical Materialism*, 1921).

'' 'Class situation' means the typical probability of (1) procuring goods (2) gaining a position in life and (3) finding inner satisfactions'' (Max Weber, *Economy and Society*, 1922, posthumously).

''It is possible to abandon one's class position through an individual or collective rise or fall in the social scale, irrespective for the moment whether this is due to personal merit, personal effort, social upheaval, or mere chance. . . . Class position is an objective fact, whether the individual in question knows his class position or not, and whether he acknowledges it or not'' (Karl Mannheim, *Essays on the Sociology of Knowledge*, 1929).

''[Class consciousness is] not only consciousness of kind, or consciousness of membership in and feeling of solidarity with a group called a class, but the possession of common interests and a common political and economic outlook or orientation'' (Richard Centers, *The Psychology of Social Classes*, 1949).

''The untouchables [in India] themselves have been partly responsible for their failure to advance farther. Some resist change for fear that it will eventually mean losing their hold on the ancestral occupation. Others reveal a natural diffidence in asserting their new rights. Though they are permitted in the temple, they don't like to go there. They do not patronize Brahmin restaurants as they are entitled to, because they do not feel comfortable in the company to be found there'' (Robert Trumbull, *As I See India*, 1956).

''The concept of class is an analytical tool which is meaningful only in the context of a class theory. 'Classes' are major interest groupings emerging from specific structural circumstances, which intervene as such in social conflicts and play a part in changes of social structure'' (Ralf Dahrendorf, *Class and Class Conflict in Industrial Society*, 1957).

''Ownership is nothing other than the right of profit and control. If one defines class benefits by this right, the communist states have seen in the final analysis, the origin of a new form of ownership or of a new ruling and exploiting class.

. . . The new class may be said to be made up of those who have special privileges and economic preferences because of the administrative monopoly they hold'' (Milovan Djilas, *The New Class*, 1957).

''The lower class boys and girls do not have access to the Country Club and, in large part, they cannot attend lodge dances because few of their parents belong. . . . The net effect is the segregation of the young people along class lines'' (August Hollingshead, *Elmtown's Youth*, 1961).

''The family, not the physical person, is the true unit of class and class theory'' (Joseph Schumpeter, *Imperialism, Social Classes*, 1961).

''Social classes are specific groups which are very large and which represent macrocosms of minor groups. The unity of these macrocosms is based on their supra-functionality, on their resistance to being penetrated by the global society, on their radical incompatibility among themselves, and on their advanced structuration with a predominant collective consciousness and specific cultural works. These groups, which first appear in industrial global societies where technical models and economic functions are specifically accentuated, have in addition the following traits: they exist de facto, are open, exist at a distance, are permanently divisive, and only have access to conditional constraint'' (Georges Davidovitch Gurvitch, *Studies on the Social Classes*, 1966, posthumously).

''In class society everyone lives as a member of a particular class, and every kind of thinking, without exception, is stamped with the brand of a class'' (Mao Tse-tung, *Quotations*, 1966).

''Three principles . . . constitute class consciousness: the *principle of identity* . . . the *principle of opposition* . . . the *principle of totality*'' (Alain Touraine, *Labor Consciousness*, 1966).

''[Much evidence casts] doubt on the widely held opinion that society is still structured along a nineteenth-century division into two fundamental classes, capitalist and proletarian, since the middle strata were being progressively assimilated with the proletariat through exploitation by Big Capital'' (Ermanno Gorrieri, *The Retributive Jungle*, 1972).

''The framework of feudal society was made up of noblemen, lords, soldiers, and priests whose wealth was based on land. The bourgeois society that took hold in the thirteenth century was made up of artisans, merchants, and free professionals whose property lay in their skills or their willingness to take risks'' (Daniel Bell, *The Coming of Post-Industrial Society*, 1973).

''If a class is indeed a concept, it does not designate a reality which can be placed in the structures; it designates the effect of an ensemble of given structures, an ensemble which determines social relations as class relations'' (Nicos Poulantzas, *Political Power and Social Classes*, 1973).

CLASS STRUGGLE

''In the Middle Ages the citizens in each town were compelled to unite against the landed nobility to save their skins. The extension of trade, the establishment of communications, led the separate towns to get to know other towns, which had asserted the same interests in the struggle with the same antagonist. Out of the many local corporations of burghers there arose only gradually the burgher *class*'' (Karl Marx and Friedrich Engels, *The German Ideology*, 1846).

''The struggle of class against class is a political struggle . . . the antagonism between the proletariat and the bourgeoisie is a struggle of class against class, a struggle which carried to its highest expression is a total revolution'' (Karl Marx, *The Poverty of Philosophy*, 1847).

''The history of all hitherto-existing society is the history of class struggles. Freeman and slave, patrician and plebeian, lord and serf, guild-master and journeyman, in a word, oppressor and oppressed, stood in constant opposition to one another, carried on an uninterrupted, now hidden, now open fight, a fight that each time ended, either in a revolutionary re-constitution of society at large, or in the common ruin of the contending classes. . . . The modern bourgeois society that has sprouted from the ruins of feudal society has not done away with class antagonisms. It has but established new classes, new conditions of oppression, new forms of struggle in place of the old ones. . . . Though not in substance, yet in form, the struggle of the proletariat with the bourgeoisie is at first a national struggle. The proletariat of each country must, of course, first of all settle matters with its own bourgeoisie'' (Karl Marx and Friedrich Engels, *Communist Manifesto*, 1847).

''The more the consciousness of authority as a feeling of superiority results in putting one class in such a position of power as to force the lower class to stay in its place, the more this latter will strive toward the attainment of equality and therefore the more indignant it becomes concerning oppression and arrogance on the part of the controlling class . . . this process is called *Klassenkampf* [class struggle]'' (Ferdinand Tönnies, *Community and Society*, 1887).

''Many of our revisionist critics believe that Marx asserted that economic development and the class struggle create, not only the conditions for socialist production, but also, and directly, the *consciousness* of its necessity. And these critics assert that . . . socialist consciousness appears to be a necessary and direct result of the proletarian class struggle. But this is absolutely untrue . . . socialism and the class struggle arise side by side and not one out of the other; each arises under different conditions'' (Karl Johann Kautsky in Nikolai Lenin, *What Is to Be Done*, 1902).

''The class struggles of Antiquity . . . were initially carried on by peasants and perhaps also artisans threatened by debt bondage'' (Max Weber, *Economy and Society*, 1922, posthumously).

''Marx would have laughed at these pompous asses [French communist ideologists] who take the class struggle for a Platonic idea or bring it in like a *Deus ex machina*'' (Jean-Paul Sartre, *The Ghost of Stalin*, 1968).

''Peaceful coexistence does not signify the revision of the laws of class struggle'' (*Soviet Military Encyclopedia,* 1980).

COHABITATION

''Coresidence without marriage [in Martinique] corresponding to the 'living with' or 'faithful concubinage' of the British West Indies, is called *ménage*. The majority of villagers have lived *en ménage*, and almost all marriages are preceded by it'' (Michael and Sylvia Horowitz in Victor Christopherson, ed., *Readings in Comparative Marriage and the Family*, 1967).

''[Among the Incas] single men and women, before deciding to marry, lived together . . . this seemed in no way a sin to them . . . after a period of considerable adolescent sexual liberty, the commoners of the empire entered a 'trial' relationship which tested the girl's work abilities and the couple's general compatibility'' (Richard Price in Victor Christopherson, ed., *Readings in Comparative Marriage and the Family*, 1967).

''[Cohabitation is] the nonlegalized heterosexual domestic unit. . . . What are some of the problems confronting cohabitors? . . . (1) painful indoctrination into nonexclusiveness by the male partner; (2) freedom for the male but not the female; (3) fear of being trapped in a monogamous relationship but without legal privileges and protection; (4) mutual consent before cohabitation; (5) experimentation with equality, influenced by women's liberation; (6) love and sex viewed as Christian sharing; and (7) the strong conviction that no cohabiting partner can fill all of his or her needs'' (Bert Adams, *The Family*, 1980).

''Cohabitants are, and regard themselves as being, more liberal about lifestyles—including sex and drugs. . . . Despite increasing cohabitation, interest in eventual marriage is still strong, though not necessarily to the person one is cohabiting with'' (Gilbert Nass and Gerald McDonald, *Marriage and the Family*, 1982).

''Human society has permitted some form of trial marriage for thousands of years, namely, betrothal, engagement, going steady, dating, and so forth. Extremist solutions are thus somewhat unnecessary. . . . Trial marriage is not a genuine experiment. If one wants to try marriage, try marriage, not trial marriage'' (Panos Bardis, *Global Marriage and Family Customs*, 1983).

''The number of unmarried couples living together has . . . risen. In 1980 the number of such couples counted by the Census Bureau had reached 1,560,000—three times the number in 1970'' (Arlene and Jerome Skolnick, *Family in Transition*, 1983).

COMMUNICATION

''If we had no voice or tongue, and wanted to communicate with others, would we not, in the fashion of deaf and dumb persons, make signs with the hands, the head, and the rest of the body?'' (Plato, *Cratylus*, c. 400 B.C.).

''You cannot talk about ice to a summer insect'' (Chuang Tzu, *Autumn Floods*, c. 300 B.C.).

"No one would talk much in society, if he only knew how often he misunderstands others" (Johann Wolfgang von Goethe, *Elective Affinities*, 1809).

"The bourgeoisie . . . by the immensely facilitated means of communication, draws all, even the most barbarian, nations into civilisation" (Karl Marx and Friedrich Engels, *Communist Manifesto*, 1847).

"[Freedom of communication tends to result in] the disease of the century [stress]. . . . [Communication is] the mechanism through which human relations exist and develop" (Charles H. Cooley, *Human Nature and the Social Order*, 1902).

"[Communication is] a device to carry on a common life-process among several distinct, though psychically interacting, individual units" (Charles Ellwood, *Sociology in Its Psychological Aspects*, 1913).

"[Modern modes of communication] wipe out those distances which formerly gave the nations a sense of security" (Edward Ross, *The Social Trend*, 1922).

"The mass media are the wholesalers; the peer-groups, the retailers of the communications industry" (David Riesman, *The Lonely Crowd*, 1950).

"When distant and unfamiliar and complex things are communicated to great masses of people, the truth suffers a considerable and often a radical distortion" (Walter Lippmann, *The Public Philosophy*, 1955).

"As the controversy proceeds, the formal media of communication—radio, television, and newspapers—become less and less able to tell people *as much* as they want to know about the controversy, or the *kinds of things* they want to know. . . . These media are simply not flexible enough. . . . At the same time, the media are restricted by normative and legal constraints" (James Coleman, *Community Conflict*, 1957).

"The medium is the message" (Marshall McLuhan, *Understanding Media*, 1964).

"Metacommunicational axiom . . . : one cannot not communicate" (P. Watzlawick et al., *Pragmatics of Human Communication*, 1967).

"There were several clear cases of votes cast not on the issues or even the personalities of the candidates. In fact, they were not really cast for the candidates at all. They were cast, so to speak, for the voters' friends . . . personal influence, with all its overtones of personal affection and loyalty, can bring to the polls votes that would otherwise not be cast or would be cast for the opposing party just as readily if some other friend had insisted" (Paul Lazarsfeld et al., *The People's Choice*, 1968).

"Within the solid framework of preestablished inequality and power, tolerance is practiced indeed. Even outrageous opinions are expressed, outrageous incidents are televised; and the critics of established policies are interrupted by the same number of commercials as the conservative advocates. Are these interludes supposed to counteract the sheer weight, magnitude, and continuity of system-publicity, indoctrination which operates playfully through endless commercials as well as through the entertainment?" (Herbert Marcuse in Robert Wolff et al., *A Critique of Pure Tolerance*, 1969).

"In communication, ideas do not fly through the air from one mind to another. Ideas (consciousness, awareness) are, in every case, attributes of the biological substance of an individual brain. They are not substances with independent existence. They are tied down to their neurones and cannot escape. Communication is always signalling from a distance through physical media" (Gardner Williams in G. Hallen and Rajeshwar Prasad, eds., *Towards Global Sociology*, 1970).

"Communication permeates every process of man's life" (Ithiel Pool and Wilbur Schramm, *Handbook of Communication*, 1973).

"The mass media in the United States are almost entirely commercial enterprises" (Alan Wells, ed., *Mass Communications*, 1974).

"Our remote ancestors were communicating animals living in small bands millions of years ago" (Melvin De Fleur and Sandra Ball-Rokeach, *Theories of Mass Communication*, 1975).

"Information technology has today become an almost completely flexible tool. Its organization can spread without encountering a major obstacle through all the configurations of power" (Simon Nora and Alain Minc, *The Informing of Society*, 1978).

"For a living being that maintains itself in the structures of ordinary language communication, the validity basis of speech has the binding force of universal and unavoidable—in this sense—transcendental—presuppositions" (Jürgen Habermas, *Communication and the Evolution of Society*, 1979).

COMMUNITY

"The ideal political community must be among those who are found at the middle level" (Aristotle, *Politics*, c. 350 B.C.).

"All those who are included in a community are parts of the whole" (Thomas Aquinas, *Summa Theologica*, 1274).

"Only within a community does the individual receive the means to develop his creative talents in an all-around manner. Only in the community does personal freedom become possible. . . . In the true community of the future, the individual, through his associations with others, will immediately receive his freedom" (Karl Marx and Friedrich Engels, *The German Ideology*, 1846).

"The exterior forms of community life as represented by natural will and *Gemeinschaft* were distinguished as house, village, and town. These are the lasting types of real and historical life . . . it is in the organization and order of the *Gemeinschaft* that folk life and folk culture persist" (Ferdinand Tönnies, *Community and Society*, 1887).

"In addition to the family we have the community as a defining agency. At present the community is so weak and vague that it gives us no idea of the former power of the local group in regulating behavior. Originally the community was practically the whole world of its members. It was composed of families related by blood and marriage and was not so large that all the members could not come together; it was a face-to-face group. I asked a Polish peasant what was the extent of an '*okolica*' or neighborhood—how far it reached. 'It reaches,' he said, 'as far as the report of a man reaches—as far as a man is talked about' '' (William Thomas, *The Unadjusted Girl*, 1923).

''*In the cosmopolitan community* the individual is the unit of social organization. Everybody looks out for himself, and selfish motivations are emphasized; the individual and the present are all that matter . . . 'community' is merely an address. . . . The cosmopolitan community emphasizes many contacts, but few of them are between 'old friends' '' (Carle Zimmerman, *The Changing Community*, 1938).

''[Unlike a region, the community] does not comprehend all the factors of time, area, and cultural conditioning'' (Howard Odum, *Understanding Society*, 1947).

''Within those early communities the relationships among people were primarily those of personal status. In a small and intimate community all people are known for their individual qualities of personality . . . men and women are known as persons, not as parts of mechanical operations'' (Robert Redfield, *The Primitive World and Its Transformations*, 1953).

''The small town is a type of community that by general agreement is embattled in the current world. The decline in importance of the small town is one of the primary reasons for the judgment by some sociologists that the community itself is going into eclipse. . . . The most general change in the theory of community is the reevaluation of the importance of locality for community'' (Don Martindale and R. Hanson, *Small Town and the Nation*, 1969).

''Control of the educational institutions, hospitals, the police force, social agencies, and other agencies serving the local neighbourhood is an essential step in ending the state of alienation and hopelessness so prevalent in many communities today'' (W. Head in J. Draper, ed., *Citizen Participation: Canada*, 1971).

''While movement of the young to large urban centres is an important phenomenon of our time, the smaller cities and towns and their associated space remain an important part of our community system'' (Carle Zimmerman and Garry Moneo, *The Prairie Community System*, 1971).

''*Middletown* is for the sociologist of the community what Durkheim's *Suicide* is for sociology as a whole. It represents a magnificent and imaginative leap forward. The Lynds' contribution is such that, just as *Suicide* has shaped the development of the whole discipline, *Middletown* has shaped the development of community studies. Both studies have provided a model for sociological analysis'' (Collin Bell and Howard Newby, *Community Studies*, 1972).

''Various criteria thought to characterize communities include a specific population living within a specific geographic area with shared institutions and values and significant social interaction'' (Roland Warren, *The Community in America*, 1978).

CONFLICT

"[The cause of conflict] lies in the want of mutual love" (Motse, *Ethical and Political Works*, c. 550 B.C.).

"There is a perpetual conflict going on among us, which must be faced with marvelous watchfulness" (Plato, *Laws*, c. 400 B.C.).

"The economic conditions have in the first place transformed the mass of the people of a country into wage workers. The domination of capital has created for this mass of people a common situation with common interests. Thus this mass is already a class, as opposed to capital, but not yet for itself. In the struggle . . . this mass unites, it is constituted as a class for itself. The interests which it defends are the interests of its class. But the struggle between class and class is a political struggle" (Karl Marx, *The Poverty of Philosophy*, 1847).

"It is the factor of imitation in the conflict that gradually assimilates and harmonizes" (Franklin Giddings, *Principles of Sociology*, 1896).

"[Conflict is practically nonexistent] among animals belonging to the same species" (Petr Alekseevich Kropotkin, *Mutual Aid*, 1896).

"[In history there is a development] from a maximum toward a minimum of conflict, from a minimum toward a maximum of helpful reciprocity" (Albion Small, *General Sociology*, 1905).

"Conflict is always conscious. Indeed it evokes the deepest emotions and strongest passions and enlists the greatest concentration of attention and of effort. Both competition and conflict are forms of struggle. Competition, however, is continuous and impersonal. Conflict is intermittent and personal" (Robert Park and Ernest Burgess, *Introduction to the Science of Sociology*, 1921).

"A classic example of the lack of class conflict was the relationship of the 'poor white trash' to the plantation owners in the Southern states" (Max Weber, *Economy and Society*, 1922, posthumously).

"The tendency to aggression is an innate, independent, instinctual disposition in man" (Sigmund Freud, *Civilization and Its Discontents*, 1930).

"The primordial social fact is conflict, actual or potential" (Hans Morgenthau, *Scientific Man vs. Power Politics*, 1946).

"Once the individual has convinced himself that there are people who ought to be punished, he is provided with a channel through which his deepest aggressive impulses may be expressed, even while he thinks of himself as thoroughly moral" (Theodor Adorno et al., *The Authoritarian Personality*, 1950).

"In every type of social structure there are occasions for conflict, since individuals and subgroups are likely to make from time to time rival claims to scarce resources, prestige or power positions" (Lewis Coser, *The Functions of Social Conflict*, 1956).

"[Society] prevents and regulates conflicts of groups and individuals" (Radhakamal Mukerjee in Baljit Singh, ed., *The Frontiers of Social Science*, 1956).

"[In conflict] movement from specific to general issues occurs whenever there are deep cleavages of values or interests in the community which require a spark to set them off'' (James Coleman, *Community Conflict,* 1957).

''Conflict theory arose as a realistic protest against many superficialities in early organismic theories. By and large, the conflict theorists retained and even intensified the positivism of early sociology. However, in place of the conception of society as an organism, social reality was thought to be a process of conflict of individuals and of groups over scarce values'' (Don Martindale, *Social Life and Cultural Change*, 1962).

''The control of conflict, especially in its violent manifestations, constitutes the crisis of our very existence'' (Clagett Smith, ed., *Conflict Resolution*, 1971).

''In the process of racial conflict, it is intended that the deliberate use of violence will lead to negotiation or some other institutional mechanism for the settlement of the issues in dispute. That is, violence is not itself the problem-solving tactic'' (Joseph Himes, *Racial Conflict in American Society*, 1973).

''When it comes to the resolution of conflict in plural nation states . . . if, in a plural society anywhere in the world, civilized people have to choose between compulsory assimilation of the melting-pot winner-take-all type, on the one hand, and, on the other, a pluralist accommodation guaranteeing group rights and consensual decision-making across group boundaries, they will naturally opt for the latter, on condition, of course, that accommodation is based on genuine democratic pluralism'' (Nic Rhoodie, ed., *Intergroup Accommodation in Plural Societies*, 1978).

''Conflict among ethnic, racial, and religious groupings is most likely in periods of rapid change in levels of living'' (Robin Williams in T. Smith and Man Das, eds., *Sociocultural Change Since 1950,* 1978).

''Social conflicts are all around us. They are inherent in human relations. But this does not mean that every social relationship is entirely or even partly conflicting all the time'' (Louis Kriesberg, *Social Conflicts*, 1982).

''The more one struggles, the more one loses his peace and calmness of mind. If this becomes excessive, one loses even the ability to regain peace and calmness of mind. The mutual hostilities among the communist states of the world are a natural consequence of their philosophy that centers around struggle and hatred'' (Masatoshi Matsushita in Professors World Peace Academy of Japan, *Challenging the Future*, 1982).

''The science of conflict is not at present generally regarded as a pure science'' (James Schellenberg, *The Science of Conflict*, 1982).

CONTROL, SOCIAL

''When class spirit has sapped the social spirit and rent society in twain, the first effect is a weakening of social control and a drifting toward disorder. . . . In respect to their fundamental character, it is possible to divide most of the supports of order into two groups. Such instruments of control as public opinion, suggestion, personal ideal, social religion, art, and social valuation draw much of their strength from the primal moral feelings. They take their shape from sentiment rather than utility. They control men in many things which have little to do with the welfare of society regarded as a corporation. They are aimed to realize not merely a social order but what one might term a *moral* order. These we may call *ethical*. On the other hand, law, belief, ceremony, education, and illusion need not spring from ethical feelings at all. They are frequently the means deliberately chosen in order to reach certain ends. They are likely to come under the control of the organized few, and be used, whether for the corporate benefit or for class benefit, as the tools of policy. They may be termed *political*, using the word 'political' in its original sense of 'pertain-to policy.' . . . In this common wrath and common vengeance [against antisocial behavior] lies the germ of a social control of the person'' (Edward Ross, *Social Control*, 1901).

''All morality appears to us as a system of rules of conduct. But all techniques are equally ruled by maxims that prescribe the behavior of the agent in particular circumstances. What then is the difference between moral rules and other rules of technique? (i) We shall show that moral rules are invested with a special authority by virtue of which they are obeyed simply because they command. . . . (ii) In opposition to Kant, however, we shall show that the notion of duty does not exhaust the concept of morality. It is impossible for us to carry out an act simply because we are ordered to do so and without consideration of its content. . . . Desirability and obligation are the two characteristics which it is useful to stress, without necessarily denying the existence of others . . . all moral acts have these two characteristics, even though they may be combined in different proportions. . . . Morality appears to us to be a collection of maxims, of rules of conduct. But there are also other rules that prescribe our behavior. All utilitarian techniques are governed by analogous systems of rules, and we must find the distinguishing characteristics of moral rules. . . . A sanction is the consequence of an act that does not result from the content of that act, but from the violation by that act of a pre-established rule. It is because there is a pre-established rule, and the breach is a rebellion against this rule, that a sanction is entailed'' (Émile Durkheim, *Sociology and Philosophy*, 1911).

''The first principle of control is to prepare for its own demise'' (D. Mukerji, *Basic Concepts in Sociology*, 1932).

''The relations of constraint and unilateral respect which are spontaneously established between child and adult contribute to the formation of a first type of logical and moral control'' (Jean Piaget, *The Moral Judgment of the Child*, 1932).

''Culturally standardized practices are not all of a piece. They are subject to a wide gamut of control. They may represent definitely prescribed or preferential or permissive or proscribed patterns of behavior. In assessing the operation of social controls, these variations—roughly indicated by the terms *prescription, preference, permission* and *proscription*—must of course be taken into account'' (Robert Merton, *Social Theory and Social Structure*, 1949).

''Social control is . . . concerned primarily with an understanding of (1) how society makes its members susceptive to its regulative system, and (2) how it makes them conform to it'' (Paul Landis, *Social Control*, 1956).

''This [labeling theory] is a large turn away from older sociology which tended to rest heavily upon the idea that deviance leads to social control. I have come to believe that the reverse idea, i.e., social control leads to deviance, is equally tenable and the potentially richer premise for studying deviance in modern society'' (Edwin Lemert, *Human Deviance, Social Problems, and Social Control*, 1967).

''Social control consists of the manner in which the interests of the individual and those of society are combined and ordered'' (Don Martindale and R. Hanson, *Small Town and the Nation*, 1969).

''The origin of the field of social control in the United States is usually traced to the pioneering work of E. A. Ross in 1901'' (Don Martindale in Joseph Roucek, ed., *Social Control for the 1980s*, 1978).

''The term '*social* control' has been used more extensively in sociology than in other disciplines, perhaps because sociologists study diverse kinds of human behavior at different levels'' (Jack Gibbs, ed., *Social Control*, 1982).

COOPERATION

''Cooperative enterprises are more successful when they benefit both parties'' (Euripides, *Iphigenia in Tauris*, c. 400 B.C.).

''Serve me, I will serve you'' (Petronius, *Satyricon*, c. 60).

''Human beings cannot create new forces, but only unite and direct those that exist'' (Jean Jacques Rousseau, *The Social Contract*, 1762).

''Egoism is the feeling which demands for self an increase of enjoyment and diminution of discomfort. Altruism is that which demands these results for others'' (Lester Ward, *Dynamic Sociology*, 1883).

''[Society] is a group of distinct individuals who render one another mutual services'' (Gabriel Tarde, *The Laws of Imitation*, 1890).

''Consciousness of kind [is] a state of consciousness in which any being, whether low or high in the scale of life, recognizes another conscious being as of like mind with itself'' (Franklin Giddings, *Principles of Sociology*, 1896).

''So far as the fruits of a common enterprise can be reaped in full by the participants, coöperation may be left entirely free'' (Edward Ross, *Social Control*, 1901).

''Our thesis is that along with out-and-out struggle, i.e., self-assertion of the extremist type—and along with the externally socialized self-assertion which recognizes the self-interest of pooling issues with others; a factor quite different in temper develops in the course of the social process. We have called this the co-operative or civilizing factor. . . . A few men dedicate themselves to causes which they regard as greater than themselves'' (Albion Small, *General Sociology*, 1905).

''[Through socialization one] consciously modifies his behavior and shapes his purposes to promote more efficient co-operative activity and to realize the higher welfare of the group'' (Ernest Burgess, *The Function of Socialization in Social Evolution*, 1916).

''[Cooperation] is eminently capable of becoming the leading principle of a social order whose possibilities of expansion and improvement are practically unlimited'' (William Thomas and Florian Znaniecki, *The Polish Peasant in Europe and America*, 1920).

''Co-operation resting on mutual need [if] carried to completion would yield a harmonious development of humanity'' (Leonard Hobhouse, *Social Development,* 1924).

''Man contains many genes making for altruism of a general kind'' (J. Haldane, *The Causes of Evolution*, 1932).

''[Altruism] solves for another a painful situation which the latter is incapable of solving for himself'' (Florian Znaniecki, *Social Actions*, 1936).

''The concept of 'One World' is not only an abstract concept but a naive one unless made real by some sort of analysis, classification, and integration of this extraordinary heterogeneous culture-world of situation and conflict'' (Howard Odum in Merrill Jensen, ed., *Regionalism in America*, 1951).

''[The] continuity and solidarity between man and universe, between the social order and the cosmic order [must be accepted before] uniting mankind'' (Radhakamal Mukerjee in Baljit Singh, ed., *The Frontiers of Social Science*, 1956).

''World community includes both a world idea and a community idea blended into one'' (Emory Bogardus, *Toward a World Community*, 1964).

''In addition to widespread proto-cooperation, which has survival value, there is a wide occurrence of group behavior among animal species . . . group behavior may facilitate some biological process'' (Don Martindale, *Institutions, Organizations, and Mass Society*, 1966).

''For millennia . . . man has proved that he is capable of altruistic cooperation and phoenix-like survival and self-renewal'' (Panos Bardis in G. Hallen and Rajeshwar Prasad, eds., *Towards Global Sociology*, 1970).

''[Altruism is] self-destructive behavior performed for the benefit of others'' (Edward Wilson, *Sociobiology*, 1975).

''Men like to live in groups . . . they use a collective method in solving problems . . . man has determined that the stronger should assist and cultivate the weaker, not as in the animal kingdom where the weaker are always enslaved by the stronger'' (Wego Chiang, *Chung-Tao and Human Nature*, 1979).

COUNSELING

''Where no counsel is, the people fall: but in the multitude of counsellors there is safety'' (Proverbs 11:14).

''As for bad counsel, it is much worse for the counselor himself'' (Hesiod, *Works and Days*, c. 750 B.C.).

''Never trust the counsel of a man who has problems'' (Aesop, *The Fox and the Goat*, c. 600 B.C.).

"It is easy for him who does not suffer to counsel and rebuke the one who suffers" (Aeschylus, *Prometheus Bound*, 478 B.C.).

"It is easy for the healthy to counsel the sick" (Terence, *Andria*, 166 B.C.).

"Good counsellors lack no clients" (William Shakespeare, *Measure for Measure*, 1605).

"The light that a man receiveth by counsel from another is drier and purer than that which cometh from his own understanding and judgment" (Francis Bacon, *Essays*, 1625).

"How difficult it is to ask another's counsel on something without coloring his judgment by the manner in which the problem is presented to him" (Blaise Pascal, *Thoughts*, 1670, posthumously).

"Counseling may be broadly and simply defined as the process of helping individuals cope with certain kinds of personal problems" (Gordon Nelson in Ernest Harms and Paul Schreiber, eds., *Handbook of Counseling Techniques*, 1963).

"While little had been done to assist parents of the mentally retarded prior to the second half of our century, the professional helping specialties have since then become increasingly conscious of the need to deal not just with the retarded child but with his entire family, especially his parents" (Robert Noland, *Counseling Parents of the Mentally Retarded*, 1979).

"Casual and unconventional marriage counseling has existed from time immemorial, perhaps for as long as the institution of marriage" (Hirsch Silverman, ed., *Marital Therapy*, 1972).

"Marriage counseling [is] any counseling with one or more clients dealing with problems related to marriage" (Ben and Constance Ard, eds., *Handbook of Marriage Counseling*, 1976).

"In contrast to family therapy, marital therapy can handle material of murderous hostilities and sexual disabilities between mates that cannot adequately be dealt with in the presence of children. Such material is traumatic to children" (Peter Martin, *A Marital Therapy Manual*, 1976).

"Several studies have shown that client gain is significantly correlated with the attitudes of congruence, accurate empathy, and positive regard" (Betty Meador and Carl Rogers in Raymond Corsini et al., *Current Psychotherapies*, 1979).

"The actual number of systems and techniques of psychotherapy in existence today is unknown . . . patients are unaware of the variety of modalities that are available. . . . An extensive search of the available literature . . . produced a list of over 350 psychotherapeutic systems and techniques" (Richie Herink, ed., *The Psychotherapy Handbook*, 1980).

COURTSHIP

"I flee the one that chases me and chase the one that flees me" (Ovid, *Amores*, c. 8).

"Those marriages generally abound most with love and constancy that are preceded by a long courtship" (Joseph Addison, *The Spectator*, 1712).

"[In modern China] the most widespread phenomenon has been the demand, on the part of youth, for premarital courtship and freedom in the selection of a life partner" (Francis Hsu in Ruth Anshen, ed., *The Family*, 1959).

"Pre-Meiji rural Japan had a high rate of divorce and yet allowed relatively free marital choice to the young peasants. This was apparently in sharp contrast with the Chinese rural pattern, in which marriage was decided and arranged by family elders" (Jesse Pitts in Harold Christensen, ed., *Handbook of Marriage and the Family*, 1964).

"[A] factor helpful to courtship progress is when each partner confirms the self-concept and the self-ideal of the other" (Thomas Kando, *Sexual Behavior and Family Life in Transition*, 1978).

"Courtship involves interaction with a person who is seen as a possible marriage partner. Hedonistic considerations count for less than in dating, and the person's family and class backgrounds count for much more" (Mark Hutter, *The Changing Family*, 1981).

"In the majority of the Philippine communities, the courtship custom known as *binalata* was of the following nature: After the young couple had selected each other, the boy informed the girl's parents or guardians about his decision to marry her. Then the parents of both parties met to make arrangements concerning the marriage of their children. Before the wedding day, the boy sent a daily gift to his girl and, on the eve of their wedding, the final gift, which consisted in the price of the wedding dress. The bridegroom also gave his bride a dowry in the form of a house, land, money, or other articles of value" (Panos Bardis, *Global Marriage and Family Customs*, 1983).

CRIMINOLOGY

"The revenger of blood himself shall slay the murderer" (Numbers 35:19).

"[The philosopher Tsang said to chief criminal judge Yang Fu:]The rulers have failed in their duties, and the people consequently have been disorganized, for a long time. When you have found out the truth of any accusation, be grieved for and pity them, and do not feel joy at your own ability" (Confucius, *Analects*, c. 500 B.C.).

"It is good, not only never to do wrong, but also never to wish to do wrong" (Fragment 62). "A man becomes more virtuous when he is guided by exhortations and persuasion rather than by laws and compulsion" (Democritus, Fragment 181, c. 400 B.C.).

"Of the causes of crime, the greatest is lust, which controls the soul when passion maddens it . . . the power of wealth creates endless desires for acquisition which are never satisfied" (Plato, *Laws*, c. 400 B.C.).

"An act is criminal and unjust if it is essentially deliberate" (Aristotle, *Rhetoric*, c. 350 B.C.).

"When a crime is successful and fortunate, we call it virtue" (Lucius Annaeus Seneca, *Mad Hercules*, c. 50).

''Punishments were designed not to destroy but to discipline our people. In fact, not to let the impious alone for long, but to punish them immediately, is a sign of great kindness'' (II Maccabees 6:12–13).

''People commit crimes either because of fear or because of hatred'' (Niccolò Machiavelli, *The Prince*, 1513).

''Crimes, like lands, are not inherited'' (William Shakespeare, *Timon of Athens*, 1608).

''Certain crimes always precede great crimes'' (Jean Baptiste Racine, *Phèdre*, 1677).

''Now, there is stealing; why should it be thought a crime? When we consider by what unjust methods property has often been acquired, and that what has unjustly got it must be unjust to keep, where is the harm in one man's taking the property of another from him? Besides, Sir, when we consider the bad use that many people make of it, it may be defended as a very allowable practice. Yet, Sir, the experience of mankind has discovered stealing to be so very bad a thing, that they make no scruple to hang a man for it'' (Samuel Johnson, 1763, in James Boswell, *Life of Johnson*, 1791).

''In order for punishment not to be in every instance, an act of violence of one or many against a private citizen, it must be essentially public, prompt, necessary, the least possible in the given circumstances, proportionate to the crimes, dictated by the laws'' (Cesare Bonesana Beccaria, *An Essay on Crimes and Punishments*, 1764).

''Most of the crimes which disturb the internal peace of society are produced by the restraints which the necessary, but, unequal laws of property have imposed on the appetites of mankind, by confining to a few the possession of those objects that are coveted by man'' (Edward Gibbon, *The Decline and Fall of the Roman Empire*, 1776).

''People spit on a petty thief, but they cannot repress a kind of respect for a great criminal' (Denis Diderot, *Rameau's Nephew*, 1823, posthumously).

''The criminal produces not only crimes but also criminal law, and with this also the professor who gives lectures on criminal law and in addition to this the inevitable compendium in which this same professor throws his lectures onto the general market as 'commodities.' . . . The criminal moreover produces the whole of the police and of criminal justice, constables, judges, hangmen, juries, etc.'' (Karl Marx, *Theories of Surplus Value*, 1863).

''Is it not clear that the repression of crime will be effectual in proportion as the punishment is severe? Yet the great amelioration in our penal code . . . has not been followed by increased criminality but by decreased criminality; and the testimonies of those who have had most experience . . . unite to show that in proportion as the criminal is left to suffer no other penalty than that of maintaining himself under such restraints only as are needful for public safety, the reformation is great: exceeding indeed, all anticipation'' (Herbert Spencer, *The Study of Sociology*, 1873).

''Let the punishment fit the crime'' (William Gilbert, *The Mikado*, 1885).

''[In England, c. 1600] authors and publishers were often nailed by the ears to the pillory, and when ready to be set at liberty the ears would frequently be cut off, and left on the post of the pillory'' (William Andrews, *Old-Time Punishments*, 1890).

''Crime is present . . . in all societies of all types. There is no society that is not confronted with the problem of criminality. Its form changes; the acts thus characterized are not the same everywhere; but, everywhere and always, there have been men who have behaved in such a way as to draw upon themselves penal repression. . . . What is normal, simply, is the existence of criminality'' (Émile Durkheim, *The Rules of Sociological Method*, 1895).

''In England [c. 1500] petty thieves, unruly servants, wife-beaters, hedge-tearers, vagrants, sabbath-breakers, revilers, gamblers, drunkards, ballad-singers, fortune-tellers, traveling musicians and a variety of other offenders, were all punished by the stocks'' (Alice Earle, *Curious Punishments of Bygone Days*, 1896).

''[Crime is] an objectively evil act, a violation of social validity, an offense against the superior [collective] dignity'' (Florian Znaniecki, *Social Actions*, 1936).

''Those who uphold the Theory of Race and deny the influence of environment on the development of the human being should spend a year in prison and observe themselves daily in a mirror'' (Arthur Koestler, *Dialogue with Death*, 1938).

''The process of making the criminal . . . is a process of tagging, defining, identifying, segregating, describing, emphasizing, making conscious and self-conscious; it becomes a way of stimulating, suggesting, emphasizing, and evoking the very traits that are complained of. . . . The person becomes the thing he is described as being'' (Frank Tannenbaum, *Crime and the Community*, 1938).

''The characteristics of white collar crime . . . depend to some extent on the corporate form of business organization. The statement is frequently made that big business is more legal and more honest than small business. No organized research has demonstrated the truth or falsity of this claim'' (Edwin Sutherland, *White Collar Crime*, 1949).

''Trusted persons become trust violators when they conceive of themselves as having a financial problem which is non-sharable, are aware that this problem can be secretly resolved by violation of the position of financial trust, and are able to apply to their own conduct in that situation verbalizations which enable them to adjust their conception of themselves as trusted persons with their conception of themselves as users of the entrusted funds'' (Donald Cressey, *Other People's Money*, 1953).

''Scientific explanations of criminal behavior may be stated either in terms of the processes which are operating at the moment of the occurrence of crime or in terms of the processes operating in the earlier history of the criminal. In the first case the explanation may be called 'mechanistic,' 'situational,' or 'dynamic,' in the second, 'historical' or 'genetic.' Both types of explanation are desirable. The mechanistic type of explanation has been favored by physical and biological scientists'' (Edwin Sutherland and Donald Cressey, *Principles of Criminology*, 1955).

''The majority of the people who make their living in crime . . . don't want to hurt anybody'' (Dave Fisher, *Killer*, 1973).

''Crime as a legal definition of human conduct is created by agents of the dominant class in a politically organized society'' (Richard Quinney, *Criminology*, 1975).

''Although Cheyennes sin when they commit murder . . . murder is expiated in the here and now, and wrongdoing builds up no burden of guilt to be borne beyond the grave'' (E. Hoebel, *The Cheyennes,* 1978).

''A single case of corporate law violation may involve millions and even billions of dollars of losses . . . in one case, the electrical price-fixing conspiracy of the 1960s, losses amounted to over $2 billion, a sum far greater than the total losses from the 3 million burglaries in any given year'' (Marshall Clinard, *Illegal Corporate Behavior*, 1979).

''Victimology focuses on the victims of crime and their role in criminal activity'' (Larry Siegel, *Criminology*, 1983).

CULTURAL LAG

''This rapidity of change in modern times raises the very important question of social adjustment. . . . The thesis is that the various parts of modern culture are not changing at the same time, some parts are changing much more rapidly than others; and that since there is a correlation and interdependence of parts, a rapid change in one part of our culture requires readjustments through other changes in the various correlated parts of culture. For instance, industry and education are correlated, hence a change in industry makes adjustments necessary through changes in the educational system'' (William Ogburn, *Social Change*, 1922).

''By 1870, many people were working in factories where industrial accidents were common. Yet, it was not until 1915 that the United States laws gave protection to working people through legally enforced safety standards and workmen's compensation'' (Ronald Federico and Janet Schwartz, *Sociology*, 1983).

CULTURE

''[Culture is] that complex whole which includes knowledge, belief, art, morals, law, custom, and any other capabilities and habits acquired by man as a member of society'' (Edward Tylor, *Primitive Culture*, 1871).

''[Without their social heritage] the white races would probably become extinct everywhere'' (Graham Wallas, *The Great Society*, 1914).

''Environment is not only unable to create cultural features, in some instances it is even incapable of perpetuating them'' (Robert Lowie, *Culture and Ethnology*, 1917).

"[Culture is] the set of attitudes and values which we call the immigrants' heritage" (Robert Park et al., *Old World Traits Transplanted*, 1921).

"They [collective representations] are common to the members of a given social group; they are transmitted to one generation from another; they impress themselves upon the individual members and awaken in them sentiments of respect, fear, adoration, and so on" (Lucien Lévy-Bruhl, *Primitive Mentality*, 1922).

"[Culture is] a collective learning process produced by the interaction of human minds . . . a process of learning and communication" (Charles Ellwood, *Cultural Evolution*, 1927).

"The culture pattern of any civilization makes use of a certain segment of the great arc of potential human purposes and motivations. . . . The great arc along which all the possible human behaviors are distributed is far too immense and too full of contradictions for any one culture to utilize even any considerable portion of it. Selection is the first requirement" (Ruth Benedict, *Patterns of Culture*, 1934).

"Every cultural system is found by the investigator to exist for certain conscious and active historical subjects, i.e., within the sphere of experience and activity of some particular people, individuals, and collectivities, living in a certain part of the human world during a certain historical period. . . . This essential character of cultural data we call the *humanistic coefficient* because such data, as objects of the student's theoretic reflection, already belong to somebody else's active experience and are such as this active experience makes them" (Florian Znaniecki, *The Method of Sociology*, 1934).

"Culture, as distinct from civilization, is based on the realization of the mind, of the philosophical and emotional self" (Alfred Weber, *Cultural History as Cultural Sociology*, 1935).

"Diversities in behavior and culture are the result of different interpretations of experience, resulting in characteristic behavior reactions and habit systems . . . a uniform course of cultural and behavior evaluation is consequently out of the question" (William Thomas, *Primitive Behavior*, 1937).

"Geographic differences are primordial, while social differentiations . . . are emergent: one is foundation, the other pinnacle. Merely by examining the geographic base one cannot tell what the social emergent will be; for, precisely because it *is* an emergent, precisely because it necessarily contains elements from other geographic regions and other cultures and other layers of historic experience, it is a new configuration, not given in the geographic complex itself. But geographic conditions nevertheless place the possibilities of cultural development within certain limits: the skills of the Eskimo are of no use in the tropical jungle" (Lewis Mumford, *The Culture of Cities*, 1938).

"The last thing which a dweller in the deep sea would be likely to discover would be water. He would become conscious of its existence only if some accident brought him to the surface and introduced him to air. Man, throughout most of his history, has been only vaguely conscious of the existence of culture and has owed even this consciousness to contrasts between the customs of his own society and those of some other with which he happened to be brought into contact'' (Ralph Linton, *The Cultural Background of Personality*, 1945).

''Barbarism is the opposite of culture only within the order of thought which it gives us. Outside of it the opposite may be something quite different, or no opposite at all'' (Thomas Mann, *Doctor Faustus*, 1947).

''[Folk culture is] the supreme product of the folk society'' (Howard Odum, *Understanding Society*, 1947).

''A . . . discrimination is that of . . . the *organic* from the *cultural*. The implicit recognition of the difference between organic qualities and processes and social qualities and processes is of long standing. The formal distinction is however recent. In fact the full import of the significance of the antithesis may be said to be only dawning upon the world. For every occasion on which some human mind sharply separates organic and social forces, there are dozens of other times when the distinction between them is not thought of, or an actual confusion of the two ideas takes place'' (Alfred Kroeber, *The Nature of Culture*, 1952).

''We do not observe 'culture,' since that word denotes . . . an abstraction'' (A. Radcliffe-Brown, *Structure and Function in Primitive Society*, 1952).

''[Culture is] the aggregate of beliefs, values, and behaviors of the members of a society and the aggregate of symbols which express and communicate such beliefs, values, and behaviors'' (Radhakamal Mukerjee in Baljit Singh, ed., *The Frontiers of Social Science*, 1956).

''What we call freedom is the irreducibility of the cultural order to the natural order'' (Jean-Paul Sartre, *The Problem of Method*, 1960).

''[Culture refers to] 'patterns' of meaning, e.g., of values, of norms, of organized knowledge and beliefs, of expressive 'forms' '' (Talcott Parsons in Talcott Parsons et al., eds., *Theories of Society*, 1961).

''With a very few notable (and mainly recent) exceptions, anthropologists have failed to give systematic attention to the problem of how specific bits of culture are transmitted from individual to individual within particular societies. Such factual material as is available in the published literature is almost wholly anecdotal in character'' (Clyde Kluckhohn, *Culture and Behavior*, 1962).

CUSTOM

''Men of talents and virtue remember the greater principles of these customs, but others, not possessing such talents and virtue, remember the smaller'' (Confucius, *Analects*, c. 500 B.C.).

''No man can overturn ancestral customs by argument, customs as old as time itself'' (Euripides, *Bacchae*, 405 B.C.).

''Custom and nature usually contradict each other. Thus, when a man hesitates to express his natural thoughts, he is forced to contradict himself'' (Plato, *Gorgias*, c. 400 B.C.).

''The custom handed down since time immemorial . . . is called the conduct of virtuous men'' (Manu, *Laws*, c. 200 B.C.).

''How many things, both just and unjust, are permitted by custom!'' (Terence, *Heautontimoroumenos*, 163 B.C.).

''Stand fast, and hold the traditions which ye have been taught'' (II Thessalonians 2:15).

''We are more sensible of what men do against custom than against nature'' (Plutarch, *Of Eating Flesh*, c. 100).

''It is difficult to abolish the custom of the masses'' (Thomas Aquinas, *Summa Theologica*, 1274).

''It is a custom more honour'd in the breach than the observance'' (William Shakespeare, *Hamlet*, 1601).

''Custom is the principal magistrate of man's life'' (Francis Bacon, *Essays*, 1625).

''The ignorant child listens with curiosity to the tales, which flow into his mind like his mother's milk . . . to the youth they account for the way of life of his tribe'' (Johann Gottfried von Herder, *Outlines of a Philosophy of the History of Man*, 1791).

''The older the custom, the more idiotic; the more miserable the times, the more the idiocies multiply'' (Denis Diderot, *Rameau's Nephew*, 1823, posthumously).

''Customs are made for customary circumstances, and customary characters'' (John S. Mill, *On Liberty*, 1859).

''A government by discussion if it can be borne, at once breaks down the yoke of custom'' (Walter Bagehot, *Physics and Politics*, 1869).

''It is surprising to find . . . how tenaciously the English race clings to that which habit and usage have established; how ancient customs hold sway in the palace, the parliament, the army, the law courts, amongst educated people as well as unlearned rustics'' (P. Ditchfield, *Old English Customs*, 1896).

''Tradition and custom become intertwined and are a strong coercion which directs the society upon fixed lines, and strangles liberty. Children see their parents always yield to the same custom and obey the same persons. They see that the elders are allowed to do all the talking, and that if an outsider enters, he is saluted by those who are at home according to rank and in fixed order. All this becomes rule for children, and helps to give to all primitive customs their stereotyped formality'' (William Sumner, *Folkways*, 1906).

''[Customs and traditions are] the objective and subjective aspects of the same process . . . [customs are] supported by traditions, that is, by the knowledge, ideas, beliefs, and standards of the group'' (Charles Ellwood, *The Psychology of Human Society*, 1925).

''Culture has never the translucidity of custom; it abhors all simplification. In its essence it is opposed to custom, for custom is always the deterioration of culture'' (Frantz Fanon, *The Wretched of the Earth*, 1961).

''[Customs are] norms governing activities not generally considered crucial to society's existence or functioning and whose violation is not associated with severe sanctions'' [same as William Sumner's *Folkways*, 1906] (Norman Goodman and Gary Marx, *Society Today*, 1982).

D

DANCE, SOCIOLOGY OF

"When an old man dances, his aged locks are grey, but he has the heart of a child" (Anacreon, *Odes*, c. 500 B.C.).

"Peaceful dances are of two kinds: one offers an escape from daily toils and dangers to good, thus giving greater pleasures; the other is celebrated for the sake of preservation and increase of former good, thus giving less exciting pleasure" (Plato, *Laws*, c. 400 B.C.).

"Imitation in the arts of dancing is by rhythm, without harmony" (Aristotle, *Poetics*, c. 350 B.C.).

"Gamblers, dancers, and singers, cruel men . . . let him instantly banish from his town" (Manu, *Laws*, c. 200 B.C.).

"And after we had been driven forth before the wind . . . the sons of Ishmael and also their wives began to make themselves merry, insomuch that they began to dance, and to sing, and to speak with much rudeness" (The Book of Mormon: I Nephi 18:9).

"The dance among savages may be considered a just indication of their character; it plays a very important part in their daily life—so important that there are races who have special dances for every day in the year and for every occasion in the day" (Lilly Grove, *Dancing*, 1895).

"Dancing is a very crude attempt to get into the rhythm of life" (George B. Shaw, *Back to Methuselah*, 1921).

"In all the ages since man's tenancy of the earth began human beings seem to have enjoyed and revered the dance; and certainly no people ever appreciated the dance more than did the ancient Greeks" (Lillian Lawler, *The Dance in Ancient Greece*, 1964).

"It has been hypothesized by aesthetic and literary scholars that in some era of prehistory all men were artists, or perhaps better that each member of society had skills which permitted him to assume the creative role at some time. The seemingly spontaneous elaboration of the primitive dance would lend credence to this view" (Robert Wilson, *The Arts in Society*, 1964).

"Before man found a means of artistic expression in measured, rhythmic movement, he enjoyed the sensation of stepping, turning, swaying, swinging, stamping and leaping. He has always done so in his folk dances, or in those dances that were fashioned into theatrical forms—simply because there is endless joy in dancing'' (Walter Sorell, *The Dance Through the Ages*, 1967).

''The dominant style of dancing among young people may have changed from the fox trot to rock, but we still generally see couples dancing—not individuals dancing in isolation'' (Carol and Melvin Ember, *Cultural Anthropology*, 1977).

DATING

''Dating refers to the early friendship activities of young people whereby they seek to have fun in pairs. It is generally distinguished from true courtship in that the latter is more definitely oriented toward marriage'' (Harold Christensen, *Marriage Analysis*, 1958).

''[Dating is] a social engagement of two young people with no commitment beyond the expectation that it will be a pleasurable event for both'' (Ernest Burgess and Harvey Locke, *The Family*, 1960).

''Adolescent clique and dating patterns are a reflection in large part of the adult social structure'' (August Hollingshead, *Elmtown's Youth*, 1961).

''In the courtship attitudes and marriage mores of Mexico there are differences between classes. Generally speaking the least changes are occurring in the lower strata and the greatest in the middle ranks'' (Norman Hayner in Victor Christopherson, ed., *Readings in Comparative Marriage and the Family*, 1967).

''The development of an extensive dating system seems to be a modern-American innovation. In the absence of historical and cross-cultural precedents, therefore, it is only natural to find that the codes have not fully crystallized'' (William Kephart, *The Family, Society, and the Individual*, 1977).

''[In the United States] the typical foreign student's attitudes toward dating and related practices are less liberal than those which he attributes to Americans, but less conservative than those which, in his opinion, are characteristic of his native home town's people'' (Panos Bardis, *Studies in Marriage and the Family*, 1978).

''Dating in the United States has been changing rapidly. The changes are so recent that it is difficult to say just where we stand'' (Gerald Leslie, *The Family in Social Context*, 1982).

''In computer dances people are not as afraid of rejection as they are in normal dating situations so their dating choices might be different from those in ordinary dating situations. . . . Good looks seem to be more important to a woman's popularity than a man's'' (Gilbert Nass and Gerald McDonald, *Marriage and the Family*, 1982).

DELINQUENCY

''In contemplating the character of all these different classes of delinquents (that is Thieves, Robbers, Cheats, and Swindlers), *there can be little hesitation in pronouncing the Receivers to be the most mischievous of the whole: inasmuch as without the aid they afford*, in purchasing and concealing every species of property stolen or fraudulently obtained, *Thieves, Robbers and Swindlers . . . must quit the trade*. . . . Deprive a Thief of a safe and ready market for his goods and he is undone'' (Patrick Colquhoun, *A Treatise on the Police of the Metropolis*, 1795).

''The young delinquent becomes bad because he is defined as bad and because he is not believed if he is good. There is a persistent demand for consistency in character. . . . The entire process of dealing with the young delinquent is mischievous insofar as it identifies him to himself or to the environment as a delinquent person'' (Frank Tannenbaum, *Crime and the Community*, 1938).

''The effectiveness of the neighborhood as a unit of control and as a medium for the transmission of the moral standards of society is greatly diminished. The boy who grows up in this area has little access to the cultural heritages of conventional society. For the most part, the organization of his behavior takes place through his participation in the spontaneous play groups and organized gangs with which he has contact . . . this area is an especially favorable habitat for the development of boys' gangs and organized criminal groups'' (Clifford Shaw, *The Natural History of a Delinquent Career*, 1951).

''Relations with gang members tend to be intensely solidary and imperious. . . . Gang members are usually resistant to the efforts of home, school and other agencies to regulate, not only their delinquent activities, but any activities carried on within the group'' (Albert Cohen, *Delinquent Boys*, 1955).

''Delinquent behavior tends to be less stable when peer supports are weak or absent'' (Richard Cloward and Lloyd Ohlin, *Delinquency and Opportunity*, 1960).

''The younger adolescent gangs [in Chicago] were shown to be responsible for the bulk of minor delinquencies. The older gangs were for the most part engaged in delinquent enterprises, and gang clubs, likewise, were often semi-criminal groups'' (Frederic Thrasher in Ernest Burgess and Donald Bogue, eds., *Contributions to Urban Sociology*, 1964).

''The socialised delinquent has no psychiatric disorder as such. It is simply that he has acquired standards which are at odds with society at large although in keeping with those of his family and immediate peer group. The unsocialised, aggressive child, however, does have a psychiatric disorder, as shown by his emotional disturbances and poor interpersonal relationships. Furthermore, his difficulties have arisen as a result of family stress and discord'' (M. Rutter, *Helping Troubled Children*, 1975).

''Many police officers decry diversion practices—especially diversion without referral as being antithetical to police goals and of no rehabilitative value. In fact, it is often suggested that to release youngsters without further action is tantamount to *rewarding* them or showing them that they can get away with their legal transgressions'' (M. Klein in R. Carter and M. Klein, eds., *Back on the Street*, 1976).

''Juvenile 'misbehavior' is a social problem experienced by all members of society, young or old, at some time in their lives. Children generally perceive their socializing agents (parents, teachers, and others) as intruding on their autonomy as people, and adults usually consider the administration of some form of social control over children as a responsibility they must discharge'' (Martin Haskell and Lewis Yablonsky, *Juvenile Delinquency*, 1978).

DEMOGRAPHY

''God said unto them, Be fruitful, and multiply, and replenish the earth'' (Genesis 1:28).

''But the number of marriages we will leave to the judgment of the rulers, so that they may keep the same number of men as nearly as possible, taking into consideration wars and diseases and all such things, and so that, as far as possible, our city may not grow too great or too small'' (Plato, *Republic*, c. 400 B.C.).

''The world could not be best peopled in rude and ignorant ages, while men lived chiefly on the spontaneous fruits of the earth, and were not instructed in agriculture . . . in whatever age we find a country grossly ignorant of agriculture, we may be assured that country must have been but thinly inhabited'' (Robert Wallace, *A Dissertation on the Numbers of Mankind*, 1753).

''Every species of animals naturally multiplies in proportion to the means of their subsistence, and no species can ever multiply beyond it'' (Adam Smith, *The Wealth of Nations*, 1776).

''In every country where the whole of the procreative power cannot be called into action, the preventive and the positive checks must vary inversely as each other'' (Thomas R. Malthus, *An Essay on the Principles of Population*, 1798).

''The bourgeoisie keeps more and more doing away with the scattered state of the population. . . . It has agglomerated population. . . . The necessary consequence of this was political centralisation. Independent, or but loosely connected provinces, with separate interests, laws, governments and systems of taxation, became lumped together into one nation, with one government, one code of laws, one national class-interest, one frontier and one customs-tariff'' (Karl Marx and Friedrich Engels, *Communist Manifesto*, 1847).

''Capitalist production collects the population in great centers'' (Karl Marx, *Das Kapital*, 1879).

''It is . . . foreign emigration that is robbing Hellas of her hardy peasantry, and this constitutes one of the most serious problems with which the Hellenic Government is at the present confronted. For Greece has *no surplus population*, and, if the country is to prosper, the services of every able-bodied man and boy are needed for the proper development of its natural resources'' (Lucy Garnett, *Greece of the Hellenes*, 1914).

''[Competition] determines the distribution of population territorially and vocationally'' (Robert Park and Ernest Burgess, *Introduction to the Science of Sociology*, 1921).

''A sudden drop of 25 per cent in the grain crop, just such a drop as has occurred time and again before . . . will make what is left of them [earth's people] awaken to the folly of negligence'' (E. East, *Mankind at the Crossroads*, 1923).

''Monks, nuns, long-term spinsters and bachelors and permanent homosexuals are all, in a reproductive sense, aberrant. Society has bred them, but they have failed to return the compliment'' (Desmond Morris, *The Naked Ape*, 1967).

''In most populations the numbers of males and females tend to be nearly equal, with males outnumbering the females at the younger ages and females outnumbering the males at the older ages'' (Donald Bogue, *Principles of Demography*, 1969).

''The first result of the reduction of births was greatly to increase differential fertility between social, economic and educational groups'' (F. Osborn in Carl Bajema, ed., *Natural Selection in Human Populations*, 1971).

''Reproduction, whether at high or low levels, is so important to the family and society everywhere that its level is more or less controlled by cultural norms about family size and such related matters as marriage, timing of intercourse, and abortion. In each society, the cultural norms about these vital matters are consistent with social institutions in which they are deeply embedded. Changes in fertility are unlikely without prior or, at least, simultaneous changes in these institutions'' (Ronald Freedman in M. Micklin, ed., *Population, Environment, and Social Organization*, 1973).

''The actual or potential shortages of food or other natural resources, the actual or potential destruction of the natural environment, are serious problems—far too serious to be dealt with by those who substitute an apocalyptic stance for the expertise they lack'' (William Petersen, *Population*, 1975).

''Demography may be broadly defined as the study of human populations. More specifically, demography is primarily concerned with the size, composition, and geographic distribution of populations'' (Howard Taylor, ed., *Human Reproduction: Population*, 1976).

''In the European industrial nations . . . 'demographic transition' began in the last century with a reduction in mortality followed by a lesser, and then a more marked reduction in the number of births. Initially this produced an acceleration and then a contraction in the natural growth of population until a stable reproductive pattern became established in which births and deaths stood in approximate balance'' (Wolfgang Köllmann, in David Eversley and Wolfgang Köllmann, eds., *Population Change and Social Planning*, 1982).

''Currently, population estimation is a flourishing business because states have joined the federal government in requiring estimates before allocating funds to local agencies, and because businesses have increased their use of small area [subcounty] estimates in decision making. The environmental statements required for many kinds of construction require detailed estimates. Courts have begun to demand population estimates by race for small areas before permitting the reconstitution of political entities, and juries are frequently challenged as to their representativeness'' (Everett Lee and Harold Goldsmith, eds., *Population Estimates*, 1982).

DEVIANCE

"[Hobos] are mostly the misfits of society. They can't or won't fit in. And however much they may boast of their freedom, they are always on the defensive against the condemnation of a larger society, sensitive to the opinion of a larger world" (Harvey Zorbaugh, *The Gold Coast and the Slum*, 1929).

[Deviance is] "the tendency on the part of one or more of the component actors to behave in such a way as to disturb the equilibrium of the interactive process" (Talcott Parsons, *The Social System*, 1951).

"Social groups create deviance by making the rules whose infraction constitutes deviance, and by applying those rules to particular people and labeling them as outsiders" (Howard Becker, *Outsiders*, 1963).

"Deviant roles are socially disvalued roles . . . not all disvalued roles are deviant . . . the role of slave, hunchback, moron, sick person, and the blind are disvalued, but socially they are felt to be different from such roles as coward, thief, scab or adulterer. What the latter have in common is the notion of a person who knows what he is doing and is capable of doing otherwise, but who *chooses* to violate some normative rule. . . . By contrast, no one in his right mind chooses to be a moron" (Albert Cohen, *Deviance and Control*, 1966).

" 'Deviance' refers to conduct which the people of a group consider so dangerous or embarrassing or irritating that they bring special sanctions to bear against the persons who exhibit it. Deviance is not properly *inherent in* any particular kind of behavior; it is a property *conferred upon* that behavior by the people who come into direct or indirect contact with it. The only way an observer can tell whether or not a given style of behavior is deviant, then, is to learn something about the standards of the audience" (Kai Erickson, *Wayward Puritans*, 1966).

"Primary deviation is assumed to arise in a variety of social, cultural, and psychological contexts, and at best has only marginal implication for the psychic structure of the individual; it does not lead to symbolic organization at the level of self-regarding attitudes and social roles. Secondary deviation is deviant behavior or social roles based upon it, which becomes a means of defense, attack, or adaptation to the overt and covert problems created by the societal reaction to the primary deviation" (Edwin Lemert, *Human Deviance, Social Problems, and Social Control*, 1967).

"It is when a system of cultural values extols, virtually above all else, certain common success-goals for the population at large while the social structure rigorously restricts or completely closes access to approved modes of reaching goals for a considerable part of the same population, that deviant behavior ensues on a large scale" (Robert Merton, *Social Theory and Social Structure*, 1968).

"Deviants, like other humans, have hopes and aspirations, fears and insecurities, habits and daydreams. . . . These facts are often lost sight of in the hot pursuit of justice and revenge, when the deviant becomes a faceless object to be dealt with" (Jerry Simmons, *Deviants*, 1969).

''Deviance is created through processes of social definition and rule making through . . . interaction with individuals and organizations, including agents and agencies of social control, that affect the development of deviant self-concepts among individual rule-breakers. . . . Human behavior is deviant to the extent that it comes to be viewed as involving a personally discreditable departure from a group's normative expectation, and it elicits interpersonal and collective reactions that serve to 'isolate,' 'treat,' 'correct' or 'punish' individuals engaged in such behavior'' (Edwin Schur, *Labeling Deviant Behavior*, 1971).

''The politicized 'deviant' gains a new identity, an heroic self-image as a crusader in the political cause'' (R. Humphreys, *Out of the Closets*, 1972).

''Under the guise of diagnosing disease, the psychiatrist disqualifies deviance'' (Thomas Szasz, *The Second Sin*, 1973).

''The chance that a group will get community support for its definition of unacceptable deviance depends on its relative power position. The greater the group's size, resources, efficiency, unity, articulateness, prestige, coordination with other groups, and access to the mass media and to decision-makers, the more likely it is to get its preferred norms legitimated'' (F. Davis in F. Davis and R. Stivers, eds., *The Collective Definition of Deviance*, 1975).

''Actually, labeling theory, as it is characterized by its critics, never existed. Its approach may better be called the 'interactionist perspective.' This term covers a broader canvas than that implied by the term labeling. . . . If I were to write an article entitled 'The Myth of Labeling Theory,' I would argue that all good sociology of deviant behavior is labeling theory. It does not exist any longer—if, indeed, it ever did—as a distinct perspective. Its central ideas have been absorbed into mainstream sociology . . . its exaggerations and excesses . . . have been discarded'' (Erich Goode, *Deviant Behavior*, 1978).

''To study deviance is to study the creation, structure, and change of *morally condemned* differences in a society. And, unlike many other areas of social science, the study of deviance poses a major philosophical question—the one of what is right and wrong among a group of people'' (Morris Rosenberg et al., eds., *The Sociology of Deviance*, 1982).

''Sociological efforts to define deviance are less concerned with particular kinds of deviance than they are with what all forms of deviance have in common'' (James Orcutt, *Analyzing Deviance*, 1983).

DIFFUSION

''Before going out for breakfast he [the American man] glances through the window, made of glass invented in Egypt, and if it is raining puts on overshoes made of rubber discovered by the Central American Indians and takes an umbrella, invented in southeastern Asia'' (Ralph Linton, *The Study of Man*, 1936).

''Any feature of culture once established will automatically tend to spread to the cultures of other societies, just as it will tend to persist in its own. The principle is empirical, but so great is the mass of experience, both contemporary and historical, on which it is based that it has the force of an axiom'' (Alfred Kroeber, *Anthropology*, 1948).

''The German *Kulturkreis* school looked for nonfunctional relationships to establish diffusion or migration. The form criterion of this school demanded that the culture variables (originally material objects) have resemblances in form not caused by the materials from which they were made or the uses to which they were put. The greater the quantity of such resemblances among a number of societies, the greater the probability of diffusion or migration'' (Harold Driver in John Honigmann, ed., *Handbook of Social and Cultural Anthropology*, 1973).

''The source of new cultural elements in a society may be another society. The process by which cultural elements are borrowed from another society and incorporated into the culture of the recipient group is called *diffusion*'' (Carol and Melvin Ember, *Cultural Anthropology*, 1977).

''Diffusion is the process by which items of culture spread from one society to another through culture contact. Not all traits are equally likely to be accepted by members of another society. In general, technology is most easily diffused, for it is a matter of simple observation whether or not a new technique is more efficient than another'' (Beth Hess et al., *Sociology*, 1982).

DISCRIMINATION

''The Jewish question still exists. It would be foolish to deny it. It is a remnant of the Middle Ages, which civilized nations do not even yet seem able to shake off, try as they will. . . . The Jewish question exists wherever Jews live in perceptible numbers. Where it does not exist, it is carried by Jews in the course of their migrations. We naturally move to those places where we are not persecuted, and there our presence produces persecution. This is the case in every country, and will remain so, even in those highly civilized—for instance, France—until the Jewish question finds a solution on a political basis'' (Theodor Herzl, *The Jewish State*, 1896).

''A 'good' man treats any human being and community as a basically positive social value'' (Florian Znaniecki, *The People of Today and the Civilization of Tomorrow*, 1934).

''No excuse for other forms of social segregation and discrimination is so potent as the one that sociable relations on an equal basis between members of the two races [blacks and whites] may possibly lead to intermarriage'' (Gunnar Myrdal, *An American Dilemma*, 1944).

''[The goals of India's Anti-Untouchability Organizations are] carrying propaganda against untouchability and taking immediate steps to secure as early as practicable that all public wells . . . roads, schools, crematoriums . . . and all public temples be declared opened to the depressed classes, provided that no compulsion or force shall be used and that only peaceful persuasion shall be adopted towards this end'' (B. Ambedkar, *What Congress and Gandhi Have Done to the Untouchables*, 1946).

"There are . . . two vitally important considerations to bear in mind concerning persecution-produced traits. (1) They are not all unpleasant traits—some of them are pleasing and constructive. (2) Just what ego defenses will develop is largely an individual matter. Every form of ego defense may be found among members of every persecuted group" (Gordon Allport, *The Nature of Prejudice*, 1954).

"It is ironic that the white South was extremely successful in minimizing the impact of the desegregation decision of the federal court without arousing the indignation of the rest of the nation. As much as the White Citizens Council and the Ku Klux Klan are evoked as symbols of the southern resistance, they and their extra-legal tactics did not make this possible. Far more effective were the legal stratagems, evasions, and delays that led Negroes to realize that although they had won a new statement of principle they had not won the power to cause this principle to be implemented" (Lewis Killian, *The Impossible Revolution?*, 1968).

"Starting in the mid-1950's and increasing more or less steadily into the early 1960's—white violence grew against the now lawful and protected efforts of Negroes to gain integration. And so did direct action and later violence undertaken by blacks, in a reciprocal process that moved into the substantial violence of 1965–67" (James Davies in Hugh Graham and Ted Gurr, eds., *Violence in America*, 1969).

"One does find an evidence of discrimination against black athletes on integrated basketball teams" (Harry Edwards, *Sociology of Sport*, 1973).

"Dominant peoples everywhere have resorted to various devices for restricting economically, politically, and socially the racial and ethnic groups over whom they have set themselves" (Brewton Berry and Henry Tischler, *Race and Ethnic Relations*, 1978).

"[In South Africa] white sophisticates no longer need to be convinced that old-style segregationist policies have become counterproductive . . . classic apartheid can only generate White-Black confrontation" (Nic Rhoodie, ed., *Conflict Resolution in South Africa*, 1980).

"Discrimination is an *act* or a series of acts taken toward another group—or toward people from that group—that are unfair when compared with our behavior toward other groups" (Charles Morris, *Psychology*, 1982).

"The greater the prejudice and discrimination directed toward the minority, the less its structural assimilation" (Edward Murguia, *Chicano Intermarriage*, 1982).

DIVISION OF LABOR

"We must put each laborer to a task for which nature designed him, every man thus performing an expert task, which leads to specialization, not versatility . . . a shoemaker will be a shoemaker and not a pilot also, and a farmer will be a farmer and not a dicast also, and a soldier will be a soldier and not a trader also" (Plato, *Republic*, c. 400 B.C.).

"Let everything be in its place and every talent be put to its most appropriate use" (Han Fei Tzu, *Complete Works*, c. 250 B.C.).

"This great increase in the quantity of work, which, in consequence of the division of labour, the same number of people are capable of performing, is owing to three different circumstances; first, to the increase of dexterity in every particular workman; secondly, to the saving of the time which is commonly lost in passing from one species of work to another; and lastly, to the invention of the great number of machines which facilitate and abridge labour, and enable one man to do the work of many" (Adam Smith, *The Wealth of Nations*, 1776).

"The master manufacturer, by dividing the work to be executed into different processes, each requiring different degrees of skill or of force, can purchase exactly the precise quantity of both which is necessary for each process; whereas, if the whole work were executed by one workman, that person must possess sufficient skill to perform the most difficult, and sufficient strength to execute the most laborious of the operations into which the art is divided" (Charles Babbage, *On the Economy of Machinery and Manufactures*, 1832).

"The accumulation of capital increases the division of labour . . . just as the division of labour increases the accumulation of capital. With this division of labour on the one hand and the accumulation of capital on the other, the worker becomes ever more exclusively dependent on labour, and on a particular, one-sided, machine-like labour at that . . . he is thus depressed spiritually and physically to the condition of a machine and from being a man becomes an abstract activity and a belly" (Karl Marx, *Economic and Philosophic Manuscripts*, 1844).

"The division of labour inside a nation leads at first to the separation of industrial and commercial from agricultural labour, and hence to the separation of town and country and a clash of interests between them. Its further development leads to the separation of commercial from industrial labour. At the same time through the division of labour there develop further, inside these various branches, various divisions among the individuals co-operating in definite kinds of labour. The relative position of these individual groups is determined by the methods employed in agriculture, industry and commerce (patriarchalism, slavery, estates, classes). These same conditions are to be seen (given a more developed intercourse) in the relations of different nations to one another. The various stages of development in the division of labour are just so many different forms of ownership. . . . The first form of ownership is tribal ownership. . . . The second form is the ancient communal and State ownership which proceeds especially from the union of several tribes into a city by agreement or by conquest, and which is still accompanied by slavery. . . . The third form of ownership is feudal or estate-property" (Karl Marx and Friedrich Engels, *The German Ideology*, 1846).

"Owing to the ever more extended use of machinery and the division of labour, the work of these proletarians has completely lost its individual character and therewith has forfeited all its charm for the workers. The worker has become a mere appendage to a machine'' (Karl Marx and Friedrich Engels, *Communist Manifesto*, 1847).

''We have much studied and perfected, of late, the great civilised invention of the division of labour; only we give it a false name. It is not, truly speaking, the labour that is divided; but the men: divided into mere segments of men—broken into small fragments and crumbs of life; so that all the little piece of intelligence that is left in a man is not enough to make a pin, or a nail, but exhausts itself in making the point of a pin, or the head of a nail'' (John Ruskin, *The Stones of Venice*, 1853).

''[The division of labor] creates among men an entire system of rights and duties which link them together in a durable way [solidarity]. . . . [A spontaneous division of labor is achieved] only if society is constituted in such a way that social inequalities exactly express natural inequalities. . . . The sexual division of labor is the source of conjugal solidarity. . . . It has made possible perhaps the strongest of all unselfish inclinations'' (Émile Durkheim, *The Division of Labor in Society*, 1893).

''[Competition explains] the division of labor and all the vast organized interdependence of individuals and groups of individuals characteristic of modern life'' (Robert Park and Ernest Burgess, *Introduction to the Science of Sociology*, 1921).

''Though with many individual exceptions, technological advance almost always leads to increasingly elaborate division of labor and the concomitant requirement of increasingly elaborate organization'' (Talcott Parsons, *The Social System*, 1951).

''Only rarely is any division of labor within an industry . . . encountered among nonliterate folk. Such intra-industrial specialization would be encountered only in the production of such larger capital goods as houses, canoes, or fish-weirs . . . in groups where the primary division of labor is along sex lines, every man or woman not only will know how to do all those things that men or women habitually do among them, but must be able to do them efficiently . . . except under the most unusual circumstances, we do not find the kind of organization where one woman characteristically specializes in gathering the clay, another in fashioning it, and a third in firing the pots; or, where one man devotes himself to getting wood, a second to roughly blocking out the proportions of a stool or figure, and a third to finishing it'' (Melville Herskovits, *Economic Anthropology*, 1960).

''The division of labor among capitalists, and the market, make capitalists dependent upon one another and act collectively vis-à-vis the labor force'' (C. Lefort, *Elements of a Critique of Bureaucracy*, 1971).

''When it is stated that one sex must perform certain tasks, this also means that the other sex is forbidden to do them'' (Claude Lévi-Strauss in Harry Shapiro, ed., *Man, Culture and Society*, 1971).

''The common reality is that the household involves a simple but highly important division of labor. With the receipt of the income, in the usual case, goes the *basic* authority over its use . . . a natural authority resides with the person who earns the money. This entitles him to be called the head of the family'' (John K. Galbraith, *Economics and the Public Purpose*, 1973).

''[In the Soviet Union the division of labor aims at] the fulfillment of the production program, since under all conditions management must take as its point of departure the priority of production requirements as the first and principal task of the enterprise'' (V. Podmarkov, *Introduction to Industrial Sociology*, 1973).

''Important processes both stemming from, and adding to, the division of labor are the growth of formal organizations and the growth of technology. Since an intensified division of labor provides a reduction in the cost of organization, the division of labor and growth has been intrinsically connected in the historical evolution of the industrial system in the process of power concentration'' (Volker Bornschier, *Growth, Concentration, and Multinationalization of Industrial Enterprises*, 1976).

DIVORCE

''When a man hath taken a wife, and married her, and it come to pass that she find no favour in his eyes, because he hath found some uncleanness in her: then let him write her a bill of divorcement'' (Deuteronomy 24:1).

''Hipponicus assembled a number of witnesses and put away his wife, saying that this man had been entering his house, not as her brother, but as her spouse'' (Lysias, *Contra Alcibiades*, c. 400 B.C.).

''If a man and a woman are quite incompatible because of unhappy dispositions, they must be under the constant control of 10 middle-aged guardians of the law and also of 10 women who are in charge of marriage; and if they are able to reconcile them, let their marriage stand, but if their souls are tossed greatly with passion, let the officials find, so far as possible, another suitable mate for each of them'' (Plato, *Laws*, c. 400 B.C.).

''Whosoever shall put away his wife, saving for the cause of fornication, causeth her to commit adultery: and whosoever shall marry her that is divorced committeth adultery. . . . What therefore God hath joined together, let no man put asunder'' (Matthew 5:32; 19:6).

''Romulus introduced several laws. One of them, which was quite severe, forbids a wife to leave her spouse, but gives a husband the right to divorce his wife for poisoning her children, for falsifying his keys, and for adultery'' (Plutarch, *Romulus*, c.100).

''[Caesar] chose for tribunes Vatinius and Clodius Pulcher, although Clodius had been suspected of an affair with Caesar's wife [Pompeia] during a religious ceremony of women; but Caesar did not prosecute him, since he was extremely popular, although he divorced his wife; others, however, prosecuted Clodius for his impiety during the religious ceremony, Cicero being the counsel for the prosecution. And when Caesar was called as a witness, he did not testify against Clodius'' (Appianus, *Civil Wars*, c. 150).

''A man must give his wife a divorce if she desires it on his taking an additional wife'' (Talmud: Levirate Marriage 65a).

''Divorce must be pronounced and then a woman must be retained in honour or released in kindness. And it is not lawful for you that ye take from women aught of that which ye have given them'' (Koran: The Cow, 229).

''He counsels a divorce; a loss of her that, like a jewel, has hung twenty years about his neck'' (William Shakespeare, *Henry VIII*, 1613).

''Our marriage is dead, when the pleasure is fled'' (John Dryden, *Songs*, 1673).

''Better a tooth out than always aching'' (Thomas Fuller, *Gnomologia*, 1732).

''Perhaps divorce is of almost the same age as marriage, but I believe that marriage is a few weeks older'' (François Marie Arouet Voltaire, *Philosophical Dictionary,* 1764).

''Divorce is so natural that, in many houses, it sleeps every night between two spouses'' (Sébastien Roch Nicolas Chamfort, *Maxims and Thoughts*, c. 1800, posthumously).

''Whosoever shall put away his wife, saving for the cause of fornication, causeth her to commit adultery; and whoso shall marry her who is divorced committeth adultery'' (The Book of Mormon: III Nephi 12:32).

''[Since intemperance is involved] in nearly a fifth of the divorces [we] ought to invigorate the temperance movement in all its branches'' (Edward Ross, *Changing America*, 1912).

''The institution of divorce, like sickness, has largely settled down in Middletown to the status of a means of livelihood for a profession, with the public officials supplying seemly rituals and the official seal'' (Robert and Helen Lynd, *Middletown in Transition*, 1937).

''They [the Lakher of Southeast Asia] consider that the child of a properly married man is exclusively his and that his divorced wife has absolutely no rights in the child whatsoever'' (Edmund Leach, *Rethinking Anthropology*, 1961).

''In thirty of the forty [non-European] cultures surveyed it was impossible to detect any substantial difference in the rights of men and women to terminate an unsatisfactory alliance. The stereotype of the oppressed aboriginal woman proved to be a complete myth'' (George Murdock in Victor Christopherson, ed., *Readings in Comparative Marriage and the Family*, 1967).

''The divorce rate in the United States seems to be of considerable concern. For a generation, Americans have been told that their family system is disintegrating, as evidenced by the fact that so many marriages are breaking up. . . . Practically all societies make some arrangement for divorce'' (J. Udry, *The Social Context of Marriage*, 1974).

''[In ancient Egypt] when a woman committed adultery, not only was a divorce obtained by her husband, but her nose was cut or bitten off'' (Panos Bardis, *History of the Family*, 1975).

"The popular notion that it was the well-to-do who divorced was originally based on fact, for it was once only they who could afford it. Nevertheless, there was no reason to suppose that the marital stability of the lower strata was greater at our time in our history. The popular picture of lower-class family life as stable, warm, and inviting, with frequent exchange of kinship obligations and tightly knit against the outside world, was a literary stereotype, often used by authors who had never observed a lower-class family. Lower-class instability was probably expressed in separation and desertion when divorce was very difficult. These forms of dissolution continue to be more common among the lowest strata" (William Goode in Robert Merton and Robert Nisbet, eds., *Contemporary Social Problems*, 1976).

"Although divorced parents often do not try to explain to their children the reasons for the divorce, the deserted person usually can give no explanation because he himself doesn't know what it is. The deserted spouse also cannot remarry until a divorce is secured" (M. and L. Smart, *Families*, 1976).

"In earlier times, the collapse of a marriage was far more likely to deprive both spouses of a great deal more than the pleasure of each other's company. Since family members performed so many functions for one another, divorce in the past meant a farmer without a wife to churn the cream into butter or care for him when he was sick, and a mother without a husband to plow the fields and bring her the food to feed their children. Today, when emotional satisfaction is the bond that holds marriages together, the waning of love or the emergence of real incompatibilities and conflicts between husband and wife leave fewer reasons for a marriage to continue. Schools and doctors and counselors and social workers provide their supports whether the family is intact or not. One loses less by divorce today than in earlier times, because marriage provides fewer kinds of sustenance and satisfaction" (Kenneth Keniston, *All Our Children*, 1977).

"There are three predominant types of separation. The first is separation as a preliminary to divorce. . . . The second type of separation is a substitute for divorce. . . . Separation of the third kind is the desertion by one of the spouses" (Benjamin Schlesinger, *The One-Parent Family*, 1978).

"It is conceivable, although not provable, that the national figures for the 1920s and 1930s understate the actual number of divorces by 50 percent or more and that the widely lamented increase in the American divorce rate in the past half of the century is partly a myth" (Theodore Caplow et al., *Middletown Families*, 1982).

"The divorced were most likely to have ulcers and the remarried high blood pressure" (Leonard Cargan and Matthew Melko, *Singles*, 1982).

E

ECOLOGY

''All creatures are content with their pasturage; trees and plants are flourishing. The birds, flying from their nests, stretch out their wings in praise to thy spirit'' (*Hymn to Aton*, c. 1400 B.C.).

''For, lo, the winter is past, the rain is over and gone; the flowers appear on the earth; the time of the singing of birds is come, and the voice of the turtle is heard in our land; the fig tree putteth forth her green figs, and the vines with the tender grape give a good smell'' (Song of Solomon 2:11–13).

''What a great dream in the mallow and the asphodel'' (Hesiod, *Works and Days*, c. 750 B.C.).

''The whole black earth is oppressed beneath the storm . . . all the rivers flow in flood, and many hillsides are furrowed deeply by the torrents, and they rush to the purple sea from the mountains, roaring mightily, and the fields of men are wasted'' (Homer, *Iliad*, c. 750 B.C.).

''Dear is the light of the sun, and lovely to the eye is the placid ocean-flood, and the earth in the bloom of spring'' (Euripides, *Danae*, c. 450 B.C.).

''I say that Asia and Europe differ extremely in the natures of all inhabitants and all plants of the land . . . the cause of these is the climate'' (Hippocrates, *On Airs, Waters, Places*, c. 400 B.C.).

''Since the land is the parent, let the citizens take care of her more carefully than children do their mother'' (Plato, *Laws*, c. 400 B.C.).

''The first and greatest knowledge, and also common to all men, is the division and order of our environment'' (Polybius, *Histories*, 130 B.C.).

''There are also kinds of water that cause death, as they run through harmful juices in the soil and become poisonous'' (Vitruvius, *On Architecture*, c. 50 B.C.).

''It is undeniable that every organic whole must have an ultimate ideal of perfection. As in vines or in cattle we see that, unless obstructed by some force, nature progresses on a certain path of her own to her goal of full development'' (Cicero, *On the Nature of the Gods*, c. 45 B.C.).

''Hail, great mother of fruits, land of Saturn, great mother of men!'' (Vergil, *Georgics*, c. 30 B.C.).

''It is said that the people of Massalia fenced the vineyards with bones, and that the soil, after the corpses had wasted away in it and the rains had fallen on it during the winter, grew so rich . . . that it produced a great crop'' (Plutarch, *Caius Marius*, c. 110).

''[Social ecology is] a synoptic study of the balance of plant, animal, and human communities, which are systems of correlated working parts in the organization of the region'' (Radhakamal Mukerjee, *Regional Sociology*, 1926).

''Light being the main necessity of plants, the dominant plant of a community is the tallest member, which can spread its green energy-trap above the heads of the others. What marginal exploitation there is to be done is an exploitation of the dimmer light below this canopy . . . in the wheat field the dominating form is the wheat, with lower weeds among its stalks'' (Herbert G. Wells, *The Science of Life*, 1934).

''There is continuity in the life patterns of all organic forms. . . . The word ecology is derived from the Greek *oikos*—a house or place to live in. . . . Ernst Haeckel, the German biologist, is credited with being the first to use the term *ecology*, employing it in his study of plants in 1868 [*History of Creation*] . . . ecology is but a new name for an old subject'' (Amos Hawley, *Human Ecology*, 1950).

''Pessimists now believe that environmental pollution and the depletion of natural resources are taking industrial societies on a suicidal course and that the year 2000 might well be the beginning'' (William White and Frank Little, eds., *North American Reference Encyclopedia of Ecology and Pollution*, 1972).

''The cedar forests of Lebanon supplied the best wood not only for the construction of Solomon's Temple in Jerusalem, but also for numerous cities of the Near East. Today a few tiny, protected groves manage to survive among whole mountain ranges of dry, eroding rock'' (J. Hughes, *Ecology in Ancient Civilizations*, 1975).

''Properly managed, forests can enrich human life in a variety of ways which are both material and psychological. Poorly managed, they can be a source for the disruption of the environment of an entire region. However, through the centuries we have seen a pattern repeated. The misuse of axe or saw, of fire or grazing, causes forest destruction. This leads to disruption of watersheds, to the erosion or loss of fertility of soils, to siltation and flooding in stream valleys, and to loss of the continued productivity of the land on which man must depend'' (Raymond Dasmann, *Environmental Conservation*, 1976).

''In the German parliament, as in the American Congress, there is already a majority in favor of changing the law so as to permit the passage of high-priority legislation controlling the impact of industry and technology upon the environment'' (Bernhard Grzimek, ed., *Encyclopedia of Ecology*, 1976).

''The science of ecology is no longer something of interest only to ecologists or a subject to be studied only for its intellectual fascination (although that still exists). Many of the major problems the world faces—pollution, overpopulation, the wise use of resources—are at heart ecological problems. Ecologists will help to find solutions to these problems, but so will everybody else'' (Richard Brewer, *Principles of Ecology*, 1979).

''The ecological man . . . attempts to meet the problems of the present and the challenge of the future . . . [he is] a bundle of sensitivities which are in the process of continuous refinement. . . . The ecological man directs himself to root causes and not to symptoms'' (Henryk Skolimowsky, *The Ecological Man*, no date).

''Organisms exist under the influence of external conditions which in total constitute the environment. . . . The consequences of disturbing the balance of an ecosystem are well documented throughout history in the extinction of species'' (Sybil Parker, ed., *McGraw-Hill Encyclopedia of Environmental Science*, 1980).

''From a strictly ecological viewpoint nuclear power is almost certainly the most benign of all the main available or prospective energy supply technologies'' (Ian Barbour et al., *Energy and American Values*, 1982).

''The idea that there is a link between the health of man and the weather has a very long heritage . . . weather is one of the determinants of man's health . . . for man depends on the atmospheric environment for his well-being, in fact for his very survival. . . . It was Smuts' (1926) *Holism and Evolution* which provided the philosophical basis for the concepts that were to become human ecology. . . . It was Smuts' philosophy and the ideas of Huntington and Petersen which guided the botanist Bews (1935) in writing the first book to be entitled *Human Ecology*'' (Frederick Sargent, *Hippocratic Heritage*, 1982).

ECONOMIC SOCIOLOGY

''Silver is useful only because it helps us satisfy our physical needs'' (Plato, *Eryxias*, c. 400 B.C., spurious).

''If you wish to make Pythocles wealthy, do not give him more money, but diminish his desire for money'' (Epicurus, *To Idomeneus*, c. 300 B.C.).

''A hired servant or workman who, without being ill, out of pride fails to perform his work according to the agreement, shall be fined'' (Manu, *Laws*, c. 200 B.C.).

''Men do not realize that thrift is a great income'' (Cicero, *Paradoxes of the Stoics*, 46 B.C.).

''The love of money is the root of all evil'' (I Timothy 6:10).

''Allah hath blighted usury and made almsgiving fruitful'' (Koran: The Cow 276).

''If money go before, all ways do lie open'' (William Shakespeare, *The Merry Wives of Windsor*, 1601).

''Every individual necessarily labours to render the annual revenue of the society as great as he can. He generally, indeed, neither intends to promote the public interest, nor knows how much he is promoting it. . . . By directing that industry in such a manner as its produce may be of the greatest value, he intends only his own gain, and he is in this, as in many other cases, led by an invisible hand to promote an end which was no part of his intention. Nor is it always the worse for the society that it was no part of it. By pursuing his own interest he frequently promotes that of the society more effectually than when he really intends to promote it. . . . High taxes, sometimes by diminishing the consumption of the taxed commodities, and sometimes by encouraging smuggling, frequently afford a smaller revenue to government than what might be drawn from more moderate taxes'' (Adam Smith, *The Wealth of Nations*, 1776).

``In those countries where the labouring classes have the fewest wants, and are contented with the cheapest food, the people are exposed to the greatest vicissitudes and miseries'' (David Ricardo, *On the Principles of Political Economy and Taxation*, 1817).

``Property, after having robbed the laborer by usury, murders him by slow starvation'' (Pierre Joseph Proudhon, *What Is Property?* 1840).

``The bourgeoisie has through its exploitation of the world market given a cosmopolitan character to production and consumption in every country'' (Karl Marx and Friedrich Engels, *Communist Manifesto*, 1847).

``No social order is ever destroyed before all the productive forces for which it is sufficient have been developed, and new superior relations of production never replace older ones before the material conditions for their existence have matured within the framework of the old society'' (Karl Marx, *A Contribution to the Critique of Political Economy*, 1859).

``The fact is that the work which improves the condition of mankind, the work which extends knowledge and increases power and enriches literature, and elevates thought, is not done to secure a living. It is not the work of slaves, driven to their task by the lash of a master or by animal necessities. It is the work of men who perform it for their own sake, and not that they may get more to eat or drink, or wear, or display'' (Henry George, *Progress and Poverty*, 1879).

``[In a democratic republic] wealth wields its power indirectly, but all the more effectively'' (Friedrich Engels, *The Origin of the Family, Private Property, and the State*, 1884).

``[Private commerce and industry are] similar to . . . surrendering the functions of political government to kings and nobles for their personal glorification'' (Edward Bellamy, *Looking Backward*, 1888).

``The man of wealth is reproved if he lives the life of a poor man, but also if he seeks the refinements of luxury overmuch. Economists may protest in vain; public feeling will always be scandalized if an individual spends too much wealth for wholly superfluous use, and it even seems that this severity relaxes only in times of moral disturbance'' (Émile Durkheim, *Suicide*, 1897).

``In order to stand well in the eyes of the community, it is necessary to come up to a certain, somewhat indefinite, conventional standard of wealth. . . . Those members of the community who fall short of this . . . suffer in the esteem of their fellowmen; and consequently they suffer also in their own esteem'' (Thorstein Veblen, *The Theory of the Leisure Class*, 1899).

''I don't like to work—no man does—but I like what is in work—the chance to find yourself'' (Joseph Conrad, *Youth*, 1902).

''The pursuit of wealth, stripped of its religious and ethical weaving, tends to become associated with purely mundane passions, which often actually give it the character of sport'' (Max Weber, *The Protestant Ethic and the Spirit of Capitalism*, 1905).

''The economic problem is the fundamental one, out of which all other social and moral problems have grown'' (Thomas Carver, *Essays in Social Justice*, 1915).

''The omnipotence of 'wealth' is thus more secure in a democratic republic, since it does not depend on the poor political shell of capitalism. A democratic republic is the best possible political shell for capitalism, and therefore, once capital has gained control . . . of this very best shell, it establishes its power so securely, so firmly that no change, either of persons, or institutions, or parties in the bourgeois republic can shake it'' (Nikolai Lenin, *The State and Revolution*, 1917).

''Commercialization is the increasing subjection of any calling or function to the profits motive'' (Edward Ross, *Principles of Sociology*, 1920).

''When work is no longer only a means of gaining a living that has become a primary need in life . . . only then can the narrow bourgeois horizons of law be completely surpassed and society can emblazon on its flag: from each according to his abilities, to each according to his need'' (Leon Trotsky, *Terrorism and Communism*, 1920).

''What is one man's luxury is another man's necessity'' (Leonard Hobhouse, *The Elements of Social Justice*, 1922).

''When the number of competitors increases in relation to the profit span, the participants become interested in curbing competition. Usually one group of competitors takes some externally identifiable characteristic of another group of (actual or potential) competitors—race, language, religion, local or social origin, descent, residence, etc.—as a pretext for attempting their exclusion'' (Max Weber, *Economy and Society*, 1922, posthumously).

''Production for profit really subserves the general welfare'' (Edward Ross, *The Russian Soviet Republic*, 1923).

''The economic system forms men . . . under certain circumstances men can also form their economic and social systems'' (Karl Mannheim, *Essays on the Sociology of Knowledge*, 1929).

''We are being afflicted with a new disease of which some readers may not yet have heard the name, but of which they will hear a great deal in the years to come—namely, *technological unemployment*'' (John M. Keynes, *Essays in Persuasion*, 1931).

''[The profit-account is] one of the basest inventions with which the devil has yet deceived mankind. . . . [Advertising is] one of the most unfortunate phenomena of our times'' (Werner Sombart, *A New Social Philosophy*, 1934).

''The endless stimulation of desires originating in a competitive system, where the producers try to outdo each other by creating cravings for new kinds of goods [opposes the spirit of Christianity]'' (Karl Mannheim, *Diagnosis of Our Time*, 1943).

''[We must stress social planning] not for a classless society but for one that abolishes the extremes of wealth and poverty'' (Karl Mannheim, *Freedom, Power, and Democratic Planning*, 1950, posthumously).

''Expenditure rises to meet income'' (C. N. Parkinson, *The Law and the Profits*, 1960).

''What is good for the worker is good for them [businessmen] too'' (John Zervas in D. Kalitsounakis, ed., *Economy and Society*, 1961).

''To understand and predict any aspect of social life, we cannot ignore economic matters'' (Neil Smelser, *The Sociology of Economic Life*, 1963).

''[In the Soviet Union] the manager must know the policy of the Party, master Marxist-Leninist theory, have a broad political orientation, and be able to combine correctly current economic work with political activity'' (F. Aunapu, *What Management Is*, 1967).

''The state is strongly concerned with the stability of the economy. And with its expansion of growth. And with education. And with technical and scientific advance. And, most notably, with the national defense. . . . It requires stability in demand for its planning. Growth brings promotion and prestige. It requires trained manpower. It needs government underwriting of research and development'' (John K. Galbraith, *The New Industrial State*, 1967).

''From an economy of goods, which America was as recently as World War II, we have changed into a knowledge economy. . . . The economic history of the last hundred years in the advanced and developed countries could be called 'from agriculture to knowledge' '' (Peter Drucker, *The Age of Discontinuity*, 1969).

''The inequality of salaries produces strong inequalities in the distribution of work revenues. On the one hand, workers in the advanced sector enjoy high incomes and want consumer goods in a manner typical of industrial aggregates. On the other hand, workers in the semi-artisan sector have much more modest incomes and cannot purchase in adequate quantities even the most elementary goods, and thus contribute to the lowering of the average level of consumption for society as a whole'' (A. Graziani et al., *Evolution of an Open Economy*, 1972).

''[The Soviet economy] is not capitalism, it is not socialism, it is not even on its way to either of these two forms; the Soviet economy represents a historically new type, and its name matters little if its essential features are understood'' (Cornelius Castoriadis, *The Bureaucratic Society*, 1973).

''[In the Soviet Union] at the present time it is difficult to find any important problem which is decided by enterprise management exclusively on its own without first ascertaining collective opinion'' (V. Ermuratskii, *Social Activities of Workers in Industrial Enterprises*, 1973).

''Multinational corporations, as the central institution of the modern world economy, imply—due to their internal division of labor across countries—an *internalization* of economic relationships previously regarded as *international*'' (Volker Bornschier, *Multinational Monopolies*, 1980).

''If we made an income pyramid out of a child's blocks, with each layer portraying $1,000 of income, the peak would be far higher than the Eiffel Tower, but almost all of us would be within a yard of the ground'' (Paul Samuelson in P. Blumberg, *Inequality in an Age of Decline*, 1980).

''One salient feature of today's economic life is not the enjoyment offered by the use of modern achievements, but the everlasting effort to obtain more and more novel goods'' (Xenophon Zolotas, *Economic Growth and Declining Social Welfare*, 1981).

EDUCATIONAL SOCIOLOGY

''Education is an ornament for those who are fortunate, and a refuge for those who are unfortunate. . . . Nature and teaching are very similar; for teaching transforms man, and in the process of transforming him makes him natural. . . . More people become superior through training than through heredity. . . . A teacher is more successful when he uses exhortations and persuasion rather than rules and compulsion'' (Democritus, Fragments, c. 400 B.C.).

''A good education is that which improves both mind and body'' (Plato, *Laws*, c. 400 B.C.).

''When one is wealthy enough not to have to work, it is very profitable to educate one's daughter in Greek and Latin. But if, because of lack of means, she is obliged to engage in manual labor, she should be taught to read her own language, for much wisdom may be obtained from reading good books'' (Desiderius Erasmus, *The Institution of Christian Marriage*, 1526).

''Everything is good as it comes from the hand of the Creator; everything degenerates in the hands of man'' (Jean Jacques Rousseau, *Émile*, 1762).

''The artificial mode of the schools, which everywhere crowds in this array of words . . . instead of the easier and slower method of nature . . . endows men with an artificial show of acquirement, which varnishes over their lack of inner natural powers, but at the same time satisfied the people of the present century'' (Johann Heinrich Pestalozzi, *Evening Hour of a Hermit*, 1780).

''There is scarcely a town of considerable note in Great Britain, which is not sometimes visited by . . . travelling lecturers, who, by means of portable apparatus, and a facility in communicating instruction, import the benefits of useful knowledge to hundreds and thousands who might otherwise remain destitute of its advantages'' (John Griscom, *A Year in Europe*, 1824).

''Every individual must, in order to acquire the art of reading in the shortest possible time, be taught quite apart from any other, and therefore there must be a separate method for each'' (Leo Nikolaevich Tolstoi, *On Teaching the Rudiments*, c. 1865).

''If the great benefits of scientific training are sought, it is essential that such training be real: that is to say, that the mind of the scholar should be brought into direct relation with fact, that he should not merely be told a thing, but made to see. . . . Don't be satisfied with telling him that a magnet attracts iron. Let him see that it does'' (Thomas Huxley, *Scientific Education*, 1869).

''Universal education [is] the one clear, overshadowing, and immediate social duty to which all others are subordinate'' (Lester Ward, *Dynamic Sociology*, 1883).

''[All should receive] the completest education that the nation can give'' (Edward Bellamy, *Looking Backward*, 1888).

''The class is a small society. . . . Since the child comes to understand the rule through the teacher and since it is the teacher who reveals it to him, it can have only such authority as the teacher communicates to it'' (Émile Durkheim, *Moral Education*, 1906).

''[True education is based on] the habits and atmosphere of a school, not from the school textbooks'' (William Sumner, *Folkways*, 1907).

''The humanities need to be defended today against the encroachments of physical science, as they once needed to be defended against the encroachments of theology'' (Irving Babbitt, *Literature and the American College*, 1908).

''Lack of interest in study, habits of inattention and procrastination, positive aversion to intellectual application, dependence upon sheer memorizing and mechanical routine with only a modicum of understanding by the pupil of what he is about, show that the theory of logical definition, division, gradation, and system does not work out practically'' (John Dewey, *How We Think*, 1910).

''Not only does social life demand teaching and learning for its own permanence, but the very process of living together educates'' (John Dewey, *Democracy and Education*, 1916).

''[Education is] the influences exercised by adult generations on those that are not yet ready for social life. Its object is to arouse and to develop in the child a certain number of physical, intellectual and moral states which are demanded of him both by the political society as a whole and the special milieu for which he is specifically destined'' (Émile Durkheim, *Education and Sociology*, 1922, posthumously).

''[Effective education will restructure] the whole complex of our social life, or our civilization within the comparatively short space of one or two generations'' (Charles Ellwood, *Christianity and Social Science*, 1923).

''The key to the regeneration of Mexico [is popular education]'' (Edward Ross, *The Social Revolution in Mexico*, 1923).

''I should like to go one step further now and say, 'Give me a dozen healthy infants, well-formed, and my own specified world to bring them up in and I'll guarantee to take any one at random and train him to become any type of specialist' '' (John Watson, *Behaviorism*, 1925).

''[True education gives social studies] the central place in the curriculum of our schools, flanked on one side by language and on the other by the natural sciences'' (Charles Ellwood, *Man's Social Destiny in the Light of Science*, 1929).

''An adequate education or instruction of the young (in the sense of the complete transmission of all experiential stimuli which underlie pragmatic knowlege) would encounter a formidable difficulty in the fact that the experiential problems of the young are defined by a different set of adversaries from those of their teachers'' (Karl Mannheim, *Essays on the Sociology of Knowledge*, 1929).

''The teacher represents the established social order in the school, and his interest is in maintaining that order, whereas pupils have only a negative interest in that feudal superstructure'' (Willard Waller, *The Sociology of Teaching*, 1932).

''[Education based on sociology makes a person] many times more effective socially than he is at the present time . . . [adds] something to the life of the group . . . [and it does not merely] emancipate the individual and develop his capacities'' (Charles Ellwood, *Methods of Sociology*, 1933).

''[Public education will be based on] the values of Jewish culture and the achievements of science, of love of the homeland, and loyalty to the Jewish State and the Jewish people, on practice in agricultural work and in handicraft, on pioneer training, and on striving for a society built on freedom, equality, tolerance, mutual assistance, and a love of mankind'' (*State Education Law*, Israel, 1953).

''Schools bring little influence to bear on a child's development that is independent of his background and general school context'' (James Coleman et al., *Equality of Educational Opportunity*, 1966).

''Any teacher who knows his job . . . divides his course into 'thematic units,' that is, lessons . . . he makes one or more outlines to explain these units . . . the original root of each fundamental outline can be found in a form of social behavior almost as old as the human race'' (Juan Tusquets, *Theory and Practice in Comparative Education*, 1968).

''[Middle-class high schools] increase a student's chances of making college-oriented friends. This raises the probability that the student will go to college. On the other hand, middle-class high schools have higher academic standards than working-class high schools. This means that if a student at any given ability level enters a middle-class school, he is likely to rank lower in this class than if he enters a working-class school'' (Christopher Jencks et al., *Inequality*, 1972).

''Faith in the powers of education [in Italy] was probably never so strong as at the end of the 1950s. Modern priests praised its virtues. Supported and financed by governments and foundations, sociologists and economists invested their best energies in this fascinating enterprise. . . . Nevertheless, the old conceptual edifices having fallen new ones have yet to appear'' (Marzio Barbagli, *Intellectual Unemployment and the School System in Italy*, 1973).

''[Four main industries comprise higher education], one is the general education industry, which formed the base line from which the others have differentiated. A second is the research industry, which is concerned with enhancing the cognitive capacity of society through adding to the cultural base on which it operates. A third is graduate training of the personnel who will be the successors of current academicians. A fourth industry is training in capacity to apply knowledge to practical problems'' (Talcott Parsons and Gerald Platt, *The American University*, 1973).

''[As for continuing education] in the process of teaching the stress could be laid on the development of creative and expressive talents, on the furthering of the motivation for further learning, on the ability to review critically and refresh one's already acquired knowledge'' (*Report on the State of Education in the People's Republic of Poland*, 1973).

''In French society there is greater inequality of educational opportunities between young people from the lower and the upper classes than is the case in Greece'' (Jane Lambiri, *Toward a Greek Sociology of Education*, 1974).

''[In China] formerly we put intellectual development first and kept a closed door. . . . The students did not know how the workers worked or how the peasants plowed the fields. Under chairman Mao's revolutionary lines, we develop the children morally, intellectually, and physically. The students are educated to serve the people wholeheartedly . . . to combine theory with practice'' (William Kessen, ed., *Childhood in China*, 1975).

''[In India] the student community now includes a large proportion of persons whose motivation is minimal and whose competence to profit from higher education . . . is also questionable. . . . Student unrest has thus become a major factor which makes it extremely difficult to run university administration'' (J. Naik in S. Dube, ed., *India Since Independence,* 1977).

''Society affects the schools mainly through the attitudes of parents, values derived from the media and the changed approach to moral questions generally associated with the 'permissive society' '' (Scottish Education Department, *The Pack Report*, 1977).

''The weight of class structure . . . does not determine student aspiration as effectively as the variables linked to scholarly stratification'' (Mohamed Cherkaoui, *The Paradoxes of the Social Issue*, 1979).

''If children are to develop self-confidence they must first have confidence in the adults around them'' (Her Majesty's Inspectorate, *Aspects of Secondary Education in England*, 1979).

''[It is] important for the Japanese to get to know more about other cultures in order to reflect rigorously upon ourselves. Thus, 'internationalization of education' has become the order of the day'' (Nobuyuki Kubota in Professors World Peace Academy of Japan, *The Pacific Era*, 1979).

''While American education has been used as an instrument of social justice almost all groups have looked to the educational system for legitimation'' (Don Martindale and Raj Mohan, eds., *Ideals and Realities*, 1980).

''Educators have concentrated their efforts too often and too long on the individual'' (Joseph Scimecca, *Education and Society*, 1980).

''[It is still debatable] whether the function of the History of Education is a formative and informative one . . . for future teachers . . . or is to be a strictly scientific-historical discipline'' (José Doménech, *The Sciences of Education Under Examination*, 1981).

''Plumbers install plumbing, and, when something goes wrong with the plumbing, they fix it. They don't care how the pipes feel about it. Teaching reading and arithmetic is much more like plumbing than you probably think. If you know how to read and cipher, you can, if you want to, teach those skills to almost any child in America'' (Richard Mitchell, *The Graves of Academe*, 1981).

''It is natural for children to rise to meet higher expectations, but only if those expectations are set before them and made both reasonable and attractive'' (Mortimer Adler, *The Paideia Proposal*, 1982).

''Catholic school students are less likely to come from father-absent families . . . [public schools] are most successful with the affluent while Catholic schools are most successful with the poor'' (Andrew Greeley, *Catholic High Schools and Minority Students*, 1982).

''Much has already been done for secondary and higher education in Brazil in terms of financial support, participation of the private sector, scholarships, loans to be repaid after graduation, diversification of curricula, and professional instruction. We need to develop similar policies for the primary level, especially in the rural zone . . . to make it easier for Brazilians to finish primary school'' (José Pastore, *Inequality and Social Mobility in Brazil*, 1982).

''College teaching is the only profession for which there is no professional training'' (B. F. Skinner in Robert Epstein, ed., *Skinner for the Classroom*, 1982).

ELITE

''Aristocracy is government of the best with the consent of the many'' (Plato, *Menexenus*, c. 400 B.C.).

''All artistocratic governments are free oligarchies'' (Aristotle, *Politics*, c. 350 B.C.).

''High people, Sir, are the best; take a hundred ladies of quality, you'll find them better wives, better mothers'' (Samuel Johnson, 1778, in James Boswell, *The Life of Samuel Johnson*, 1791).

''Men of talent are constantly forced to serve the rest. They make the discoveries and inventions, order the battles, write the books, and produce the art'' (William Sumner, *Folkways*, 1907).

''In virtue of class-circulation, the governing *élite* is always in a state of slow and continuous tranformation. It flows on like a river, never being today what it was yesterday. From time to time sudden and violent disturbances occur. There is a flood—the river overflows its banks. Afterwards, the new governing *élite* again resumes its slow transformation. The flood has subsided, the river is again flowing normally in its wonted bed'' (Vilfredo Pareto, *The Mind and Society*, 1916).

''The discovery that in all large-scale societies the decisions at any given time are typically in the hands of a small number of people, confirms a basic fact:

Government is always government by the few, whether in the name of the few, the one, or the many'' (Harold Lasswell and Daniel Lerner, *The Comparative Study of Elites*, 1952).

''If we took the one hundred most powerful men in America, the one hundred wealthiest, and the one hundred most celebrated away from the institutional positions they now occupy, away from their resources of men and women and money, away from the media of mass communication . . . they would be powerless and poor and uncelebrated. For power is not of a man. Wealth does not center in the person of the wealthy. Celebrity is not inherent in any personality. To be celebrated, to be wealthy, to have power, requires access to major institutions . . . [Elites] are in positions to make decisions having major consequences'' (C. W. Mills, *The Power Elite*, 1956).

''The tiny group, consisting primarily of men, that directs the political economy of the United States is overwhelmingly recruited from the wealthier families of society. Few persons reach elite positions in political and economic life unless they are born to wealth, acquire it fairly early in life, or at least have access to it'' (K. Prewitt and A. Stone, *The Ruling Elites*, 1973).

''[In Jodhpur, India] the elite differed not only from the general adult population of the city, but perhaps from one another also . . . the elite emerged from among those who possessed the valued social characteristics'' (Sheo Lal, *The Urban Elite*, 1974).

''[In India] the specialist elites (doctors and engineers) do not have matching status, power and promotion opportunities vis-à-vis the generalist elites . . . the former harbour a feeling of relative deprivation against the latter'' (S. Pande, *Relative Deprivation Among Career Elites*, 1979).

''[In India] slowly but surely, and at an increasing pace, a new 'elite class' seems to be developing which seeks to gear itself to a 'modernized culture' and which may be able to operate and meet the changed situation'' (Carle Zimmerman and Mitra Das in Harald Niemeyer, ed., *Social Relations Network*, 1980).

''[In Japan] ascriptive factors and achievement factors had independent effects on political status'' (Masaaki Takane, *Political Elite in Japan*, 1981).

EQUALITY

''By nature men are nearly all alike; by practice they get to be wide apart'' (Confucius, *Analects*, c. 500 B.C.).

''The statutes about war, as well as freedom of speech in poetry, must apply equally to men and women'' (Plato, *Laws*, c. 400 B.C.).

''Nature has made all men equal'' (Aristotle, *Politics*, c. 350 B.C.).

''If these riches are distributed equally, it is certain that they will not long remain in this state of equality, or that, if they did, they would be as if nonexistent for those who possessed them'' (Jean Jacques Rousseau, *Political Fragments*, c. 1750).

"Wherever there is great property, there is great inequality" (Adam Smith, *The Wealth of Nations*, 1776).

"A human being as he comes originally from the hand of nature, is everywhere the same" (William Robertson, *History of America*, 1777).

"The communist revolution . . . abolishes the rule of all classes with the classes themselves, because it is carried through by the class which no longer counts as a class in society, is not recognised as a class, and is in itself the expression of the dissolution of all classes, nationalities, etc." (Karl Marx and Friedrich Engels, *The German Ideology*, 1846).

"The condition for the emancipation of the working class is the abolition of every class" (Karl Marx, *The Poverty of Philosophy*, 1847).

"Distribute the earth as you will, the principal question remains inexorable—Who is to dig it? Which of us, in brief word, is to do the hard and dirty work for the rest" (John Ruskin, *Sesame and Lilies*, 1865).

"The good of any one individual is of no more importance, from the point of view (if I may say so) of the Universe, than the good of any other" (Henry Sidgwick, *The Methods of Ethics*, 1874).

"[Invention is] the source of privileges, monopolies, and aristocratic inequalities" (Gabriel Tarde, *The Laws of Imitation*, 1890).

"Men share equally in the free gifts of nature" (Edward Bellamy, *Equality*, 1897).

"Both propertied and propertyless people can belong to the same status group, and frequently they do" (Max Weber, *Economy and Society*, 1922, posthumously).

"There can be no equality in uniformity" (D. Mukerji, *Basic Concepts in Sociology*, 1932).

"The one undebatable strategy that is needed now is somehow to equalize opportunity and re-distribute resources and the good things of life to the end that we may have a genuine regional equalization and balance of men" (Howard Odum in Merrill Jensen, ed., *Regionalism in America*, 1951).

"Where everyone is equal there is no politics, for politics involves subordinates and superiors" (Hans Gerth and C. W. Mills, *Character and Social Structure*, 1953).

"Under Communism inequality resulting from different qualifications, unequal endowments and ability will be a thing of the past" (G. Glezerman in F. Konstantinov et al., *Building of Communism and Development of Social Relations*, 1966).

"Complete equalization of the cultural experiences of people will probably never occur and it would not be desirable" (Antonina Kloskowska, *Mass Culture*, 1982).

"From the most primitive communities to the industrial societies of the contemporary world, social inequality has always been present among people" (José Pastore, *Inequality and Social Mobility in Brazil*, 1982).

ETHNOCENTRISM

"[Ethnocentrism is the] view of things in which one's own group is the center of everything and all others are scaled and rated with references to it. . . . Each group nourishes its own pride and vanity, boasts itself superior, exalts its own divinities, and looks with contempt on outsiders. Each group thinks its own folkways the only right ones, and it observes that other groups have other folkways; these excite its scorn" (William Sumner, *Folkways*, 1907).

"The social sciences in various countries only sporadically take account of the achievements of their neighbours. In particular, German research into the problem of generations has ignored results obtained abroad" (Karl Mannheim, *Essays on the Sociology of Knowledge*, 1929).

"Ethnocentrism describes a type of prejudice that says simply, my culture's ways are right and other cultures' ways, if they are not like mine, are wrong. Racism (a particular race is superior to others) and sexism (one sex is superior) are related to ethnocentrism but are more specific types of prejudice" (Judson Landis, *Sociology*, 1983).

ETHNOMETHODOLOGY

"I shall exercise a theorist's preference and say that meaningful events are entirely and exclusively events in a person's behavioral environment. . . . Hence there is no reason to look under the skull since nothing of interest is to be found there but brains" (Harold Garfinkel in O. Harvey, ed., *Motivation and Social Interaction*, 1963).

"The cry of pain, then, is [Harold] Garfinkel's triumphal moment. . . . The demonstration is the message and the message seems to be that anomic normlessness is no longer merely something that the sociologist studies in the social world, but is now something that he inflicts upon it and is the basis of his method of investigation" (Alvin Gouldner, *The Coming Crisis of Western Sociology*, 1971).

"The ethnomethodologist employs glosses while operating within the mundaneity principle at different levels, and these glosses forever remain a member's account of practices said to make up the properties of mundane reasoning. Because these glosses recommend that a sense of 'stepping back' is possible . . . the ethnomethodologist is also vulnerable to the charge of having adopted a privileged position" (Aaron Cicourel, *Cognitive Sociology*, 1974).

"I do not suggest that social scientists cease studying human phenomena, only that they begin to use methods that are more becoming to the mysterious phenomena ethnomethodology has unearthed. To become one's own phenomenon is such a method" (Hugh Mehan and Houston Wood, *The Reality of Ethnomethodology*, 1975).

"The meanings of terms one uses should be unequivocal. In other words, their meaning should remain stable from one situation to another'' (Harold Garfinkel in Kenneth Leiter, *A Primer on Ethnomethodology*, 1980).

''Ethnomethodology does not begin with the assertion that what people know and use is wrong. Rather, it begins by proposing that we need to study what people know and use, commonsense knowledge, because the use of such knowledge by the members of a society produces the sociological phenomena studied by sociologists. . . . Where sociology studies the causes of social action, ethnomethodology is the study of how members perceive behavior as social action'' (Kenneth Leiter, *A Primer on Ethnomethodology*, 1980).

ETHOLOGY

''[Psychology is] the science of the elementary laws of the mind. . . . [Ethology is] the ulterior science which determines the kind of character produced in conformity to those general laws, by any set of circumstances, physical and moral'' (John S. Mill, *A System of Logic*, 1843).

''If we defend the title to our land or the sovereignty of our country, we do it for reasons no different, no less innate, no less ineradicable, than do lower animals'' (Robert Ardrey, *The Territorial Imperative*, 1966).

''According to two of its most prominent founders, Konrad Lorenz and Nikolaas Tinbergen, the field of ethology can be defined as 'the Biology of Behaviour.' It places emphasis on the notion that the behaviour of animals and its physiological basis has evolved phylogenetically and should be studied as one aspect of evolution'' (M. von Cranach et al., eds., *Human Ethology*, 1979).

''The science of animal behavior has special attractions, but it also puts unusual demands on our understanding. Everyday speech includes presumptions about animals which, for scientific analysis, have to be discarded. It is natural to say of a captive animal that it wants freedom . . . such ways of speaking can hinder understanding. All are examples of anthropomorphism'' (S. Barnett, *Modern Ethology*, 1981).

''Ethology is distinguished from other approaches to the study of behaviour in seeking to combine functional and causal types of explanation. . . . Traditionally, ethologists have sought to combine observations of the form of behaviour, and hypotheses about its causation, with speculation and experiment concerning the function of the behaviour'' (David McFarland, ed., *The Oxford Companion to Animal Behavior*, 1982).

EUGENICS

''Jacob took him rods of green poplar, and of the hazel and chestnut tree; and pilled white strakes in them. . . . And he set the rods which he had pilled before the flocks. . . . And the flocks conceived before the rods, and brought forth cattle ringstraked, speckled and spotted'' (Genesis 30:37–39).

"The preponderance of male or female semen determines the gender of the child" (Alcmaeon, Fragment, c. 500 B.C.).

"A noble father sires a noble son" (Euripides, *Alcmene*, c. 410 B.C.).

"Like other diseases it [epilepsy] is determined by hereditary factors" (Hippocrates, *On the Sacred Disease*, c. 400 B.C.).

"You, then, I said, their legislator, as you selected the men, will also select and give to them women as much as possible of the same nature . . . the best men should be united with the best women as often as possible, while the opposite should be done with the worst men and women, and the children of the former should be reared, but not those of the latter, if the flock is to be as superior as possible. . . . And the number of marriages we will leave to the discretion of the rulers . . . so that our state may not become too large or too small" (Plato, *Republic*, c. 400 B.C.).

"The legislator must begin by considering how the bodies of the children reared may be very sound . . . he should take care of marriage, and decide when and who must be united. In legislating on this union, he must consider the persons and their length of life, so that their ages may reach the same period together, and their powers may not be different in that the man is still capable of begetting offspring but the woman is not, or the woman capable and the man not . . . also he must consider the succession of the children, for the children must be neither much younger than their fathers (for to the old ones the gratitude of the children is unprofitable, and so is the fathers' help to the children) nor too near them (for this involves much inconvenience, since in such cases there is less respect, as among equals in age, and also such proximity causes complaints concerning the management of the household) . . . consideration must be given to the bodies of the new-born children, so that they may be in accordance with the wish of the legislator" (Aristotle, *Politics*, c. 350 B.C.).

"Changes sometimes occur spontaneously in fruits. . . . Some herbaceous plants return to their wild state if they are not tended for some time" (Theophrastus, *On the Causes of Plants*, c. 300 B.C.).

"The husband should be at least 25 and the wife at least 16 years old before they have children, so that their offspring will be healthy" (*Susruta Grihya Sutra*, c. 200 B.C.).

"It often happens that children resemble their grandparents or have traits like those of their great-grandparents" (Lucretius, *On the Nature of Things*, c. 60 B.C.).

"An equal degree of heat in the semen of the parents produces a boy that resembles the father; an equal degree of cold produces a girl that resembles the mother" (Censorinus, *On the Day of Birth*, 238).

"My advice to a woman who wants a male child is to lie on her right side immediately after coitus" (Conrad von Megenberg, *Treatise on Nature*, c. 1350).

"The power of man over animal life, in producing whatever varieties of form he pleases, is enormously great . . . talent is transmitted by inheritance in a very remarkable degree" (Francis Galton, *Hereditary Talent and Character*, 1865).

"The power by which Eugenic reforms must chiefly be effected is that of Popular Opinion" (Francis Galton, *Essays in Eugenics*, 1909).

"He [Francis Galton, 1822–1911] proposed the utopian ideal that the quality of mankind be improved by the deliberate application of the techniques of breeding. He coined the term 'eugenics' as the name of the science which would study the conditions under which hereditary characters could be perfected in future generations" (Hans Stubge, *History of Genetics*, 1972).

"Lessening the incidence of hereditary disorders through prevention of child bearing, i.e., *negative eugenics*, has an unsavory history that is primarily related to the enforced sterilization of persons considered 'unfit' " (Arthur and Elaine Mange, *Genetics*, 1980).

EUTHANASIA

"Genetically, a body still circulating blood is in some sense a 'human life,' if genetic membership in the human species is the norm. Then if the moral aim is to preserve whatever genetically counts as 'individual human life,' then an artificially sustained body meets the standard. But if the moral concern is with personhood—thus presupposing our electrically active brain—then, in the absence of brain activity, no 'person' is present" (Daniel Callahan, *Abortion*, 1970).

"In Nazi Germany gassing 70,000 people to death was not murder, but 'euthanasia.' Hitler's definition of the act of killing was accepted by enough of his countrymen to accomplish this mass slaughter. Thousands of 'useless eaters' (Hitler-ese for chronically ill people) were also killed deliberately" (Robert Kastenbaum and Ruth Aisenberg, *The Psychology of Death*, 1972).

"If we can contemplate the precarious possibility that in *some* cases killing may be an act of merciful love and an expression of God's humanizing intentions for life, then we are resting neither in a life worship which is blind to life's quality nor in a death fear which is blind to transcendent hope" (James Nelson, *Human Medicine*, 1973).

"The doctor is less mysterious and less absolute in the home than he is in the hospital. This is because in the hospital he is part of a bureaucracy whose power depends on discipline, organization, and anonymity. These hospital conditions have given rise to a new model of medicalized death" (Philippe Ariès, *The Hour of Our Death*, 1977).

"The terms 'euthanasia' and 'prolongation of life' are not necessarily antithetical. Both aims can be seen generally as expressions of the aspirations of modern culture to control the forces of nature" (Gerald Gruman in Warren Reich, ed., *Encyclopedia of Bioethics*, 1978).

"In Talmudic times . . . euthanasia was rejected even for the terminally ill, who were considered complete living persons" (Panos Bardis, *History of Thanatology*, 1981).

"The American attitude toward dealing humanely with persons who are diagnosed as irreversibly, terminally ill is ambiguous" (Lynne DeSpelder and Albert Strickland, *The Last Dance*, 1982).

EVOLUTION

"All things change and nothing remains unaltered" (Heraclitus, *On Nature*, c. 500 B.C.).

"In the beginning, undifferentiated forms of earth arose" (Empedocles, Fragment, c. 450 B.C.).

"It is evolution that is for the sake of the object, not the object for the sake of evolution" (Aristotle, *Parts of Animals*, c. 350 B.C.).

"All things change and nothing ever remains like to itself. Nature alters all and forces each thing to change its form" (Lucretius, *On the Nature of Things*, c. 60 B.C.).

"Several animals which possess something of the cat, like the lion, tiger, and lynx, could have been of the same race and could be now like new subdivisions of the ancient species of cats" (Gottfried Wilhelm von Leibniz, *Protogaea*, 1691).

"All animals undergo perpetual transformations which are in part produced . . . in consequence of their desires and aversions, of their pleasures and their pains, or of irritations, or of associations; and many of these acquired forms or propensities are transmitted to their posterity" (Erasmus Darwin, *Zoonomia*, 1794).

"Every change that is wrought in an organ through a habit of frequently using it, is subsequently preserved by reproduction, if it is common to the individuals who unite together in fertilization" (Jean Baptiste Pierre Antoine de Monet Lamarck, *Zoological Philosophy*, 1809).

"Progress is the law of life, man is not man as yet" (Robert Browning, *Paracelsus*, 1835).

"The progress of the individual mind is not only an illustration, but an indirect evidence of that of the general mind. The point of departure of the individual and of the race being the same, the phases of the mind of a man correspond to the epochs of the mind of the race. Now, each of us is aware, if he looks back upon his own history, that he was a theologian in his childhood, a metaphysician in his youth, and a natural philosopher in his manhood" (Auguste Comte, *Positive Philosophy*, 1842).

"It is only in an order of things in which there are no more classes and class antagonisms that *social evolutions* will cease to be *political revolutions*" (Karl Marx, *The Poverty of Philosophy*, 1847).

"During the period in which the Earth has been peopled, the human organism has grown more heterogeneous among the civilized divisions of the species . . . the species, as a whole, has been growing more heterogeneous in virtue of the multiplication of races and the differentiation of these races from each other'' (Herbert Spencer, 1857, *Essays*, 1915).

''As natural selection works solely by and for the good of each being, all corporeal and mental endowments will tend to progress towards perfection'' (Charles Robert Darwin, *Origin of Species*, 1859).

''The Asiatic, ancient, feudal and modern bourgeois modes of production may be designated as epochs marking progress in the economic development of society. The bourgeois mode of production is the last antagonistic form of the social process of production'' (Karl Marx, *A Contribution to the Critique of Political Economy*, 1859).

''[Social evolution began when families], temporarily organized among all the higher gregarious mammals, became in the case of the highest mammal permanently organized'' (John Fiske, *Outlines of Cosmic Philosophy*, 1874).

''It is an error to imagine that evolution signifies a constant tendency to increased perfection'' (Thomas Huxley, *The Struggle for Existence in Human Society*, 1888).

''[Superorganic evolution originated with] all those processes and products which imply the co-ordinated actions of many individuals'' (Herbert Spencer, *The Principles of Sociology*, 1896).

''Darwin's theory has no more to do with philosophy than any other hypothesis in natural science'' (Ludwig Josef Johann Wittgenstein, *Tractatus Logico-philosophicus*, 1921).

''One of the most important powers gained during the evolution of animal life is the ability to make decisions from within instead of having them imposed from without'' (William Thomas, *The Unadjusted Girl*, 1923).

''[The laws of cultural evolution] are only indirectly affected by the laws of organic evolution'' (Charles Ellwood, *Cultural Evolution*, 1927).

''Most of the important problems in human social evolution cannot be solved by narrow scientific methods'' (Charles Ellwood, *A History of Social Philosophy*, 1938).

''We are seemingly between two epochs: the dying Sensate culture of our magnificent yesterday and the coming Ideational culture of the creative tomorrow'' (Pitirim Sorokin, *Social and Cultural Dynamics*, 1941).

''We act as we do for reasons of our evolutionary past, not our cultural present, and our behavior is as much a mark of our species as is the shape of a human thigh bone'' (Robert Ardrey, *The Territorial Imperative*, 1966).

''Continuing social evolution further involved creating systems of human order able to persist and develop within this basic contingent relation between the divine and human conditions'' (Talcott Parsons, *Societies*, 1966).

''Errors which destroy the individual are also the origin of species. Without these errors there would be no evolution'' (Jacob Bronowski, *Nature and Knowledge*, 1969).

''As part of organic evolution, the phenomenon of human evolution . . . amounts to a fact, but as yet its detailed path is not known with great certainty'' (Bernard Campbell, *Human Evolution*, 1974).

''The modern theory of evolution emerged in the 1930s and 1940s as a synthesis of genetic knowledge and the Darwinian concept of natural selection'' (Theodosius Dobzhansky et al., *Evolution*, 1977).

''One of the difficulties in thinking about evolution is that the word itself has evolved. Lately the word 'evolution' has been extended to encompass the origin of life and even the transformation of inorganic matter as solar systems develop'' (C. Harris, *Evolution*, 1981).

''Mutations that can lead to evolution may stem from changes in the sequences of DNA molecules in the chromosomes and thus upset their positions'' (Carleton Coon, *Racial Adaptations*, 1982).

''For 3 billion years biological evolution has been powered by discrimination. Even mere survival in the absence of evolutionary change depends on discrimination'' (Garrett Hardin, *Naked Emperors*, 1982).

F

FAMILY

"It is better to dwell in a corner of the housetop, than with a brawling woman in a wide house" (Proverbs 21:9).

"The age of parents must be remembered, both for joy and anxiety" (Confucius, *Analects*, c. 500 B.C.).

"We have adopted ways of preventing every man from knowing who his child is, thus helping all people imagine that they belong to one family" (Plato, *Timaeus*, c. 400 B.C.).

"A family is a society established by nature for daily support" (Aristotle, *Politics*, c. 350 B.C.).

"In temperate climates, where the charms of women are best preserved, where they arrive later at maturity, and have children at a more advanced season of life, the old age of their husband in some degree follows theirs; and as they have more reason and knowledge at the time of marriage, if it be only on account of their having continued longer in life, it must naturally introduce a kind of equality between the two sexes; and, in consequence of this, the law of having only one wife" (Charles de Secondat Montesquieu, *The Spirit of the Laws*, 1748).

"The most ancient of all societies, and the only natural one, is that of the family" (Jean Jacques Rousseau, *The Social Contract*, 1762).

"The bourgeoisie has torn away from the family its sentimental veil, and has reduced the family relation to a mere money relation" (Karl Marx and Friedrich Engels, *Communist Manifesto*, 1847).

"Each individual peasant family is almost self-sufficient; it itself directly produces the major part of its consumption and thus acquires its means of life more through exchange with nature than in intercourse with society" (Karl Marx, *The Eighteenth Brumaire of Louis Bonaparte*, 1852).

"Ye shall defend your families even unto bloodshed" (The Book of Mormon: Alma: 47).

"Students of comparative institutions have generally regarded the family as the unit or germ from which the higher forms of social organism have been evolved" (George Howard, *A History of Matrimonial Institutions*, 1904).

"We were guests in the home of a family counting sixty-eight members. It was one of the few remaining family *zadruga*, or collectives, in Serbia. We met about forty of the members, including the *stareshina*, or head of the family, a patriarch of seventy and absolute ruler of the group. The enormous household, with a considerable tract of ground and a twenty-room house, was all but self-sufficient economically. Every member above ten had his or her special duty to attend to. Six women and girls, supervised by the *stareshina's* wife, did nothing but cook and bake. Eight other females only spun, weaved, sewed, and embroidered. Five men and boys attended to all the sheep, goats, buffaloes, cattle, and horses. One man was the family shoemaker. The husbands were all the *stareshina's* brothers, sons, and grandsons; their wives had married into the *zadruga* from near-by villages'' (Louis Adamic, *The Native's Return*, 1934).

''The family in historical times has been, and at present is, in transition from an institution to a companionship. In the past, the important factors unifying the family have been external, formal, and authoritarian, as the law, the mores, public opinion, tradition, the authority of the family head, rigid discipline, and elaborate ritual. At present, in the new emerging form of the companionship family, its unity inheres less and less in community pressures and more and more in such interpersonal relationships as the mutual affection, the sympathetic understanding, and the comradeship of its members'' (Ernest Burgess and Harvey Locke, *The Family*, 1945).

''When the family and the home no longer functioned as an economic unit, women, children, and old people were placed in an ambiguous position outside the occupational world. For children, the shift to industrial work, and the removal of the father from the home, also meant that the mother became more of a central figure. Little boys could no longer observe and participate in father's work. This created a strain on both child and mother'' (Talcott Parsons, *Essays in Sociological Theory, Pure and Applied*, 1949).

''The Law of Family Interaction. . . . Within every family, there are two variables which submit to precise mathematical determination. One of these is the number of members . . . the other is the number of personal relationships. . . .

Number of persons	2, 3, 4, 5, 6, 7, 8
Number of personal relationships	1, 3, 6, 10, 15, 21, 28

The mathematical formula involved may be set forth as follows:

x = the number of personal relationships;
y = the number of persons;

$$x = \frac{y^2 - y}{2}\text{''}$$

(James Bossard and Eleanor Boll, *The Sociology of Child Development*, 1966).

''The family has provided the link of continuity in the evolution of Indian culture from Mohenjo-Daro times to the present day'' (S. Chandrasekhar in

Victor Christopherson, ed., *Readings in Comparative Marriage and the Family*, 1967).

''The essence of this firmly rooted, latent group consciousness in Japanese society is expressed in the traditional and ubiquitous concept of *ie*, the household, a concept which penetrates every nook and cranny of Japanese society'' (Chie Nakane, *Japanese Society*, 1970).

''The Greek family is . . . progressive when concerning the young men, traditional when concerning the young women'' (Jane Lambiri, *Toward a Greek Sociology of Education*, 1974).

''[In China] if a couple is quarreling, the children, sometimes even children of eight or nine, will come to the residents' committee to ask for help. Whoever is available will go. We will talk separately with the husband and with the wife and then all talk together. If the children are at home, they will attend, and if other people live in the home, they may attend, too'' (Ruth Sidel, *Families of Fengsheng*, 1974).

''As I delved further into the data that describe what Americans do and how they live, I became less sure that the family was in trouble'' (Mary Bane, *Here to Stay*, 1976).

''[In the Soviet Union] the decline of male supremacy in a number of families is . . . fraught with certain negative consequences. Although this is in a way a counterweight to the former tradition of unlimited male supremacy, it implies a belittling of the husband's functions and in a number of cases signifies a weakening of his position as responsible head of the family, a fact which can spell trouble'' (Feiga Blekher, *The Soviet Woman in the Family and in Society*, 1979).

''The family has been slowly coming apart for more than a hundred years. The divorce crisis, feminism, and revolt of youth originated in the nineteenth century, and they have been the subject of controversy ever since'' (Christopher Lasch, *Haven in a Heartless World*, 1979).

''[In England] the family and the education system are used in concert to sustain and reproduce the social and economic status quo'' (Miriam David, *The State, the Family and Education*, 1980).

''The latest reports of the imminent death of the family [have] been greatly exaggerated'' (Andrew Cherlin, *Marriage, Divorce, Remarriage*, 1981).

''My struggle to understand why the Chinese working family [in Hong Kong] is so powerful led me away from views of societal convergence and directly to the concept of a centripetal family regime and its determination by an overarching institutional framework'' (Janet Salaff, *Working Daughters of Hong Kong*, 1981).

''The Middletown family is in exceptionally good condition. Tracing the changes from the 1920s to the 1970s, we discovered increased family solidarity, a smaller generation gap, closer marital communication, more religion, and less mobility. With respect to the major features of family life, the trend of the past two generations has run in the opposite direction from the trend nearly everyone perceives and talks about'' (Theodore Caplow et al., *Middletown Families*, 1982).

"If we know only our own family system, we do not really know our own family system. To understand it much better, we must also know something about other family systems, both past and present, in various cultures and civilizations" (Panos Bardis, *Global Marriage and Family Customs*, 1983).

"The youth culture has not taken over, and closed marriages still abound. Despite a continuing increase in the number of working mothers and single-parent families, there is evidence of a growing interest in preserving the traditional family" (Rita Kramer, *In Defense of the Family*, 1983).

FASHION, SOCIOLOGY OF

"[Adam and Eve] knew that they were naked; and they sewed fig leaves together, and made themselves aprons" (Genesis 3:7).

"It seems that every day brings in a different fashion" (Ovid, *The Art of Love*, c. 8).

"At home you know the name, abroad the costume" (Talmud: Sabbath 145 b).

"Some women may be excused from sin, if their clothing is not due to vanity, but to a fashion . . . even if such a fashion is not praiseworthy" (Thomas Aquinas, *Summa Theologica*, 1274).

"The fashion wears out more apparel than the man" (William Shakespeare, *Much Ado About Nothing*, 1599).

"The present fashion is always handsome" (Thomas Fuller, *Gnomologia*, 1732).

"Fashion determines use" (Karl Marx, *Economic and Philosophic Manuscripts*, 1844).

"[Fashion imitation is terminated] by putting pupil-peoples upon the same level, both in their armaments and in their arts and sciences, with their master-people" (Gabriel Tarde, *Social Laws*, 1898).

"When seen in the perspective of half-a-dozen years or more, the best of our fashions strike us as grotesque, if not unsightly" (Thorstein Veblen, *The Theory of the Leisure Class*, 1899).

"Even in the first years the [Puritan] settlers paid close attention to their attire, to its richness, its elegance, its modishness, and watched narrowly also the attire of their neighbors, not only from a distinct liking for dress, but from a careful regard of social distinctions and from a regard for the proprieties and relations of life" (Alice Earle, *Two Centuries of Costume in America*, 1903).

"Covering of the body, which keeps abreast with civilization, continuously arouses sexual curiosity" (Sigmund Freud, *Three Contributions to the Theory of Sex*, 1905).

"Fashions . . . are only induced epidemics" (George B. Shaw, *The Doctor's Dilemma*, 1913).

"From the type of their dress it is possible to distinguish three clans or ranks [among the Retennu, Upper Euphrates]. One wore the apron-like garment; the second wrapped material round the body; the third wore tailored garments'' (Carl Köhler, *A History of Costume*, 1928).

''When the classical Roman dress began to be superseded by the barbarian type, the conservativeness of religion asserted itself by retaining these old-fashioned garments for the minister after laymen had abandoned them'' (Herbert Norris, *Church Vestments*, 1949).

''Just as the habits and dress of an individual frequently give a true impression of his character and type of mind, so the salient characteristics of a nation are reflected in the external details of their manners and their costume'' (Ethel Abrahams and Lady Evans, *Ancient Greek Dress*, 1964).

''Everywhere man adorns and dresses himself, and everywhere the nature of his attempts to modify his appearance is related to his social circumstances'' (Mary Roach and Joanne Eicher, eds., *Dress, Adornment, and the Social Order*, 1965).

''In the twelfth century a sharp contrast did exist between the labourer's appearance and that of his master [in England]'' (Phillis Cunnington and Catherine Lucas, *Occupational Costume in England*, 1967).

''There is no traditional rabbinical dress apart from the Polish fur hat, which was popular up to the nineteenth century'' (Alfred Rubens, *A History of Jewish Costume*, 1967).

FEMINISM

''All place your hands on the wine cup . . . and repeat after me. . . . There is no adulterer, or husband who can approach me with amorous intentions'' (Aristophanes, *Lysistrata*, 411 B.C.).

''By now you must have realized that women can be militant, too'' (Sophocles, *Electra*, c. 411 B.C.).

''Therefore, the women should be taught these arts and that of war and also be employed in the same manner . . . present custom would make much of what is being said now appear ridiculous, if what we are saying is going to be practiced . . . we must not fear the ironies of the wits, no matter how much and what they would say about gymnastics and culture, and mostly about the bearing of arms and the riding of horses . . . what appeared ridiculous to the eyes vanished before what reason presented as a superior custom'' (Plato, *Republic*, c. 400 B.C.).

''In all civilized countries the laws have been framed so as to discriminate severely against the personal and proprietary rights of women. . . . Woman is scarcely a greater sufferer from her condition than man is, and there is, therefore, nothing either improper or inexplicable in man's espousing the cause of woman's emancipation'' (Lester Ward, *Dynamic Sociology*, 1883).

''The working woman . . . has a far better chance to work out her economic salvation through solidarity and co-operation with her own class'' (B. Hutchins and A. Harrison, *A History of Factory Legislation*, 1903).

''An inevitable by-product of the liberation of women from men, and of both from tradition, is a rank individualism which makes a lasting union impossible, and thus defeats the end for which marriage exists'' (Edward Ross, *Changing America*, 1912).

''Women are equal because they are not different any more'' (Erich Fromm, *The Art of Loving*, 1956).

''[In communist China, two of the changes involving women are] the opening of administrative and supervisory positions to women in places where members of both sexes work together, which means that men may be taking orders from women superiors, which is something unusual if not intolerable in traditional public life. Secondly, a whole class of women formerly sheltered by a favoured economic position from having to work are now being compelled by new circumstances to join society's working force'' (C. Yang, *The Chinese Family in the Communist Revolution*, 1959).

''Since our culture gives women no firm role except an erotic one, but rather surrounds them with ambiguities, they fit readily into tree-houses or any other kind of commercial fantasy'' (Jules Henry, *Culture Against Man*, 1963).

''In a Greek country town . . . many of the factory women did not make full use of the new opportunities for leading a freer life because of the restraining influence of the family . . . they used the new financial opportunities mainly to enhance the status quo, i.e., to build up their dowries'' (Jane Lambiri, *Social Change in a Greek Country Town*, 1965).

''Lower-class men concede fewer rights ideologically than their women in fact *obtain*, and the more educated men are likely to concede *more* rights ideologically than they in fact grant'' (William Goode, *World Revolutions and Family Patterns*, 1970).

''Radical Feminism recognizes the oppression of women as a fundamental political oppression wherein women are categorized as an inferior class based upon their sex'' (J. Hole and E. Levine, *Rebirth of Feminism*, 1971).

''Despite the brave efforts by feminists to teach women how to avoid or resist sexual harassment in the universities, it can be expected to continue so long as families, religions and local communities train their young women to look at men, particularly at men with reputations in positions of authority, with stars in their eyes, assuming respectful and obedient attitudes toward those in authority'' (Don Martindale, *Ideals and Realities of Ph.D. Advising*, 1980).

''Cooptation into existing power structures continually mutes their [women in the Third World] potential contribution to the future'' (Elise Boulding in Roslyn Dauber and Melinda Cain, eds., *Women and Technological Change in Developing Countries*, 1981).

''The contemporary feminist revolution constitutes a current example of new demands being made on the environment as lifeways and identities change'' (Suzanne Keller, ed., *Building for Women*, 1981).

''The feminism of the 1960s and 1970s has altered irrevocably the consciousness of many Americans'' (Janet and Larry Hunt in Joan Aldous, ed., *Two Paychecks*, 1982).

"The women's liberation movement has given us a totally new way to understand women's psychology" (Luise Eichenbaum and Susie Orbach, *Understanding Women*, 1983).

"There are women who renounce interest or at least explain their lack of interest in politics on grounds of their womanhood or femininity" (Virginia Sapiro, *The Political Integration of Women*, 1983).

FOLKLORE

"Science proves conclusively that the popular traditions which have come down to us in the form whether of myths strictly so called or of folklore generally, embody the whole thought of primitive man on the vast range of physical phenomena" (George Cox, *An Introduction to the Science of Comparative Mythology and Folklore*, 1883).

"Folk-lore—in other words, the records of man's beliefs and customs—begins only with the traces or records of his thought. The term *Folk-lore* was first suggested by the late Mr. Thoms, in 1846, to designate 'that department of the study of antiquities and archaeology which embraces everything relating to ancient observances and customs, to the notions, beliefs, traditions, superstitions, and prejudices of the common people' " (Marian Cox, *An Introduction to Folk-Lore*, 1904).

"She [Demeter, goddess of vegetation] is a real person, not the personification of any natural force. The tiller of the land foresees his yearly gain from cornfield and vineyard; the shepherd on the mountainside expects the yearly increase of his flock; but by neither is any principle inferred therefrom, much less is such a principle personified; the blessing which rests on field and fold is the work of a living goddess' hand" (J. Lawson, *Modern Greek Folklore and Ancient Greek Religion*, 1910).

"One of the great debts which we owe to students of folklore has been the collection and elucidation of folktales . . . the underlying motives of many of these stories can be traced back for hundreds, even thousands, of years" (Macleod Yearsley, *The Folklore of Fairy-Tale*, 1924).

"Developments in philology in folklore . . . contributed to the broadening of the disciplinary bases converging on the study of man" (Fred Voget in John Honigmann, ed., *Handbook of Social and Cultural Anthropology*, 1973).

"A wealth of folklore accumulated over the centuries expresses real life experiences, furnishing study material that is attractive and of vital interest to children" (Beatrice Landeck, *Learn to Read, Read to Read*, 1976).

FOLKWAY

"The result [of man's traits inherited from animals] is mass phenomena; currents of similarity, concurrence, and mutual contribution; and these produce folkways [which are] the widest, most fundamental, and most important operation by which the interests of men in groups are served'' (William Sumner, *Folkways*, 1907).

''The folkways provide a limitless number of signposts throughout society, guiding the individual of the given culture area to the accepted, practical, successful way of doing things. It is the folkways which dictate that a man tip his hat when he meets a lady'' (Paul Landis, *Social Control*, 1956).

''Folkways are the less serious norms, which, when broken, bring only mild disapproval from others. Slurping your soup would clearly fall into this category'' (Reid Luhman, *The Sociological Outlook*, 1982).

FOOD, SOCIOLOGY OF

''The Egyptians might not eat bread with the Hebrews; for that is an abomination unto the Egyptians'' (Genesis 43:22).

''[Confucius] did not eat much. . . . When eating, he did not converse'' (Confucius, *Analects*, c. 500 B.C.).

''Other men live to eat, but I eat to live'' (Socrates, c. 420 B.C.), in Stobaeus, *Anthology*, c. 420).

''People become accustomed to all kinds of food and drink that they at first disliked'' (Plato, *Laws*, c. 400 B.C.).

''Let him [a Brahman] never eat food . . . in which hair or insects are found, nor what has been touched intentionally with the foot'' (Manu, *Laws*, c. 200 B.C.).

''What is food to one man may be strong poison to another'' (Lucretius, *On the Nature of Things*, c. 60 B.C.).

''[Garlic] fosters love and drives away enmity'' (Talmud: The First Gate 82a).

''He hath forbidden you only carrion, and blood, and swineflesh, and that which hath been immolated to the name of any other than Allah'' (Koran: The Cow 173).

''No person ever desires meat or drink without limit'' (Thomas Aquinas, *Summa Theologica*, 1274).

''A depraved taste in food . . . is a species of disease'' (François Marie Arouet Voltaire, *Philosophical Dictionary*, 1764).

''Man is a carnivorous production, and must have meals, at least one meal a day'' (Lord Byron, *Don Juan*, 1824).

''Man has been distinguished from other animals in various ways; but perhaps there is no particular in which he exhibits so marked a difference from the rest of creation . . . as in the objection to raw food, meat, and vegetables'' (W. Hazlitt, *Old Cookery Books and Ancient Cuisine*, 1886).

''It is largely through food and drink that man derives his highest mental efficiency and physical well-being'' (George Ellwanger, *The Pleasures of the Table*, 1902).

''By whomsoever a people is fed . . . to him their allegiance is due . . . the legitimate source of political authority is to be traced to the capacity for satisfying the appetites of the community . . . the pledge cup has been the accompaniment of the banquet'' (Frederick Hackwood, *Good Cheer*, 1911).

''[In old England, spoons] were an indispensable item of personal equipment. Hosts were under no obligation to supply them to their guests, and the man who went out to dine took his spoon with him. . . . Pepys, when he dined with the Lord Mayor, carried his own table implements to the feast'' (Charles Cooper, *The English Table*, 1929).

''The history of man from the beginning has been the history of his struggle for daily bread'' (Josué de Castro, *Geography of Hunger*, 1955).

''Food may be defined as all solid and fluid substances which permit the human organism to grow and maintain its health throughout life . . . cannibalism probably has a very long history, [it] may have been adopted to a greater or lesser degree by a number of ancient peoples and finally, might even have played a useful dietary role in times of a protein crisis'' (Don and Patricia Brothwell, *Food in Antiquity*, 1969).

''In Shao-shan [China] it has been decided that guests are to be served with only three kinds of animal food, namely, chicken, fish and pork. It is also forbidden to serve bamboo shoots, kelp and lentil noodles. In Hengshan county it has been resolved that eight dishes and no more may be served at a banquet'' (K. Chang, ed., *Food in Chinese Culture*, 1977).

''This country [the United States] has been witness to a significant change in dietary patterns away from raw fruits, vegetables, dairy products and proteins of meat origin. For too many, today's diet is still high in cholesterol, and other lipids, sugar, and refined grains—almost 20 percent refined sugar and 45 percent fat'' (Ruth Weg, *Nutrition and the Later Years*, 1978).

''Even though food and clothing may serve as symbols, symbols cannot replace food and clothing, at least not for normal individuals and not in the long run'' (Antonina Kloskowska, *Sociology and Culture*, 1982).

FUTUROLOGY

''Thou knowest not what a day may bring forth'' (Proverbs 27:1).

''You will know the future when it has come; forget it now'' (Aeschylus, *Agamemnon*, 458 B.C.).

''We must not let the future discourage us'' (Plato, *Sophist*, c. 400 B.C.).

''No man can foretell the future'' (Demosthenes, *Against Leptines*, c. 350 B.C.).

''It is great wisdom not only to see the present clearly, but also to foresee what future things will be'' (Terence, *Adelphi*, 160 B.C.).

''Do not be concerned about future things'' (Marcus Aurelius, *Meditations*, c. 160).

''We can know the future by knowing its present causes'' (Thomas Aquinas, *Summa Theologica*, 1274).

"To know that which before us lies in daily life is the prime wisdom" (John Milton, *Paradise Lost,* 1667).

"Today's utopia is tomorrow's flesh and blood" (Victor Marie Hugo, *Les Misérables*, 1862).

"A triumph of practical interests . . . shall sweep away the present barriers of language, national pride, and natural uncongeniality, and unite all nations in one vast social aggregate with a single political organization" (Lester Ward, *Dynamic Sociology*, 1883).

"As this revolution [woman's emancipation] is completed, both men and women will find themselves on a far higher plane, and in a stage that, for want of a better term, may be called gynandrocratic, a stage in which both men and women shall be free to rule themselves" (Lester Ward, *Pure Sociology*, 1903).

"A new universal civilization will develop, a civilization which will not only save everything that is worthy to be saved from national civilizations, but even will elevate mankind to the level higher than all dreams of utopians; or national civilizations will fall apart . . . their greatest systems, most valuable patterns will lose all significance for the life of human communities for a span of many generations" (Florian Znaniecki, *The People of Today and the Civilization of Tomorrow*, 1934).

"The only way to predict the future is to have power to shape the future" (Eric Hoffer, *The Passionate State of Mind*, 1954).

"The chief pleasure of a forecaster of future events lies in finding that his predictions are correct" (Harrison Brown et al., *The Next Hundred Years*, 1963).

"For at least six thousand years . . . men have persistently and ingeniously sought to foretell the future. The ancient Chinese tried to read their fate by studying cracks in dried turtle-shells. The Babylonians developed the art of astrology. . . . The ancient Greeks visited the oracle of Apollo at Delphi. . . . The Roman augurs examined the entrails of animals and birds. . . . The Christians of medieval Europe relied on the Bible and its interpreters" (Burnham Beckwith, *The Next 500 Years*, 1967).

"[An important] objective for a long-range study is to anticipate some problem early enough for effective planning" (Herman Kahn and Anthony Wiener, *The Year 2000*, 1967).

"The first real optimistic interest in the future was exhibited by the Jews. Lacking a glorious past, their interest was held by a succession of prophets whose names and stories they cherished" (W. Armytage, *Yesterdays Tomorrows*, 1968).

"That I have lived through this era of shattering change is one qualification for trying to predict its future course" (Stuart Chase, *The Most Probable World*, 1968).

"At one end . . . will be a minority of the people whose work will keep intact the technology that sustains the multitude at a high standard of living. In the middle . . . will be found a type, largely unemployed, for whom the distinction between the real and the illusory will still be meaningful and whose prototype is the beatnik. . . . At the other end . . . will be a type largely unemployable for whom the boundary of the real and the imagined will have been largely dissolved, at least to the extent compatible with his physical survival. His prototype is the hippie. His interest in the world will be rather small, and he will derive his satisfaction mainly from drugs or, once this has become technologically practicable, from direct electrical inputs into his nervous system. This spectral distribution . . . bears some considerable resemblance to the Alphas, Betas, and Gammas in Aldous Huxley's *Brave New World*'' (G. Stent, *The Coming of the Golden Age*, 1969).

''There is no serious danger of utopians taking charge in America today'' (Herbert Muller, *The Children of Frankenstein*, 1970).

''It has become a truism of our time that we concurrently face the portents of unprecedented disaster and the potentialities of remarkable fulfillment'' (C. Wallia, ed., *Toward Century 21*, 1970).

''[Some forecasting methods are] trend extrapolation: the concept that the historical changes and forces of change will continue into at least the near future. . . . Historical analogy: the study of historical events and circumstances surrounding certain periods of change in an effort to generalize about what might happen under similar circumstances in the future. . . . Delphi: an interactive survey process whereby group intuitive judgment is the basis for plausibility ratings for future developments. Scenario writing: a process that demonstrates the possibility of future developments by exhibiting a chain of events that might lead them, and the interaction of complex factors in this chain'' (Brian Berry and John Kasarda, *Contemporary Urban Ecology*, 1977).

''After the war, Japan formulated several broad plans, mostly economic plans. Then a demand arose for more vigorous research and prediction of the uncertain future, and the need for long-range planning based on predictions was soon recognized'' (Yujiro Hayashi in Jib Fowles, ed., *Handbook of Future Research*, 1978).

''Today, any consumer of electricity can instantly obtain the electric power he needs without worrying about where it comes from or how much it costs. There is every reason to believe that the same will be true in the future of 'telematics.' Once the initial connections are made, the network will spread by osmosis. . . . Traditional data processing was hierarchical, isolated, and centralized. . . . From now on, data processing can be deconcentrated, decentralized, or autonomous: it is a matter of choice'' (Simon Nora and Alain Minc, *The Informing of Society*, 1978).

''A new harmony between spirit and matter is most likely to evolve out of the combined strengths of Eastern and Western civilizations'' (Professors' World Peace Academy of Japan, *Japan at the Turning Point*, 1981).

''A revitalized America—revitalized in terms of traditional values, of worldwide status and influence and of citizenship and morale, as well as of economic improvement—seems to be very probable, and with sensible social and economic policies, a near certainty'' (Herman Kahn, *The Coming Boom*, 1982).

G

GEMEINSCHAFT

"I call all kinds of association in which natural will predominates Gemeinschaft . . . the essence of both Gemeinschaft and Gesellschaft is found interwoven in all kinds of associations . . . when I become conscious of my most urgent needs and find that I can neither satisfy them out of my own volition nor out of a natural relation, this means that I must do something to satisfy my need; that is, engage in free activity which is bound only by the requirement or possibly conditioned by the need but not by consideration for other people. Soon I perceive that I must work on other people in order to influence them to deliver or give something to me which I need. Possibly in restricted individual cases my mere requests will be granted, as, for example, in the case of a piece of bread or a glass of water. However, as a rule when one is not receiving something in a Gemeinschaft-like relationship, such as from within the family, one must earn or buy it by labor, service, or money which has been earned previously as payment for labor or service. . . . [In] natural relationships it is self-evident that action will take place and be willed in accordance with the relationship, whether it be what is contained on the one hand in the simplest relationships resulting from desire and inclination, from love or habit, or on the other hand from reason or intellect contained in the feeling of duty. These latter types of natural will change into one another, and each can be the basis of Gemeinschaft. . . . *Gemeinschaft-like relationships*. a. Fellowship type. The simplest fellowship type is represented by a pair who live together in a brotherly, comradely, and friendly manner, and it is most likely to exist when those involved are of the same age, sex, and sentiment, are engaged in the same activity or have the same intentions, or when they are united by one idea. In legend and history such pairs occur frequently. The Greeks used to honor such friendships as those of Achilles and Patroclus, Orestes and Pylades, Epaminondas and Pelopidas, to the extent that to Aristotle is ascribed the paradox: He who has friends has no friend. . . . b. Authoritative type. The relationship of father to child, as observations in everyday life will prove, is to be found in all the strata of society in all stages of culture. The weaker the child and the more it is in need of help, the greater the extent to which the relationship is represented by protection. . . . c. Mixed relationships.

In many Gemeinschaft-like relationships the essence of authority and that of fellowship are mixed. This is the case in the most important of the relationships of Gemeinschaft, the lasting relationship between man and woman which is conditioned through sexual needs and reproduction, whether or not the relationship is called marriage'' (Ferdinand Tönnies, *Community and Society*, 1887).

``Gemeinschaft communities are characterized by personalized, face-to-face relationships such as those in the family, the rural village, and the small town'' (George Ritzer et al., *Sociology*, 1982).

GERONTOLOGY

``The hoary head is a crown of glory, if it be found in the way of righteousness'' (Proverbs 16:31).

``The relations between old and young may not be neglected'' (Confucius, *Analects*, c. 500 B.C.).

``Old men are always young enough to learn'' (Aeschylus, *Agamemnon*, 458 B.C.).

``Young men in the state often honor old people'' (Plato, *Laws*, c. 400 B.C.).

``Older people tend to have negative attitudes toward things'' (Aristotle, *Rhetoric*, c. 350 B.C.).

``I have no reason to complain about old age'' (Cicero, *On Old Age*, c. 44 B.C.).

``Old age and infancy present the same degree of weakness'' (Thomas Aquinas, *Summa Theologica*, 1274).

``An old man is twice a child'' (William Shakespeare, *Hamlet*, 1601).

``Age does not bring childhood back again, it only shows that we remain children'' (Johann Wolfgang von Goethe, *Faust*, 1808).

``To an old man, any warm place is homeland'' (Maxim Gorky, *The Lower Depths*, 1903).

``If life is a good thing then to have more of it is to be better off'' (Edward Ross, *Seventy Years of It*, 1936).

``[In Japan] old people are respected for their wisdom and their experience. The old are proud of themselves because everyone is proud of them. If they reach ninety or so, they become the darlings of the community. It is a lovely way to end a life'' (Pearl Buck, *The People of Japan*, 1966).

``Historic changes in population distribution, in community planning, and in the designing and marketing of houses affect the residential setting of older people today'' (Matilda Riley and Anne Foner, *Aging and Society*, 1968).

``If an old man sees that you are really interested in his personal life, you will see a wonderful transformation take place in him. Just like the child, the old man needs to be spoken to and listened to in order to become a person, to become aware of himself, to live and grow. You will have brought about something that no social service can do of itself: you will have promoted him to the rank of person'' (Paul Tournier, *Learning to Grow Old*, 1971).

''For most Americans, some major difficulties of growing old are associated with retirement from the work force. For Indians there is usually no work to retire from. Old age is the continuation of a state of near and actual destitution which most Indians over 65 have had ample time to accustom themselves to'' (Robert Benedict, *Minority Aged in America*, 1972).

''Of course, all elderly people have problems, but so have preschoolers. Of course, some elderly people are difficult to deal with. But is this not true of adolescents and young adults? Of course, the aging and aged are often pessimistic and negative. But is this not also true of those in middle age who see the years slipping away with their dreams, ideals, and goals, unfulfilled?'' (Dorothy Fritz, *Growing Old Is a Family Affair*, 1972).

''[In Jodhpur, India] the traditional idea that wisdom belongs to age was perceptible when the elite were distributed in various age groups which revealed that most of the elite were rather mature in age'' (Sheo Lal, *The Urban Elite*, 1974).

''A society that cuts off older people from meaningful contact with children . . . is greatly endangered'' (Margaret Mead, *Blackberry Winter*, 1975).

''Both children and old people are barred from various opportunities because it is *believed* that they are not fully capable. It can be easily demonstrated that such beliefs often mask large individual differences and produce individual injustices'' (Robert Atchley and Mildred Seltzer, *The Sociology of Aging*, 1976).

''The aging of a population is indicated by increased average (or median) age and by a larger proportion of old persons'' (Philip Hauser in Robert Binstock and Ethel Shanas, eds., *Handbook of Aging and the Social Sciences*, 1976).

''Most men and women over 65 are healthy enough to carry on their normal activities—only 15 percent are not. Less than 5 percent of the elderly are in institutions, nursing homes for the aged'' (Barbara Silverstone and Helen Hyman, *You and Your Aging Parent*, 1976).

''Developmental psychology usually refers to the differentiation of the organism up to the age of physical maturity, and aging refers to the changes or differentiation after the age of physical maturity'' (James Birren and V. Renner in James Birren and K. Schaie, eds., *Handbook of the Psychology of Aging*, 1977).

''We tend to assume that youth will not venerate age. Modern psychology has taught us to expect trouble between age and youth'' (David Fischer, *Growing Old in America*, 1977).

''Older Americans spend proportionately more of their income on food, shelter, and medical care and less on other items in a pattern generally similar to that of other low-income groups'' (Marquis Academic Media, *Sourcebook on Aging*, 1977).

''Aging may well be the result of coding error or point mutation in DNA'' (F. Sinex in Caleb Finch and Leonard Hayflick, eds., *Handbook of the Biology of Aging*, 1977).

''The study of aging is a tremendously varied field. It is, of necessity, multidisciplinary, and this is both its strength and its weakness'' (Russell Ward, *The Aging Experience*, 1979).

''The major reason that aging is an anthropologist's subject is that anthropology covers the entire range of subdisciplines that are relevant to successful gerontology'' (Paul Bohannan in Christine Fry, ed., *Aging in Culture and Society*, 1980).

''Age discrimination, of which retirement is a particular variant, dates from the last quarter of the eighteenth century. Not until a century later, however, did either the larger phenomenon of age discrimination or the specific mechanism of retirement come to affect large numbers of persons'' (William Graebner, *A History of Retirement*, 1980).

''Human sexuality is natural and should continue into old age'' (George Wharton, *Sexuality and Aging*, 1981).

''Social gerontology exhibits a very complex conceptual structure, which reflects the interdisciplinary nature of gerontology, the levels of analysis implied by the different disciplines, and the policies of government on all levels concerning the delivery of services and the administration of programs'' (David Mangen et al. in David Mangen and Warren Peterson, eds., *Clinical and Social Psychology*, 1982).

''Aging is inevitable. We grow older every second, minute, hour, day, week, and month. Marking our age in years by our birthdate tends to obscure the slow but steady march of time upon our beings. The usual stages of life are marked by infancy, childhood, adolescence, and adulthood. These stages indicate not only skills and responsibilities but also freedoms and opportunities. Within our century . . . we have begun to explore and analyze another stage to life: 'old' '' (Georgia Barrow and Patricia Smith, *Aging, the Individual, and Society*, 1983).

GESELLSCHAFT

''I call all kinds of association . . . which are formed and fundamentally conditioned by rational will, Gesellschaft . . . in the purest and most abstract contract relationship and the contracting parties are thought of as separate, hitherto and otherwise independent, as strangers to each other, and perhaps even as hitherto and in other respects inimical persons. *Do, ut des* (I give, so that you will give) is the only principle of such a relationship. What I do for you, I do only as a means to effect your simultaneous, previous, or later service for me. Actually and really I want and desire only this. To get something from you is my end; my service is the means thereto, which I naturally contribute unwillingly. Only the aforesaid and anticipated result is the cause which determines my volition. This is the simplest form of rational will. Relationships of [this] type are to be classified . . . under the concept of Gesellschaft. . . . The Gesellschaft-like authority attains its consummation in the modern state, a consummation which many predecessors strove to attain until the democratic republic came into existence and allowed for development beyond the Gesellschaft-like foundation'' (Ferdinand Tönnies, *Community and Society*, 1887).

''Gesellschaft (meaning 'association') is characterized by impersonal patterns of interaction. Formal written agreements replace tradition as a social bond. Utilitarian values prevail'' (Peter Rose et al., *Sociology*, 1982).

GROUP

''Emotionally, mobs are very similar to children'' (Euripides, *Orestes*, 408 B.C.).

''Nothing can be more uncertain or unpredictable than a crowd's emotions'' (Livy, *Annals of the Roman People*, c. 10 B.C.).

''In no country in the world has the principle of association been more successfully used or applied to a greater multitude of objects than in America. Besides the permanent associations which are established by law . . . a vast number of others are formed and maintained by the agency of private individuals'' (Alexis Charles Henri Maurice Clérel de Tocqueville, *Democracy in America*, 1840).

''A nation can be maintained only if, between the state and the individual, there is intercalated a whole series of secondary groups near enough to the individuals to attract them strongly in their sphere of action and drag them in this way, into the general torrent of social life'' (Émile Durkheim, *The Division of Labor in Society*, 1893).

''The conception of 'primitive society' which we ought to form is that of small groups scattered over a territory. The size of the groups is determined by the conditions of the struggle for existence. The internal organization of each group corresponds to its size. A group of groups may have some relation to each other (kin, neighborhood, alliance, connubium and commercium) which draws them together and differentiates them from others. Thus a differentiation arises between ourselves, the we-group, or in-group, and everybody else, or the others-groups, out-groups. The insiders in a we-group are in a relation of peace, order, law, government, and industry, to each other. Their relation to all outsiders, or others-groups, is one of war and plunder, except so far as agreements have modified it. If a group is exogamic, the women in it were born abroad somewhere. Other foreigners who might be found in it are adopted persons, guest friends, and slaves'' (William G. Sumner, *Folkways*, 1906).

''By primary group I mean those characterized by intimate face-to-face association and cooperation. They are primary in several senses, but chiefly in that they are fundamental in forming the social nature and ideals of the individual. The result of intimate association, psychologically, is a certain fusion of individualities in a common whole, so that one's very self, for many purposes at least, is the common life and purpose of the group. . . . [In primary groups a person receives] his earliest and completest experience of social unity'' (Charles Cooley, *Social Organization*, 1909).

"A closed group of colonists may allow free use of the land or sanction and guarantee permanent appropriation of separate holdings" (Max Weber, *Economy and Society*, 1922, posthumously).

"Internally the gang may be viewed as a struggle for recognition. It offers the underprivileged boy probably the best opportunity to acquire status and hence it plays an essential part in the development of his personality. . . . For this reason the gang boy's conception of his role is more vivid with reference to his gang than to other social groups" (Frederic Thrasher, *The Gang*, 1927).

"By a concrete group . . . we mean the union of a number of individuals through naturally developed or consciously willed ties" (Karl Mannheim, *Essays on the Sociology of Knowledge*, 1929).

"We belong to a group not only because we are born into it, not merely because we confess to belong to it, not finally because we give it our loyalty and allegiance, but primarily because we see the world and certain things in the world the way it does" (Karl Mannheim, *Ideology and Utopia*, 1929).

"The individual experiences himself as such, not directly, but indirectly, from the particular standpoints of other individual members of the same group, or from the generalized standpoint of the social group as a whole to which he belongs" (George H. Mead, *Mind, Self, and Society*, 1934, posthumously).

"[Among the Tswana] since every adult in the tribe must belong to one [age-regiment], a regiment consists of all tribesmen of the same sex and of about the same age. The initiation ceremonies they undergo simultaneously, the name given to their regiment and identifying it ever afterwards, their organization into a single body under the leadership of some member of the royal family, and the numerous activities they as a body are subsequently called upon to carry out, give them a strong feeling of group solidarity cutting across the parochial loyalties of family, ward, village, and tribal community" (I. Schapera, *A Handbook of Tswana Law and Custom*, 1938).

"The size of the group by reference to which a particular person evaluates his behavior may vary considerably; when a person's immediate reference group is small and select, and does not share the values of the majority of persons in his social class, it may sometimes appear that he is making an independent self-evaluation, and displaying 'inner-directed' behavior, whereas he may be, in fact, highly dependent on the actual or fantasied approval or disapproval of a few individuals whose judgments he values highly" (Albert Bandura and Richard Walters, *Social Learning and Personality Development*, 1963).

"All Greek social groups were also religious unions" (W. Lacey, *The Family in Classical Greece*, 1968).

"There is no definite cutting point in the continuum between a collection of individuals, such as one might find waiting for a bus on a corner, and a fully organized 'group.' There is also no definite cutting point between the small, intimate, face-to-face group and the large, formal group" (A. Hare, *Handbook of Small Group Research*, 1976).

"There is no clear-cut dividing line between small and large groups. A group having ten or fewer members is certainly a small group; one with thirty or more members is definitely a large group. But there is a gray area between ten and thirty'' (Marvin Shaw, *Group Dynamics*, 1976).

``Groups can be characterized as units of analysis and . . . group characteristics can be seen to have an effect on individual characteristics'' (Raymond Boudon, *The Crisis in Sociology*, 1980).

``The number of primary groups of which we are members is far less than the many secondary groups to which we belong. The interaction in secondary groups is of an impersonal, superficial, and utilitarian nature'' (Ronald Smith and Frederick Preston, *Sociology*, 1982).

H

HISTORICAL SOCIOLOGY

''These events are very likely, in accordance with human nature, to repeat themselves at some future time exactly or similarly'' (Thucydides, *Histories*, c. 410 B.C.).

''To ignore what happened before your birth is to remain always a child'' (Cicero, *Orator*, 46 B.C.).

''It is not surprising that, in the long course of history, as fortune unfolds itself, many coincidences occur spontaneously'' (Plutarch, *Sertorius*, c. 100).

''He who examines the past is warned of the future'' (Lope de Vega, *Eclogue for Claudio*, c. 1600).

''History . . . is indeed little more than the register of the crimes, follies, and misfortunes of mankind'' (Edward Gibbon, *Decline and Fall of the Roman Empire*, 1776).

''History is the essence of innumerable biographies'' (Thomas Carlyle, *On History*, 1830).

''Peoples and governments have never been taught anything by history. . . . The history of the world is nothing but the development of the idea of freedom'' (Georg Wilhelm Friedrich Hegel, *The Philosophy of History*, 1837).

''History is nothing if it is not the activity of men in pursuit of their objectives'' (Karl Marx and Friedrich Engels, *The Holy Family*, 1845).

''If now in considering the course of history we detach the ideas of the ruling class itself and attribute to them an independent existence, if we confine ourselves to saying that these or those ideas were dominant at a given time, without bothering ourselves about the conditions of production and the producers of these ideas, if we thus ignore the individuals and world conditions which are the sources of the ideas, we can say, for instance, that during the time that the aristocracy was dominant, the concepts honour, loyalty, etc. were dominant, during the dominance of the bourgeoisie the concepts freedom, equality, etc. The ruling class itself on the whole imagines this to be so. This conception of history, which is common to all historians, particularly since the eighteenth century, will necessarily come up against the phenomenon that increasingly abstract ideas hold sway, i.e., ideas which increasingly take on the form of universality'' (Karl Marx and Friedrich Engels, *The German Ideology*, 1846).

'' 'One event is always the son of another, and we must never forget the parentage,' was a remark made by a Bechuana chief. . . . Thus at all times historians, so far as they have aimed at being more than mere chroniclers, have done their best to show not merely succession, but connexion, among the events upon their record. Moreover, they have striven to elicit general principles of human action, and by these to explain particular events, stating expressly or taking tacitly for granted the existence of a philosophy of history'' (Edward Tylor, *Primitive Culture*, 1871).

''The Germans have taken the lead in historical enquiries, and they laugh at results which are got by groping about the woods with a pocket compass when they have made good roads'' (George Eliot, *Middlemarch*, 1872).

''History always enunciates new truths'' (Friedrich Wilhelm Nietzsche, *The Will to Power*, 1888).

''The person who seeks the connecting threads in the history of his life has already . . . created a coherence in that life. . . . The power and breadth of our own lives and the energy with which we reflect on them are the foundations of historical vision'' (Wilhelm Dilthey, *Pattern and Meaning in History*, 1910).

''The movement of history is due to the deeply rooted though complex instinct which pushes man in all ways to ameliorate his condition incessantly, to develop in all ways the sum of his physical, moral, and intellectual life. And all the phenomena of his social life are closely cohesive. . . . By virtue of this cohesion, political, moral, and intellectual progress are inseparable from material progress, and so we find that the phases of his material development correspond to intellectual changes'' (John Bury, *The Idea of Progress*, 1920).

''All the diplomatic fussing [1814–1914], posturing, and scheming, all the intrigue and bloodshed of these years, all the monstrous turmoil and waste of kings and armies, all the wonderful attitudes, deeds, and schemes of the Cavours, Bismarcks, Disraelis, Bonapartes, and the like 'great men,' might very well have been avoided altogether had Europe but had the sense to instruct a small body of ordinarily honest ethnologists, geographers, and sociologists to draw out its proper boundaries and prescribe suitable forms of government in a reasonable manner'' (Herbert G. Wells, *Outline of History*, 1920).

''Feudality belongs to the category of what might be called the 'natural occurrences' or 'natural facts' of history. Its formation was determined by quasi-mechanical forces and proceeded step by step'' (J. Calmette, *The Feudal Society*, 1932).

''Identically recurrent sociocultural processes are impossible. . . . But a linear trend limited in time (whose duration is different for different systems and processes) is to be expected and is factually found in almost all sociocultural processes. . . . Since practically all the sociocultural systems have limited possibilities of variation of their essential forms, it follows that all the systems that continue to exist after all their possible forms are exhausted are bound to have recurrent rhythms. . . . Other conditions being equal, the more limited the possibilities of variation of main forms, the more frequent, conspicuous, and grasping are the rhythms in the process of the system, and the simpler the rhythms from the standpoint of their phases. . . . Thus history ever repeats itself and never repeats itself; both seemingly contradictory statements are true and are not contradictory at all, when properly understood'' (Pitirim Sorokin, *Social and Cultural Dynamics*, 1941).

''There is no history of mankind, there are only many histories of all kinds of aspects of human life'' (Karl Popper, *The Open Society and Its Enemies*, 1950).

''The investigators who are developing modern sciences of cultural data do not function as introspective psychologists, but as *historians*; and while their techniques for gathering evidence differ, depending on how near or how distant the past they investigate, their methodological approach is the same'' (Florian Znaniecki, *Cultural Sciences*, 1952).

''History is the shank of social study . . . all sociology worthy of the name is 'historical sociology' . . . we need the fuller range that can be provided only by knowledge of the historical varieties of human society. . . . A-historical studies usually tend to be static or very short-term studies of limited milieux. . . . Knowing that what we are studying is subject to change, on the simplest of descriptive levels we must ask: What are the salient trends? . . . Longer-term trends are usually needed, if only in order to overcome historical provincialism: the assumption that the present is a sort of autonomous creation'' (C. W. Mills, *The Sociological Imagination*, 1959).

''There is no known law of historical determinism'' (Arnold Joseph Toynbee, *A Study of History*, 1961).

''Sociology and history are different academic disciplines, unlike each other in origin and intention, but dealing with the same subject matter: human interaction. This makes them partners and competitors at the same time'' (Werner Cahnman and Alvin Boskoff, eds., *Sociology and History*, 1964).

''The society in which he [man] lives is itself a product of historical process, not a pattern of life designed and constructed by rational minds. All of us, in fact, are creatures of history'' (Sukhbir Singh, *A History of Political Thought*, 1966).

''No study of the dynamics of community change can conceivably be complete that omits a historical review'' (Don Martindale and R. Hanson, *Small Town and the Nation*, 1969).

''Until very recently the relationship between history and sociology has been about as distant as any that might be found in academic disciplines in American universities. Even at the present time historians and sociologists are more likely to be regarded as cousins than as sisters under the skin, and as late as the Nineteen-Forties the two disciplines were as remote from one another as they had been in the Eighteen-Nineties, when the social sciences were first becoming departmentalized in American universities'' (Robert Nisbet in G. Hallen and Rajeshwar Prasad, eds., *Towards Global Sociology*, 1970).

''Human life and thought is always situated in history'' (Peter Berger, *The Heretical Imperative*, 1980).

''It is difficult to conceive the possibility of sociology without the prior developments of historiography, beginning in classical Greece'' (Don Martindale, *The Nature and Types of Sociological Theory*, 1981).

HOMOSEXUALITY

''The men of the city, even the men of Sodom . . . called unto Lot, and said unto him, Where are the men which came in to thee this night? bring them out unto us, that we may know them'' (Genesis 19:4–5).

''Achilles spoke to him [Patroclus]: 'Wherefore, beloved head, have you come here. . . . But do stand closer; though it be but for a short time, let us clasp our arms together, about one another, and take our fill of dire lamenting' '' (Homer, *Iliad*, c. 750 B.C.).

''Ah! Love, the looser of limbs, stirs me, that bittersweet and irresistible creature, but you, Atthis, have come to hate me, and run instead after Andromeda'' (Sappho, *To Atthis*, c. 600 B.C.).

''Some say that homosexuals are shameless, but this is false, since their behavior is not due to shamelessness, but is caused by the fact that they are brave and masculine, and have a manly countenance, and thus pursue what is like them'' (Plato, *Symposium*, c. 400 B.C.).

''This kind of love was so approved by them that even young girls sought lovers among good and noble women'' (Plutarch, *Lycurgus*, c. 100).

''There is absolutely no justification for distinguishing a special homosexual instinct. What constitutes a homosexual is a peculiarity not in his instinctual life but in his object-choice'' (Sigmund Freud, *Analysis of a Phobia in a Five-Year-Old Boy*, 1909).

''Nature's attempt to get rid of soft boys is by sterilizing them'' (F. S. Fitzgerald, *The Crack-Up*, 1945).

''Males do not represent two discrete populations, heterosexual and homosexual. The world is not to be divided into sheep and goats. Not all things are black nor all things white. It is a fundamental of taxonomy that nature rarely deals with discrete categories. . . . The sooner we learn this concerning human sexual behavior the sooner we shall reach a sound understanding of the realities of sex'' (Alfred Kinsey et al., *Sexual Behavior in the Human Male*, 1948).

''In increasing numbers, distinguished as well as ordinary homosexuals in every walk of life are openly declaring their sexual orientation and demanding that the centuries old persecution and discrimination against them cease'' (Evelyn Hooker in William Parker, *Homosexuality*, 1971).

''Social oppression, at least as directed against those who reveal a preference for their own sex, takes three basic forms: *legal-physical*, in which certain behavior common to the stigmatized group is proscribed under threat of physical abuse or containment; *occupational-financial*, limiting the options for employment and financial gain for those stigmatized; and *ego-destructive*, by which the individual is made to feel morally inferior, self-hatred is encouraged, and a sense of valid identity is inhibited'' (R. Humphreys, *Out of the Closets*, 1972).

''Some authors are inclined to view a person's genetic endowment as the chief predisposing factor giving rise to homosexuality. Others emphasize the parental relationship'' (Martin Weinberg and Alan Bell, eds., *Homosexuality*, 1972).

''Homosexuality has been called among other things a sin, an illness, a way of life, a normal variant of sexual behavior, a behavior disturbance, and a crime'' (Vern Bullough, *Homosexuality*, 1979).

''Three types of theories explain homosexuality; biological, psychological, and environmental. Usually, the biological and nonbiological theories are regarded as being mutually exclusive. But, as with most phenomena, here, too, biological and environmental factors may be working together. There are countless subtle ways in which heredity and environment interact to produce a unique homosexual person. The homosexual world is so heterogeneous that it is impossible to speak of one etiology. Causation is complex'' (Panos Bardis in Harald Niemeyer, ed., *Social Relations Network*, 1980).

''[The homosexual] is motivated in adult life by a definite preferential erotic attraction to members of the same sex and . . . usually (but not necessarily) engages in overt sexual relations with them'' (Judd Marmor, ed., *Homosexual Behavior*, 1980).

HUMOR, SOCIOLOGY OF

''Clumsy humor is no joke'' (Aesop, *Fables*, c. 550 B.C.).

''The ludicrous is simply a subdivision of the ugly. . . . Comedy aims at representing men as worse, Tragedy as better than in real life'' (Aristotle, *Poetics*, c. 350 B.C.).

''A man met a pedant and said: 'Mr. Pedant, I saw you in my dream.' 'By the gods,' said the pedant, 'I was too busy to notice you' '' (Philistion, *Philogelos*, c. 50 B.C.).

''Humor often decides important matters more effectually and cheerfully than seriousness'' (Horace, *Satires*, 30 B.C.).

''[Humor is a means of] dissipating melancholy impressions, of unbending the mind from too intense application, of renewing its powers and recruiting its strengths'' (Quintilian, *Principles of Oratory*, c. 90).

''Every humour hath its adjunct pleasure'' (William Shakespeare, *Sonnets*, 1609).

''Laughter to be without offence, must be at absurdities and infirmities abstracted from persons. To laugh too much at the defects of others bespeaks pusillanimity, for in so doing we attain superiority only by virtue of the inferiority of others'' (Thomas Hobbes, *Leviathan*, 1651).

''In the case of jokes. . . . the play begins with the thoughts which occupy the body so far as they admit of sensible expression'' (Immanuel Kant, *Critique of Judgment*, 1790).

''The cause of laughter in every case is simply the sudden perception of the incongruity between a concept and the real objects which have been thought through it in some relation, and laughter itself is just the expression of this incongruity'' (Arthur Schopenhauer, *The World as Will and Idea*, 1818).

''Man is the only animal that laughs and weeps; for he is the only animal that is struck with the difference between what things are and what they ought to be'' (William Hazlitt, *Lectures on the English Comic Writers*, 1819).

''Every contrast between what is essential and its appearance, the object and its instrument, may be ridiculous'' (Georg Wilhelm Friedrich Hegel, *Lectures on Aesthetics*, 1838, posthumously).

''The mere possibility of employing laughter as a weapon shows that it presupposes power'' (Harald Höffding, *Outlines of Psychology*, 1891).

''The attitudes, gestures, and movements of the human body are laughable in exact proportion as that body reminds us of a mere machine'' (Henri Bergson, *Laughter*, 1900).

''Humor is not resigned; it is rebellious. It signifies the triumph not only of the ego, but also of the pleasure principle'' (Sigmund Freud, *Jokes and Their Relation to the Unconscious*, 1905).

''Probably no human reaction has given rise to so many conflicting opinions as those found in works dealing with laughter'' (Ralph Piddington, *The Psychology of Laughter,* 1963).

''[Ancient jokes] are found only among the ancient Greeks, the great theoreticians and teachers of all nations'' (Andreas Thierfelder, *Philologos,* 1968).

''In spite of the social character of laughter, its ubiquity and universality in social relations and situations, its social effects, especially its social potencies and functions, and its contrived uses for social ends, relatively little attention has been paid to it by social scientists, particularly sociologists'' (Joyce Hertzler, *Laughter*, 1970).

''In the ancient Greek city-states, jokes, and the often deep irony expressed by them, had acquired a great significance in politics'' (Evangelos Stamatis, *Philogelos*, 1970).

''The average man is . . . firmly committed to the belief that having a reputation for a keen sense of humour is something to be treasured and protected'' (Antony Chapman and Hugh Foot, eds., *Humour and Laughter*, 1976).

''Human societies treasure laughter and whatever can produce it. Without laughter everyday living becomes drab and lifeless'' (Charles Gruner, *Understanding Laughter*, 1978).

I

IDEAL TYPE

''An ideal type is formed by the one-sided accentuation of one or more points of view and by the synthesis of a great many diffuse, discrete, more or less present and occasionally absent *concrete individual* phenomena, which are arranged according to those one-sidedly emphasized viewpoints into a unified *analytical* construct. . . . This procedure can be indispensable for heuristic as well as expository purposes. The ideal typical concept will help to develop our skill in imputation in *research*: it is no 'hypothesis' but it offers guidance to the construction of hypotheses. It is not a *description* of reality but it aims to give unambiguous means of expression to such a description'' (Max Weber, *The Methodology of the Social Sciences*, 1917).

''The ideal type has the merit of offering us a conceptual device with which we can measure real development'' (Julien Freund, *The Sociology of Max Weber*, 1968).

''*Ideal types* enable one to construct hypotheses linking them with the conditions that brought the phenomenon or event into prominence, or with consequences that follow from its emergence'' (Lewis Coser, *Masters of Sociological Thought*, 1977).

''[Ideal types are] deliberate exaggerations of more subtle trends which are exaggerated in order to abstract out the form of the pure, unadulterated phenomenon'' (Mark Abrahamson, *Sociological Theory*, 1981).

''It is unfortunate that Weber never developed his methodology apart from [various] theoretical and philosophical issues. . . . This has not promoted the clear isolation of theoretical and philosophical issues from methodological issues. It is partly the reason for the numerous conflicting interpretations that have arisen in connection with Weber's method of the ideal type'' (Don Martindale, *The Nature and Types of Sociological Theory*, 1981).

IDEOLOGY

''So died these men as became Athenians. You, their survivors, must determine to have as unfaltering a resolution in the field, though you may pray that it may have a happier issue. And not contended with ideas derived only from words of the advantages which are bound up with the defense of your country, though these would furnish a valuable text to a speaker even before an audience so alive to them as the present, you must yourselves realize the power of Athens, and feed your eyes upon her from day to day till love of her fills your hearts" (Thucydides, *Histories*, c. 410 B.C.).

"Among the wisest of the ancients and among their disciples you will find conflicting theories, many holding the conviction that heaven does not concern itself with the beginning or the end of our life, or, in short, with mankind at all . . . others, on the contrary, believe that, though there is a harmony between fate and events, yet it is not dependent on wandering stars, but on primary elements, and on a combination of natural causes" (Publius Cornelius Tacitus, *Annals*, c. 119).

"There is no doctrine will do good where nature is wanting" (Ben Jonson, *Timber*, 1640, posthumously).

"Scripture does not teach philosophy . . . all it contains has been adapted to the understanding and established opinions of the multitude. Those, therefore, who wish to adapt it to philosophy, must needs ascribe to the prophets many ideas which they never even dreamed of, and give an extremely forced interpretation to their words: those on the other hand, who would make reason and philosophy subservient to theology, will be forced to accept as Divine utterances the prejudices of the ancient Jews" (Baruch Spinoza, *Theologico-Political Treatise*, 1670).

"Even when ideas have no manner of influence on the will as passions, truth and reality are still requisite, in order to make them entertaining to the imagination" (David Hume, *A Treatise of Human Nature*, 1739).

"General and abstract ideas are the source of the greatest errors of mankind" (Jean Jacques Rousseau, *Émile*, 1762).

"The History of the World is the discipline of the uncontrolled natural will, bringing it into obedience to a Universal principle and conferring subjective freedom. The East knew and to the present day knows only that *One* is free; the Greek and Roman world, that *some* are free; the German World knows that *All* are free. The first political form therefore which we observe in History is *Despotism*, the second *Democracy* and *Aristocracy*, the third *Monarchy*" (Georg Wilhelm Friedrich Hegel, *The Philosophy of History*, 1837).

"The bourgeoisie has more in common with every other nation of the earth than with the workers in whose midst it lives. The workers speak other dialects, have other thoughts and ideas, other customs and moral principles, a different religion and other politics than those of the bourgeoisie" (Friedrich Engels, *The Condition of the Working Class in England*, 1845).

"We set out from real, active men, and on the basis of their real life process we demonstrate the development of the ideological reflexes and echoes of this life process. The phantoms formed in the human brain are also, necessarily, sublimates of their material life process, which is empirically verifiable and bound to material premises. Morality, religion, metaphysics, all the rest of ideology and their corresponding forms of consciousness, thus no longer retain the semblance of independence. . . . The ideas of the ruling class are in every epoch the ruling ideas, i.e., the class which is the ruling *material* force of society, is at the same time its ruling *intellectual* force. The class which has the means of material production at its disposal, has control at the same time over the means of mental production, so that thereby, generally speaking, the ideas of those who lack the means of mental production are subject to it. The ruling ideas are nothing more than the ideal expression of the dominant material relationships, the dominant material relationships grasped as ideas; hence of the relationships which make the one class the ruling one, therefore, the ideas of its dominance'' (Karl Marx and Friedrich Engels, *The German Ideology*, 1846).

''The ruling ideas of each age have ever been the ideas of its ruling class'' (Karl Marx and Friedrich Engels, *Communist Manifesto*, 1847).

''Upon the different forms of property, upon the social conditions of existence, rises an entire superstructure of distinct and peculiarly formed sentiments, illusions, modes of thought and views of life. The entire class creates and forms them through tradition and upbringing'' (Karl Marx, *The Eighteenth Brumaire of Louis Bonaparte*, 1852).

''The mode of production of material life dominates the development of social, political and intellectual life generally [this] is very true for our own times, in which material interests preponderate, but not for the middle ages, in which Catholicism, nor for Athens and Rome, where politics, reigned supreme'' (Karl Marx, *Das Kapital*, 1879).

''All those who talk about 'overrating the importance of ideology,' about exaggerating the role of the conscious element, etc., imagine that the labour movement pure and simple can elaborate, and will elaborate, an independent ideology for itself, if only the workers 'wrest their fate from the hands of the leaders.' But this is a profound mistake. . . . Since there can be no talk of an independent ideology formulated by the working masses themselves in the process of their movement, the *only* choice is—either bourgeois or socialist ideology. There is no middle course (for mankind has not created a 'third' ideology, and, moreover, in a society torn by class antagonisms there can never be a non-class or an above-class ideology) . . . bourgeois ideology is far older in origin than socialist ideology . . . it is more fully developed . . . it has at its disposal *immeasurably* more means of dissemination. And the younger the socialist movement in any given country, the more vigorously it must struggle against all attempts to entrench non-socialist ideology, and the more resolutely the workers must be warned against the bad counsellors who shout against 'overrating the conscious element' '' (Nikolai Lenin, *What Is to Be Done*, 1902).

''[We must explore] the concrete setting of an historical-social situation out of which individually differentiated thought only very gradually emerges. . . . [The socialist-communist ideology] denies the possibility of exact calculations of events in advance of their happening'' (Karl Mannheim, *Ideology and Utopia*, 1929).

''Insofar as [human] actions reflect a mutual adjustment between ideology and social realities, an understanding of ideology becomes a necessary condition for the understanding of the action'' (Alex Inkeles, *Public Opinion in Soviet Russia*, 1950).

''We are now again in an epoch of wars of religion, but a religion is now called an 'ideology' '' (Bertrand Russell, *Unpopular Essays*, 1950).

''Political ideology refers to concepts that (1) deal with the questions; Who will be the rulers? How will the rulers be selected? By what principles will they govern? (2) constitute an argument; that is, they are intended to persuade and to counter opposing views; (3) integrally affect some of the major values of life; (4) embrace a program for the defense or reform or abolition of important social institutions; (5) are, in part, rationalizations of group interest—but not necessarily the interest of all groups espousing them; (6) are normative, ethical, moral in tone and content; (7) are (inevitably) torn from their context in a broader belief system, and share the structural and stylistic properties of that system'' (Robert Lane, *Political Ideology*, 1962).

''The different extremist groups have ideologies which correspond to those of their democratic counterparts. The classic fascist movements have represented the extremism of the center. Fascist ideology, though antiliberal in its glorification of the state, has been similar to liberalism in its opposition to big business, trade unions, and the socialist state. It has also resembled liberalism in its distaste for religion and other forms of traditionalism . . . the social characteristics of Nazi voters in pre-Hitler Germany and Austria resembled those of the liberals much more than they did those of the conservatives'' (Seymour Lipset, *Political Man*, 1963).

''Conservative religious systems, due to the traditional indoctrination and socialization that they emphasize, usually preclude the adoption of liberal ideologies by their adherents'' (Panos Bardis in T. Smith and Man Das, eds., *Sociocultural Change Since 1950*, 1978).

''No one has played a more important role in the postwar attempts to dethrone scientific theory as the core of sociology and replace it with ideology than Alvin W. Gouldner, Max Weber Research Professor of Social Theory at Washington University of St. Louis. It is an anomaly that a man occupying a chair in the name of Max Weber felt called upon to denounce Weber as a monster and to describe anyone who consults his views on the relations of values and social science as displaying 'the first sign of professional senility' '' (Don Martindale, *The Nature and Types of Sociological Theory*, 1981).

''In Marxism, the slightest doctrinal deviation risks derailing the Revolution from the track of History'' (Daniel Bell, *The Social Sciences Since the Second World War*, 1982).

ILLEGITIMACY

''A bastard shall not enter into the congregation of the Lord: even to his tenth generation shall he not enter'' (Deuteronomy 23:2).

''If a female slave has intercourse with a male slave, freeman or freedman, the child will always belong to the slave's master. If a free woman has intercourse with a male slave, the child will belong to the master'' (Plato, *Laws*, c. 400 B.C.).

''The most important moral and legal rule concerning the physiological side of kinship is that no child should be brought into the world without a man—and one man at that—assuming the role of sociological father. . . . Broadly speaking, an unmarried mother is under a ban, a fatherless child is a bastard. This is by no means only a European or Christian prejudice; it is the attitude found amongst most barbarous and savage peoples as well'' (Bronislaw Malinowski in V. Calverton and S. Schmalhausen, eds., *The New Generation*, 1930).

''The most pervading feature of the Arab family is the strong code governing relations between the sexes. The highest value is placed upon premarital chastity in women and upon their marital fidelity. . . . Loss of chastity in a girl is still viewed, in all classes and communities, as the gravest kind of misbehavior, to be punished by her father and brothers: the penalty varies from severe disgrace to banishment and even to death'' (Morroe Berger, *The Arab World Today*, 1962).

''The implementation of fun morality as a means to learning, child-rearing, and production goals . . . serves as a source of permissive attitudes concerning illicit sexual relationships, making it possible for such attitudes to coexist unnoticed with censorious attitudes towards illicit pregnancies'' (Clark Vincent, *Unmarried Mothers*, 1963).

''For all purposes of the law in New Zealand the relationship between every person and his father and mother shall be determined irrespective of whether the father and mother are or have been married to each other, and all relationships shall be determined accordingly'' (New Zealand Government, *Status of Children Act*, 1969).

''The current belief that illegitimacy will be reduced if teenage girls are given an effective contraceptive is an extension of the same reasoning that created the problem in the first place. It reflects an unwillingness to face problems of social control and social discipline, while trusting some technological device to extricate society from its difficulties'' (K. Davis in C. Westoff and R. Parke, eds., *Research Reports*, 1972).

''Illegitimacy, generally viewed as a welfare problem or as a psychological problem of parents, may be studied as a societal phenomenon. Reasons for high or low levels of illegitimacy are related to differences in human group life. How is it possible that some social groups are able to organize so as to obtain conformity to the 'principle of legitimacy,' while other groups give lip service to the ideal when in fact their members produce up to 70 percent of all births out of wedlock?'' (Shirley Hartley, *Illegitimacy*, 1975).

'' 'Bastard' is more than an insult; it is also a bad word, vulgar, coarse, obscene, almost a swear word. 'Bastard' is bad language, whereas 'illegitimate' is not. Hence red-blooded he-men use the word 'bastard' continually, sometimes even as a term of endearment. . . . About 8 or 9 per cent of people in Britain are born out of wedlock. This proportion is in no way atypical or startling. Over Europe as a whole over the last 100 years the proportion has varied from between 2 and 3 per cent . . . up to 37 per cent'' (Jenny Teichman, *Illegitimacy*, 1982).

INCEST

''None of you shall approach to any that is near of kin to him, to uncover their nakedness'' (Leviticus 18:6).

''And I saw the mother of Oedipus, beautiful Epicaste, who unknowingly wrought a dreadful deed by marrying her own son; and he married her after having murdered his own father'' (Homer, *Odyssey*, c. 750 B.C.).

''Those born at the same time will be called brothers and sisters, and they will not intermarry'' (Plato, *Republic*, c. 400 B.C.).

''My grandfather had married his sister born of a different mother'' (Demosthenes, *Eubulides*, c. 350 B.C.).

''On failure of issue by her husband a woman . . . may obtain . . . the desired offspring by cohabitation with a brother-in-law'' (Manu, *Laws*, c. 200 B.C.).

''It is said that the Egyptians, contrary to mankind's general custom, passed a law which permitted men to marry their sisters'' (Diodorus Siculus, *Library of History*, c. 20 B.C.).

''This Ptolemy fell in love with his full sister Arsinoe and married her, following not Macedonian customs, but those of the Egyptians, over whom he ruled'' (Pausanias, *Periegesis of Greece*, c. 150).

''Incest with one's mother or stepmother or daughter-in-law [will be punished by execution by stoning]'' (Talmud: Courts 7:4).

''Incest is a most monstrous sin'' (Thomas Aquinas, *Summa Theologica*, 1274).

''The Trobrianders . . . show horror at the idea of violating the rules of exogamy . . . they believe that sores, disease and even death might follow clan incest'' (Bronislaw Malinowski, *Crime and Custom in Savage Society*, 1926).

''[In Egypt] in the XVIIIth Dynasty, seven kings married their sisters; in the XIXth Dynasty all but three are known to have done so; in the XXth Dynasty every king married his sister'' (Robert Briffault, *The Mothers*, 1927).

''No closer human relationship exists than mother and son. So considering this essential and compelling closeness, it is indeed remarkable that mother/son incest is not far more prevalent than other forms—which it is not'' (Karl Menninger, *Man Against Himself*, 1938).

''The Greek hero [Oedipus] killed his father and married his mother. That he did so unknowingly, since he did not recognize them as his parents, constitutes a deviation from the analytical subject matter which is easily intelligible and indeed inevitable'' (Sigmund Freud, *An Outline of Psychoanalysis*, 1940).

''Mom all too often deliberateley makes her sons so dependent that they fear to lose her in exactly the same way (and for the same sexual reasons) that a man fears losing his wife'' (Phillip Wylie, *A Generation of Vipers*, 1942).

''[Among Comanches] when a man was on the warpath, his brother could sleep with his wife'' (E. Wallace and E. Hoebel, *The Comanches*, 1952).

''Mill and his psychologistic school of sociology . . . would try to explain [exogamy] by an appeal to 'human nature,' for instance to some sort of instinctive aversion against incest . . . something like this would also be the naive or popular explanation. [From Marx's] point of view . . . however, one could ask whether it is not the other way round, that is to say, whether the apparent instinct is not rather a product of education, the effect rather than the cause of the social rules and traditions demanding exogamy and forbidding incest'' (Karl Popper, *The Open Society and Its Enemies*, 1957).

''If a woman [among the Lakher of Southeast Asia] has a son and a daughter by two different husbands the children are deemed unrelated to one another. Therefore they may marry without restraint. In contrast, the son and daughter of one man by two different mothers stand in an incestuous relationship to one another'' (Edmund Leach, *Rethinking Anthropology*, 1961).

''A Pharaoh safeguarded himself from abdication by marrying every heiress without any regard to consanguinity, so that if the chief heiress died, he was already married to the next in succession and thus retained the sovereignty . . . the throne went strictly in the female line'' (Margaret Murray, *The Splendor That Was Egypt*, 1963).

''[The Ptolemy Dynasty in ancient Egypt] practised marriage between brother and sister for three hundred years without noticeably bad physical effects'' (Richard Lewinsohn, *A History of Sexual Customs*, 1964).

''The earliest hominids were perhaps unable to commit incest [due to demographic limits] very often even if they wanted to. In the simplest ecologies (and similar ones exist today) most of the people most of the time mate out, not because of the problem of inbreeding and competition, but in order to mate at all. . . . We have already built up our societies on the premise that people will breed out of the family, and we cannot easily reverse this. . . . So the taboo persists'' (R. Fox, *Kinship and Marriage*, 1967).

''The poor, the ignorant, and the incompetent [who engage in incest] come to official attention, while people of higher socioeconomic status are able either to keep their incestuous acts hidden or, if discovered, to keep the discovery from becoming part of the official record'' (M. Hunt, *Sexual Behavior in the 1970s*, 1974).

''[As for] the origin of incest taboo and the biological effects of incest, scholars have always disagreed. Freud, for instance, hypothesized that, originally, the son's sexual attraction to his mother was suppressed, and that the father forced his son to leave the parental home and to seek an outside woman. Westermarck, on the other hand, asserted that inbreeding has undesirable physical effects, and that familiarity generates sexual revulsion. Briffault, on the basis of his matriarchal theory, concluded that the jealousy of the mother forced her sons to marry exogamously. Then, the theory of economic determinism emphasizes the economic gains resulting from exogamy. Somewhat similarly, the Tylor-White theory, stressing the collective aspects of marriage, mentions the advantages of interfamily alliance, which accompanies exogamy. Wilson Wallis, however, has cited the partial unavailability of mates within the consanguineal unit, which rendered endogamy problematical, if not impossible. Finally, according to the Malinowski-Seligman theory, incest taboo originated with the sexual rivalry which prevailed among the members of the same family'' (Panos Bardis, *Evolution of the Family in the West*, 1983).

INDICATOR, SOCIAL

''The general goal of researchers . . . is to find those indexes which are most representative of the quality of life. And therein lies the rub. On the basis of whose value is quality to be judged?'' (T. Palys, *Social Indicators of Quality of Life in Canada*, 1973).

''The terms social indicators, social accounting, social reporting . . . have been bandied about in the literature to a considerable extent'' (D. Henderson, *Social Indicators*, 1974).

''We have heard a great deal about how accounting and economics need to be enlarged to include 'social indicators' or 'social accounting.' But I don't think the need is for more numbers, at all. The need is for the basis of justifying the numbers—the model or world view which tells us what difference the numbers make'' (C. Churchman in L. J. and L. L. Seidler, eds., *Social Accounting*, 1975).

''The technical expert, in selecting the mix of variables for inclusion in the composite index, is usurping a political decision. Even if his decision is politically legitimated, the political choice later appears as a technical necessity and obtains a spurious objectivity'' (R. Webber, *Liverpool Social Area Study 1971 Data*, 1975).

''Certain topics of broad social interest—social concerns . . . relate, directly or indirectly, to the quality of our lives. In order to reveal these relationships, the concerns which have been identified in each of the broad social areas are represented by selected statistics or statistical measures—social indicators—which describe the general status of the population with respect to certain aspects of each concern'' (United States Bureau of the Census, *Social Indicators 1976*, 1977).

''[A] rapidly growing field in social research involves the development and monitoring of *social indicators*. Just as economists use indexes such as gross national product (GNP) per capita as an indicator of a nation's economic development, we can monitor other aspects of society in a similar fashion. . . . If we wanted to compare the relative health conditions in different societies, we could compare their death rates . . . it's possible to use social indicators data either for comparisons across groups at one time or within a particular length of time. And often doing both sheds the most light on the subject'' (Earl Babbie, *The Practice of Social Research*, 1979).

"The pioneers of social indicators were inspired by their early recognition of the tremendous need for an improved flow of cogent social information to an increasingly complex public sector decision process. They responded with a ready and admirable enthusiasm and soon their efforts became a virtual 'movement.' The possibilities for doing social good by developing tools of social measurement seemed endless, and the social indicator movement grew rapidly in scope and stature. Now, fifteen years later, the mood is somewhat changed. The high hopes held out for social indicators remain for the most part unfulfilled, especially for the data needs of policy-making. Administrators have become guarded, if not pessimistic, about the usefulness of social indicators, and many researchers have turned from a concern for enlightening the policy process to a narrower, and often misunderstood, emphasis on detailed statistical manipulation" (Michael Garley, *Social Measurement and Social Indicators*, 1981).

INDUSTRIAL SOCIOLOGY

"Even at the present day, when the [factory] system is perfectly organised, and its labour lightened to the utmost, it is found nearly impossible to convert persons past the age of puberty, whether drawn from rural or from handicraft occupations, into useful factory hands. After struggling for a while to conquer their listless or restive habits, they either renounce the employment spontaneously, or are dismissed by the overlookers on account of inattention" (Andrew Ure, *The Philosophy of Manufacturers*, 1835).

"In many rooms of the cotton and flax-spinning mills, the air is filled with fibrous dust, which produces chest affections, especially among workers in the carding and combing-rooms. . . . The most common effects of this breathing of dust are bloodspitting, hard, noisy breathing, pains in the chest, coughs, sleeplessness. . . . We find here [among women working in factories]—the work of women up to the hour of confinement, incapacity as housekeepers, neglect of home and children, indifference, actual dislike to family life, and demoralization; further the crowding out of men from employment . . . early emancipation of children, husbands supported by their wives and children, etc., etc." (Friedrich Engels, *The Condition of the Working Class in England*, 1845).

"Modern industry has converted the little workshop of the patriarchal master into the great factory of the industrial capitalist. Masses of labourers, crowded into the factory, are organised like soldiers. As privates of the industrial army they are placed under the command of a perfect hierarchy of officers and sergeants. Not only are they slaves of the bourgeois class, and of the bourgeois State; they are daily and hourly enslaved by the machine, by the overlooker and, above all, by the individual bourgeois manufacturer himself. . . . The less the skill and exertion of strength implied in manual labour . . . the more modern industry becomes developed, the more is the labour of men superseded by that of women. Differences of age and sex have no longer any distinctive social validity for the working class. All are instruments of labour, more or less expensive to use, according to their age and sex. . . . The development of Modern Industry . . . cuts from under its feet the very foundation on which the bourgeoisie produces and appropriates products. What the bourgeoisie, therefore, produces, above all, is its own grave diggers'' (Karl Marx and Friedrich Engels, *Communist Manifesto*, 1847).

''The great cry that rises from all our manufacturing cities, louder than the furnace blast, is all in very deed for this—that we manufacture everything there except men'' (John Ruskin, *The Stones of Venice*, 1853).

''Never perhaps in the history of the human race has so simple a device created in so short a period so much order, virtue, goodness and happiness [among the workers in Owen's mill in New Lanark] out of so much ignorance, error and misery. [This resulted from the] contrivance of a silent monitor for each one employed in the establishment. This consisted of a four-sided piece of wood, about two inches long and one broad, each side coloured—one side black, another blue, the third yellow and the fourth white, tapered at the top, and finished with wire eyes, to hang upon a hook with either side to the front. One of these was suspended in a conspicuous place near to each of the persons employed and the colour at the front told the conduct of the individual during the preceding day to four degrees of comparison. Bad, denoted by black and No. 4—indifferent, by blue and No. 3—good, by yellow and No. 2—and excellent by white and No. 1'' (Robert Owen, *The Life of Robert Owen, by Himself*, 1858).

''With us [in Canada] the factory system has not grown slowly; it sprang into existence almost at one bound. . . . But . . . in acquiring the industries at one bound we have also become possessed, just as quickly, of the evils which accompany the factory system, and which, in other lands, were creatures of a gradual growth'' (Royal Commission on the Relations of Labour and Capital, *Report of the Royal Commission on the Relations of Labour and Capital*, 1889).

''For awhile the introduction of machinery which took away from the home so many industries deprived women of any importance as an economic factor; but presently she arose, and followed her lost wheel and loom to their new place, the mill. Today there is hardly an industry in the land in which some women are not found. Everywhere throughout America are women workers outside the unpaid labor of the home'' (Charlotte Gilman, *Women and Economics*, 1898).

''The one worker, whether man or woman, who works excessive hours sets the pace, compels others to work long hours also, and inevitably lowers the rate of pay for all'' (B. Hutchins and A. Harrison, *A History of Factory Legislation*, 1903).

''Union laborers are to be given preference at all times, but no nonsense is to be taken from them. . . . All men are expected to quit work at quitting time as promptly as they began work. . . . No smoking is allowed on the job except to finish noon smoke—not over one half hour—and no refilling of pipes. All steady pay men must see that this rule is enforced'' (Frank Gilbreth, *Field System*, 1908).

''The science of doing work of any kind cannot be developed by the workman.

Why? Because he has neither the time nor the money to do it'' (Frederick Taylor, *The Principles of Scientific Management*, 1911).

''Nine-tenths of the trouble with those of us who have been engaged in helping people to change from the older types of management to the new management—that is, to scientific management—nine-tenths of our trouble has been to 'bring' those on the management's side to do their fair share of the work and only one-tenth of our trouble has come on the workman's side. Invariably we find very great opposition on the part of those on the management's side to do their new duties'' (Frederick Taylor, *Testimony Before the Special House Committee*, 1912).

''It is not easy to define accurately the concept of the factory. We think at once of the steam engine and the mechanization of work, but the machine had its forerunner in what we call 'apparatus'—labor appliances which had to be utilized in the same way as the machine but which as a rule were driven by water power. The distinction is that the apparatus works as the servant of the man while in modern machines the inverse relation holds. The real distinguishing characteristic of the modern factory is in general, however . . . the concentration of ownership of workplace, means of work, source of power and raw material in one and the same hand, that of the entrepreneur. The combination was only exceptionally met with before the 18th century. . . . The oldest real factory which can be identified (though it was still driven by water power) was a silk factory at Derwent, near Derby, in 1719. It was conducted on the basis of a patent, the owner of which had stolen the invention in Italy. . . . The decisive factor, however, in the triumph of the mechanization and rationalization of work was the fate of cotton manufacture. The industry was transplanted from the continent to England in the 17th century and there immediately began a struggle against the old national industry established since the 15th century, namely, wool'' (Max Weber, *General Economic History*, 1920).

''[Early English factory] towns had their profitable smoke, their profitable disorder, their profitable ignorance, their profitable despair. . . . The new factories and the new furnaces were like the Pyramids, telling of man's enslavement, rather than of his power; casting their long shadow over the society that took such pride in them'' (John and Barbara Hammond, *The Rise of Modern Industry*, 1925).

''We have learned that it is neither necessary nor always efficient to organize all mass production in such a manner as to have the majority of workers confine themselves to doing one and only one of the elementary manipulations'' (Peter Drucker, *Concept of the Corporation*, 1946).

''Would it not be dangerous to call upon workers to participate in the technical and economic administration of enterprises, in view of their incompetence in this domain? Our answer would be that the difficulty here is imaginary rather than real: the functions of management councils will consist in the general direction and the running of enterprises and industries, and will not take over the functions of the technical personnel'' (Georges Davidovitch Gurvitch, *The Bill of Social Rights*, 1946).

''Industrial technology has also had certain psychological influences on the worker. Some of these are . . . fatigue, boredom, monotony, and the loss of pride on the part of the craftsman'' (I. Tsouderos in D. Kalitsounakis, ed., *Economy and Society*, 1961).

''Industrial conflict is . . . a curiously ambivalent affair, closer to the domestic battle of the sexes than to the clash of armies. Consequently, it is not difficult to build on the positive-sum or cooperative aspects of the game and to develop institutions that express this aspect'' (Kenneth Boulding, *Conflict and Defense*, 1963).

''[In the Soviet Union] the principle of one-man management in the management of production consists in the following: the leadership of each production unit (enterprise, shop, section) is assigned to a single executive who is endowed by the state with the necessary rights to manage, and who bears full responsibility for the work of the given unit. All individuals working in the unit are obligated to fulfill the instructions of the executive'' (F. Aunapu, *What Management Is*, 1967).

''[In the Soviet Union] the election of enterprise managers can become one of the forms of participation in management . . . the tactics adopted by some managers of orienting themselves not to those 'below' them . . . but to those 'above' them [indicate that] it is not the respect of the collective that is important to them but primarily the good will of their superiors. This creates bureaucrats and zealous administrators, some of whom unfortunately have not yet been removed. This situation would be fundamentally changed if the masses had the right to elect enterprise managers'' (V. Afanas'ev, *Scientific Management of Society*, 1968).

''[In the Soviet Union] today our chief weakness in the sphere of participation of the working people in the management of the production affairs of the enterprise is the frequent nonfulfillment of the recommendations of the trade union committee and the production conference. . . . Since workers and employees at the enterprise have the obligation of fulfilling the plan, they should have a deciding voice in formulating it'' (S. Ivanov, *Occupational Law and Scientific-Technical Progress*, 1974).

''A good manager must not only think of the technology of production but also be a 'guardian' of his subordinates; he must be aware of their frame of mind . . . informal relations promote . . . the democratization of management'' (D. Kaidalov and E. Suimenko, *Current Problems in the Sociology of Work*, 1974).

''Better management is impossible unless it becomes more democratic and unless the participation of the masses is considerably extended. . . . Every worker should be made to feel that he is one of the owners of the factory'' (Aleksei Kosygin in Roy Medvedev, *On Socialist Democracy*, 1975).

''Although all members of the socialist society are simultaneously 'managers' and 'managed,' the effective functioning of any subsystem of this society—such as an economic enterprise—requires the clear delineation of 'relations of subordination.' These relations prevail between those who 'direct' (or 'manage') the organization and those who 'execute' the directives of the former'' (Murray Yanowitch, *Social and Economic Inequality in the Soviet Union*, 1977).

''A strategy of industrialization relying heavily on inequality and multinational corporations is not one designed to satisfy the needs of the majority of the population in less developed countries'' (Volker Bornschier, *Multinational Monopolies*, 1980).

''Industrialization is . . . a massive force altering the organizations and values of the total society. On this background the operations of all work organizations are shaped and forged'' (Delbert Miller and William Form, *Industrial Sociology*, 1980).

''The increases in the length of working hours in the U.S.S.R. . . . ran against both the ideological promises of the Russian revolution and the trends in other industrialized societies'' (Jiri Zuzanek, *Work and Leisure in the Soviet Union*, 1980).

''The inundation of the working-class ranks [in Eastern Europe] by these poorly educated and organizationally inexperienced urban migrants helps to account for the success of the communist regimes in maintaining working-class conformism despite disorienting change and often severe deprivations. More recently, the slowing in the rates of social mobility, the consolidation of an increasingly hereditary, better educated and more organizationally sophisticated manual working stratum, and the necessary changeover from 'extensive' to 'intensive' economic growth, may lead workers to be more assertive and less amenable to manipulation'' (Jan Triska and Charles Gati, *Blue Collar Workers in Eastern Europe*, 1981).

INNOVATION

''It is morally impossible that there should be enough different devices in a machine to make it behave in all the occurrences of life as our reason makes us behave'' (René Descartes, *A Discourse on Method*, 1637).

''The man whose life is spent in performing a few simple operations . . . has no occasion to exert his understanding, or to exercise his invention. . . . He naturally . . . becomes as stupid and ignorant as it is possible for a human creature to become . . . in the barbarous societies . . . the varied occupations of every man oblige every man to exert his capacity, and to invent expedients for removing difficulties. . . . Invention is kept alive'' (Adam Smith, *The Wealth of Nations*, 1776).

''Invention then becomes a branch of business, and the application of science to immediate production aims at determining the inventions at the same time as it solicits them. But this is not the way in which machinery in general came into being, still less the way that it progresses in detail. This way is a process of analysis—by subdivisions of labour which transforms the worker's operations more and more into mechanical operations, so that, at a certain point, the mechanism can step into his place'' (Karl Marx, *Pre-capitalist Economic Formations*, 1858).

''The Analytical Engine [a computing machine] is therefore a machine of the most general nature. Whatever formula it is required to develop, the law of its development must be communicated to it by two sets of cards. . . . Thus the Analytical Engine will possess a library of its own'' (Charles Babbage, *Passages from the Life of a Philosopher*, 1864).

''There is no security . . . against the ultimate development of mechanical consciousness, in the fact of machines' possessing little consciousness now. A mollusk has not much consciousness. Reflect upon the extraordinary advance which machines have made during the last few hundred years, and note how slowly the animal and vegetable kingdoms are advancing. The more highly organized machines are creatures not so much of yesterday as of the last five minutes, so to speak, in comparison with past time. Assume for the sake of argument that conscious beings have existed for some twenty million years: See what strides machines have made in the last thousand! May not the world last twenty million years longer? If so, what will they not in the end become? Is it not safer to nip the mischief in the bud and to forbid them further progress? . . . But the servant [the machine] glides by imperceptible approaches into the master'' (Samuel Butler, *Erewhon*, 1872).

''The relics of the instruments of labor are of no less importance in the study of vanished socioeconomic forms than fossil bones are in the study of the organization of extinct species. . . . Darwin has aroused our interest in the history of natural technology, that is to say in the origin of the organs of plants and animals as productive instruments utilized for the life purposes of those creatures. Does not the history of the origin of the productive organs of men in society, the organs which form the material basis of every kind of social organization, deserve equal attention? . . . Technology reveals man's dealings with nature, discloses the direct productive activities of his life, thus throwing light upon social relations and the resultant mental conceptions'' (Karl Marx, *Das Kapital*, 1879).

''Invention is a question followed by an answer [sociological statistics must determine] the beneficial or harmful effects which result from the imitation of given inventions. [Invention is] intermittent, rare, and eruptive only at certain infrequent intervals. . . . There is in every period a current of inventions which is in a certain general sense religious or architectural or sculptural or musical or philosophical'' (Gabriel Tarde, *The Laws of Imitation*, 1890).

''Cultural horizon [implies that] the process of invention is a function of the stage of development of the science which deals with the natural principles governing the phenomena under consideration, and fundamental to the integration of any new cultural pattern or invention in the field considered'' (Francis Chapin, *Cultural Change*, 1928).

''Some of the conservative old men try to pass laws to stop change. One might as well brush back the tides with a broom. Passing laws will never do it. If they want to stop change, they will have to break up the machine or, better still, poison all inventors'' (William Ogburn, *Recent Social Trends*, 1934).

''The machine does us both harm and good. It saves our lives, but maims our limbs. It brings us comforts, but causes us unhappiness. The problem before the human race is to see if we can increase our friendly relations to the machine and diminish its hostility'' (William Ogburn, *You and Machines*, 1934).

''Society has been revolutionized several times by technology, for most modern social changes are precipitated by mechanical invention and scientific discovery'' (William Ogburn, *The Social Effects of Aviation*, 1946).

''Let us remember that the automatic machine . . . as the precise economic equivalent of slave labor must accept the economic condition of slave labor. It is perfectly clear that this will produce an unemployment situation, in comparison with which . . . the depression of the thirties will seem a pleasant joke'' (Norbert Wiener, *The Human Use of Human Beings*, 1950).

''Even peoples whose equipment is of the simplest . . . employ mechanical principles that are quite complex. The boomerang of the Australian, the heavy knobkerrie of the South African Bantu, the spear-thrower—all show a shrewd utilization of physical forces that give the individual added flexibility and power in using his physical capacities. The use of the principle of the spring in the manufacture of the compound bow is another instance of this. Even the simpler type of bow, made of one piece of wood, recognizes and allows for the elasticity of wood, while the bow-string compounds the same principle, and the feathered arrow insures better aim'' (Melville Herskovits, *Cultural Anthropology*, 1952).

''Laboratory work, even in pure science, requires a great inventive effort'' (Abbott Usher, *A History of Mechanical Inventions*, 1959).

''Almost always the men who achieve these fundamental inventions of a new paradigm have been either very young or very new to the field whose paradigm they change. And perhaps that point need not have been made explicit, for obviously these are the men who, being little committed by prior practice to the traditional rules of normal science, are particularly likely to see that these rules no longer define a playable game and to conceive another set that can replace them'' (Thomas Kuhn, *The Structure of Scientific Revolutions*, 1962).

''Because a French priest in the thirteenth century found that he could read an important document better by looking at it through curved glass, hundreds of millions of human lives were eventually saved'' (Jerome Meyer, *Great Inventions*, 1962).

''Invention is partly caused, hampered, promoted, steered by *social* factors and institutions'' (S. Gilfillan, *The Sociology of Invention*, 1963).

''When *Homo sapiens* appeared on the Earth, more or less in his present shape, innovation began'' (Dennis Gabor, *Innovations*, 1970).

''Western society has accepted as unquestionable a technological imperative that is quite as arbitrary as the most primitive taboo: not merely the duty to foster invention and constantly to create technological novelties, but equally the duty to surrender to these novelties unconditionally, just because they are offered, without respect to their human consequences'' (Lewis Mumford, *The Pentagon of Power*, 1970).

''In order to make discoveries, the most essential thing is not merely to obtain a gleam of light here and there that other people have missed, but to drive straight for your goal, and damn everything else'' (Simone de Beauvoir, *The Prime of Life*, 1973).

''Approximately two thirds of the technological basic innovations that will be produced in the second half of the twentieth century will occur in the decade around 1989'' (G. Mensch, *The Technological Stalemate*, 1975).

''Almost everyone in the world is directly or indirectly affected by computers. Those few people who remain untouched will soon feel their influence. Because of the ever-increasing role that the computer plays in our world, it is extremely important that every adult know something about these machines'' (Martin Holoien, *Computers and Their Societal Impact*, 1977).

''The superb efficiency of future automation will facilitate the exercise of intolerance—either overtly by governments or as a by-product of other well-meaning social forces. The automation of intolerance is an alarming prospect . . . the computerized society will have to become a far more tolerant society than most societies of the past if true freedom is to survive'' (Simon Nora and Alain Minc, *The Informing of Society*, 1978).

''[Reinvention is] the degree to which innovation is changed by the adopter in the process of adoption and implementation after its original development. We stress that reinvention is a matter of degree; the ultimate in reinvention would be the independent generation of a new idea that someone else had already created. The range of reinvention that we studied is much less than such parallel invention'' (E. Rogers in M. Radnor et al., eds., *The Diffusion of Innovations*, 1978).

''Scientists serendipitously stumble on or logically create working hypotheses, test them, and draw conclusions'' (Marvin Wolfgang in Edward Sagarin, *Raskolnikov and Others*, 1981).

''[Serendipity, or accidental innovation, is of two kinds.] In the first kind, the inventor is actively engaged in problem-solving but is unable to go past a certain point in his progress. A freak occurrence or chance observation then provides the answer. In the second type, the inventor suddenly gains a valuable insight or discovers a new principle not related to the work in which he is engaged but to some other area'' (Gilbert Kivenson, *The Art and Science of Inventing*, 1982).

INSTINCT

''The skill that art gives to the craftsman is given to the animal by nature'' (Lucius Annaeus Seneca, *To Lucilius*, c. 50).

''Without any learning, the duck will swim, because, as Hippocrates says, animal instincts are unlearned. So it seems to me that the other animals develop their skills by instinct, not by reason'' (Galen, *On the Use of Parts*, c. 150).

''Animals, by means of their members, act from natural instinct, not through knowledge of the relations of their members to these actions'' (Thomas Aquinas, *Summa Theologica*, 1274).

''By a divine instinct men's minds mistrust ensuing dangers'' (William Shakespeare, *Richard III*, 1593).

''Instinct is therefore better proportioned to the needs of beasts, than reason is to our own, and that is why it ordinarily seems so sure'' (Étienne Bonnot de Condillac, *Treatise on Animals*, 1755).

''Chickens should be able to walk by a few efforts almost immediately after their nativity: whilst the human infant in those countries where he is not incumbered with clothes, as in India, is five or six months, and in our climate almost a twelvemonth, before he can safely stand upon his feet'' (Erasmus Darwin, *Zoonomia*, 1796).

''Those who defend instinct as a 'divine something, a kind of inspiration,' are, indeed, worthy of ridicule'' (Thomas Brown, *Observations on the Zoonomia of Erasmus Darwin*, 1798).

''The establishment of those compound reflex actions which we call instincts, is comprehensible on the principle that inner relations are, by perpetual repetition, organized into correspondence with outer relations'' (Herbert Spencer, *Principles of Psychology*, 1855).

''However mysterious some animals' instincts may appear to us, our instincts will appear no less mysterious to them'' (William James, *Principles of Psychology*, 1890).

''Well-bred instinct meets reason half-way'' (George Santayana, *The Life of Reason*, 1906).

''Instincts are more than innate tendencies or dispositions to certain kinds of movement . . . even the most purely instinctive action is the outcome of a distinctly mental process'' (William McDougall, *An Introduction to Social Psychology*, 1908).

''The law of original behavior, or the law of instinct, is then that *to any situation an animal will, apart from learning, respond by virtue of the inherited nature of its reception-, connection-, and action-systems*'' (Edward Thorndike, *Animal Intelligence*, 1911).

''Human civilization rests upon two pillars, of which one is the control of natural forces and the other the restriction of our instincts. The ruler's throne rests upon fettered slaves. Among the instinctual components which are thus brought into service, the sexual instincts, in the narrower sense of the word, are conspicuous for their strength and savagery. Woe, if they should be set loose! The throne would be overturned and the ruler trampled under foot'' (Sigmund Freud, *The Resistances to Psycho-Analysis*, 1925).

''The behaviourist view of man as a helpless pawn in the fell clutch of circumstance is paralleled in its anti-Humanism by the recurrently popular doctrine which traces human conduct to blind instinctive urges, notably that of aggression, arising from a primordial and predatory ancestry. From social Darwinists through classical Freudians to the new school of ethological determinists led by Konrad Lorenz, the instinctive theory of aggression has served to reinforce a fashionable pessimism concerning the human potential for rationality, responsibility and resourcefulness'' (Floyd Matson in Paul Kurtz, ed., *The Humanist Alternative*, 1973).

``So-called instinctual behavior could be molded or, as Pavlov put it, conditioned'' (Henry Tischler et al., *Introduction to Sociology*, 1983).

INSTITUTION, SOCIAL

``Religion has lost most of its power. And government, instead of regulating economic life, has become its tool and servant. The most opposite schools, orthodox economists and extreme socialists, unite to reduce government to the role of a more or less passive intermediary among the various social functions'' (Émile Durkheim, *Suicide*, 1897).

``The more rational an institution is the less it suffers by making concessions to others'' (George Santayana, *The Life of Reason*, 1906).

``Always and everywhere there are individual cases of breaking social rules, cases which exercise some disorganizing influence on group institutions and if not counteracted are apt to multiply and to lead to a complete decay [of social institutions]'' (William Thomas and Florian Znaniecki, *The Polish Peasant in Europe and America*, 1920).

``All our social institutions are cut to the pattern of people with a unified, normal Ego, which one can classify as good or bad, and which either fulfills its function or is disabled by an overpowering influence'' (Sigmund Freud, *The Question of Lay Analysis*, 1926).

``An institution like the treasury of a state is for the citizens primarily a number of active 'minds' (if not a single 'collective mind'), that may and do, if necessary, utilize human bodies, e.g., the bodies of policemen, to coerce citizens into paying taxes, but whose own bodily composition is of no importance to the taxpayer as compared with their 'mental' capacities and dispositions'' (Florian Znaniecki, *Social Actions*, 1936).

``We belong to associations, but not to an institution. . . . [Institutions are] the established forms or conditions of procedure characteristic of group activity'' (Robert MacIver, *Society*, 1937).

``Institutionalization has integrative functions on various levels, both with reference to the different roles in which any one actor is involved, and to the coordination of the behavior of different individuals'' (Talcott Parsons, *The Social System*, 1951).

``Institutions are the patterned responses of pluralities of persons to common problems. The survival of human groups depends on the efficacy of their institutions, their solutions to three general problems of social life: socialization, the mastery of nature, and social control'' (Don Martindale and R. Hanson, *Small Town and the Nation*, 1969).

''Social institutions form an element in a more general concept, known as social structure'' (Alan Wells, *Social Institutions*, 1970).

''The ways in which society organizes and structures its social institutions—and particularly its health and welfare systems—encourage or discourage the altruistic in man'' (Richard Titmuss, *The Gift Relationship*, 1971).

''Institutions are the accepted solutions to social problems. They always, in varying degrees, reflect conscious planning and adaptive readjustment. When institutions are first established or subject to radical revision the role of conscious planning looms large. But always in the course of operation little problems that could not altogether be foreseen crop up. Every institution, thus, no matter how rationally established in the first place, acquires an encrustation of expedient readjustments. These may, in time, blur or obscure the original plan'' (Don and Edith Martindale, *Psychiatry and the Law*, 1973).

''The nation is a peculiar type of community, a system of institutions constituting a more or less complete way of life for a population'' (Raj Mohan and Don Martindale, eds., *Handbook of Contemporary Developments in World Sociology*, 1975).

''The force behind the continuing growth of institutionism seems to be the . . . need of a rapidly developing technology requiring to have at its base the most modern technological achievements'' (R. Wroczynski, *Continuing Education*, 1976).

''New institutions, as social historians and historical sociologists know, usually emerge in periods of social unrest and disorganization'' (Lowry Nelson in T. Smith and Man Das, eds., *Sociocultural Change Since 1950*, 1978).

''[As for social institutions] until now those who have not theorised about the state or macrosocial structure have concentrated almost exclusively upon the formal institutions of society: marriage and the family, industry and employment, education, medicine, social services and the institutions of law . . . But what is missing from previous accounts is the implicit and hidden contribution of informal institutions. How can we look at marriage and the family, for example, and ignore extra-marital affairs which may maintain the very existence of many families?'' (Stuart Henry, ed., *Informal Institutions*, 1981).

''Changes in institutional strategies and goals often occur as adaptations or adjustments to problems'' (Richard Blanton et al., *Ancient Mesoamerica*, 1982).

''In analysing an institutional change's effects one can restrict oneself to the study of the convergence or lack of convergence between these effects and the specific objectives that the actors responsible for the change had in mind'' (Raymond Boudon, *The Unintended Consequences of Social Action*, 1982).

''Public decision-making occurs in an institutional context, and institutions, as ongoing organizations, structure the way in which policies are debated, formulated, and implemented'' (Carl Lieberman, *Institutions and Processes of American National Government*, 1983).

INTERACTION, SOCIAL

"If I keep from meddling with people, they take care of themselves. If I keep from commanding people, they behave themselves. If I keep from preaching at people, they improve themselves. If I keep from imposing on people, they become themselves" (Lao-tse, *Teaching of Tao, c.* 550 B.C.).

"Man is by nature a social animal" (Aristotle, *Nicomachean Ethics*, c. 350 B.C.).

"Either companionship or death" (Talmud: Fast 23a).

"Man is a social animal" (Thomas Aquinas, *Summa Theologica*, 1274).

"Let all the powers and elements of nature conspire to serve and obey one man . . . he will still be miserable, till you give him some person at least with whom he may share his happiness, and whose esteem and friendship he may enjoy" (David Hume, *A Treatise of Human Nature*, 1740).

"Man, thou livest not for thyself alone. Nature educates thee for intercourse of those about thee. The domestic relations are the first and most important ties of nature" (Johann Heinrich Pestalozzi, *Evening Hour of a Hermit*, 1780).

"Act in such a way that you always treat humanity, whether in your own person or in the person of any other, never simply as a means but always at the same time as an end" (Immanuel Kant, *Fundamental Principles of the Metaphysics of Morals*, 1785).

"In the social production of their life, men enter into definite relations that are indispensable and independent of their will" (Karl Marx, *A Contribution to the Critique of Political Economy*, 1859).

"Really, universally, relations stop nowhere, and the exquisite problem of the artist is eternally but to draw, by a geometry of his own, the circle within which they shall happily *appear* to do so" (Henry James, *Roderick Hudson*, 1876).

"If no one turned round when we entered, answered when we spoke, or minded what we did, but if every person 'cut us dead,' and acted as if we were nonexisting things, a kind of rage and impotent despair would ere long well up in us, from which the cruellest bodily tortures would be a relief; for these would make us feel that, however bad might be our plight, we had not sunk to such a depth as to be unworthy of attention at all" (William James, *The Principles of Psychology*, 1890).

"Accommodation is the natural issue of conflicts . . . [it is related to] changes in habit, which are transmitted, or may be transmitted, sociologically, that is, in the form of social tradition. . . . [Competition involves] interaction without social contact . . . [it is one] of the four great types of interaction [the others are accommodation, assimilation, and conflict]" (Robert Park and Ernest Burgess, *Introduction to the Science of Sociology*, 1921).

"The fundamental patterns of life and behavior are everywhere the same, whether among the ancient Greeks, the modern Italians, the Asiatic Mongols, the Australian blacks, or the African Hottentots'' (Robert Park et al., *Old World Traits Transplanted*, 1921).

''Connections with our fellows furnish both the opportunities for action and the instrumentalities by which we take advantage of opportunity. . . . If the standard of morals is low, it is because the education given by the interaction of the individual with his social environment is defective. . . . If a child gets on by peevishness and intrigue, then others are his accomplices who assist in the habits which are built up'' (John Dewey, *Human Nature and Conduct*, 1922).

''Every observable phase of human society is statistically a pluralistic field. . . . [Human behavior involves] the approximately simultaneous reaction of a considerable number of individuals that happen to be in the same situation or circumstance'' (Franklin Giddings, *The Scientific Study of Human Society*, 1924).

''The interaction of ego and alter is the most elementary form of a social system. The features of this interaction are present in more complex form in all social systems. In interaction ego and alter are each objects of orientation for the other. The basic differences from orientations to nonsocial objects are two. First, since the outcome of ego's action (e.g., success in the attainment of a goal) is a contingent on alter's reaction to what ego does, ego becomes oriented not only to alter's probable *overt* behavior but also to what ego interprets to be alter's expectations relative to ego's behavior'' (Talcott Parsons and Edward Shils, eds., *Toward a General Theory of Action*, 1951).

''We might define sociology as the study of human groups, or of human interaction'' (Ely Chinoy, *Sociological Perspective*, 1954).

''Relations between people contain a built-in reciprocity. I smile at you; if you smile back, I speak to you; you respond, and a relationship has begun. At each step, my reaction is contingent upon yours, and yours, in turn, contingent upon mine. If you fail to smile, but scowl instead, I may say a harsh word; you respond in kind, and another chain of mutual reinforcement builds up—this time toward antagonism'' (James Coleman, *Community Conflict*, 1957).

''Every new inmate learns to dog-face, that is to assume an apathetic, *characterless* facial expression and posture when viewed by authority. The dog-face is acquired easily when everyone freezes. . . . Relaxation comes when inmates are alone: there is an exaggeration of the smiling effervescence of the 'friendly' party. The face that is protective by day is aggressively hardened and hate-filled by night against the stationed or pacing guard'' (Erving Goffman, *Behavior in Public Places*, 1963).

''Human beings act toward things on the basis of the meanings that these things have for them . . . the meaning of such things is derived from, or arises out of, the social interaction that one has with one's fellows . . . these meanings are handled in, and modified through, an interpretive process used by the person in dealing with the things he encounters'' (Herbert Blumer, *Symbolic Interactionism*, 1969).

''The decline in the *average* duration of human relationships is a likely corollary of the increase in the number of such relationships. The average urban individual today probably comes into contact with more people in a week than the feudal villager did in a year, perhaps even a lifetime'' (Alvin Toffler, *Future Shock*, 1970).

''Interaction is the process whereby, in order to give content and form to their behavior, individuals take the actions of others into account'' (Ritchie Lowry and Robert Rankin, *Sociology*, 1972).

INTERVIEW

''Interviewer 'bias'—that is, systematic errors on the part of many or even all interviewers—may enter . . . in the asking of questions and the eliciting and recording of responses'' (Claire Selltiz et al., *Research Methods in Social Relations*, 1951).

''Every interview has its own balance of revelation and of withholding of information. Only under very unusual circumstances is an interview so completely expository that every phrase can be taken at face value'' (Pauline Young, *Scientific Social Surveys and Research*, 1966).

''The general advantages of interviews include . . . a high response participation rate . . . , an ability to collect data from persons incapable of completing a questionnaire without assistance . . . , an ability to clarify questions or probe for additional information . . . , an ability to verify or cross-check certain verbal responses with the observed conditions. The general disadvantages of interviews include . . . the relatively high cost of interviewing respondents . . . , the possibility that the interviewer-interviewee relationship may produce reliability and validity measurement problems . . . , the possibility that interviewers may subtly change the intended meaning of questions'' (Kenneth Eckhardt and M. Ermann, *Social Research Methods*, 1977).

''Dozens of occupations depend upon the interview as a major source of information needed to carry out their central task. A police officer investigating an auto accident, a teacher having a conference with a parent, a nurse talking with a patient, a lawyer getting information from a client . . . all are using interviewing'' (Raymond Gorden, *Interviewing*, 1980).

''Interviews are a much more flexible data collection method than questionnaires; therefore, what is gained in scope of information must be weighed against the fact that the data are not as uniform. . . . Experience indicates that most respondents are cooperative, seem to enjoy the interview experience, and appear to take it seriously'' (Ann and Hubert Blalock, *Introduction to Social Research*, 1982).

''Interviews are two-way exchanges between an interviewer and a respondent. The interviewer seeks responses to questions or other verbal stimuli that she or he presents orally. The exchanges can be face-to-face, with the interviewer physically present in interaction with the respondent, or they can be by telephone. Unlike questionnaires that are completed by respondents, interviews are recorded by the interviewer. In addition, interviewers observe visual as well as auditory cues that may be emitted by respondents. . . . Interview schedules are forms in which responses to interviews are recorded'' (Tony Tripodi, *Evaluative Research for Social Workers*, 1983).

K

KINSHIP

''Friendship between kinsmen lasts longer'' (Thomas Aquinas, *Summa Theologica*, 1274).

''[Kinship constitutes] the sole possible ground of community in political functions'' (Henry Maine, *Ancient Law*, 1861).

''If you wish to live among the Nuer you must do so on their terms, which means that you must treat them as a kind of kinsmen and they will treat you as a kind of kinsman. Rights, privileges, and obligations are determined by kinship. Either a man is a kinsman, actually or by fiction, or he is a person to whom you have no reciprocal obligations and whom you treat as a potential enemy'' (E. Evans-Pritchard, *The Nuer*, 1940).

''In our own society [the United States], where its [kindred's] members are collectively called 'kinfolk' or 'relatives,' it includes that group of near kinsmen who may be expected to be present and participant on important ceremonial occasions, such as weddings, christenings, funerals, Thanksgiving and Christmas dinners, and 'family reunions.' Members of kindred visit and entertain one another freely, and between them marriage and pecuniary transactions for profit are ordinarily taboo. One turns first to them for aid. . . . A particular disadvantage of the kindred appears in the instances in which an individual belongs to the kindreds of two other persons and thereby becomes involved in conflicting or incompatible obligations'' (George Murdock, *Social Structure*, 1949).

''Social and political cohesion [in Tonga society] is achieved through a wide network of relationships between individuals and small kin groups rather than a structured ranking and coordination of clearly defined and permanent local or kinship units'' (J. Van Velsen, *The Politics of Kinship*, 1964).

''Ceremonial Kinship [in Portugal]. The institution of the *compadrio* (co-parenthood) constitutes a triangular relationship between the baptismal godparents and godchild on the one hand, and between the biological parents and the co-parents on the other. *Compadre* and *comadre* are . . . 'spiritual parents' of the godchild'' (Emilio Willems in Victor Christopherson, ed., *Readings in Comparative Marriage and the Family*, 1967).

''The chances of middle class separation from kin are moderately great, but

. . . this eventuality does not result in isolation from kin of orientation. On the other hand, working class migration and separation from kin, though less frequent, is apt to result in virtual isolation from all kin except parents'' (Bert Adams in M. Anderson, *The Sociology of the Family*, 1971).

''Recent historical studies show the myth of the extended family household to be just that—a myth. The nuclear family, consisting of parents living with their own children and no other adults, has been the predominant family in America since the earliest period. . . . Relationships among relatives appear to have been historically what they are now: complex patterns of companionship and help that only occasionally involve sharing bed and board . . . sociologists have been showing that contemporary families have very real kinship networks'' (Mary Bane, *Here to Stay*, 1976).

''An efficient kinship system leaves few people out in the cold and is especially protective in the two helpless phases of the life cycle, infancy and extreme age. An inefficient system produces neglected orphans and lonely old people, as well as isolation and anomie in other phases of the life cycle. Such situations are not unknown in contemporary Middletown, but they are comparatively rare'' (Theodore Caplow et al., *Middletown Families*, 1982).

KNOWLEDGE, SOCIOLOGY OF

''Am I indeed possessed of knowledge? I am not knowing'' (Confucius, *Analects*, c. 500 B.C.).

''I know only one thing: that I know nothing'' (Socrates, c. 420 B.C., in Plato, *Phaedrus*, c. 400 B.C.).

''We know nothing, for the truth is found in the depths of reality'' (Democritus, Fragments, c. 400 B.C.)

''The knowledge of things must not be derived from names. Things must be studied and investigated in themselves'' (Plato, *Cratylus*, c. 400 B.C.).

''True opinion is knowledge'' (Plato, *Theaetetus*, c. 400 B.C.).

''Knowledge is a principle of power'' (Aristotle, *Rhetoric*, c. 350 B.C.).

''All who speak about the natures of things, have in fact only their phenomena to reason from, and the value of a phenomenon is in its being natural'' (Mencius, *Book of Mencius*, c. 300 B.C.).

''Human knowledge comes from sensible objects'' (Thomas Aquinas, *Summa Theologica*, 1274).

''Knowledge is power'' (Francis Bacon, *Sacred Meditations*, 1597).

''Where there is much desire to learn, there of necessity will be much arguing, much writing, many opinions; for opinion in good men is but knowledge in the making'' (John Milton, *Areopagitica*, 1644).

''All that men can know is but limited and imperfect, like man himself'' (Giovanni Battista Vico, *On the Method of the Studies of Our Time*, 1709).

''The circle of knowledge, through which every man in his own place becomes blessed, begins immediately around him, from his own being, and from his closest relations. It extends from this beginning, and at every increase must have a reference to truth, that central point of all blessed powers'' (Johann Heinrich Pestalozzi, *Evening Hour of a Hermit*, 1780).

''There can be no doubt that all our knowledge begins with experience. For [otherwise] how should our faculty of knowledge . . . work up the raw materials of our sensible impressions into that knowledge of objects which is called experience?'' (Immanuel Kant, *Critique of Pure Reason*, 1781).

''The investigation of knowledge cannot proceed except by knowing and that is as absurd as learning to swim without going into the water'' (Georg Wilhelm Friedrich Hegel, *Encyclopedia of Philosophy*, 1817).

''Anyone who sets out . . . to hunt down final and ultimate truths . . . will bring home little, apart from platitudes and commonplaces of the sorriest kind; for example, that generally speaking man cannot live except by labor'' (Friedrich Engels, *Anti-Dühring*, 1878).

''Ideas (which themselves are but parts of our experience) become true just in so far as they help us to get into satisfactory relations with other parts of our experience'' (William James, *Pragmatism*, 1907).

''If we take on the attitude of the radical skeptic, if we occupy a point of view outside every knowledge and demand to be led back, by whatever force, into the area of knowledge, then we require something impossible, and our skepticism can never be refuted. For, every refutation must begin with a piece of knowledge shared by the disputants; on bare doubt no reasons grow. Therefore, the philosophical critique of knowledge must not be destructive in this way, if it is to lead to results. There is no *logical* argument against absolute skepticism'' (Bertrand Russell, *The Problems of Philosophy*, 1912).

''[The sociology of knowledge is] a discipline which explores the functional dependence of each intellectual standpoint on the differentiated social group reality standing behind it, which sets itself the task of retracing the evolutions of the various standpoints. . . . Social groups emerging within the social process are always in a position to project new directions of that 'intentionality,' that vital tension, which accompanies all life'' (Karl Mannheim, *Essays on the Sociology of Knowledge*, 1929).

''Knowledge is from the very beginning a co-operative process of group life, in which everyone unfolds his knowledge within the framework of a common fate, a common activity, and the overcoming of common difficulties (in which, however, each has a different share)'' (Karl Mannheim, *Ideology and Utopia*, 1929).

''We should not pretend to understand the world only by the intellect; we apprehend it just as much by feeling. Therefore the judgment of the intellect is, at least, only the half of the truth'' (Carl Jung, *Modern Man in Search of a Soul*, 1933).

''The realist assumes that our knowledge of the universals is, so to speak, the contact between the universals and the mind; we must put them in the mind, but they must also have their existence outside. And yet, many of these universals do not have an existence, in our ordinary use of that term. We imply that a thing is at some point and at some definite time when we say that it exists'' (George H. Mead, *Movements of Thought in the Nineteenth Century*, 1936, posthumous).

''When we ask whether there is a unity in science, we mean this as a question of logic, concerning the logical relationships between the terms and the laws of the various branches of science. Since it belongs to the logic of science, the question concerns scientists and logicians alike . . . the class of observable thing-predicates is a sufficient reduction basis for the whole of the language of science'' (Rudolf Carnap in O. Neurath et al., eds., *Foundations of the Unity of Science*, 1938).

''[The sociologist] is not entitled to make any judgments concerning the validity of any systems of knowledge except sociological systems'' (Florian Znaniecki, *The Social Role of the Man of Knowledge*, 1940).

''Knowledge is power'' (Navaho Indians in Clyde Kluckhohn in F. Northrop, ed., *Ideological Differences and World Order*, 1949).

''The tragedies of Aeschylus and Sophocles . . . were essentially 'the work of Athens,' and the decay of Greek tragedy the immediate result of the dissolution of the Greek *polis*'' (W. Stark, *The Sociology of Knowledge*, 1958).

''The *thing in itself* is unknowable: we can only know its appearances which are to be understood . . . as resulting from the thing in itself and from our own perceiving apparatus. Thus the appearances result from a kind of interaction between the things in themselves and ourselves. This is why one thing may appear to us in different forms, according to our different ways of perceiving it'' (Karl Popper, *The Logic of Scientific Discovery*, 1959).

''Just when men become certain they have distinguished the true path from the false, as in enlightenment theories of the progress of mind and society, a doubt begins to engulf them'' (Irving Horowitz, *Philosophy, Science and the Sociology of Knowledge*, 1961).

''The phenomenologist does not deny the existence of the outer world, but for his analytical purpose he makes up his mind to suspend belief in its existence—that is, to refrain intentionally and systematically from all judgments related directly or indirectly to the existence of the outer world'' (Alfred Schutz, *The Problem of Social Reality*, 1962).

L

LANGUAGE, SOCIOLOGY OF

"His lips are date-syrup, his tongue is a deadly dagger" (Amenemapt, *Teaching*, c. 2200 B.C.).

"Therefore is the name of it called Babel; because the Lord did there confound the language of all the earth" (Genesis 11:9).

"In language it is simply required that it convey the meaning" (Confucius, *Analects*, c. 500 B.C.).

"There are three gods, chaos and clouds and language" (Aristophanes, *Clouds*, 423 B.C.).

"Our ancestors used iota and delta very well . . . this is especially true of women, who, more than anybody else, retain ancient speech. But now, instead of iota, people use epsilon iota or eta, and, instead of delta, they use zeta, as if these were more magnificent" (Plato, *Cratylus*, c. 400 B.C.).

"The cause of learning is language" (Aristotle, *On Sense and the Sensible*, c. 350 B.C.).

"There's language in her eye, her cheek, her lip, nay, her foot speaks" (William Shakespeare, *Troilus and Cressida*, 1602).

"There are a thousand kinds of ideas which it is impossible to translate into the language of the people" (Jean Jacques Rousseau, *The Social Contract*, 1762).

"The dement of thought itself—the element of thought's living expression—language—is of a sensuous nature" (Karl Marx, *Economic and Philosophic Manuscripts*, 1844).

"[Language is] a system of *signs*, different from the things signified but able to suggest them" (William James, *Principles of Psychology*, 1890).

"The more I think of Korea and the Koreans the more I find myself concluding that language is the key, or rather the denial of a key, to the Korean character. The Korean language historically is a weaver of mind-numbing one-shot Chinese ideographs and the Koreans' own thoroughly sensible and serviceable *hangul* phonetics. Whatever the Koreans really are in psyche gets all tangled up in linguistic incompatibles" (Homer Hulbert, *The Passing of Korea*, 1906).

"[Language is] a purely human and non-instinctive method of communicating ideas, emotions, and desires by means of a system of voluntarily produced symbols'' (Edward Sapir, *Language*, 1921).

''Language does not simply symbolize a situation or object which is already there in advance; it makes possible the existence or appearance of that situation or object, for it is part of the mechanism whereby that situation or object can be created'' (George H. Mead, *Mind, Self, and Society*, 1934, posthumous).

''What justification is there for a word which is simply the opposite of some other word? A word contains its opposite in itself. . . . If you have a word like 'good,' what need is there for a word like 'bad'? 'Ungood' will do just as well . . . if you want a stronger version of 'good,' what sense is there in having a whole string of vague useless words like 'excellent' and 'splendid' and all the rest of them? 'Plusgood' covers the meaning; or 'doubleplusgood' if you want something stronger. . . . Don't you see that the whole aim of Newspeak is to narrow the range of thought? In the end we shall make thought crime literally impossible because there will be no words to express it'' (George Orwell, *Nineteen Eighty-Four*, 1949).

''On the surface, human and animal speech, in spite of the enormously greater richness and complexity of the former, are much alike. Both express emotions, possibly ideas, in sounds formed by bodily organs and understood by the hearing individual. But the difference between the so-called language of brutes and that of men is infinitely great'' (Alfred Kroeber, *The Nature of Culture*, 1952).

''We dissect nature along lines laid down by our native languages. The categories and types that we isolate from the world of phenomena we do not find there because they stare every observer in the face; on the contrary, the world is presented in a kaleidoscopic flux of impressions which has to be organized by our minds—and this means largely by the linguistic systems in our minds'' (Benjamin Whorf, *Language, Thoughts, and Reality*, 1956).

''There are words as murderous as gas chambers'' (Simone de Beauvoir, *Force of Circumstance*, 1965).

''Language is an institution, and institutions are sociocultural systems'' (Joyce Hertzler, *A Sociology of Language*, 1965).

''The methodology of kinesics is still extremely crude. At its present stage of development, kinesics . . . cannot yet be judged worthy of the appellation *kinesiology*'' (Ray Birdwhistell, *Kinesics and Context*, 1970).

''Gestures are almost always used unconsciously'' (Robert Saitz and Edward Cervenka, *Handbook of Gestures*, 1972).

''Bodily communication . . . plays a central part in human social behaviour'' (Michael Argyle, *Bodily Communication*, 1975).

''[I distinguish between linguistic issues] that appear to be within the reach of approaches and concepts that are moderately well understood—what I will call 'problems'; and others that remain as obscure to us today as when they were originally formulated—what I will call 'mysteries' '' (Noam Chomsky, *Reflections on Language*, 1975).

''Human language, being a complex and living force, changes constantly.

And this is something we must always keep in mind, especially when we are tempted to advocate a return to old linguistic forms'' (Panos Bardis, *The Future of the Greek Language in the United States*, 1976).

''Language has been perhaps the most important influence on the directions in which man has developed'' (Joseph Kess, *Psycholinguistics*, 1976).

''While there were undoubted difficulties in any policy aimed at imposing the use of national languages as the principal languages of instruction [in Africa] . . . and while it was necessary to maintain contacts with the outside world by means of an international language, the educational and cultural advantages of using those languages were such that every effort should be made to overcome those obstacles'' (UNESCO, *Education in Africa in the Light of the Lagos Conference*, 1977).

''The vocabulary of the child is enriched continually. While during the first year it consists of only 3 words, on the average, in the following years it reaches, respectively, 272, 896, and 1,540 words. In the fifth year, the child knows almost 2,200 words. . . . Children from the upper socioeconomic classes present a higher degree of linguistic development'' (Nikolaos Giannoulis and Polynices Bardis, *Instruction in the Kindergarten*, 1978).

''Words are forms of agreements. Thus one cannot give arbitrary meanings to words. These agreements are the definitions. Naturally the definitions are not absolute or constant. Even the wrong usage, if it becomes customary, can become the accepted definition'' (Masatoshi Matsushita in Professors World Peace Academy of Japan, *Challenging the Future*, 1982).

LAW, SOCIOLOGY OF

''Injustice must not win with technicalities'' (Aeschylus, *Eumenides*, 458 B.C.).

''The legislator must ordain laws wisely'' (Plato, *Laws*, c. 400 B.C.).

''It is easier to get one or a few sensible and able men to legislate and adjudge than to get many'' (Aristotle, *Rhetoric*, c. 350 B.C.).

''Let a man not do what his own sense of righteousness tells him not to do'' (Mencius, *Book of Mencius*, c. 300 B.C.).

''That man who obeys the law prescribed in the revealed texts and in the sacred tradition, gains fame in this world and after death unsurpassable bliss'' (Manu, *Laws*, c. 200 B.C.).

''Sometimes it is evil to obey the law as it stands'' (Thomas Aquinas, *Summa Theologica*, 1274).

''We must not make a scarecrow of the law'' (William Shakespeare, *Measure for Measure*, 1605).

''There are people who teach that all laws cease at war. This, however, cannot be admitted. Rather, no war should be commenced except for the assertion of the right, or be carried on except according to the measure of law and good faith. Demosthenes sensibly said that it is against those who refuse to be bound by judicial decree that war is rightly waged'' (Hugo Grotius, *On the Law of War and Peace*, 1625).

''English legislation is like an old tree, on which the legislators have incessantly grafted the strangest cuttings'' (Alexis Charles Henri Maurice Clérel de Tocqueville, *Democracy in America*, 1840).

''What perhaps is most remarkable in the legal nature of social relations is that reciprocity, the give-and-take principle, reigns supreme'' (Bronislaw Malinowski, *Crime and Custom in Savage Society*, 1926).

''Language-families originate territorially in a dominant race-stock; so do law-systems'' (John Wigmore, *Panorama of the World's Legal Systems*, 1928).

''[The supernaturalist] carries his tom-tomery into legislative lobbies and gets his tabooery into statute law. He formulates creeds and demands subscription to them by the teachers, professors, and college presidents'' (Franklin Giddings, *The Mighty Medicine*, 1929).

''[Among the Barotse of Rhodesia] large parts of the judgments read like sermons, for they are all lectures on the theme 'your station and its duties.' The standards publicly stated for the parties are the norms involved in their social positions and relationships. . . . The essence of the judicial process is to state these norms to the world and to assess against them the behaviour of the parties'' (M. Gluckman, *The Judicial Process Among the Barotse of Northern Rhodesia*, 1954).

''Civilization . . . cannot exist under a regime of uninhibited absolutism, contemptuous of law'' (Palmer Edmunds, *Law and Civilization*, 1959).

''It was a long time before anybody made any law. For ages man's conduct was governed by nothing more than the accumulated experience of his forefathers'' (René Wormser, *The Story of the Law and the Men Who Made It*, 1962).

''Unless a clearly defined, internationally organized, legal regime is established in the early stages of space exploration, the crystallization of universal practices infringing upon the rights of the several nations of the world . . . may have gone too far'' (Andrew Haley, *Space Law and Government*, 1963).

''As our society has grown increasingly complex, the legal tools for social control have indeed increased beyond the possible total comprehension of a single individual. And the lawyers, like the scientists, have increasingly, although on a much smaller scale, met the problem of specialization within large law firms'' (Erwin Smigel, *The Wall Street Lawyer*, 1964).

''Law provides the framework of formal norms within which complex societies function'' (Richard Schwartz and Jerome Skolnick, eds., *Society and the Legal Order*, 1970).

''The freedom protected by the system of law is the freedom of those who can afford it. The law serves their interests, but they are not 'society'; they are one element of society. They may in some complex societies even be a majority (though this is very rare), but the myth that the law serves the interests of 'society' misrepresents the facts'' (William Chambliss and Robert Seidman, *Law, Order and Power*, 1971).

''Law is an important and ubiquitous presence in society. So many lives are touched by it each year. . . . The United States may be unusually litigious; yet, in every major country, there is a great mass of legal process'' (Lawrence Friedman, *Law and Society*, 1977).

''The . . . subdivision of criminology known as the sociology of law consists at present of four parts: (1) sociology of civil law, (2) sociology of criminal law, (3) sociological jurisprudence, and (4) anthropology of law'' (Robert Rich, *The Sociology of Law*, 1978).

''The sociology of law is in a state of ferment'' (William Evan, ed., *The Sociology of Law*, 1980).

''Until recently, in English law faculties, there has rarely been any reference to the 'law in context,' to the relationships of law to society'' (Adam Podgórecki and Christopher Whelan, eds., *Sociological Approaches to Law*, 1981).

LEADERSHIP

''It is not good to have many rulers. Let there be one ruler, one king'' (Homer, *Iliad*, c. 750 B.C.).

''A leader is best when people barely know that he exists, not so good when people obey and acclaim him, worst when they despise him. . . . But of a good leader, who talks little when his work is done, his aim fulfilled, they will all say: 'We did this ourselves' '' (Lao-tse, *Teaching of Tao*, c. 550 B.C.).

''By his generosity he [the leader] won all. By his sincerity, he made the people repose trust in him. By his earnest activity, his achievements were great. By his justice, all were delighted'' (Confucius, *Analects*, c. 500 B.C.).

''It will be realized that there are some natures who must study philosophy and become leaders of the state'' (Plato, *Republic*, c. 400 B.C.).

''If a person is superior to all others in a community in virtue and the ability for active life, it is proper to follow him and right to obey him'' (Aristotle, *Politics*, c. 350 B.C.).

''Let the cock watch for the dawn, let the cat watch for the rats, and the sovereign need do nothing at all'' (Han Fei Tzu, *Complete Works*, c. 250 B.C.).

''The man who leads efficiently must have obeyed others in the past, and he who obeys dutifully is worthy of becoming a leader'' (Cicero, *Laws*, c. 50 B.C.).

''[The leader] should appear pious, faithful, humane, religious, and sincere, and should indeed be all of these, but should ever be ready, if need be, to change to the contrary. . . . A prince, and especially a new prince, cannot observe all those qualities for which men are esteemed good. If it be necessary to maintain the state, he must be ready to violate faith, charity, humanity, and religion. However, he must have a mind ready to veer with every wind and variation of Fortune'' (Niccolò Machiavelli, *The Prince*, 1513).

''We cannot all be masters, nor all masters cannot be truly followed'' (William Shakespeare, *Othello*, 1605).

''All people are equally in need of leadership'' (Jean Jacques Rousseau, *The Social Contract*, 1762).

''The ablest men in the United States are rarely placed at the head of affairs'' (Alexis Charles Henri Maurice Clérel de Tocqueville, *Democracy in America*, 1840).

''A man is a capitalist, not because he is a leader of industry, but, on the contrary, he is a leader of industry because he is a capitalist'' (Karl Marx, *Das Kapital*, 1879).

''The term 'charisma' will be applied to a certain quality of an individual personality, by virtue of which he is set apart from ordinary men and treated as endowed with supernatural, superhuman, or at least specifically exceptional powers or qualities . . . it will be necessary to treat a variety of different types as being endowed with charisma in this sense. It includes the state of a 'berserker' whose spells of maniac passion have, apparently wrongly, sometimes been attributed to the use of drugs. . . . It includes the 'shaman,' the kind of magician who in the pure type is subject to epileptoid seizures as a means of falling into trances. Another type is that of Joseph Smith, the founder of Mormonism. . . . In its pure form charismatic authority has a character specifically foreign to everyday routine structures. The social relationships directly involved are strictly personal, based on the validity and practice of charismatic personal qualities'' (Max Weber, *The Theory of Social and Economic Organization*, 1922, posthumously).

''Charismatic authority, involving the acceptance of a ruler because of his singular personal attributes, was held to disrupt the process of rationalization when existing routines proved inadequate'' (Alvin Gouldner in Robert Merton et al., eds., *Reader in Bureaucracy*, 1952).

''The leading men in each of the three domains of power—the warlords, the corporation chieftains, and the political directorate—tend to come together to form the power elite of America'' (C. W. Mills, *The Power Elite*, 1956).

''Even when force is employed, there is always some degree of popular approval. In fact, no state can survive if the leader's authority isn't based—at least to some extent—on the people's will, customs, beliefs, and convictions . . . even Cesare Borgia, the man who was an accomplished murderer at the age of twenty-five, the man who believed in limitless and absolute force, the man who was Machiavelli's ideal despot . . . failed at the age of thirty-one! '' (Panos Bardis, *Ivan and Artemis*, 1957).

''Out of several hundred persons named from all sources, between one hundred and two hundred were consistently chosen as top leaders and considered by all informants to be of national policy-making stature'' (Floyd Hunter, *Top Leadership, U.S.A.*, 1959).

''Mao wished to destroy a party linking a well-defined structure, the principle of working-class leadership and the role of technical expertise. . . . By attaining even partial success he has broken the concentration of power at the top and in the hands of bureaucratically oriented cadres'' (J. Lewis, *Party Leadership and Revolution in China*, 1970).

''An inseparable feature of the style of leadership is courtesy, friendliness, and tact. Instructions issued in a firm but courteous manner always lead to better results than those issued rudely'' (D. Kaidalov and E. Suimenko, Current Problems in the Sociology of Work, 1974).

''A multiplicity of themes is likely to appear in any one leadership study. Leadership itself may be the independent, dependent, on intervening variable'' (Bernard Bass, *Stogdill's Handbook of Leadership*, 1981).

''In totalitarian circumstances the only interest which really counts is that of the established political leadership'' (Alexander Shtromas, *Political Change and Social Development*, 1981).

''We are all worms. But I do believe I am a glowworm'' (Winston Churchill in Ted Morgan, *Churchill*, 1982).

''A leader is *one who has followers*. . . . Leadership and management are not necessarily the same thing. While managers ideally should have leadership ability, and vice versa, this is in reality often not the case. And managers are certainly not leaders (able to get others to follow them) by definition or job title. A manager can make excellent plans, get all of the resources allocated and organized, and implement effective control systems—and still not inspire others to want to follow'' (Lin Bothwell, *The Art of Leadership*, 1983).

LEISURE

''The difference between slaves and freemen is found in leisure, which a freeman is always able to command'' (Plato, *Theaetetus*, c. 400 B.C.).

''Nature demands that we be both properly employed and able to enjoy leisure with dignity'' (Aristotle, *Politics*, c. 350 B.C.).

''In what manner . . . is this precious time expended by those of no mental cultivation? . . . We shall often see them just simply annihilating those portions of time. They will for an hour, or for hours together . . . sit on a bench, or lie down on a bank or hillock . . . yielded up to utter vacancy and torpor . . . practising some impertinence, or uttering some jeering scurrility, at the expense of persons going by'' (John Foster, *An Essay on the Evils of Popular Ignorance*, 1821).

''The relation of football to physical culture is much the same as that of the bullfight to agriculture'' (Thorstein Veblen, *The Theory of the Leisure Class*, 1899).

''There is no country and no people, I think, who can look forward to the age of leisure and of abundance without a dread. It is a fearful problem for the ordinary person, with no special talents, to occupy himself, especially if he no longer has roots in the soil or in custom or in the beloved conventions of a traditional society'' (John M. Keynes, *Essays in Persuasion*, 1931).

''Leisure, instead of being a vacuum representing a break with society, is literally stuffed with technical mechanisms of compensation and integrations. . . . [Leisure] is a mechanized time . . . and leaves man no more free than labor itself'' (Jacques Ellul, *The Technological Society*, 1967).

''The *humanistic* model of leisure sees it as an end in itself, illustrated by the contemporary Chinese and the ancient Greeks. . . . The *therapeutic* model of leisure sees it as a means, an instrument, a control. . . . The *quantitative* model of leisure views it as the time left over when the work necessary for maintaining life is finished. . . . The *institutional* conception of leisure seeks to distinguish it from such behavior and value patterns as the religious, marital, educational, or political. . . . The *epistemological* conception of leisure relates activities and meanings to the assumptive, analytic, and aesthetic views of the world . . . the *sociological* conception, following the lead of Max Weber, sees leisure as a construct with such elements as an antithesis to the work of the participant, a perception of the activity as voluntary or free, a pleasant expectation and recollection, a full range of possibilities from withdrawal in sleep or drink to highly creative tasks'' (Max Kaplan, *Leisure*, 1975).

''When the first Olympiad took place in the year 776 B.C., the Hellenic world had already moulded . . . a cohesion of fascinating legends and mythical traditions. . . . The highest ideal was . . . 'Always be the best and excel over others so as not to disgrace the race of your fathers.' . . . But what was of the greatest importance, both as regards those very ancient contests which were also of a religious nature . . . was mainly that these Panhellenic contests were the means of declaring, above all, *the integrity of the national conscience and the spiritual unity of the Hellenes*. Athletes from all the national centres of Hellenism . . . took part'' (Takis Papayannopoulos, *The Olympic Idea and the Voice of Peace*, 1980).

''Leisure lack is widespread in our society as well as the rest of the world. It besets the young and the old . . . the poor and the rich, and members of the majority and all the different minorities. . . . What is most threatening is that it is on the increase'' (John Neulinger, *To Leisure*, 1981).

''The act of participating in sports either as a player or as a spectator is a collective striving to grasp life as a totality, to make sense out of the fragmented, alienating nature of the differentiation and specialization that are the attributes of modernity—an organic solidarity'' (Phillip Bosserman in Robert Rankin, ed., *Social Approaches to Sport*, 1982).

''Sport takes place in social settings and has a profound influence on the social life of large numbers of Americans of all ages'' (D. Eitzen and George Sage, *Sociology of American Sport*, 1982).

LITERATURE, SOCIOLOGY OF

''Is it, then, only the poets that we must censor and force to include in their poems the image of the good character or else not to write poetry among us, or must we also censor other craftsmen and prevent them from presenting the evil character, the licentious, the illiberal, the ugly?'' (Plato, *Republic*, c. 400 B.C.).

''Literature flourishes best when it is half a trade and half an art'' (William Inge, *Outspoken Essays*, 1922).

''What used to be the quest for individual wisdom, an attempt at self-knowledge, is now the search for aggregate wisdom. In literature, our societies seem, as a rule, to lack self-knowledge'' (Robert Escarpit, *Sociology of Literature*, 1965).

''Sociology of literature is a proper name for the study of the origin, history, and constitution of literary society, but it does not by any means circumscribe all the elements from which it draws. For literary sociology can explain literature only with the assistance of related disciplines such as economics, psychology, history and philosophy'' (Ernest Pick in Robert Escarpit, *Sociology of Literature*, 1965).

''The sociological study of literature has not developed, either in terms of its theory or in its methods of analysis, but has remained in some kind of limbo, suspended between literature as literature and sociology as social science'' (Diana Laurenson and Alan Swingewood, *The Sociology of Literature*, 1972).

''One of the functions of science fiction is to serve as an early warning system. In fact, the very act of description may prevent some features, by a kind of exclusion principle. Far from predicting the future, science fiction often exorcises it. At the very least, it makes us ask ourselves: What kind of future do we really want? No other type of literature poses such fundamental questions, at any rate explicitly'' (Arthur Clarke in A. Bolger, ed., *The Telephone's First Century and Beyond*, 1977).

''The perceptions and observations of a creative writer are more vivid, direct and authentic in a study and analysis of society than the methods used normally in social science research. . . . Post-1950 writing in Hindi widely reflects a social change in various ways: basically it expresses a feeling of constant disillusionment of the modern man. . . . [The contemporary writer is] a realist who moves round the society and expresses himself among the struggling masses. It is here that his deep feelings are aroused and help to make him . . . a writer in participation'' (Raghuvir Sinha, *Social Change in Contemporary Literature*, 1979).

''Coming back to the arts and literature, their subsequent forms have been closely connected with social development: with the growing size of societies, the emergence of literacy, differing sources of patronage, etc.'' (Ronald Fletcher, *Sociology*, 1981).

''The world of literature and the world of criminology look at the same social realities and grapple with similar problems about the human being and the human condition. Yet these two worlds are hardly on speaking terms with each other'' (Edward Sagarin, *Raskolnikov and Others*, 1981).

''Dostoyevsky is the pioneer of the Russian literature of the city and its social problems. . . . He focused on the sufferings of the city's small and impoverished people oppressed by capitalism, and created the modern 'Divine Comedy' of crime, poverty, tragedy, and fear. In his works he analyzes the modern city dweller's sickly neurosis with an intensity and thoroughness that surprises even professional psychologists and psychiatrists'' (Nobori Shomu and Akamatsu Katsumaro, *The Russian Impact on Japan*, 1981).

LOVE

''Let him kiss me with the kisses of his mouth: for thy love is better than wine'' (Song of Solomon 1:2).

''Brilliant-throned, immortal Aphrodite. . . . O come to me again, release me from this agony, do whatever my heart desires'' (Sappho, *Hymn to Aphrodite*, c. 600 B.C.).

[Buddha's hymn to love, equivalent to Saint Paul's I Corinthians 13.] ''An all-embracing love for all the universe in all its heights and depths and breadth, unstinted love, unmarred by hate within, not rousing enmity'' (Buddha, *Collection of Sermons*, c. 500 B.C.).

''It is only the truly virtuous man that can love. . . . To love a man means to wish him to live'' (Confucius, *Analects*, c. 500 B.C.).

''Love, resistless, unconquered in battle'' (Sophocles, *Antigone*, 441 B.C.).

''From love no injury must come, but advantage to both parties'' (Plato, *Phaedrus*, c. 400 B.C.).

''In love, to have one's affection returned is preferable to coitus. Accordingly, love is closer to friendship than to having coitus'' (Aristotle, *Prior Analysis*, c. 350 B.C.).

''Love conquers all, and we must submit to love'' (Vergil, *Aeneid*, 19 B.C.).

''Though I speak with the tongues of men and of angels, and have no charity [*agape*: love], I am become as sounding brass, or a tinkling cymbal'' (I Corinthians 13:1).

''Who ever loved, that loved not at first sight?'' (William Shakespeare, *As You Like It*, 1600).

''In general, it may be affirmed that there is no such passion in human minds as the love of mankind, merely as such, independent of personal qualities, of services, or of relation to oneself'' (David Hume, *A Treatise of Human Nature*, 1740).

''I love thee to the level of every day's most quiet need, by sun and candle-light'' (Elizabeth Browning, *Sonnets from the Portuguese*, 1850).

''Egoism is the feeling which demands for self an increase of enjoyment and diminution of discomfort. Altruism is that which demands these results for others'' (Lester Ward, *Dynamic Sociology*, 1883).

''Not to love before one gains full knowledge of the thing loved presupposes a delay which is harmful. When one finally reaches cognition, he neither loves nor hates properly; one remains beyond love and hatred. One has investigated instead of having loved'' (Sigmund Freud, *Leonardo da Vinci*, 1910).

''[In modern Africa] the making of love-philtres is a very common occupation of the witch-doctor, to whom both men and women apply for means whereby they may enjoy the love of some particular person'' (E. Budge, *Osiris*, 1911).

''[Altruism occurs when a person] solves for another a painful situation which the latter is incapable of solving for himself [or when people] cooperate for a common objective purpose'' (Florian Znaniecki, *Social Actions*, 1936).

''The old men of China did not succeed in eliminating love from the life of the young women. . . . Poor and middle-class families could not afford to keep men and women in separate quarters'' (Olga Lang, *Chinese Family and Society*, 1946).

''Immature love says: 'I love you because I need you.' Mature love says: 'I need you because I love you.' . . . There is hardly any activity, any enterprise, which is started with such tremendous hopes and expectations, and yet which fails so regularly, as love'' (Erich Fromm, *The Art of Loving*, 1956).

''[Conjugal love] grows as the marriage progresses, thrives on companionship, common experiences, and the number of happy episodes which are scattered throughout a rich marriage'' (Evelyn Duvall and Reuben Hill, *Being Married*, 1960).

''Love is of very great importance to the Gypsies, who are fundamentally complete romantics. And if love somewhat defies tradition, it is the oversight most easily forgiven. But being romantics, Gypsies are nonetheless quick-blooded, and love needs to be strictly governed by laws'' (Jean-Paul Clébert, *The Gypsies*, 1961).

''American family sociologists [have neglected the study of conjugal love because] (a) love has been considered a subjective, vague, elusive feeling which defies operationalization and measurement; (b) it has been treated as a *constant* by American social scientists, since Americans are presumed to marry for love and stay in love until death or divorce; (c) male family sociologists have considered love a 'soft feminine' variable that cannot be treated like 'hard' variables. [In Ghana] love and sex *outside* marriage are becoming institutionalized . . . there is . . . a decreasing emphasis among educated young men upon the importance of love *within* the marital relationship'' (Christine Oppong in Mark Cook and Glenn Wilson, eds., *Love and Attraction*, 1979).

''Love is the primary reason people give for marrying and the major factor they cite as contributing to personal happiness. . . . Americans, Canadians, and Britons [give six kinds of love]: *Eros*: love of beauty. . . . *Ludis*: playful love. . . . *Storge*: companionate love. . . . *Mania*: obsessive love. . . . *Pragma*: realistic love. . . . *Agape*: altruistic love'' (Gilbert Nass and Gerald McDonald, *Marriage and the Family*, 1982).

M

MAGIC, SOCIOLOGY OF

"If a man has charged a man with sorcery and then has not proved it against him, he who is charged with the sorcery shall go to the holy river; he shall leap into the holy river and, if the holy river overwhelms him, his accuser shall take and keep his house; if the holy river proves that man clear of the offense and he comes back safe, he who has charged him with sorcery shall be put to death; he who leapt into the holy river shall take and keep the house of the accuser" (Hammurabi, *Code*, c. 1750 B.C.).

"There shall not be found among you any one that maketh his son or his daughter to pass through the fire, or that useth divination, or an observer of times, or an enchanter, or a witch" (Deuteronomy 18:10).

"Fortune-tellers . . . he should know to be thorns in the side of his people" (Manu, *Laws*, c. 200 B.C.).

"Away with your astrology! The planets have no influence over Israel" (Talmud: Sabbath 156a).

"No operation of witchcraft has a permanent effect among us. And this is the proof thereof: For if it were so, it would be effected by the operation of demons. But to maintain that the devil has power to change human bodies or to do them permanent harm does not seem in accordance with the teaching of the Church. For in this way they could destroy the whole world" (Heinrich Kramer and James Sprenger, *Malleus Maleficarum*, 1486).

"A sorcerer is he who, by Diabolical means, has a full intention of achieving his own goals" (Jean Bodin, *Demonomania of Sorcerers*, 1580).

"Garden magic . . . is in the Trobriands a public and official service. It is performed by the garden magician . . . for the benefit of the community . . . among the forces and beliefs which bear upon and regulate gardening, magic is the most important, apart, of course, from the practical work. . . . To each village community this magic . . . is a very precious possession and a symbol of its social integrity as well as of its standing in the tribal hierarchy" (Bronislaw Malinowski, *Coral Gardens and Their Magic*, 1935).

"Magic suggests aid from sources lying in the unseen and in the unknown" (C. Loomis, *White Magic*, 1948).

''Commerce between human beings and evil spirits . . . is the very core and kernel of Witchcraft'' (Montague Summers, *The History of Witchcraft and Demonology*, 1956).

''The problem of survival means in the first place that man must try to bend the forces of nature to his own will. Before this was done in ways that we could now describe as scientific, man practised magic. The underlying general notion is the same in the two cases. For magic is an attempt to obtain specific results on the basis of certain rigidly defined rites. It is based on a recognition of the principle of causality, that given the same antecedent conditions, the same results will follow. Magic is thus proto-science'' (Bertrand Russell, *Wisdom of the West*, 1959).

''Plato's spiritual doctrine, borrowed from memories of his initiation at the hands of the Magi, had suffered, like most other things, from the disintegrating effects of political revolutions'' (Paul Christian, *A History and Practice of Magic*, 1963).

''Not all disturbances of social relations arise from breaches of rules of right conduct. A marked characteristic of tribal society is that natural misfortunes are ascribed to evil wishes of witches or sorcerers, to the anger of spirits affronted by neglect of themselves . . . and to rightful curses by appropriate persons'' (M. Gluckman, *The Ideas of Barotse Jurisprudence*, 1965).

''Both Increase and Cotton Mather were impressed by the inability of science to explain the phenomena they studied. To them, science left the ultimate mysteries untouched. Lacking a scientific explanation for many baffling events in human affairs, they were driven to the conviction that demons were constantly at work among men'' (John Miller, *This New Man, The American*, 1974).

''Magic is as old as man. It is found as far back as evidence of human existence runs and has influenced religion, art, agriculture, industry, science, government and social institutions. The western tradition of magic was born in the Roman world. . . . Magic is an attempt to exert power through actions which are believed to have a direct and automatic influence on man, nature and the divine'' (Richard Cavendish, *A History of Magic*, 1977).

MARRIAGE

''Have they not sped? have they not divided the prey; to every man a damsel or two'' (Judges 5:30).

''Every man must contract a marriage that is not most pleasing to himself, but most beneficial to the state'' (Plato, *Laws*, c. 400 B.C.).

''The right age for marriage is 18 for a woman and about 37 for a man'' (Aristotle, *Politics*, c. 350 B.C.).

''In marrying a wife, how ought a man to proceed? He must inform his parents'' (Mencius, *Book of Mencius*, c. 300 B.C.).

''A husband must be constantly worshipped as a god by a faithful wife'' (Manu, *Laws*, c. 200 B.C.).

''When Socrates [c. 420 B.C.] was asked whether it was better to marry or not, he answered: 'Whichever you do, you will regret it' '' (Diogenes Laertius, *Socrates*, c. 250).

''In marriage woman is not so inferior to man that she ought not share his authority. Husbands act ill when they make servants of their wives'' (Erasmus, *The Institution of Christian Marriage*, 1526).

''A young man married is a man that's marred'' (William Shakespeare, *All's Well That Ends Well*, 1603).

''Women in hot climates are marriageable at eight, nine, or ten years of age; thus, in those countries, infancy and marriage generally go together. They are old at twenty; their reason therefore never accompanies their beauty'' (Charles de Secondat Montesquieu, *The Spirit of the Laws*, 1748).

''Nor have the Americans ever supposed that one consequence of democratic principles is the subversion of marital power, or the confusion of the natural authorities in families'' (Alexis Charles Henri Maurice Clérel de Tocqueville, *Democracy in America*, 1840).

''Bourgeois marriage is in reality a system of wives in common'' (Karl Marx and Friedrich Engels, *Communist Manifesto*, 1847).

''Marriage has always been an elastic and variable usage, as it now is. Each pair, or other marital combination, has always chosen its own 'ways' of living within the limits set by the mores. In fact the use of language reflects the vagueness of marriage, for we use the word 'marriage' for wedding, nuptials, or matrimony. . . . No rules or laws can control it. They only affect the condition against which the individuals react. No laws can do more than specify ways of entering into wedlock, and the rights and duties which the society will enforce'' (William Sumner, *Folkways*, 1907).

''[A] social atmosphere frosty toward foolish and frivolous ideals of marriage [will strengthen the family]'' (Edward Ross, *Principles of Sociology*, 1920).

''The companionship concept of marriage (with its emphasis upon affection, comradeship, democracy, and happiness of members of the family) is replacing the old-time notion of [institutional] marriage as a relation stressing respect, obedience, authority, and duty. This new concept has arisen as the result of many factors, including the loss of economic and other functions by the family, the growth of the urban way of life, the rising status of women, the continued decline in parental control of children's marriage, and the application of democracy in marital and familial relations'' (Ernest Burgess and Harvey Locke, *The Family*, 1945).

''[In Greece] the man's [wedding] ring is of gold and symbolizes the sun, whereas the woman's ring is of silver and symbolizes the moon'' (Panos Bardis in Irwin Sanders, *Rainbow in the Rock*, 1962).

''The marriage laws of Ancient Egypt were never formulated and knowledge of them can be obtained only by working out the marriages and genealogies'' (Margaret Murray, *The Splendor That Was Egypt*, 1963).

''Every society controls to some extent who may mate with whom'' (William Goode, *The Family*, 1964).

''Taking a child bride as a form of marriage was still common in many rural sections throughout China proper in the early years of Communist rule. . . . A very young girl, sometimes even an infant, was purchased by a poor family which could raise her along with the young son. When they both reached marriageable age, they were married with a simple ceremony'' (C. Yang, *Chinese Communist Society*, 1965).

''The future of marriage is as assured as any social form can be. . . . For men and women will continue to want intimacy, they will continue to want to celebrate their mutuality, to experience the mystic unity which once led the church to consider marriage a sacrament'' (Jessie Bernard, *The Future of Marriage*, 1972).

''[In India] the students will not marry against the wishes of their parents'' (Sheo Lal and Umed Nahar, *Higher Education*, 1978).

''In no human society is marriage simply the private business of the spouses'' (Pierre van den Berghe, *Human Family Systems*, 1979).

''Loneliness is the most often cited consequence of singleness'' (J. Barkas, *Single in America*, 1980).

''Historically in all cultures . . . marriage unions, have been very much controlled in one way or another by the parents of the bride and groom. Exceptions have always existed, as when living parents were lacking or could not prevail, but these were seldom the mode until modern times. . . . [In India] the upper caste groups monopolize this method [matrimonial advertisements] of mate selection'' (Carle Zimmerman and Mitra Das in Harald Niemeyer, *Social Relations Network*, 1980).

''Marriage is not necessarily connected with either romantic love or the pair-bond. The instinct that more directly underlies it is that of sequestering a mate and protecting her from other males so that the husband can be sure of his paternity'' (Glenn Wilson, *Love and Instinct*, 1981).

MARRIAGE, MIXED

''Samson went down to Timnath, and saw a woman in Timnath of the daughters of the Philistines. And he came up, and told his father and his mother, and said, I have seen a woman in Timnath of the daughters of the Philistines: now therefore get her for me to wife. Then his father and his mother said unto him, Is there never a woman among the daughters of thy brethren, or among all my people, that thou goest to take a wife of the uncircumcised Philistines?'' (Judges 14:1–3).

''These restrictions [on social intercourse due to status] may confine normal marriages to within the status circle and may lead to complete endogamous closure'' (Max Weber, *Economy and Society*, 1922, posthumously).

''Minority groups that advocate the letting down of barriers in fraternities and sororities must accept the responsibility for an increase in intermarriage that follows naturally therefrom'' (Albert Gordon, *Intermarriage*, 1964).

''Quite generally the marriage patterns of any American ethnic group are a reliable guide to the speed with which such a group is fading into the larger American society'' (Frank Mittelbach et al., *Intermarriage of Mexican-Americans*, 1966).

''The more significant to a society are the differences between two categories of people, the less will they intermarry'' (J. Udry, *The Social Context of Marriage*, 1966).

''For most ethnic groups in the United States and elsewhere, the incidence of exogamous marriages has been a reliable guide to the extent and speed of assimilation. . . . Conversely, endogamy can be viewed as a reflection of the rigidity of boundaries around the subpopulation'' (Leo Grebler et al., *The Mexican American People*, 1970).

''Those who are interested in studying American ethnic groups often say that the ethnic groups vanish after intermarriage, but there is no evidence to support such an assertion. The child of a Polish mother and an Italian father may choose to define himself as Polish or Italian or Italian-Polish or even only as American, but he is not likely to think of himself as Anglo-Saxon'' (Andrew Greeley, *Ethnicity in the United States*, 1974).

MEDICAL SOCIOLOGY

''The sage does not wait for men to become ill before caring for them. He guides them when they are in good health'' (Huang Ti, *The Theory of Internal Disease*, 2650 B.C.).

''If a physician operate on a man for a severe wound with a bronze lancet and cause the man's death; or open an abscess of a man with a bronze lancet and destroy the man's eye, they shall cut off his fingers'' (Hammurabi, *Code*, c. 1750 B.C.).

''The child . . . was very sick. David therefore besought God for the child; and David fasted, and went in, and lay all night upon the earth'' (II Samuel 12:15–16).

''Just as in all other arts the workers vary much in both skill and knowledge, so also do physicians'' (Hippocrates, *Ancient Medicine*, c. 420 B.C.).

''There is a theory according to which one cannot treat the head alone . . . good physicians, when a patient comes with pain in the eyes, tell him that it is impossible to treat only the eyes, but that it is necessary to treat the head, also, if the eyes are to get well; and if a physician believes that he can treat the head without considering the entire body, he is very foolish'' (Plato, *Charmides*, c. 400 B.C.).

''Some cures are worse than the disease'' (Publilius Syrus, *Maxims*, c. 50 B.C.).

''The rationalists also tell us to consider customs, occupations, and the physiological conditions for each patient, since all of them together indicate the most effective treatment'' (Galen, *On Medical Sects*, c. 150).

''The diversity of countries and dwellings . . . necessarily predisposes bodies to diseases differently'' (Rhazes, *Foundations of Medicine*, c. 900).

''Moderation in food as to both quantity and quality is part of the art of medicine'' (Thomas Aquinas, *Summa Theologica*, 1274).

''If you look at almost any literature before the latter part of the nineteenth century, you find that a hospital is popularly regarded as much the same thing as a prison, and an old-fashioned, dungeon-like prison at that. A hospital is a place of filth, torture and death, a sort of ante-chamber to the tomb. No one who was not more or less destitute would have thought of going into such a place for treatment'' (George Orwell, *How the Poor Die*, 1950).

''Further improvements in the environment, reductions in self-imposed risk, and a greater knowledge of human biology are necessary if more Canadians are to live a full, happy, long and illness-free life'' (M. Laconde, *A New Perspective on the Health of Canadians*, 1974).

''Illness, illness behavior, and reactions to the ill are aspects of an adaptive social process in which participants are often actively striving to meet their social roles and responsibilities, to control their environment, and to make their everyday circumstances less uncertain and, therefore, more tolerable and predictable'' (David Mechanic, *Medical Sociology*, 1978).

''The social sciences have been underemphasized in medical education in favor of the biological and physical sciences'' (John Knowles in Howard Freeman et al., eds., *Handbook of Medical Sociology*, 1979).

''In the actual behavioural situations, in departure from the formally prescribed conduct . . . the social and ethnical values set up by doctors and nurses govern the larger activities of the hospital in spirit as far as the supplementary functions are concerned'' (R. Venkataratnam, *Medical Sociology in an Indian Setting*, 1979).

''For the longest part of their history professional codes have been paternalistically nonegalitarian'' (Bernard Barber, *Informed Consent in Medical Therapy and Research*, 1980).

''Primitive medicine is spared the conflicts which in modern times have called psychosomatic medicine into being. Primitives do not in general make a distinction between organic, functional, and mental diseases. For them there is only disease and its treatment. . . . This holistic or unitary character is one of the outstanding traits of primitive medicine. Diagnostics is at the same time therapeutics, organic treatment is used in mental disease, and the mental approach is applied to organic disease'' (Erwin Ackerknecht, *A Short History of Medicine*, 1982).

''Medical care and cure has become big business, with the inevitable development of interest groups, lobbies, political pressures, and deviance'' (Emily Mumford, *Medical Sociology*, 1983).

METHODOLOGY

''Those . . . who aspire not to guess and divine, but to discover and know, who propose not to devise mimic and fabulous worlds of their own, but to examine and dissect the nature of this very world itself, must go to facts themselves for everything'' (Francis Bacon, *The Great Instauration*, c. 1600).

''I frame no hypotheses . . . it is enough that gravity does really exist and act according to the laws which we have explained'' (Isaac Newton, *Principia*, 1687).

''Nothing can be more ludicrous than the sort of parodies on experimental reasoning which one is accustomed to meet with, not in popular discussion only, but in grave treatises, when the affairs of nations are the theme. . . . Whoever makes use of an argument of this kind, not intending to deceive, should be sent back to learn the elements of some one of the more easy physical sciences'' (John S. Mill, *A System of Logic*, 1843).

''The social statistics of Germany and the rest of Continental Western Europe are, by comparison with those of England, wretchedly compiled. But they raise the veil just enough to let us catch a glimpse of the Medusa head behind it'' (Karl Marx, *Das Kapital*, 1879).

''[Life-histories are] the perfect type of sociological material. . . . We shall presently follow the life-history of an individual who, living amidst this process of change, finds in his environment no place for himself, because his fundamental attitudes correspond entirely to the old type of social organization whereas by his social status he no longer belongs to this organization and is thrown without any permanent guidance into various new conditions to which he can adapt himself always only partially and imperfectly'' (William Thomas and Florian Znaciecki, *The Polish Peasant in Europe and America*, 1920).

''It is only quantity we can measure, but it is only quality we can experience . . . the range of the measurable is not the range of the knowable. . . . [Science that only measures is] a means to power, not to understanding'' (Robert MacIver, *The Elements of Social Science*, 1921).

''The first thing that students in sociology need to learn is to observe and record their own observations: to read, and then to select and record the materials which are the fruits of their readings; to organize and use, in short, their own experience'' (Robert Park and Ernest Burgess, *Introduction to the Science of Sociology*, 1921).

''Relations of toleration, the reactions of conflict, and the reactions of adjustment are notoriously contingent upon forms of association, and these contingencies in a great number of instances admit of quantitative determination'' (Franklin Giddings, *The Scientific Study of Human Society*, 1924).

''It is a good plan in any study to observe for a while carefully but with no definite purpose'' (Charles Cooley, *Life and the Student*, 1927).

''[We must stress] scientific imagination in methods of research. . . . [Imagination is] the basis of all culture, of religion, of good citizenship'' (Charles Ellwood, *Man's Social Destiny in the Light of Science*, 1929).

''The individual life history is only a component in a series of . . . life histories'' (Karl Mannheim, *Ideology and Utopia*, 1929).

''Of all recognized sources of information, oral 'evidence' . . . has proved to be the least profitable. Considering the time spent in listening to it, or even in rapidly reading and analysing these interminable questions and answers—still more, the money spent over them—the yield of fact is absurdly small'' (Sidney and Beatrice Webb, *Methods of Social Study*, 1932).

''Observation and experiment are subject to a very popular myth. The knower is seen as a kind of conqueror, like Julius Caesar winning his battles according to the formula 'I came, I saw, I conquered.' A person wants to know something, so he makes the observation or experiment and then he knows. Even research workers who have won many a scientific battle may believe this naive story when looking at their own work in retrospect'' (L. Fleck, *Origin and Development of Scientific Data*, 1935).

''At a time like the present, when experience forces us to seek a newer and more solid foundation, the physicist cannot simply surrender to the philosopher the critical contemplation of the theoretical foundations; for, he himself knows best'' (Albert Einstein, *Out of My Later Years*, 1936).

''When scientific observation begins to transcend common sense, and becomes to a degree methodologically sophisticated there emerge explicit schemata which may be called descriptive frames of reference . . . descriptive frames of reference in this sense are fundamental to all science'' (Talcott Parsons, *The Structure of Social Action*, 1937).

''Research without an actively selective point of view becomes the dirty bag of an idiot, filled with bits of pebbles, straws, feathers, and other random hoardings'' (Robert Lynd, *Knowledge for What?*, 1939).

''The fundamental unit of study for sociology is the region'' (Radhakamal Mukerjee, *Social Ecology*, 1945).

''[Regionalism is] the study and planning of each region with special reference to the integration of all regions into the societal whole. . . . [The region is] the smallest unit for study that combines all the factors of time, geography, and folk behavior essential to complete analysis'' (Howard Odum, *Understanding Society*, 1947).

''In applying the humanistic coefficient, an inductive student of culture does not accept the doctrine that his own active experience constitutes the main and the most reliable source of knowledge about the data which he experiences'' (Florian Znaniecki, *Cultural Sciences*, 1952).

''This cult [stresses] mechanical test . . . statistical operations . . . 'mathematical models of robots,' and pseudo-experimental studies of mechanical man and his 'mindless mind,' 'emotionless emotions,' 'will-less will' . . . the unhesitating extension upon man of conditioned reflexes or the mechanisms of learning observed in rats, mice, dogs, rabbits, or other animals . . . the still more mechanistic interpretation of man's psychology and behavior by the principles of cybernetics, with its 'feed back' and extension of control and communication in the machine upon man'' (Pitirim Sorokin, *Fads and Foibles in Modern Sociology*, 1956).

''Intelligence is what Intelligence tests measure'' (H. Eysenck, *Uses and Abuses of Psychology*, 1958).

''The naive empiricist thinks that we begin by collecting and analysing our experiences, and so ascend the ladder of science. . . . But if I am ordered to record what you are now experiencing, I shall hardly know how to obey that ambiguous order. Am I to report what I am writing; that I hear a bell ringing; a newsboy shouting; a loudspeaker droning; or am I to report, perhaps, that these noises irritate me? A science needs points of view, and theoretical problems'' (Karl Popper, *The Logic of Scientific Discovery*, 1961).

''There are sociologists who frankly deny the need, utility, or even the possibility of formal methodological rigor in sociology; who make no apology for comparing their work to that of novelists and journalists'' (Elbridge Sibley, *The Education of Sociologists in the United States*, 1963).

''The fundamental methodological problem of any human science lies in the division of the object of study. . . . Once this division has been made and accepted, the results will be practically predictable'' (Lucien Goldmann, *Marxism and Human Sciences*, 1970).

''The ideal of objectivity is much more complex and elusive than the pedlars of methodological gimmicks would have us believe'' (Stanislav Andreski, *Social Sciences as Sorcery*, 1972).

''Comparative research is only just beginning, and it would be extremely imprudent to draw conclusions from it so soon, given the material at one's disposal and the great difficulties, both linguistic and otherwise, that arise in replications, not to mention the long initiation necessary for mastery of the test procedures, which are increasingly difficult to use the more closely they relate to operational functioning'' (Jean Piaget, *Psychology and Epistemology*, 1972).

''The pretence is made to examine an object by means of an instrument of research, which, through its own formulation, decides what the object is; in other words, we are faced with a simple circle'' (Theodor Adorno et al., *The Positivist Dispute in German Sociology*, 1976).

''Paul Radin has said that no one quite knows how one goes about fieldwork. . . . But when I was a serious young student in London I thought that I would get a few tips from experienced fieldworkers before setting out to Central America. I first sought advice from Westermarck. All I got from him was 'don't converse with an informant for more than 20 minutes because if you aren't bored by that time he will be.' . . . I sought instruction from Haddon, a man foremost in field research. He told me that it was really quite simple; one should always behave as a gentleman. . . . My teacher, Seligman, told me to take ten grains of quinine every night and to keep off women. The famous egyptologist, Sir Flinders Petri, just told me not to bother about drinking dirty water as one soon became immune to it. Finally I asked Malinowski and was told not to be a bloody fool.

So there is no clear answer, much will depend on the man, on the society he is studying, and the conditions in which he is to make it'' (E. Evans-Pritchard, *Witchcraft, Oracles and Magic Among the Azande*, 1976).

''In view of the multiple sources of bias, from the side of both the researcher and the subjects, it might seem that the safest route to scientific objectivity is to limit scientific research to neutral individuals (that is, those individuals without intense commitments). However, human affairs are never simple'' (Don Martindale, *The Nature and Types of Sociological Theory*, 1981).

''Many of the variables of greatest interest to us are extremely difficult to measure, even where they have been defined with great precision'' (Hubert Blalock, *Conceptualization and Measurement in the Social Sciences*, 1982).

''Contemporary sociological research . . . is characterized . . . by methodological pluralism'' (Jane Lambiri, *Methodology of Sociology*, 1982).

MIDDLE-RANGE THEORY

''Theories of the middle range [are] theories that lie between the minor but necessary working hypotheses that evolve in abundance during day-to-day research and the all-inclusive systematic efforts to develop a unified theory that will explain all the observed uniformities of social behavior, social organization and social change. Middle-range theory is principally used in sociology to guide empirical inquiry. It is intermediate to general theories of social systems which are too remote from particular classes of social behavior, organization and change to account for what is observed and to those detailed orderly descriptions of particulars that are not generalized at all'' (Robert Merton, *Social Theory and Social Structure*, 1968).

MILITARY SOCIOLOGY

''If a recruiting officer or adjutant levies men exempt from service or has accepted and dispatches a hired man as a substitute for a mission of the king, that recruiting officer or adjutant shall be put to death'' (Hammurabi, *Code*, c. 1750 B.C.).

''The entire military art . . . is hunting by force'' (Plato, *Sophist*, c. 400 B.C.).

''The occupation of a soldier is both to wear armor and to fight'' (Thomas Aquinas, *Summa Theologica*, 1274).

''Soldiers' stomachs always serve them well'' (William Shakespeare, *I Henry VI*, 1592).

''[Soldiers] owe their existence to social evils'' (Karl Marx, *Das Kapital*, 1879).

''The men of Mars set the pace for the rest of the world'' (Edward Ross, *The Social Trend*, 1922).

''[An army career was] the only opportunity for an adventurous and uneducated man, either Egyptian or alien, to achieve a position of importance or affluence'' (C. Aldred, *The Egyptians*, 1956).

''Insofar as the structural clue to the power elite today lies in the enlarged and military state, that clue becomes evident in the military ascendancy. The warlords have gained decisive political relevance, and the military structure of America is now in considerable part a political structure'' (C. W. Mills, *The Power Elite*, 1956).

''[Militarism] presents a vast array of customs, interests, prestige and actions . . . it displays qualities of caste and cult, authority and belief'' (Alfred Vagts, *A History of Militarism*, 1959).

''The practice of appointing military personnel to politically responsible posts, although it continues, has declined sharply since 1950'' (Morris Janowitz, *The Professional Soldier*, 1960).

''The adjustments of a nation's economy to a program of selective military service occur for the economy as a whole, and also in the economic lives of the persons directly affected by the program'' (Kenneth McGill in D. Kalitsounakis, ed., *Economy and Society*, 1961).

''[The military-industrial complex] is an organization or a complex of organizations and not a conspiracy. . . . In the conspiratorial view, the military power is a coalition of generals and conniving industrialists. The goal is mutual enrichment. . . . There is some enrichment and some graft. . . . Nonetheless, the notion of a conspiracy to enrich the corrupt is gravely damaging to an understanding of military power'' (John K. Galbraith, *How to Control the Military*, 1969).

''Military personnel are often viewed as transients with whom persisting relationships are futile'' (Roger Little, ed., *Handbook of Military Institutions*, 1971).

''The military profession today . . . is recruited on the basis of education and skill rather than on the basis of social origins'' (Bengt Abrahamsson, *Military Professionalization and Political Power*, 1972).

''The subject matter of military sociology is best defined by reference to organized violence'' (Kurt Lang, *Military Institutions and the Sociology of War*, 1972).

''The greater the difference and distinction between periphery and centre, and the greater the tendency of the centre to mobilize and control the periphery, or the more that the centre and periphery struggle over mutual control, the more will the distinction between civil and military authorities tend to develop'' (S. Eisenstadt in Harold Schiffrin, ed., *Military and State in Modern Asia*, 1976).

''The deployment of nuclear weapons represents the 'perfection' of the modern military by vastly increasing its effectiveness. At the same time, advanced technology carries the 'seeds of its own destruction,' since the outbreak of total nuclear war can no longer be perceived as in the national interest'' (Morris Janowitz, *The Last Half-century*, 1978).

''If a nation has no stong combat force, but it has a vast land, a mass population, and a united will to successfully conduct a sustained war, it will win a victory'' (Wego Chiang, *How Generalissimo Chiang Kai-shek Won the Eight-Year Sino-Japanese War, 1937–1945*, 1979).

''There is no such thing as absolute security. There are many methods to seek security, but there is simply no complete security. This fact forces us to make a decision. One argument is that since there is no absolute security, we must succumb to invasion and become slaves. . . . Another is to do everything possible to approach complete security, and accept the consequence when it fails. If people are prepared to face destruction, they have greater chances of escaping it'' (Masatoshi Matsushita in Professors World Peace Academy of Japan, *Challenging the Future*, 1982).

''The study of civic education in the military faces two opposite tendencies—either becoming ultra-theoretical or ultra-empirical. One tendency is to lose ourselves in abstract generalizations about ideology and patriotism. . . . The other tendency is to concern ourselves with unique conditions peculiar to one army at one period in time'' (Charles Moskos in Morris Janowitz and Stephen Wesbrook, eds., *The Political Education of Soldiers*, 1983).

MINORITY

''Then said they unto him, Say now Shibboleth: and he said Sibboleth: for he could not frame to pronounce it right. Then they took him, and slew him'' (Judges 12:6).

''All earlier movements have been movements of minorities, or movements in the interest of minorities. The proletarian movement is an independent movement of the overwhelming majority in the interest of that majority'' (Karl Marx and Friedrich Engels, *Communist Manifesto*, 1847).

''Ethnic coexistence, based on mutual repulsion and disdain, allows each ethnic community to consider its own honor as the highest one'' (Max Weber, *Economy and Society*, 1922, posthumously).

''The problems and principles of race relations are remarkably similar, regardless of what groups are involved and . . . only by an integrated study of all minority peoples in the United States can a real understanding and sociological analysis of the involved social phenomena be achieved'' (Donald Young in Gunnar Myrdal, *An American Dilemma*, 1944).

''Tolerant people, with a passion for justice, often deny that any distinctive traits exist among minority-group members. They find them 'just like' everybody else. And in a broad sense this judgment is sound. . . . Differences within groups are almost always greater than differences between groups'' (Gordon Allport, *The Nature of Prejudice*, 1954).

''There seems to be no historical exception to the rule that when peoples come into contact and occupy the same area there is a mixture of blood'' (Brewton Berry, *Race and Ethnic Relations*, 1965).

''Minority pupils, except for Orientals, have far less conviction than whites that they can affect their own environments and futures. When they do, however, their achievement is higher than that of whites who lack that conviction. . . . Those Negroes in schools with a higher proportion of whites have a greater sense of control'' (James Coleman et al., *Equality of Educational Opportunity*, 1966).

''Minority groups are usually disadvantaged in terms of favoring environmental conditions'' (J. Zanden, *American Minority Relations*, 1966).

''Government programs concerned with improving academic performance of blacks or other minority groups should give as much attention, if not more, to the environment—both family and neighborhood—in which the minority child lives'' (David Armor in Frederick Mosteller and Daniel Moynihan, eds., *On Equality of Educational Opportunity*, 1972).

''The emergence of the Mexican American community is in large part due to the continued expansion of widespread alienation and meaninglessness'' (Charles Loomis in T. Smith and Man Das, eds., *Sociocultural Change Since 1950*, 1978).

''For the practitioner the question of whether the minorities ought, or ought not, to remain ethnically distinct should be irrelevant. The fact is that they are'' (Roger Ballard in Saifullah Khan, ed., *Minority Families in Britain*, 1979).

''When the problems of Blacks and other minorities became critical, the educational system once more was relied upon as a primary instrument of social justice'' (Don Martindale and Raj Mohan, eds., *Ideals and Realities*, 1980).

''[In South Africa] in terms of key criterial indexes such as language, race, ethnicity, and culture, a unitarian system will condemn the Afrikaners to multiple minority status. Such an onerous handicap, added to the lack of major historically evolved, geographically defined power bases, could have disastrous consequences for Afrikaner national survival'' (Nic Rhoodie, ed., *Conflict Resolution in South Africa*, 1980).

''In the last 180 years, a momentous change has occurred in the social conditions and the political role of the Jews. At the time of the Napoleonic Wars, the Jews as a people were peripheral. Most lived in semiautonomous defenseless communities or in ghettos, isolated from the mainstream of general political and economic development. By World War I, large numbers of Jews were participating in important ways in the general economic, social and intellectual development of advanced Western countries'' (Daniel Shimshoni, *Israeli Democracy*, 1982).

MOBILITY

''In the case of economic disasters . . . declassification occurs which suddenly casts certain individuals into a lower state than their previous one . . . their moral education has to be recommenced. . . . It is the same if the source of the crisis is an abrupt growth of power and wealth'' (Émile Durkheim, *Suicide*, 1897).

''Our epoch is a period of intensive social mobility. . . . At the present moment the Western peoples remind one of a pot of boiling water in which the water particles move up and down, to and fro, with great rapidity. To this is due the illusion that our present societies are as though not stratified, in spite of the fact that they are actually stratified. . . . Great mobility, with its intensive transposition of the individuals, makes such an illusion natural and inevitable. . . . When a man throughout his life works at the same occupation and has the same economic and social status, his mind is decidedly marked . . . he is doomed to think and to look at the world through the glasses of his 'social box.' . . . Another picture is given by the mind of a man who passes from occupation to occupation'' (Pitirim Sorokin, *Social Mobility*, 1927).

''[Due to World War II] upward economic mobility increased tremendously in amount and speed; women advanced to jobs never before available to them, ethnic and racial groups raised the ceiling on their job expectations, unskilled workers learned new skills'' (W. Warner et al., *Democracy in Jonesville*, 1949).

''High social mobility . . . reflected anomie in nineteenth-century France, while low social mobility reflects anomie in twentieth-century America'' (Ephraim Mizruchi, *Success and Opportunity*, 1964).

''There is uncommon agreement that types and rate of mobility are crucial to an understanding of modern society. And there are hints that work-life mobility may be more fateful than intergeneration mobility. It is therefore remarkable that detailed work histories which cover a decade or more have been reported in only about a dozen studies'' (Harold Wilensky in T. Burns, ed., *Industrial Man*, 1969).

''Greek young people follow more often than French youth do the road to upward social mobility through the channel of higher education'' (Jane Lambiri, *Toward a Greek Sociology of Education*, 1974).

''Adopting a diachronic or biographical perspective on mobility produces a very different picture from that derived from the synchronic, cross-sectional view of a conventional mobility table . . . a wide diversity exists in the actual routes and sequences of worklife movement that men have followed even between similar origins and destinations'' (John Goldthorpe et al., *Social Mobility and Class Structure in Modern Britain*, 1980).

''[In Brazil] social origin, although not a direct determinant of the individual's status, plays a large, indirect role in that it limits education and, therefore, occupation and upward mobility. . . . Brazil tends more toward the countries which progressed a great deal in terms of mobility (Austria, England, Italy, and the United States) than toward those which progressed slightly (Indonesia, Argentina, West Germany, and Switzerland)'' (José Pastore, *Inequality and Social Mobility in Brazil*, 1982).

MODERNIZATION

''The citizens of modern societies are socialized to shift constantly among various social units such as the family, the community and the work unit. The relatively high separation and low scope of all these units allows the typically modern mode of managing tension to operate. Tensions generated in one unit are released in another by changing partners, thus 'localizing' rather than 'totalizing' conflicts and by shifting back and forth between social units'' (Amitai Etzioni, *Modern Organizations*, 1964).

''How are families to be protected from market fluctuations? Whereas such integrative exigencies were faced by kinsmen, neighbors, and local largesse in pre-modern settings, development gives birth to dozens of institutions and organizations geared to these new integrative problems—labor recruitment agencies and exchanges, labor unions, government regulation of labor allocation, welfare and relief arrangements, co-operation societies, and savings institutions'' (Neil Smelser in Amitai and Eva Etzioni, eds., *Social Change*, 1964).

''In the modernization of advanced countries, national leadership puts emphasis on spiritual reform prior to economic change. Modernization efforts bore fruit only when the energy of a nation was effectively integrated into a single objective by superb leadership from above. In the case of Korea, this modernization process was reversed'' (Park Chung Hee, *To Build a Nation*, 1971).

''Four assumptions in particular deserve mention regarding the concept of modernization: the importance attributed to the capacities relevant to modernization developed by a society before the modern era; the role of the advancement of knowledge . . . the capacity of a society in political, economic, and social terms to take advantage of the possibilities for development offered by the advancement of knowledge; and the utility of various policies that the political leaders of a society may follow in seeking both to convert its heritage of values and institutions to modern requirements and to borrow selectively from more modern societies'' (Cyril Black, ed., *Comparative Modernization*, 1976).

''Whether or not one accepts our analysis of why neo-Confucian cultures are so competent in industrialization, the impressive data that support the final thesis are overwhelming. The performance of the People's Republic of China; of both North and South Korea; of Japan, Taiwan, Hong Kong, and Singapore; and of the various Chinese ethnic groups in Malaysia, Thailand, Indonesia, and the Philippines, discloses extraordinary talent . . . for economic development . . . all of them seem amenable to modernization under current conditions'' (Herman Kahn, *World Economic Development*, 1979).

'' 'Modernization' is one of the most widely used words nowadays. Because of that, it is also, perhaps, one of the most abused words in contemporary vocabulary. Often people talk about 'modernization' as if it had a universal meaning. . . . Economists in our part of the world tend to interpret 'modernization' as the progress of the capitalistic economic system'' (Professors World Peace Academy of Japan, *Emerging Asia*, 1981).

''[In Japan] modernization has been attained within the persisting framework of the traditional social structure'' (Masaaki Takane, *Political Elite in Japan*, 1981).

"A movement away from family traditionalism and toward family modernism . . . may be expressed in *individual* as well as in structural terms" (Alex Inkeles, *Exploring Individual Modernity*, 1983).

MOS, MORES

"*Lex* [law] is the written ordinance. *Mos* [singular of mores] is custom approved by its antiquity, or unwritten *lex*. For *lex* is derived from *legere* (to read) because it is written. *Mos* is old custom and is drawn merely from *mores*. *Consuetudo* (custom) is a sort of *jus* [right] established by *mores*" (Isidore of Seville, *Etymologies*, c. 600).

"They [mores] are the ways of doing things which are current in a society to satisfy human needs and desires, together with the faiths, notions, codes, and standards of well living which inhere in those ways, having a genetic connection with them. By virtue of the latter element the mores are traits in the specific character (ethos) of a society or a period. They pervade and control the ways of thinking in all the exigencies of life, returning from the world of abstractions to the world of action, to give guidance and to win revivification. . . . The mores are social ritual in which we all participate unconsciously. The current habits as to hours of labor, meal hours, family life, the social intercourse of the sexes, propriety, amusements, travel, holidays, education, the use of periodicals and libraries, and innumerable other details of life fall under this ritual. . . . The mores come down to us from the past. Each individual is born into them as he is born into the atmosphere, and he does not reflect on them, or criticize them any more than a baby analyzes the atmosphere before he begins to breathe it . . . we must conceive of the mores as a vast system of usages, covering the whole of life, and serving all its interests! Also containing in themselves their own justification by tradition and use and wont, and approved by mystic sanctions until, by rational reflection, they develop their own philosophical and ethical generalizations, which are elevated into 'principles' of truth and right. . . . At every turn we find new evidence that the mores can make anything right" (William Sumner, *Folkways*, 1907).

"[Schools] are controlled by the mores of their time and place from which they cannot escape even if they would" (Charles Ellwood, *Man's Social Destiny in the Light of Science*, 1929).

"The whole mores of African life make a high and sustained level of effort in a given length of working day a greater burden both physically and psychologically than in Europe" (F. Wells and W. Warmington, *Studies in Industrialization*, 1962).

"Mores are defined by the group as being very important or as having high value. We are particularly ethnocentric about our mores" (Glenn Vernon, *Human Interaction*, 1972).

MOVEMENT, SOCIAL

''Do not say that social movement excludes political movement. There is never a political movement which is not at the same time social'' (Karl Marx, *The Poverty of Philosophy*, 1847).

''All great movements in history are preceded and accompanied by strong feelings. And it is those persons whose feelings have been most violent that have exerted the greatest influence upon the tone and character of society. Purely intellectual feeling is never sufficient directly to sway the multitude'' (Lester Ward, *Dynamic Sociology*, 1883).

''The lack of a great, new, creative idea means at all times a limitation of the fighting power. The conviction of the justification of using even the most brutal weapons is always dependent on the presence of a fanatical belief in the necessity of the victory of a revolutionary new order on this globe. A movement which does not fight for such highest aims and ideals will therefore never take the ultimate weapon'' (Adolf Hitler, *Mein Kampf*, 1925).

''[The historical method reveals] the cultural development of any people . . . the forces and factors, the possibilities and the probabilities, of any social movement or condition'' (Charles Ellwood, *Methods in Sociology*, 1933).

''All mass movements . . . irrespective of the doctrine they preach and the program they project, breed fanaticism, enthusiasm, fervent hope, hatred, and intolerance'' (Eric Hoffer, *The True Believer*, 1951).

''All the demons that communism believed it had banished from the forthcoming as well as the real world, have crept into the soul of communism and become part of its being. Communism, once a popular movement that in the name of science inspired the toiling and oppressed people of the world with the hope of creating the kingdom of heaven on Earth, that launched and continues to launch millions to their deaths in pursuit of this inextinguishable primaeval dream, has become transformed into national political bureaucracies and states squabbling among themselves for prestige and influence, for the source of wealth and for markets'' (Milovan Djilas, *The Unperfect Society*, 1969).

''In a social movement change does not usually have the form of an organized campaign, but of a transformation as many persons more or less independently are appraising situations in a new but paralleled manner'' (Don and Edith Martindale, *Psychiatry and the Law*, 1973).

''Social movements are forced to adapt themselves to present social norms and institutions in the ambient society, and yet they must maintain their own sense of apartness and purity, their own distinct identity, to retain membership commitment and avoid the dilution of co-optation'' (John Wilson, *Introduction to Social Movements*, 1973).

''The sociology of knowledge . . . may be the best approach . . . toward the development of concepts and theory on social movements'' (Ron Roberts and Robert Kloss, *Social Movements*, 1979).

[On students of the 1960s] ''It was foolish and naive. You cannot change humankind's nature by slogans. It was important to explain to overwrought 18–year-olds that the world crushes naive idealists. Darwin taught us that any species unable to adapt to things as they are becomes extinct'' (William McGill, *The Year of the Monkey*, 1982).

''Countercultures combine three forms of protest: direct opposition to the dominant values, but opposition also to the power structures and opposition to patterned exchanges that are entangled with those values'' (J. Yinger, *Countercultures*, 1982).

''One of the most difficult problems in analyzing social movements is defining exactly what a social movement is. . . . Nonetheless, there are some common themes and elements. . . . Spontaneity and structure are the most important elements'' (Jo Freeman, ed., *Social Movements of the Sixties and Seventies*, 1983).

MUSIC, SOCIOLOGY OF

''It is by the Odes that the mind is aroused. . . . It is from Music that the finish is received'' (Confucius, *Analects*, c. 500 B.C.).

''It is said that music is a more recent art, the reason being that it was born, not as a response to necessity, but of what was left over'' (Democritus, Fragments, c. 400 B.C.).

''Music is the counterpart of gymnastic, and trains the guardians through habit, making them harmonious through harmony and rhythmical through rhythm, but it does not give them science'' (Plato, *Republic*, c. 400 B.C.).

''If the king's love of music were very great, the kingdom of Chi would be near to a state of good government!'' (Mencius, *Book of Mencius*, c. 300 B.C.).

''Music is a part of us, either ennobling us or degrading our deeds'' (Anicius Manlius Severinus Boethius, *Elements of Music*, c. 505).

''Music oft hath such a charm to make bad good, and good provoke to harm'' (William Shakespeare, *Measure for Measure*, 1605).

''[Music is] the only adequate, final, and impeccable utterance of man's unutterable ecstasy of concord of Being and Becoming'' (Radhakamal Mukerjee, *The Dynamics of Morals*, 1950).

''The musician is conceived of as an artist who possesses a mysterious artistic gift setting him apart from all other people. Possessing this gift he should be free from control by outsiders who lack it. The gift is something which cannot be acquired through education'' (Howard S. Becker, *Outsiders*, 1963).

''[Pop] is sensitive to change, indeed it could be said that it is sensitive to nothing else. . . . It draws no conclusions. It makes no comments. It proposes no solutions. It admits to neither past nor future, not even its own'' (George Melly, *Revolt into Style*, 1970).

''The nineteenth century created the musical environment in which twentieth-century musicians and listeners have grown up. . . . The twentieth century has modified the system without changing or substantially adding to its essential nature'' (Henry Raynor, *Music and Society*, 1972).

"The history of music is . . . part of the vast, unwieldy complex that is history; we can break it into its own departments of harmony, form and textures" (Henry Raynor, *A Social History of Music*, 1972).

"A sociology of music is . . . knowledge of the relation between music and the socially organized individuals who listen to it" (Theodor Adorno, *Introduction to the Sociology of Music*, 1976).

"A prominent reason for the relative absence of systematic treatment of youth and music in standard sociological sources, no doubt, is the historic specificity of the subject. Another reason might be the conceptual ambiguity surrounding both terms. . . . Where does 'youth' begin and end, and what, indeed, is the sociologically relevant meaning of music?" (K. Etzkorn in T. Smith and Man Das, eds., *Sociocultural Change Since 1950*, 1978).

"Rock is made in order to have emotional, social, physical, commercial results" (Simon Frith, *Sound Effects*, 1981).

"The Greek civilization placed great importance on the study of music, making it for the educated man as important as the study of mathematics. The very term *music* comes from the Greek word *Muses*, the nine goddesses of song and poetry" (Nick Rossi, *Music Through the Ages*, 1981).

MYTH, SOCIOLOGY OF

"Since we are not certain about ancient events, we use mythology to make falsehood appear as the truth, which is practical and useful" (Plato, *Republic*, c. 400 B.C.).

"Mythology is the handmaid of literature; and literature is one of the best allies of virtue and promoters of happiness. Without a knowledge of mythology much of the elegant literature of our own language cannot be understood and appreciated" (Thomas Bulfinch, *The Age of Fable*, 1855).

"Myths are not believed in, they are conceived and understood" (George Santayana, *Little Essays*, 1920).

"[The function of myth] is to reveal models and, in so doing, to give meaning to the World and to human life . . . through myth . . . the ideas of *reality, value, transcendence* slowly dawn. Through myth, the World can be apprehended as a perfectly articulated, intelligible, and significant Cosmos. In telling how things were made, myth reveals by whom and why they were made and under what circumstances. All these 'revelations' involve man more or less directly, for they make up a Sacred History" (M. Eliade, *Myth and Reality*, 1964).

"It is remarkable that in an environment of desert wastes and infertile soil, as well as in well-watered country, the imagination of the [Australian] Aborigines should produce tales that are both beautiful and amusing, and that they should find human characteristics and poetry in bird and beast, in the sky above them, in sun, moon, and stars, and even in reptiles and insects" (A. Reed, *Myths and Legends of Australia*, 1965).

''Myths provide charters for social institutions'' (Clifford Geertz in M. Banton, ed., *Anthropological Approaches to the Study of Religion*, 1966).

''It is, in a way, a paradox that myth, which is definitely a form of tradition stemming from the depth of the past, should have become a favorite subject of structuralism. But as historical methods in this field seemed to add up to more and more complications and uncertainties, it was possible to hope for a break-through by structural analysis of myth as an elaborate nonfactual communication system'' (Walter Burkert, *Structure and History in Greek Mythology and Ritual*, 1979).

N

NEED

"The state . . . is established because each of us happens to be not self-sufficient, but in need of many things. . . . In this way, then, one man taking another for a service and another for another, having many needs, many of us gathered together as partners and helpers in one habitation, and to this common dwelling we gave the name state. . . . Now the first and greatest need is the provision of food for existence and life. . . . The second is the dwelling and the third, clothing and the like" (Plato, *Republic*, c. 400 B.C.).

"Needs hold a living being together more strongly than anything else does" (Epictetus, *Discourses*, c. 80).

"A community has many needs which one individual alone cannot satisfy; the community as a whole, however, meets these needs, as one person satisfies one need and another person another" (Thomas Aquinas, *Summa Theologica*, 1274).

"Allow not nature more than nature needs" (William Shakespeare, *King Lear*, 1606).

"A want [is], according to my idea, contra-distinguished from a mere desire by a positive physical pain, instead of mental uneasiness accompanying it" (Henry Mayhew, *London Labour and the London Poor*, 1861).

"Just as the savage must wrestle with Nature to satisfy his wants, to maintain and reproduce life, so must civilised man, and he must do so in all social formations and under all possible modes of production. With his development this realm of physical necessity expands as a result of his wants; but, at the same time, the forces of production which satisfy these wants also increase" (Karl Marx, *Das Kapital*, 1879).

"All the [animal] organism needs is that the supplies of substance and energy constantly employed in the vital process should be periodically renewed by equivalent quantities; that replacement be equivalent to use. When the void created by existence in its own resources is filled, the animal, satisfied, asks nothing further. . . . This is not the case with man, because most of his needs are not dependent on his body or not to the same degree. Strictly speaking, we may consider that the quantity of material supplies necessary to the physical maintenance of a human life is subject to computation, though this be less exact than in the preceding case and a wider margin left for the free combinations of the will'' (Émile Durkheim, *Suicide*, 1897).

''A decade ago, and all the more so before then, one could speak of a marked tendency in psychological and sociological theory to attribute the faulty operation of social structures to failures of social control over man's imperious biological drives. The imagery of the relations between man and society implied by this doctrine is as clear as it is questionable'' (Robert Merton, *Social Theory and Social Structure*, 1949).

''Needs may lead to cooperation, conflict, inventions, and other phenomena . . . as further factors in social change'' (Panos Bardis in D. Kalitsounakis, ed., *Economy and Society*, 1961).

''A quasi-need persists if the task has not been completed *to the subject's own* satisfaction'' (Bluma Zeigarnik in William Sahakian, *History and Systems of Psychology*, 1975).

''Needs assessment has risen from opportunistic and empirical sources. It is not 'owned' by any one discipline. As a result, it has no unique theoretical frameworks. Also, perhaps as a result of its 'odd' birth, it is not well grounded in either a theoretical literature or in research findings. There is missing the scholarly first step of finding out what went before'' (Daniel Bell, *The Cultural Contradictions of Capitalism*, 1976).

NORM, SOCIAL

''What you do not want done to yourself, do not do to others'' (Confucius, *Analects*, c. 500 B.C.).

''You cannot put the same shoe on every foot'' (Publilius Syrus, *Opinions*, c. 50 B.C.).

''All things whatsoever ye would that men should do to you, do ye even so to them'' (Matthew 7:12).

''A normative law is a rule and measure of conduct, whereby a person is induced to act or is forbidden to act'' (Thomas Aquinas, *Summa Theologica*, 1274).

''Any fool can make a rule and every fool will mind it'' (Henry D. Thoreau, *Journal*, 1860).

''A decrease in the influence of existing social rules of behavior upon individual members of the group [leads to social disorganization]'' (William Thomas and Florian Znaniecki, *The Polish Peasant in Europe and America*, 1920).

''Morality is thus the generally accepted definition of the situation, whether expressed in public opinion and the unwritten law, in a formal legal code, or in religious commandments and prohibitions'' (William Thomas, *The Unadjusted Girl*, 1923).

''In a certain sense neither logical nor moral norms are innate in the individual mind. We can find, no doubt, even before language, all the elements of rationality and morality'' (Jean Piaget, *The Moral Judgment of the Child*, 1932).

''[Preparation for social living is achieved] by learning to obey coercive rules and regulations that arise out of the constant threat and pressure of the external environment and the inadequacy of [man's] nature'' (Radhakamal Mukerjee, *The Theory and Art of Mysticism*, 1937).

''No society lacks norms governing conduct. But societies do differ in the degree to which the folkways, mores and institutional controls are effectively integrated with the goals which stand high in the hierarchy of cultural values'' (Robert Merton, *Social Theory and Social Structure*, 1949).

''Variation [from culture to culture] rages rampant as to details of proscribed instrumentalities and sanctions'' (Ralph Linton in Ruth Anshen, ed., *Moral Principles of Action*, 1952).

''No one has ever attempted to ascertain quantitatively the extent to which and the specific conditions under which determined government action can through coercion bring about changes in the norms of any community of persons'' (Richard LaPiere, *A Theory of Social Control*, 1954).

''It is . . . the very ancient problem whether social laws are 'natural' or 'conventional' '' (Karl Popper, *The Open Society and Its Enemies*, 1957).

''Norms may be violated without surrendering allegiance to them. . . . They may be evaded rather than radically rejected'' (David Matza, *Delinquency and Drift*, 1964).

''*Mores* are the most important norms in a society; they are the basic rules that govern the society and hold it together. When mores are violated, the punishment is usually severe. . . . Less-important norms are called *folkways*, and the punishments for violating them are much less severe . . . *redefinition of norms* . . . often happens when the person who is deviating has high status in the group. But norms are also redefined as part of the normal interaction among group members, and this is one of the major reasons for the changing nature of groups . . . norms [are] expectations and standards that regulate interactions among people. Norms are more specific than values in that they are embodied in codes, rules, laws, and etiquette, all of which are designed to promote behavior that the values define as good'' (Neil Smelser, *Sociology*, 1981).

O

OCCUPATIONAL SOCIOLOGY

''In the sweat of thy face shalt thou eat bread'' (Genesis 3:19).

''No kind of work is a disgrace, but idleness is a disgrace'' (Hesiod, *Works and Days*, c. 750 B.C.).

''Those who work with their hands are the third class. These are not politicians and do not have much to live upon'' (Plato, *Republic*, c. 400 B.C.).

''One occupation only the lord prescribed to the Sudra, to serve meekly even these three castes [Brahmans, Kshatriya, Vaisya]'' (Manu, *Laws*, c. 200 B.C.).

''The sovereign . . . with all the officers both of justice and war who serve under him, the whole army and navy, are unproductive labourers. They are servants of the public, and are maintained by a part of the annual produce of the industry of other people. . . . In the same class must be ranked some of the gravest and most important and some of the most frivolous professions: churchmen, lawyers, physicians, men of letters of all kinds; players, buffoons, musicians, opera-singers, opera-dancers, etc. . . . Like the declamation of the actor, the harangue of the orator, or the tune of the musician, the work of them all perishes in the very instant of its production. . . . Unproductive labourers, and those who do not labour at all, are all maintained by revenue. . . . [To make a pin] one man draws out the wire, another straightens it, a third cuts it, a fourth points it, a fifth grinds it at the top for receiving the head; to make the head requires two or three distinct operations; to put it on, is a peculiar business, to whiten the pins is another; it is even a trade by itself to put them into the paper'' (Adam Smith, *The Wealth of Nations*, 1776).

''Serious occupation is work that has reference to some need'' (Georg Wilhelm Friedrich Hegel, *The Philosophy of History*, 1837, posthumously).

''Every medieval artisan could . . . find his entire fulfillment in his work. He had to work in soulful servitude, and he was subsumed under his work far more than is the modern worker. The modern worker is indifferent to his work. . . . The occupation assumes an independent existence owing to division of labor'' (Karl Marx and Friedrich Engels, *The German Ideology*, 1846).

''The bourgeoisie has robbed of their haloes various occupations hitherto regarded with awe and veneration. Doctor, lawyer, priest, poet, and scientist, have become its wage-labourers'' (Karl Marx and Friedrich Engels, *Communist Manifesto*, 1847).

''In order to modify the human organism, so that it may acquire skill and handiness in a given branch of industry, and become labour-power of a special kind, a special education or training is requisite, and this, on its part, costs an equivalent in commodities of a greater or less amount. This amount varies according to the more or less complicated character of the labour-power. The expenses of this education (excessively small in the case of ordinary labour-power), enter *pro tanto* into the total value spent in its production'' (Karl Marx, *Das Kapital*, 1879).

''Every man's work, whether it be literature or music or pictures or architecture or anything else, is always a portrait of himself'' (Samuel Butler, *The Way of All Flesh*, 1903).

''[Admitting technical men of the lower schools into the university] leads them to court a specious appearance of scholarship and so to invest their technological discipline with a degree of pedantry and sophistication; whereby it is hoped to give these schools and their work some scientific and scholarly prestige'' (Thorstein Veblen, *The Higher Learning in America*, 1918).

''It used to be that every worker aspired to be a self-employed businessman. However, this is less and less feasible'' (Max Weber, *Economy and Society*, 1922, posthumously).

''[No matter what] the different temporary bases of inter-occupational stratification at different times and in different societies, side by side with these partially changing bases there seem to exist some bases which are *permanent* and *universal*. . . . At least two conditions seem to have been fundamental: *First, the importance of an occupation for the survival and existence of a group as a whole; second, the degree of intelligence necessary for the successful performance of an occupation*'' (Pitirim Sorokin, *Social Mobility*, 1927).

''It is not difficult to account in general for the emergence of the new professions. Large-scale organization has favored specialization. Specialized occupations have arisen around the new scientific knowledge'' (A. Carr-Saunders, *Professions*, 1928).

''I felt I was moving among two groups—comparable in intelligence, identical in race, not grossly different in social origin, earning about the same incomes, who had almost ceased to communicate at all, who in intellectual, moral and psychological climate had so little in common that instead of going from Burlington House or South Kensington to Chelsea, one might have crossed an ocean'' (C. P. Snow, *The Two Cultures and the Scientific Revolution*, 1959).

''Work expands to fill the time available for its completion'' (C. Parkinson, *Parkinson's Law*, 1962).

''There was a certain contempt for trade among the Athenian upper classes, although they undoubtedly benefited from its operations'' (A. Andrewes, *Greek Society*, 1967).

''[A profession] involves the application of general principles to specific problems, and it is a feature of modern societies that such general principles are abundant and growing . . . the two primary bases for specialization within a profession are (1) the substantive field of knowledge that the specialist professes to command and (2) the technique of production or application of knowledge over which the specialist claims mastery'' (Wilbert Moore, *The Professions*, 1970).

''Do not wait for a subordinate to be the first to show friendship and affability, but take the initiative yourself. Even if the subordinate does not immediately respond, your affability will ultimately be worthwhile'' (D. Kaidalov and E. Suimenko, *Current Problems in the Sociology of Work*, 1974).

''The centrality of an individual's occupation to his life is a fact that requires little verification'' (Richard Hall, *Occupations and the Social Structure*, 1975).

''[In India] students are drifting away from their traditional occupations . . . students will not like to adopt the occupations of their parents . . . traditional occupations are slowly but steadily breaking down'' (Sheo Lal and Umed Nahar, *Higher Education*, 1978).

''The socialist state [in the Soviet Union] found itself . . . very soon in need of a re-emphasis of the values of work'' (Jiri Zuzanek, *Work and Leisure in the Soviet Union*, 1980).

OPINION, PUBLIC

''When the multitude detests a man, inquiry is necessary; when the multitude likes a man, inquiry is equally necessary'' (Confucius, *Analects*, c. 500 B.C.).

''Their opinions about good and evil differ . . . there would be no conflicts among them, if there were no such differences'' (Plato, *Euthyphro*, c. 400 B.C.).

''Each of the many by himself may not be of a good quality, but when all of them come together, it is possible that, collectively and as a group, but not individually, they may surpass the quality of the few best'' (Aristotle, *Politics*, c. 350 B.C.).

''The love of the people constitutes the best fortress; for although you may have fortresses, they will not save you if the people hate you'' (Niccolò Machiavelli, *The Prince*, 1513).

''[Public opinion is] the organic will of the community expressed in the public wills of its members'' (Jean Jacques Rousseau, *The Social Contract*, 1762).

''There are times when public opinion is the worst kind of opinion'' (Sébastien Roch Nicolas Chamfort, *Maxims and Thoughts*, c. 1800).

''The idea of what the public will think prevents the public from ever thinking at all, and acts as a spell on the exercise of private judgment'' (William Hazlitt, *Table Talk*, 1822).

''*Public opinion* is to be understood largely in terms of the social differences between citizens—differences in age, occupation, education, social class, religion, and race. In general, opinions of youth tend to support radical changes whereas the opinions of older people tend to retain the status quo'' (Ritchie Lowry and Robert Rankin, *Sociology*, 1972).

''The task of defining public opinion is an elusive one. Political science is a relatively young discipline and precise, commonly accepted definitions for many of its terms are lacking. This is certainly true of the term *public opinion*. . . . At least three categories of publics are common in contemporary American society: (1) single-issue publics, (2) organizational publics, and (3) ideological publics. . . . In defining the term *public opinion*, the public can be described as a collection of individuals who share a common attitude, and an opinion can be described as an expressed attitude. Public opinion therefore can be defined as *the shared opinions of a collection of individuals on a common concern*'' (Jerry Yeric and John Todd, *Public Opinion*, 1983).

ORGANIZATION, SOCIAL

''Civil society was established not merely in order that its members might live, but that they might live well'' (Aristotle, *Politics*, c. 350 B.C.).

''Social justice is achieved when inferiors obey their superiors'' (Thomas Aquinas, *Summa Theologica*, 1274).

''What man loses through the social contract is his natural liberty . . . what he gains is civil liberty'' (Jean Jacques Rousseau, *The Social Contract*, 1762).

''If man is social by nature, he will develop his true nature only in society'' (Karl Marx and Friedrich Engels, *The Holy Family*, 1845).

''[The] most important category of pure or theoretical sociology is the social organization or corporate body, a social body or union known by many other names. It is never anything natural, neither can it be understood as a mere physical phenomenon. It is completely and essentially a social phenomenon and must be considered as composed of several individuals'' (Ferdinand Tönnies, *Community and Society*, 1887).

''[Public opinion is] a co-operative product of communication and reciprocal influence'' (Charles Cooley, *Human Nature and the Social Order*, 1902).

''[The members of a successful social organization become] more rational, more sympathetic, with an ever-broadening consciousness of kind'' (Franklin Giddings, *Descriptive and Historical Sociology*, 1904).

''[We must invent the] means of organizing the conflicting wills of individuals and classes within each nation more effective than reliance upon any single 'principle,' whether representation, property, or professionalism'' (Graham Wallas, *The Great Society*, 1914).

''[Higher social organization] renders group life the great ennobling influence by aid of which man alone rises a little above the animals and may even aspire to fellowship with the angels'' (William McDougall, *The Group Mind*, 1920).

''In the face of the increasing importance which individual efficiency assumes in all domains of cultural life [social organization suffers]'' (William Thomas and Florian Znaniecki, *The Polish Peasant in Europe and America*, 1920).

''The meager output of genuine wisdom about organizations from modern managers is startling'' (James March, ed., *Handbook of Organizations*, 1965).

''Contemporary men increasingly experience themselves in confrontation with organizations composed of thousands of specialized positions'' (Don Martindale, *Institutions, Organizations, and Mass Society*, 1966).

''Where both the 'production' of specialized outputs and their consumption or ultimate utilization occur within the same structural unit there is no need for the differentiations of specialized organization. Primitive societies, in so far as their units are 'self-sufficient' in both economic and other senses, generally do not have clear-cut differentiated organizations in the present sense'' (Talcott Parsons in O. Grusky and G. Miller, eds., *The Sociology of Organizations*, 1970).

''From its outset the United States has been a society of organizations'' (James Wood in Thomas Drabek and J. Haas, *Understanding Complex Organizations*, 1974).

''The comparative analysis of organizations will lead to a richer and more precise organizational theory'' (Amitai Etzioni, *A Comparative Analysis of Complex Organizations*, 1975).

''When subordinates are given more autonomy their emotional commitment to the organizational program often increases in a dramatic way'' (Theodore Caplow, *How to Run Any Organization*, 1976).

''Many psychologists appear to accept the goals organizations give them as aspects of performance. Most sociologists do not. To them the organization is merely an instrument of society that can be used or misused. The success of an organization, then, depends upon its contribution to society'' (Richard Osborn et al., *Organization Theory*, 1980).

P

PARADIGM

''Codification is the orderly and compact arrangement of systematized fruitful experience with procedures of inquiry and with the substantive findings which result from the use of these procedures. . . . I use the device of the *analytical paradigm* for presenting codified materials'' (Robert Merton, *Social Theory and Social Structure*, 1957).

''[A paradigm may be improved by] extending the knowledge of those facts that the paradigm displays as particularly revealing . . . increasing the extent of the match between those facts and the paradigm's predictions . . . further articulation of the paradigm itself'' (Thomas Kuhn, *The Structure of Scientific Revolutions*, 1970).

''That sociology does not have a paradigm . . . is clear . . . from a random selection of any issue of the major journals. But, to be in the preparadigmatic stage is not to be lost in the wilderness. We do have some paths—our theoretical orientations. These, or any one of them, may develop into a basic paradigm'' (Jerald Hage, *Techniques and Problems of Theory Construction in Sociology*, 1972).

''If a given science has one widely agreed upon paradigm, its efforts are spent doing those things we usually think of as the 'normal' scientific process: developing theories, testing them, revising them, retesting, and so on'' (Janet Chafetz, *A Primer on the Construction and Testing of Theories in Sociology*, 1978).

''A paradigm is a fundamental image of the subject matter within a science. It serves to define what should be studied, what questions should be asked, and what rules should be followed in interpreting the answers obtained. The paradigm is the broadest unit of consensus within a science and serves to differentiate one scientific community (*or sub-community*) from another. It subsumes, defines, and interrelates the exemplars, theories, and methods and tools that exist within it'' (George Ritzer, *Sociology*, 1980).

''It was the scientific circle, in its role in both the promotion and obstruction of scientific growth, that Thomas Kuhn discovered in his notion of the revolutions of science. . . . However, upon close examination, paradigm, the central notion in Kuhn's interpretation, proved to be ambiguous. One philosopher traced out more than twenty different senses in which the term was used. Kuhn was forced to admit that he had used the term loosely'' (Don Martindale, *The Nature and Types of Sociological Theory*, 1981).

PARENTHOOD

''Honour thy father and thy mother'' (Exodus 20:12).

''Tsai Wo asked about the three years' mourning for parents, saying that one year was long enough . . . the Master said. . . . 'It is not till a child is three years old that it is allowed to leave the arms of its parents. And the three years' mourning is universally observed throughout the empire' '' (Confucius, *Analects*, c. 500 B.C.).

''Work, if work it be, is nothing when done for the sake of parents'' (Sophocles, *Oedipus at Colonus*, 401 B.C.).

''No man should have children if he is unwilling to persevere to the end in their upbringing and education'' (Plato, *Crito*, c. 380 B.C.).

''Mothers are more devoted to their children than fathers are because they suffer more in giving them birth and are more certain that they are their own'' (Aristotle, *Nicomachean Ethics*, c. 350 B.C.).

''[Alexander the Great to Olympias, his mother, when she was requesting something persistently:] 'The rent you request for my 10–month stay in your womb is exorbitant' '' (Alexander, c. 330 B.C., in Leo Sternbach, *Gnomologium Vaticanum*, 1963).

''The manifestation of love must begin with our parents'' (Mencius, *Book of Mencius*, c. 300 B.C.).

''He who forsakes his mother, his father . . . must be avoided'' (Manu, *Laws*, c. 200 B.C.).

''The father who subordinates the interests of his son to his own convenience is unwise'' (Plautus, *The Three Penny Day*, c. 200 B.C.).

''Leave the honouring of your mother and honour your father, because both you and your mother have the duty of honouring him'' (Talmud: Sanctification 31a).

''Your Lord hath made a sacred duty for you . . . that ye do good for parents'' (Koran: Cattle 152).

''It is a wise father that knows his own child'' (William Shakespeare, *The Merchant of Venice*, 1597).

''When a woman is 20, a child deforms her; when she is 30, he preserves her; and when 40, he makes her young again'' (Léon Blum, *On Marriage*, 1907).

''The mealy look of men today is the result of momism'' (Philip Wylie, *Generation of Vipers*, 1942).

''Parentage is a very important profession; but no test of fitness for it is ever imposed in the interest of the children'' (George B. Shaw, *Everybody's Political What's What*, 1944).

''In all societies except the United States, and, to a lesser degree the countries facing her across the Atlantic, at all periods except during the last hundred years . . . the proper way to bring up children is the way we were brought up. . . . When a woman bore her first child, she had the accumulated wisdom of her whole society to help her; the grandmothers, the midwives, the neighbors all spoke with one voice; every baby she had seen since she could first notice anything was being brought up in the same way'' (Geoffrey Gorer, *The American People*, 1948).

''The difference [between the German father and Victorian patriarch] lies in the German father's essential lack of true inner authority—that authority which results from an integration of cultural ideal and educational method'' (Erik Erikson, *Childhood and Society*, 1950).

''Our society, like most, if not all, societies, glorifies the experience of parenthood. Children, especially in the period of early childhood, are culturally idealized as 'bundles of joy.' Parents who fail to regard them as such run the risk in many groups of being judged at best as unconventional and at most as immoral or abnormal. Consequently persons who find the satisfactions from their offspring outweighed by the various demands and restrictions of parenthood may be reluctant to state that the net result of having a child has been a decrease rather than an increase in their happiness. This might account for the high proportion of parents who reported a strong favorable reaction to having a child'' (Ernest Burgess and Paul Wallin, *Engagement and Marriage*, 1953).

''The mother-child relationship is paradoxical and, in a sense, tragic. It requires the most intense love on the mother's side, yet this very love must help the child grow away from the mother, and to become fully independent'' (Erich Fromm, *The Sane Society*, 1955).

''No parent wakes up in the morning planning to make his child's life miserable. . . . Yet, in spite of good intentions, the unwanted war breaks out again. Once more we find ourselves saying things we do not mean, in a tone we do not like. All parents want their children to be secure and happy. . . . Yet in the process of growing up, many children acquire undesirable characteristics and fail to achieve a sense of security'' (Haim Ginott, *Between Parent and Child*, 1965).

''The divided perception of parental authority carries over into social action. On the one hand, authorities invite contempt because they allow so many violations of their own rules; on the other hand, they threaten to exact a terrifying revenge . . . in the future'' (Christopher Lasch, *Haven in a Heartless World*, 1977).

''One-parent families can be the outcome of marriage, death, divorce or the birth of a child to an unmarried woman'' (Benjamin Schlesinger, *The One-Parent Family*, 1978).

''[In the Soviet Union] an underestimation of the prime function of a woman, that is, motherhood and all that this involves, works against the interests of the mother and child, as well as of society as a whole'' (Feiga Blekher, *The Soviet Woman in the Family and in Society*, 1979).

''[Parent education] does have effects upon its participant clientele and upon their children. There is clear, although not abundant, evidence showing that the children of participants are influenced . . . parent education affects participating parents in a generally positive direction. Changes have been observed . . . in knowledge, attitudes, and child-rearing practices of parents . . . however, the line is not as distinct as one would wish. It is unclear how durable such changes are . . . whether they are all functions of participation; and . . . whether the presumed sequence of knowledge to attitudes to behaviors is valid'' (E. Harman and O. Brim, *Learning to Be Parents*, 1980).

''Parents in a relatively static society would have less difficulty than those in one in which social change is rapid and deep. . . . Parents are not the only source of wisdom and propriety in modern society. The schools, the mass media, the youth peer groups all tell the youth what he or she should think and behave . . . parents today are being judged by higher standards—by their children, by professionals such as schoolteachers, psychologists, and social workers, and by parents themselves'' (E. LeMasters and John DeFrain, *Parents in Contemporary America*, 1983).

PEACE

''Let the mutual goodwill of the old days be restored, and let peace and plenty prevail'' (Homer, *Iliad*, c. 750 B.C.).

''Better beans and bacon in peace than cakes and ale in fear'' (Aesop, *Fables*, c. 550 B.C.).

''Peace will never come to the victors of a civil war before they stop sentencing men to exile and death and taking revenge on the opposition party'' (Plato, *Letters*, c. 400 B.C., perhaps spurious).

''Peace is liberty in tranquility'' (Cicero, *Philippics*, 43 B.C.).

''Now the hoes, the hard mattocks, and beaked plowshares are the wealth of the countryside . . . while weapons grow dirty with mould!'' (Ovid, *Calendar*, c. 10 B.C.).

''The God of peace shall bruise Satan'' (Romans 6:20).

''We who were filled with war and mutual slaughter and every wickedness have each of us in all the world changed our weapons of war . . . into plows, and spears into agricultural instruments'' (Justin Martyr, *Dialogue with Trypho*, c. 155).

''We no longer take up sword against nation, nor do we learn war any more, having become children of peace'' (Origen, *Against Celsus*, 250).

''Be of the disciples of Aaron, loving peace and pursuing peace'' (Talmud: Chapters of the Fathers 1:12).

''The peace of the commonwealth is good in itself, and is not made evil by those few who use it evilly; for many more people use it well; and peace prevents much greater evils, such as homicides and sacrilege, than the evils it occasions'' (Thomas Aquinas, *Summa Theologica*, 1274).

''The proper work of the human race, taken as a whole, is to set in action the whole capacity of that understanding which is capable of achievement. . . . The condition requisite for the accomplishment of this purpose is universal peace'' (Dante Alighieri, *On Monarchy*, 1312).

''People like serenity, and for this reason they like peaceful princes'' (Niccolò Machiavelli, *The Prince*, 1513).

''A peace is of the nature of a conquest; for then both parties nobly are subdued, and neither party loser'' (William Shakespeare, *II Henry IV*, 1598).

''The passions that incline men to peace are fear of death, desire of such things as are necessary to commodious living, and a hope by their industry to obtain them'' (Thomas Hobbes, *Leviathan*, 1651).

''They [Antonines] preserved peace by a constant preparation for war'' (Edward Gibbon, *Decline and Fall of the Roman Empire*, 1788).

''You should love peace as a means to new wars, and the short peace more than the long one'' (Friedrich Wilhelm Nietzsche, *Thus Spake Zarathustra*, 1885).

''[Peace will be promoted by] an organization provided with the means of adjudicating [international] disputes and enforcing awards'' (Edward Ross, *The Social Trend*, 1922).

''Mankind has grown strong in eternal struggles and it will only perish through eternal peace'' (Adolf Hitler, *Mein Kampf*, 1924).

''It [the world] has neither the spirit of unity, nor the clear sense of a common interest, nor an adequate mechanism which might at least maintain the externals of orderly peace'' (Leonard Hobhouse, *Social Development*, 1924).

''The deliberate aim at Peace very easily passes into its bastard substitute, Anaesthesia'' (Alfred N. Whitehead, *Adventures of Ideas*, 1935).

''The rhetoric of peace is, in the last analysis, preferable to that of war'' (Gerardo Zampaglione, *The Idea of Peace in Antiquity*, 1967).

''The association of peace with the military term 'strategy' is not a simple rhetoric, but has its significance . . . you need a correct strategy in order to maintain peace as much as in order to win a war'' (Masatoshi Matsushita in Professors World Peace Academy of Korea, *Strategy for Peace*, 1975).

''There is a long, painful, slow but very persistent historical movement from stable war into unstable war into unstable peace into stable peace. The main object of peace policy is to speed up the transition by deliberate decision'' (Kenneth Boulding, *Stable Peace*, 1978).

''The theoretical concept of international peacekeeping is that the control of violence in interstate and intrastate conflict is possible without resort to the use of force or enforcement measures'' (International Peace Academy Publication, *Peacekeeper's Handbook*, 1978).

''Irenology [is] the science of peace'' (Panos Bardis in Pacific Cultural Foundation, *In Search of a New World Order*, 1980).

''Education for peace . . . should be one of the basic objectives of every country, of all international organizations and of all mass communications media'' (Presidential Commission on the University for Peace, Costa Rica, *University for Peace*, 1980).

''Russians are not so much concerned with the goals of peace and security as with the ways and means to obtain it'' (John Yin, *The Soviet Views on the Use of Force in International Law*, 1980).

''[We need a] new international order [where citizens of nations] accept an international decision as unhesitatingly as residents of states and provinces today accept a federal government decision'' (John Barton, *The Politics of Peace*, 1981).

''We define *peace* as the absence of war. . . . This is obviously an extremely narrow usage. The term peace is commonly employed in much broader ways. It often covers various levels below international relations and contains specifications for substantive justice. . . . Peace may also include an affective or emotional component'' (Francis Beer, *Peace Against War*, 1981).

''No matter how the terms are defined, peace is considered desirable, war undesirable'' (Leonard Doob, *The Pursuit of Peace*, 1981).

PERSONALITY

''Do we not think of a human being as a moral person?'' (Plato, *Laws*, c. 400 B.C.).

''A person's character depends on the way in which he exercises his powers'' (Aristotle, *Nicomachean Ethics*, c. 350 B.C.).

''I shall never cease to marvel, why it has come about that, albeit the whole of Greece lies in the same clime and all Greeks have a like upbringing, we have not the same constitution of character'' (Theophrastus, *Characters*, c. 300 B.C.).

''Personality is more important than surroundings'' (Lucius Annaeus Seneca, *Letters*, 63).

''Cold air constringes the extremities of the external fibres of the body; this increases their elasticity, and favors the return of blood from the extreme parts to the heart. . . . People are therefore more vigorous in cold climates. . . . [This makes] them patient and intrepid, and qualifies them for arduous enterprises'' (Charles de Secondat Montesquieu, *The Spirit of the Laws*, 1748).

''Nature develops all the human faculties by practice, and their growth depends upon their exercise. Men, fathers, force not the faculties of your children into paths too distant before they have attained strength by exercise; avoid harshness and overfatigue'' (Johann Heinrich Pestalozzi, *Evening Hour of a Hermit*, 1780).

''[Personality develops in heredity and] in the stream of communication, both of which flow from the corporate life of the race'' (Charles Cooley, *Human Nature and the Social Order*, 1902).

''Higher education, travel, self-direction, professional pursuits, participation in intellectual and public life [make men less suggestible than women]'' (Edward Ross, *Social Psychology*, 1908).

''The human personality is both a continually producing factor and a continually produced result of social evolution, and this double relation expresses itself in every elementary social fact'' (William Thomas and Florian Znaniecki, *The Polish Peasant in Europe and America*, 1920).

''Reorganization of human nature takes place in response to the folkways and the mores, the traditions and conventions of the group'' (Robert Park and Ernest Burgess, *Introduction to the Science of Sociology*, 1921).

''The (negative-) authoritarian character's fight against authority is essentially defiance. It is an attempt to assert himself and to overcome his own feelings of powerlessness by fighting authority, although the longing for submission remains present, whether consciously or unconsciously'' (Erich Fromm, *Escape from Freedom*, 1941).

''[We need] planning for gradual transformation of society in order to encourage the growth of personality'' (Karl Mannheim, *Freedom, Power, and Democratic Planning*, 1950, posthumously).

''Among the learned elements of personality in certain respects the stablest and most enduring are the major value-orientation patterns and there is much evidence that these are 'laid down' in childhood and are not on a large scale subject to drastic alteration during adult life'' (Talcott Parsons, *The Social System*, 1951).

''A society in order to persist must regularly fulfil the supreme values of personality'' (Radhakamal Mukerjee in Baljit Singh, eds., *The Frontiers of Social Science*, 1956).

''Experimental psychologists have long been surprised that so many personality theorists, despite claims to being scientists, have been content to raise elaborate theoretical edifices on a basis of everyday observation only'' (Raymond Cattell and Frank Warburton, *Objective Personality and Motivation Tests*, 1967).

''The word 'personality' comes from the Latin *persona*. Originally it referred to the masks worn in the theatre; later the term came to include the wearers of the masks'' (John Burnham in Edgar Borgatta and William Lambert, eds., *Handbook of Personality Theory and Research*, 1968).

''When American sociologists turned their attention to the problem of personality around the turn of the century, they developed theories springing from a position close to the religious view of man. The presuppositions of their theories appear to have included the small town and the individual as an autonomous moral agent'' (Don Martindale, *American Society*, 1972).

''The biological basis of personality can be studied from four points of view: neurophysiology, psychophysiology, behavioral pharmacology, and behavior genetics'' (Jochen Fahrenberg in Raymond Cattell and Ralph Dreger, eds., *Handbook of Modern Personality Theory*, 1977).

''As the shape of the oceans delimits the land, and the map of land delimits the shape of the ocean, so a proper grasp of genetics tells us more precisely the shape of what we have to explain by learning'' (Raymond Cattell, *The Inheritance of Personality and Ability*, 1982).

''The Japanese tend to be overly emotional and weak in their contemplative capacity. We like to stop our thinking at a point which falls short of logical soundness'' (Masatoshi Matsushita in Professors World Peace Academy of Japan, *Challenging the Future*, 1982).

POLITICAL SOCIOLOGY

''We should be taught the art of politics, which is extremely important, so that we may undertake the labors from which spring the great and shining acts of men'' (Democritus, Fragments, c. 400 B.C.).

''The politician who curries favor with the citizens and indulges them . . . is considered a great statesman'' (Plato, *Republic*, c. 400 B.C.).

''The goal of political science is the greatest good, that is, justice'' (Aristotle, *Politics*, c. 350 B.C.).

''If men had the use of reason they pretend to, their Commonwealths might be secured, at least, from perishing by internal diseases'' (Thomas Hobbes, *Leviathan*, 1651).

''For forms of government let fools contest; What'er is best administered is best'' (Alexander Pope, *An Essay on Man*, 1733).

''Man is born free, and everywhere we look we see him in chains. . . . Were there a people of Gods, their government would be democratic. So perfect a government is not for men'' (Jean Jacques Rousseau, *The Social Contract*, 1762).

''The voice of the people has been said to be the voice of God; and however generally this maxim has been quoted and believed, it is not true in fact. The people are turbulent and changing, they seldom judge or determine right'' (Alexander Hamilton, *Records of the Federal Convention*, 1797).

''The anticipation of criticism from the Many, particularly of public criticism, has the effect of inducing officials to devote their best attention beforehand to their duties and the schemes under consideration, and to deal with these only in accordance with the purest of motives'' (Georg Wilhelm Friedrich Hegel, *The Philosophy of Right*, 1821).

''Democratic nations care little for what has been, but they are haunted by visions of what will be; in this direction their unbounded imagination grows and dilates beyond all measure. . . . Democracy, which shuts the past against the poet, opens the future before him'' (Alexis Charles Henri Maurice Clérel de Tocqueville, *Democracy in America*, 1840).

''English economists are amazed to see the workers sacrifice a good part of their wages in favour of associations, which, in the eyes of these economists, are established solely in favour of wages. In this struggle—a veritable civil war—all the elements necessary for a coming battle unite and develop. Once it has reached this point, association takes on a political character. . . . The working class, in the course of its development, will substitute for the old civil society an association which will exclude classes and their antagonism, and there will be no more political power properly so-called, since political power is precisely the official expression of antagonism in civil society'' (Karl Marx, *The Poverty of Philosophy*, 1847).

''The state is . . . by no means a power imposed on society from the outside. . . . Rather, it is a product of society at a certain stage of development; it is the admission that this society has become entangled in an insoluble contradiction with itself, that it is cleft into irreconcilable antagonisms which it is powerless to dispel. But in order that these antagonisms, classes with conflicting economic interests, may not consume themselves and society in sterile struggle, a power apparently standing above society becomes necessary, whose purpose it is to moderate the conflict and keep it within the bounds of 'order'; and this power arising out of society, but placing itself above it, and increasingly separating itself from it, is the state'' (Friedrich Engels, *The Origin of the Family, Private Property, and the State*, 1884).

''The spread of socialism, then, is but the latest phase of the universal tendency for the people to endeavor to control government for their own benefit'' (Edward Ross, *Changing America*, 1912).

''He who says organization says oligarchy. . . . [This is the] iron law of oligarchy'' (Robert Michels, *Political Parties*, 1915).

''Under socialism all will govern in turn and will soon become accustomed to no one governing'' (Nikolai Lenin, *The State and Revolution*, 1917).

''Since a party always struggles for *Herrschaft* [political control], its organization too is frequently strict and 'authoritarian' '' (Max Weber, *Economy and Society*, 1922, posthumously).

''[Autocracy] keeps the people politically children'' (Charles Ellwood, *Man's Social Destiny in the Light of Science*, 1929).

''[Nationality is] a type of community sentiment, a sense of belonging together, created by historical circumstances and supported by common spiritual possessions, of such an extent and so strong that those who feel it desire to have a common government peculiarly or exclusively their own'' (Robert MacIver, *Society*, 1937).

''[In the Soviet system] the character of the economy as a whole . . . depends upon the character of state power'' (Leon Trotsky, *The Revolution Betrayed*, 1937).

''Repression works only to strengthen and knit the oppressed'' (John Steinbeck, *The Grapes of Wrath*, 1939).

''Community of language and culture . . . does not necessarily give rise to political unity, any more than linguistic and cultural dissimilarity prevents political unity'' (M. Fortes and E. Evans-Pritchard, *African Political Systems*, 1940).

''Most of our calamities can only be removed once we have understood that politics form a set of problems which can never be solved by prejudice, but only by a gradual and conscientious study of society'' (Karl Mannheim, *Man and Society in an Age of Reconstruction*, 1940).

''In any political order, we may expect to find both 'conscience' and 'coercion' '' (Hans Gerth and C. W. Mills, *Character and Social Structure*, 1953).

''Like everything that concerns the human condition, liberty is ambiguous and ambivalent. It can decompose as well as construct, push toward perversity as well as generosity, turn to good as well as evil, lead to degeneration as well as to leaps ahead'' (Georges Davidovitch Gurvitch, *Social Determinisms and Human Liberty*, 1955).

''It takes time for people to learn to govern themselves'' (Bernard Baruch, *The Public Years*, 1960).

''Because of overlapping county and city jurisdictions, some of the consequences may be conflict, expensive duplication, insufficient supervision, and exploitative control over one local government by the other. Complete or partial consolidation of the two units may alleviate the problem, as San Francisco and New York proved in 1856 and 1897, respectively. Another solution, which St. Louis adopted in 1876, is absolute separation between county and city jurisdictions'' (Panos Bardis in Instituto de Ciencias Sociales, *The County*, 1966).

''*The functional deficiencies of the official structure generate an alternative (unofficial) structure to fulfil existing needs somewhat more effectively*. Whatever its specific historical origins, the political machine persists as an apparatus for satisfying otherwise unfulfilled needs of diverse groups'' (Robert Merton, *Social Theory and Social Structure*, 1968).

''In a vast country such as Russia with its mainly peasant and petty-bourgeois population, its economic backwardness and ignorance . . . after a socialist revolution a mainly authoritarian regime was inevitable, and not only the old tsarist officials and specialists, who had perforce to be utilized by the new regime, were bureaucrats'' (Roy Medvedev, *On Soviet Democracy*, 1972).

''The production of political thought in a given country has very little in common with the ways in which politics is actually carried out; or rather it reflects politics by contrast, by covering up or by evading the issue'' (Alessandro Pizzorno in F. Cavazza and S. Graubard, eds., *The Italian Case*, 1974).

''[In South Africa] considering . . . the nexus between territorialism, demographic size and effective political power, the Afrikaners' survival chances hinge on the extent that they succeed in establishing a democratic pluralist White-Black accommodation that can provide them with a viable geographically defined power base'' (Nic Rhoodie, ed., *Conflict Resolution in South Africa*, 1980).

''Political sociology is crosscut by several different visions of what society and politics are all about'' (Anthony Orum, *Introduction to Political Sociology*, 1983).

POVERTY, SOCIOLOGY OF

''That which is thine with thy brother thine hand shall release; save when there shall be no poor among you'' (Deuteronomy 15:3–4).

''To be poor without murmuring is difficult. To be rich without being proud is easy'' (Confucius, *Analects*, c. 500 B.C.).

''A community without poverty will always have the noblest principles'' (Plato, *Laws*, c. 400 B.C.).

''Is it only the mouth and belly which are injured by hunger and thirst? Men's minds are also injured by them'' (Mencius, *Book of Mencius*, c. 300 B.C.).

''Whatever a man has in superabundance is owed, of natural right, to the poor for their sustenance'' (Thomas Aquinas, *Summa Theologica*, 1274).

''Poor and content is rich and rich enough'' (William Shakespeare, *Othello*, 1605).

''Poverty does not prevent the procreation of children, but is on the other hand extremely unfavorable to the rearing of children. . . . No society can surely be flourishing and happy of which the far greater part of the members are poor and miserable'' (Adam Smith, *The Wealth of Nations*, 1776).

''[The poor] compose the greatest part of the dangerous classes . . . [due to] their vices, their ignorance, and their poverty. . . . Idleness and debauchery were the predominant vices of the poor . . . because they give into their passions and do not work'' (Honoré Frégier, *On the Dangerous Classes*, 1840).

''Poverty often dwells in hidden alleys close to the palaces of the rich; but, in general, a separate territory has been assigned to it, where removed from the sight of the happier classes, it may struggle along as it can'' (Friedrich Engels, *The Condition of the Working Class in England*, 1845).

''In proportion as the bourgeoisie, i.e., capital, is developed, in the same proportion is the proletariat, the modern working class, developed—a class of labourers, who live only so long as they find work, and who find work only so long as their labour increases capital. These labourers, who must sell themselves piecemeal, are a commodity, like every other article of commerce, and are consequently exposed to all the vicissitudes of competition, to all the fluctuations of the market. . . . The modern labourer . . . instead of rising with the progress of industry, sinks deeper and deeper below the conditions of existence of his own class. He becomes a pauper, and pauperism develops more rapidly than population and wealth'' (Karl Marx and Friedrich Engels, *Communist Manifesto*, 1847).

''Under the term 'poor' I shall include all those persons whose incomings are insufficient for the satisfaction of their wants'' (Henry Mayhew, *London Labour and the London Poor*, 1861).

''Poverty protects against suicide because it is a restraint in itself. No matter how one acts, desires have to depend upon resources to some extent; actual possessions are partly the criterion of those aspired to. So the less one has the less he is tempted to extend the range of his needs indefinitely'' (Émile Durkheim, *Suicide*, 1897).

''*The average stature of the poor of a given race, sex, and age must be lower in comparison with the stature of rich people of the same race, sex, and age*'' (Pitirim Sorokin, *Hunger as a Factor in Human Affairs*, 1919).

''The poorer working man, coming home after his nine and a half hours on the job, walks up the frequently unpaved street, turns in at a bare yard littered with a rusty velocipede or worn-out automobile tires, opens a sagging door, and enters the living room of his home'' (Robert and Helen Lynd, *Middletown*, 1929).

''The [Chilean] worker reaches the conclusion that going to the tavern and intoxicating oneself is the apparent solution to all these problems [poverty]'' (Salvador Allende, *The Medicosocial Reality in Chile*, 1939).

''Poverty becomes a dynamic factor which affects participation in the larger national culture and creates a subculture of its own. One can speak of a culture of the poor'' (Oscar Lewis, *Life in a Mexican Village*, 1951).

''The Negro family in the urban ghettos is crumbling. So long as this situation persists, the cycle of poverty and disadvantage will continue to repeat itself'' (Daniel Moynihan, *The Negro Family*, 1965).

''Life is marked by frustration and hopelessness, by a sense of failure, and consequently by fear and apathy . . . the welfare system has failed because it has largely ignored the human factors associated with poverty'' (Canadian Parliament, *Report of the Special Senate Committee on Poverty*, 1971).

''Once a relative view of poverty is adopted, it follows that poverty cannot be abolished, since in any society where complete social inequality does not always prevail, the label of poor can always be given to the 10 per cent or 20 per cent of the population'' (J. Kincaid, *Poverty and Equality in Britain*, 1973).

''Research studies . . . have usually concentrated on establishing the extent and range of poverty. Less attention is devoted to considering the explanation of poverty'' (Robert Holman, *Poverty*, 1978).

''[In Brazil] the poorest families are 'forced' to throw their unprepared children into the work force, where they must compete in extremely unequal situations with the children of the middle and upper classes'' (José Pastore, *Inequality and Social Mobility in Brazil*, 1982).

POWER

''The truly bad men come from the class that enjoys power'' (Plato, *Gorgias*, c. 400 B.C.).

''No man shall have too much power either because of his fortune or because of his friends'' (Aristotle, *Politics*, c. 350 B.C.).

''He who abuses the power that was given to him deserves to lose it'' (Thomas Aquinas, *Summa Theologica*, 1274).

''Every particular man is author of all the sovereign doth'' (Thomas Hobbes, *Leviathan*, 1651).

''The strongest is never strong enough to be always master, unless he transforms his strength into right, and obedience into duty'' (Jean Jacques Rousseau, *The Social Contract*, 1762).

''The accumulation of all powers, legislative, executive, and judiciary, in the same hands, whether of one, a few, or many, and whether hereditary, self-appointed, or elective, may justly be pronounced the very definition of tyranny'' (James Madison in *The Federalist*, 1788).

''The security of the state and its subjects against the misuse of power by ministers and their officials lies directly in their hierarchical organization and their answerability'' (Georg Wilhelm Friedrich Hegel, *The Philosophy of Right*, 1821).

''The classes that have hitherto won to power have tried to safeguard their newly acquired position by subjecting society at large to the conditions by which they themselves gained their possessions'' (Karl Marx and Friedrich Engels, *Communist Manifesto*, 1847).

''The only purpose for which power can be rightfully exercised over any member of a civilized community, against his will, is to prevent harm to others'' (John S. Mill, *On Liberty*, 1859).

''The second [distinguishing characteristic of the state] is the establishment of a *public force*, which is no longer absolutely identical with the population organising itself as an armed power. This special public force is necessary, because a self-acting armed organisation of the population has become impossible since the cleavage of society into classes. . . . This public force exists in every state; it consists not merely of armed men, but of material appendages, prisons and repressive institutions of all kinds'' (Friedrich Engels, *The Origin of the Family, Private Property, and the State*, 1884).

''The public power peculiar to every state is not 'absolutely identical' with the armed population, with its 'self-acting armed organisation.' . . . A standing army and police are the chief instruments of state power'' (Nikolai Lenin, *The State and Revolution*, 1917).

'' 'Classes,' 'status groups,' and 'parties' are phenomena of the distribution of power within a community'' (Max Weber, *Economy and Society*, 1922, posthumously).

''Antagonistic classes exist in society everywhere, and a class deprived of power inevitably strives to some extent to swerve the governmental course in its favor'' (Leon Trotsky, *History of the Russian Revolution*, 1932).

''In all societies . . . two classes of people appear—a class that rules and a class that is ruled. The first class, always the less numerous, performs all of the political functions, monopolizes power, and enjoys the advantages that power brings, whereas the second, the more numerous class, is directed and controlled by the first'' (Gaetano Mosca, *The Ruling Class*, 1939).

''Interpersonal influence stemming from specialized expertness typically involves some social distance between the advice-giver and the advice-seeker'' (Robert Merton in Paul Lazarsfeld and Frank Stanton, eds., *Communications Research*, 1949).

''[Democracy is based on] a theory of power aimed at defining ways of distributing and controlling communal power for maximum security, efficiency, and freedom'' (Karl Mannheim, *Freedom, Power, and Democratic Planning*, 1950, posthumously).

''The simple Marxian view makes the big economic man the *real* holder of power; the simple liberal view makes the big political man the chief of the power system; and there are some who would view the warlords as virtual dictators. Each of these is an oversimplified view. It is to avoid them that we use the term 'power elite' rather than, for example, 'ruling class.' . . . *Power* is simply the probability that men will act as another man wishes'' (C. W. Mills, *The Power Elite*, 1956).

''Power may be defined as the production of intended effects'' (Bertrand Russell, *Power*, 1960).

''The belief that an 'economic elite' controls governmental and community affairs, by means kept hidden from the public, is one that can be traced at least as far back in American history as the political attacks of some Jeffersonians on some Hamiltonians at the end of the eighteenth century'' (Arnold Rose, *The Power Structure*, 1967).

''The Stalin and post-Stalin periods formed the bureaucracy into a separate social group, a separate stratum . . . power is in the hands of a social group standing above society'' (Roy Medvedev, *On Soviet Democracy*, 1972).

''[In Jodhpur, India] power was essentially fragmented in three sections: the political, the specialist and the economic elites'' (Sheo Lal, *The Urban Elite*, 1974).

''The state is the system of political institutions that exercises a monopoly over the use of power in a given territory'' (Raj Mohan and Don Martindale, eds., *Handbook of Contemporary Developments in World Sociology*, 1975).

PREJUDICE

''Dogs bark at the one they do not know'' (Heraclitus, *On Nature*, c. 500 B.C.).

''Mother, it is right that Greeks rule barbarians, but not that barbarians rule Greeks'' (Euripides, *Iphigeneia in Aulis*, c. 405 B.C.).

''Prejudices annihilate all tender attitudes'' (Charles de Secondat Montesquieu, *The Spirit of the Laws*, 1748).

''Prejudice is the child of ignorance'' (William Hazlitt, *Sketches and Essays*, 1839).

''Law, morality, religion are to the proletarian so many bourgeois prejudices, behind which lurk in ambush just as many bourgeois interests'' (Karl Marx and Friedrich Engels, *Communist Manifesto*, 1847).

''I was myself much impressed . . . during my travels in Africa. The mistakes the negroes made in their own matters were so childish, stupid, and simpleton-like, as frequently to make me ashamed of my own species. I do not think it any exaggeration to say, that their C is as low as our E, which would be a difference of two grades'' (Francis Galton, *Hereditary Genius*, 1869).

''The source of race prejudice lies in a felt challenge to this sense of group position [a minority seen as a threat to the dominant group]. The challenge . . . may come in many different ways. It may be in the form of an affront to feelings of group superiority; it may be in the form of attempts at familiarity or transgressing the boundary line of group exclusiveness; it may be in the form of encroachment at countless points of proprietary claim; it may be a challenge to power and privilege; it may take the form of economic competition'' (Herbert Blumer in J. Masuoka and P. Valien, eds., *Race Relations*, 1961).

''There is every reason to accept the contention that authoritarianism, of the kind that is indexed by the F-scale, tends to enhance the likelihood of ethnic prejudice. But neither the authoritarian syndrome nor other related personality tendencies invariably constitute either a necessary or sufficient set of conditions for prejudice, much less discriminatory behavior'' (Robin Williams, *Strangers Next Door*, 1964).

''Since every human being depends upon his cumulative experiences with others for clues as to how he should view and value himself, children who are consistently rejected understandably begin to question and doubt whether they, their family, and their group really deserve no more respect from the larger society than they receive. These doubts become the seeds of pernicious self-and-group-hatred and the Negro's complex, debilitating prejudice against himself'' (Kenneth Clark, *Dark Ghetto*, 1965).

''The postulated connection between social mobility and prejudice represents an altogether too fragile view of people's coping capacities in modern society'' (Melvin Seeman in Morris Rosenberg and Ralph Turner, eds., *Social Psychology*, 1981).

''Prejudice is widespread, but so is a denial of prejudice. No one—not even members of the Ku Klux Klan—likes to be called prejudiced'' (Charles Morris, *Psychology*, 1982).

''The greater the structural assimilation of the minority, the less prejudice and discrimination it experiences'' (Edward Murguia, *Chicano Intermarriage*, 1982).

PROBLEM, SOCIAL

''The sage aims neither at the cultivation of what is ancient, nor at the observance of what is usual. He studies the conditions of the time and provides remedy for them'' (Han Fei Tzu, *Complete Works*, c. 250 B.C.).

''Drunkenness leads to all other vices, and in the end conquers and absorbs them all'' (Honoré Frégier, *On the Dangerous Classes*, 1840).

''You war against the vast iniquities in modern business, finance, politics, journalism, due to the ineffectiveness of public opinion in coping with the dominant types of wrong-doing in a huge, rich, highly complex industrial civilization like ours'' (Theodore Roosevelt in Edward Ross, *Sin and Society*, 1907).

''The social problem [is manifested by] the blindness and selfishness of some of our socially privileged classes, the fanatic radicalism and class hatred of some of the leaders of the non-privileged'' (Charles Ellwood, *The Social Problem*, 1915).

''Group selfishness . . . probably has had more to do with causing the disorders of our world than individual selfishness'' (Charles Ellwood, *The World's Need of Christ*, 1940).

''[There is negative social change in] the rise of gross inequalities, in industrial strife, in religious strife, in exploitation, in international war, in estrangements in the family and elsewhere, in ossification and the crystalization of the status quo, in the power of commercialized vice'' (Edward Ross, *New-Age Sociology*, 1940).

''[If the family teaches moral values and] the laws of the market compel us to become self-assertive, the consequence of these conflicting demands will be a kind of neurosis'' (Karl Mannheim, *Diagnosis of Our Time*, 1943).

''In the degree that the 'mentally ill' outside hospitals numerically approach or surpass those inside hospitals, one could say that mental patients distinctly suffer not from mental illness, but from contingencies'' (Erving Goffman, *Asylums*, 1961).

''Man has never been free of social problems. However, increased sensitivity to them has been brought about through the expansion of mass communication and mass education'' (Erwin Smigel, ed., *Handbook on the Study of Social Problems*, 1971).

''Race prejudice was one of the problems engendered by immigration'' (Emory Bogardus, *A History of Sociology at the University of Southern California*, 1972).

''Today's man . . . both a cause and a victim of problems, needs . . . a general education to enable him . . . to solve truly human problems. . . . These problems are as old, and yet as current, as man himself'' (Juan Tusquets, *Education with Reference to Problems*, 1972).

''Problems are issues which require resolution if life is to go on. The social problems with which men wrestle have a form intimately related to the properties of the society in which they occur though they are not exclusively determined by the society. In varying degrees the physical environment and the characteristics of a population may also play a role in the incidence of a problem'' (Don and Edith Martindale, *Psychiatry and the Law*, 1973).

''For every woman killed by a 'sex fiend,' several are slaughtered by their husbands; but the sex crimes attract more interest and arouse far greater anxiety'' (Paul Horton and Gerald Leslie, *The Sociology of Social Problems*, 1974).

''When sociologists speak of social problems, we are concerned with conditions or situations that in one way or another affect group life'' (Leonard Glick and Daniel Hebding, *Introduction to Social Problems*, 1980).

''For a social problem to be recognized there must be both an objective and a subjective element. The objective element is the condition itself; the subjective element is the belief that the condition should be changed'' (Joseph Julian and William Kornblum, *Social Problems*, 1983).

PROGRESS

''At first, the Olympian immortals created a golden race of mortal men . . . would that I were not among the men of the fifth race . . . for this race now is of iron'' (Hesiod, *Works and Days*, c. 750 B.C.).

''Progress results when the craftsmen of the past cannot stand comparison with the craftsmen of today'' (Plato, *Hippias Major*, c. 400 B.C., perhaps spurious).

''The five chiefs of the princes were sinners against the three kings. The princes of the present day are sinners against the five chiefs'' (Mencius, *Book of Mencius*, c. 300 B.C.).

''All that is human must retrograde if it do not advance'' (Edward Gibbon, *Decline and Fall of the Roman Empire*, 1776).

''How dangerous is the acquirement of knowledge'' (Mary Shelley, *Frankenstein*, 1818).

''Sometimes [progress] comprehends little more than simple growth—as of a nation in the number of its members and the extent of territory over which it spreads. Sometimes it has reference to quantity of material products. . . . *Social progress is supposed to consist in the making of a greater quantity and variety of the articles required for satisfying men's wants; in the increasing security of person and property; in widening freedom of action; whereas, rightly understood, social progress consists in those changes of structure in the social organism which have entailed these consequences. The current conception is a teleological one* . . . the series of changes gone through during the development of a seed into a tree, or an ovum into an animal, constitute an advance from homogeneity of structure to heterogeneity of structure . . . *this law of organic progress is the law of all progress*'' (Herbert Spencer, 1857, *Essays*, 1915, posthumously).

''As natural selection works solely by and for the good of each being, all corporeal and mental endowments will tend to progress toward perfection'' (Charles Robert Darwin, *Origin of Species*, 1859).

''The extent of 'progress' is gauged by the extent of the sacrifice that it requires'' (Friedrich Wilhelm Nietzsche, *The Genealogy of Morals*, 1887).

''Progress results from the fusion of unlike elements'' (Lester Ward, *Pure Sociology*, 1903).

''All progress means war with Society'' (George B. Shaw, *Getting Married*, 1911).

''The Progress of humanity belongs to the same order of ideas as Providence or personal immortality. It is true or it is false, and like them it cannot be proved true or false. Belief in it is an act of faith'' (John Bury, *The Idea of Progress*, 1920).

''[Dynamic education facilitates] the initiation and control of social progress'' (Charles Ellwood, *Methods of Sociology*, 1933).

''Philosophers and sociologists once thought that there was a tendency towards rational and moral progress inherent in the human mind. That this is untrue is clear . . . in the past decades, we have receded rather than advanced as far as moral and rational progress is concerned'' (Karl Mannheim, *Man and Society in an Age of Reconstruction*, 1935).

''[Through innovation, revolution may become] the main factor of cultural progress'' (Florian Znaniecki, *Social Actions*, 1936).

''The rationalism and moralism which is the driving force behind social study . . . is the faith that institutions can be improved and strengthened and that people are good enough to live a happier life'' (Gunnar Myrdal, *An American Dilemma*, 1942).

''For individuals as well as for societies, the types of decline and the causes of death are much more varied than the types of birth and of progress'' (Corrado Gini in D. Kalitsounakis, ed., *Economy and Society*, 1961).

''Progress does not mean much unless one decides where it is to start and from what it starts. But the decision as to the origin and the goal of history is capable of very different constructions depending on one's values'' (Don Martindale, *Social Life and Cultural Change*, 1962).

''In this era of rapid change in rural areas, progress is often believed strongly based on moving people away from farms and small towns into the bigger cities'' (Carle Zimmerman and Garry Moneo, *The Prairie Community System*, 1971).

''*The idea of progress holds that mankind has advanced in the past . . . is now advancing, and will continue to advance through the foreseeable future*'' (Robert Nisbet, *History of the Idea of Progress*, 1980).

PROLETARIAT

''Political economy advances the proposition that the proletarian, the same as any horse, must get as much as will enable him to work. It does not consider him when he is not working, as a human being'' (Karl Marx, *Economic and Philosophic Manuscripts*, 1844).

''Proletariat means the class of modern wage-laborers who, having no means of production of their own, are reduced to selling their labor power in order to live. . . . The proletariat is recruited from all classes of the population. . . . With the development of industry the proletariat not only increases in number, it becomes concentrated in great masses, its strength grows, and it feels that strength move. . . . Not only has the bourgeoisie forged the weapons that bring death to itself; it has also called into existence the men who are to wield those weapons, namely, the modern working class, the proletarians. . . . The proletariat will use its political supremacy to wrest, by degrees, all capital from the bourgeoisie, to centralize all instruments of production in the hands of the state, namely, of the proletariat organized as the ruling class'' (Karl Marx and Friedrich Engels, *Communist Manifesto*, 1847).

''Accumulation of capital means increase of the proletariat'' (Karl Marx, *Das Kapital*, 1879).

''Today there are many professional and service workers who do not control the means of production, but who also do not identify with the working class. . . . The working class has failed to become a militant revolutionary force, perhaps because the government and the capitalists themselves have become more responsive'' (Neil Smelser, *Sociology*, 1981).

PROSTITUTION

''[The prostitute] is like a whirlpool in a current leading man knoweth not where. To listen to her is an abominable and deadly thing'' (Ani, *Maxims*, c. 1400 B.C.).

''Her [prostitute's] house is the way to hell, going down to the chambers of death'' (Proverbs 7:27).

''I would order men to abstain from any female field in which what is sown is not likely to grow'' (Plato, *Laws*, c. 400 B.C.).

''Harlots we keep for the sake of pleasure only, concubines for daily service, but wives for bearing us legitimate children and acting as loyal guardians of our households'' (Demosthenes, *Against Neaera*, c. 350 B.C.).

''Clever prostitutes . . . he should know to be thorns in the side of his people. Having detected them by means of trustworthy persons, who, disguising themselves, pretend to follow the same occupations, and by means of spies, wearing various disguises, he must cause them to be instigated to commit offenses . . . the king shall duly punish them'' (Manu, *Laws*, c. 200 B.C.).

''A form of unlawful giving is giving for a service that is unlawful, although the giving itself is not unlawful, as when a man gives to a prostitute her hire'' (Thomas Aquinas, *Summa Theologica*, 1274).

''Get thee to a nunnery: why wouldst thou be a breeder of sinners?'' (William Shakespeare, *Hamlet*, 1601).

''Prisons are built with stones of law, brothels with bricks of religion'' (William Blake, *The Marriage of Heaven and Hell*, 1790).

''The present family finds its complement in public prostitution. The bourgeois family will vanish as a matter of course when its complement vanishes, and both will vanish with the vanishing of capital'' (Karl Marx and Friedrich Engels, *Communist Manifesto*, 1847).

''Among the Ancient Greeks . . . copulation itself was at times regarded as an act of worship. But it is in those societies where prostitution becomes an essential part of the worship of the gods that the most powerful expression of the union of sexuality and religion is to be found. The main areas where this phenomenon occurs are parts of the Mediterranean lands, Asia Minor, West Africa, and southern India. Two types of temple prostitution have to be distinguished. The first is where the individual woman performs an initial act of prostitution, and thereafter becomes married in the ordinary way. The second is when a woman is dedicated to the service of the temple as a sacred harlot. This may be for a term, or, what is more common, for her life'' (Fernando Henriques, *Prostitution and Society*, 1962).

''Erotical services are provided as part of the build-up and entertainment which speeds along the big order. The night-life of New York is very largely run on the expense account, and many of the customers are out-of-towners with wives not present'' (C. W. Mills in Irving Horowitz, ed., *Power, Politics, and People*, 1963).

''According to Chinese tradition commercial brothels were originated in the seventh century B.C. by the statesman and philosopher Kuang Chung as a means for increasing the state's income'' (Vern Bullough, *The History of Prostitution*, 1964).

''All prostitutes are in it for the money. With most uptown call girls, the choice is not between starvation and life, but between $5,000 and $25,000 or between $10,000 and $50,000. . . . You can say that they're in this business because of the difference of $40,000 a year. A businessman would say so. . . . Call girls do go into capitalism and think like capitalists'' (Kate Millett, ed., *The Prostitution Papers*, 1973).

''Despite their highly advanced code of ethics, in practice, the ancient Egyptians frequently engaged in behavior diametrically opposed to this code. Prostitution, for instance, was quite common'' (Panos Bardis, *Evolution of the Family in the West*, 1983).

''Prostitution was strongly disapproved of [among the ancient Hebrews]. . . . The law appeared more liberal regarding relations with foreign prostitutes, the so-called strange women who were often seen along highways, living in tents and sometimes working as peddlers. Solomon later liberalized the laws further, allowing foreign harlots to enter Jerusalem'' (Panos Bardis, *Global Marriage and Family Customs*, 1983).

PROTESTANT ETHIC

''Since asceticism undertook to remodel the world and to work out its ideals in the world, material goods have gained an increasing and finally an inexorable power over the lives of men as at no previous period in history. Today the spirit of religious asceticism—whether finally, who knows?—has escaped from the cage. But victorious capitalism, since it rests on mechanical foundations, needs its support no longer. . . . [The modern economy is] bound to the technical and economic conditions of machine production which today determines the lives of all the individuals . . . wherever riches have increased, the essence of religion has decreased in the same proportion . . . religion must necessarily produce both industry and frugality, and these cannot but produce riches. But as riches increase, so will pride, anger, and love of the world in all its branches . . . the Methodists in every place grow diligent and frugal; consequently they increase in goods'' (Max Weber, *The Protestant Ethic and the Spirit of Capitalism*, 1905).

''In the United States . . . even though success is often regarded as an end in itself and sometimes there is almost no positive relation between success and moral virtue, yet the success pattern is still linked to achievement, achievement is still associated with work, and work is still invested with an almost organic complex of ethical values'' (Robin Williams, *American Society*, 1951).

''It is impossible to over-dramatize the forthcoming crisis as it potentially strikes a blow at the very core of industrialized societies—the work ethic. We have based our social structures on this ethic and now it would appear that it is to become redundant along with millions of other people'' (Clive Jenkins and Barrie Sherman, *The Collapse of Work*, 1979).

''There has never been much evidence to support Max Weber's description of man as 'driving hard against the environment because of his need to prove himself before God.' The Protestant ethic may have heightened the social stigma associated with not working, but the struggle for survival offered ample motivation to work for even the most irreverent of characters'' (Sar Levitan and Clifford Johnson, *Second Thoughts on Work*, 1982).

PSYCHOLOGY, SOCIAL

''The man who has not contemplated the mind is unable to give a reason of those things that have reason'' (Plato, *Laws*, c. 400 B.C.).

''The actual perception by mind of mind itself thus subsists to eternity'' (Aristotle, *Metaphysics*, c. 350 B.C.).

''Although in operations which pass to an external effect, the object of the operation, which is taken as the term, exists outside the operator, nevertheless, in operations that remain in the operator, the object signified as the term of the operation resides in the operator; and according as it is in the operator is the operation actual'' (Thomas Aquinas, *Summa Theologica*, 1274).

''In the first place, I put for a general inclination of all mankind, a perpetual and restless desire of power after power, that ceases only in death'' (Thomas Hobbes, *Leviathan*, 1651).

''There are evidently some principles in his [man's] nature which interest him in the fortune of others, and render their happiness necessary to him'' (Adam Smith, *The Wealth of Nations*, 1776).

''Sociology alone gives a knowledge of our intellectual and moral attributes which become sufficiently appreciable only in their collective upgrowth . . . the true final science, namely, morale [*la morale*], is able to systematize the special knowledge of our individual nature, by virtue of an appropriate combination of the two points of view, the biological and the sociological'' (Auguste Comte, *System of Positive Polity*, 1854).

''What man wills, what every smallest part of a living organism wills, is a plus of power. Both pleasure and unpleasure are consequences of striving for it'' (Friedrich Wilhelm Nietzsche, *The Will to Power*, 1888).

''Pleasure accompanies neither the very intense states of conscience nor those that are too weak. There is a pain when the functional activity is insufficient, but excessive activity produces the same effects . . . human experience sees the condition of happiness in the *golden mean*'' (Émile Durkheim, *The Division of Labor in Society*, 1893).

''Under the influence of a suggestion [in a crowd], he [the individual] will undertake the accomplishment of certain acts with irresistible impetuosity'' (Gustave Le Bon, *The Crowd*, 1895).

''[Law of imitation:] the thing that is most imitated is the most superior one of those that are nearest'' (Gabriel Tarde, *Social Laws*, 1898).

''[Social psychology is the science of] the psychic interplay between man and his environing society'' (Edward Ross, *Social Control*, 1901).

''[Ideomotor theory:] The idea of an action is itself a motive to that action and tends intrinsically to produce it unless something intervenes to prevent it'' (Charles Cooley, *Human Nature and the Social Order*, 1902).

''The human mind has certain innate or inherited tendencies which are the essential springs or motive powers of all thought and action'' (William McDougall, *An Introduction to Social Psychology*, 1908).

''[Social psychology studies] the moulding of the ordinary person by his social environment'' (Edward Ross, *Social Psychology*, 1908).

''All human conduct is psychological and, from that standpoint, not only the study of economics but the study of every other branch of human activity is a psychological study and the facts of all such branches are psychological facts'' (Vilfredo Pareto, *The Mind and Society*, 1916).

''[Social psychology is] a general science of the subjective side of social culture . . . precisely the science of attitudes . . . while its methods are essentially different from the methods of individual psychology its field is as wide as conscious life'' (William Thomas and Florian Znaniecki, *The Polish Peasant in Europe and America*, 1920).

''The problem of social psychology [is] how different customs, established interacting arrangements, form and nurture different minds . . . we need to know about the social conditions which have educated original activities into definite and significant dispositions before we can discuss the psychological element in society. This is the true meaning of social psychology'' (John Dewey, *Human Nature and Conduct*, 1922).

''If men define situations as real then they will be real in their consequences'' (William Thomas, *The Unadjusted Girl*, 1923).

''It is in the form of the generalized other that the social process influences the behavior of the individuals involved in it and carrying it on, that is, that the community exercises control over the conduct of its individual members; for it is in this form that the social process or community enters as a determining factor into the individual's thinking. . . . The meaning of what we are saying is the tendency to respond to it'' (George H. Mead, *Mind, Self, and Society*, 1934, posthumously).

''If it were possible to designate a single deliberate 'founder' of social psychology as a science, we should have to nominate Comte for this honor'' (Gordon Allport in Gardner Lindzey and Elliot Aronson, eds., *The Handbook of Social Psychology*, 1968).

''It is the social process of group life that creates and upholds rules, not the rules that create and uphold group life'' (Herbert Blumer, *Symbolic Interactionism*, 1969).

''Nonsociologists sometimes express puzzlement at the fact that a branch of sociology should be called 'social psychology.' Yet . . . social psychology clearly occupies a prominent position in sociology . . . the first sociology textbook, published by Small and Vincent in 1894, devoted five chapters to social psychology . . . as early as 1908, the sociologist E. A. Ross published a book entitled *Social Psychology*; and . . . the universally acknowledged father of sociology, Auguste Comte, is also accorded paternity of the field'' (Morris Rosenberg and Ralph Turner, eds., *Social Psychology*, 1981).

Q

QUESTIONNAIRE

''Questionnaires are of various forms and types, with various goals and ways of administering them. . . . Much careful attention and experimentation are needed to produce effectively worded questions. . . . The respondent's frame of reference will influence his anwers. . . . The arrangement or ordering of the questions should receive special attention'' (Pauline Young, *Scientific Social Surveys and Research*, 1966).

''Questionnaires have advantages and disadvantages. Among the advantages are 1.They are less expensive than interviews . . . 2.They reduce respondent-researcher interaction . . . 3.They provide the respondent with a greater sense of privacy . . . 4.They generally provide the respondent with more time. . . . Some disadvantages of questionnaires are 1.Their response rates vary depending upon the method of administration . . . 2.They pose special difficulties for illiterate and marginally literate respondents . . . 3.They allow little opportunity for respondents to seek clarification of questions . . . 4.They permit respondents to respond in any manner whatsoever'' (Kenneth Eckhardt and M. Ermann, *Social Research Methods*, 1977).

''There are two main methods of administering survey questionnaires to a sample of respondents . . . *self-administered* questionnaires and . . . administered by staff interviewers'' (Earl Babbie, *The Practice of Social Research*, 1979).

''Public opinion polling had become ubiquitous. It has progressed from a curiosity to a major industry with its own professional association. . . . The increasing use of polling derives both from greater need and greater opportunity. The need arises from a universal problem: limited resources and unlimited desires. . . . The opportunity arises because the United States . . . supports an infrastructure that makes feasible cheap and extensive public opinion polling. . . . Mandatory universal education has brought the total populace to a minimum level of competency in understanding and speaking English. . . . Thus, the need to set priorities, combined with this massive technical infrastructure, creates a favorable climate for continued growth in public opinion polling and the questionnaires that provide the foundation for every poll'' (Patricia Labaw, *Advanced Questionnaire Design*, 1980).

''Interviews are a much more flexible data collection method than questionnaires. . . . Both methods rely on verbal reports of emotional, cognitive, and overt behavior, although interviews permit observations as well . . . only certain facts can be studied by means of . . . mailed questionnaires. These measuring instruments are best at obtaining present attitudes about relatively simple phenomena. They cannot be used to study actual behavior as it takes place'' (Ann and Hubert Blalock, *Introduction to Social Research*, 1982).

''Questionnaires contain a series of questions, statements, or other stimuli to which persons are asked to respond, either by writing short, narrative responses or by selecting among the structured alternatives presented. They may be brief, with only a few questions and their response alternatives, or very long, requiring from a few minutes up to an hour for their completion. They are administered in a variety of ways: by mail, over the telephone, in face-to-face interviews, and by hand delivery'' (Tony Tripodi, *Evaluative Research for Social Workers*, 1983).

R

RACE

"The black races in Ethiopia are not the product of the sun; for if black gets black with child in Scythia, the offspring is black; but if a black gets a white woman with child the offspring is grey. And this shows that the seed of the mother has power in the embryo equally with that of the father" (Leonardo da Vinci, *Notebooks*, c. 1500).

"It cannot be believed that such newly found people in the islands are of Adam's blood" (Philippus Aureolus Paracelsus, *Great Astronomy*, 1538).

"Certain nations have something peculiar in the shape of their head" (Andreas Vesalius, *The Fabric of the Human Body*, 1543).

"The people of the South are of a contrary humor and disposition to them of the North. . . . [The cause is not] the climate alone, for we see in climates that are alike and of the same elevation four notable differences of people in color" (Jean Bodin, *The Six Books of the Republic*, 1576).

"Of many colors are the species of men . . . nor are they sprung from the generative force of a single progenitor" (Giordano Bruno, *On the Immense and Innumerable*, 1590).

"The blackness of the skin is no reason why a human being should be abandoned without redress to the caprice of a tormentor" (Jeremy Bentham, *Introduction to the Principles of Morals and Legislation*, 1789).

"If the defenders of race theories prove that a certain kind of behavior is hereditary and wish to explain in this way that it belongs to a racial type they would have to prove that the particular kind of behavior is characteristic of all the genetic lines composing the race. . . . The organization of mind is practically identical among all races of man" (Franz Boas, *The Mind of Primitive Man*, 1911).

"The temperament of the Negro as I conceive it consists in a few elementary but distinctive characteristics, determined by physical organizations and transmitted biologically. These characteristics manifest themselves in a genial, sunny, and social disposition, in an interest and attachment to external, physical things rather than to subjective states and objects of introspection, in a disposition for expression rather than enterprise and action'' (Robert Park and Ernest Burgess, *Introduction to the Science of Sociology*, 1921).

''[No evidence supports differences in] degrees of mental endowment among races'' (William Thomas, *Primitive Behavior*, 1937).

''The practically complete absence of intermarriage in all states has the social effect of preventing the most intimate type of acceptance into white society: if Negroes can never get into a white family, they can never be treated as 'one of the family' '' (Gunnar Myrdal, *An American Dilemma*, 1944).

''In the relations of races there is a cycle of events which tends everywhere to repeat itself. . . . The race relations cycle, which takes the form, to state it abstractly, of contacts, competition, accommodation, and eventual assimilation, is apparently progressive and irreversible'' (Robert Park, *Race and Culture*, 1944).

''[Some so-called races are] more nearly folk societies'' (Howard Odum, *Understanding Society*, 1947).

''There is a tendency to judge a race . . . by its least worthy members'' (Eric Hoffer, *The True Believer*, 1951).

''The Negro is only an American and nothing else. He has no values and culture to guard and protect'' (Nathan Glazer and Daniel Moynihan, *Beyond the Melting Pot*, 1963).

''The only useful way of grouping individuals for anthropological analysis is to group together the people participating within the same circle of matings'' (J. Hiernaux in Ashley Montagu, ed., *The Concept of Race*, 1964).

''No argument has ever been advanced by any reasonable man against the fact of differences among men. The whole argument is about what differences exist and how they are to be gauged'' (Jacques Barzun, *Race*, 1965).

''Vulgar Marxism has a monocausal theory on the origin of racism: racism is part of the bourgeois ideology designed especially to rationalize the exploitation of nonwhite peoples of the world during the imperialistic phase of capitalism'' (Pierre Van den Berghe, *Race and Racism*, 1967).

''To deny existence of racial differences within the human species is futile. . . . I find it amusing that those who questioned the validity of racial classifications have themselves used the word 'race' '' (Theodosius Dobzhansky, *Science and the Concept of Race*, 1968).

''People keep reminding me that there is a difference in physical ability between the races [in athletics], but I think there isn't. The Negro boy practices longer and harder. The Negro has the keener desire to excel in sports because it is more mandatory for his future opportunities than it is for a white boy'' (Jack Olsen, *The Black Athlete*, 1968).

''[Black Power activity] has subsided not because the racial crisis has passed but because white power has demonstrated that open black defiance is extremely dangerous and often suicidal'' (Lewis Killian, *The Impossible Revolution, Phase II*, 1975).

''As a neighborhood moves from, say, a 10 percent population of blacks to

20 percent or more, integration should be regulated so that long-range community stability is guaranteed. . . . Institutional racism is a reality; the massive migration of blacks into a neighborhood does not bring with it social rewards but, almost exclusively, punishments'' (Michael Novak in John and Erna Perry, eds., *Social Problems in Today's World*, 1978).

''Race relations in the United States have undergone fundamental changes in recent years, so much so that now the life chances of individual blacks have more to do with their economic class position than with their day-to-day encounters with whites'' (William Wilson, *The Declining Significance of Race*, 1978).

''The coinciding of race and socio-economic boundaries is still one of the major determinants of power stratification in South Africa'' (Nic Rhoodie, ed., *Conflict Resolution in South Africa*, 1980).

''The plain fact is that at present there exists no scientifically satisfactory explanation for the differences between the IQ distributions in the black and white populations. The only genuine consensus among well-informed scientists on this topic is that the cause of the difference remains an open question'' (Arthur Jensen, *Straight Talk About Mental Tests*, 1981).

''The five primary races are the Caucasoid, Mongoloid, Australoid, Congoid (more commonly called Negroid), and the Capoid, mostly the Bushmen of southern Africa. . . . Some of my colleagues lump the last named with the Negroes, into whose ranks some of them have been absorbed. These races differ most conspicuously in skin, eye, and hair color, hair form, hairiness, and facial features. Caucasoid skins run from pink to almost black; the Mongoloids and Capoids are yellowish, while Negroids and Australoids are dark brown to black; those of other races are, with few exceptions, brown or black'' (Carleton Coon, *Racial Adaptations*, 1982).

RELIABILITY

''There are four procedures in common use for computing the reliability coefficient (sometimes called the self-correlation) of a test. These are (1) Test-retest (repetition) (2) Alternate or parallel forms (3) Split-half technique (4) Rational equivalence'' (Henry Garrett, *Statistics in Psychology and Education*, 1966).

''The concept of reliability is a complex one. The simplest definition of reliability is the degree to which a scale yields consistent scores when the attitude is measured a number of times'' (Marvin Shaw and Jack Wright, *Scales for the Measurement of Attitudes*, 1967).

''Reliability is defined as a correlation coefficient. . . . [It is] the correlation between two parallel measures'' (George Bohrnstedt in Gene Summers, ed., *Attitude Measurement*, 1970).

''One of the most unfortunately ambiguous terms in psychometry is 'reliability.' There are at least three major entities to which the term can refer: (1)

The correlation between the same person's score on the same items at two separate points in time; (2) the correlation between two different sets of items at the same time . . . and (3) the correlation between the scale items for all people who answer the items'' (John Robinson et al., *Measures of Occupational Attitudes and Occupational Characteristics*, 1976).

''An operational definition can be considered to be a detailed set of instructions enabling one to classify individuals unambiguously. The notion of reliability is thus built into this conception'' (Hubert Blalock, *Social Statistics*, 1979).

RELIGION, SOCIOLOGY OF

''The fool hath said in his heart, There is no God'' (Psalms 14:1).

''If things are going well, religion and legislation are helpful, but if not, they are of no avail'' (Solon, c. 600 B.C., in Diogenes Laertius, *Lives of Eminent Philosophers*, c. 250).

''O most great and sovereign God . . . if, in my person, I commit offenses, they are not to be attributed to you'' (Confucius, *Analects*, c. 500 B.C.).

''One man worships one god, and one another'' (Euripides, *Hippolytus*, 428 B.C.).

''The most serious offenses are those against religion'' (Plato, *Laws*, c. 400 B.C.).

''Those who are fortunate love the gods and display a kind of confidence toward the deity'' (Aristotle, *Rhetoric*, c. 350 B.C.).

''Be always studious to be in harmony with the ordinances of God'' (Mencius, *Book of Mencius*, c. 300 B.C.).

''When he has paid . . . his debts . . . to the gods, let him make over everything to his son'' (Manu, *Laws*, c. 200 B.C.).

''Pure religion . . . is this, To visit the fatherless and widows in their affliction, and to keep himself unspotted from the world'' (James 1:27).

''Religion is divine wisdom'' (Thomas Aquinas, *Summa Theologica*, 1274).

''How is it that we hear so much about reward if there is no such thing as merit? With what impudence is the obedience of those who obey the divine commands praised, and the disobedience of those who do not obey condemned? Why is there so frequent a mention of judgment in Holy Scriptures if there is no weighing of merits?'' (Desiderius Erasmus, *Discourse on Free Will*, 1524).

''I count religion but a childish toy, and hold there is no sin but ignorance'' (Christopher Marlowe, *The Jew of Malta*, 1589).

''It is religion that doth make vows kept'' (William Shakespeare, *King John*, 1597).

''In all countries, the dominant Religion, when it does not persecute anyone, in the long run engulfs all the others'' (François Marie Arouet de Voltaire, *English or Philosophical Letters*, 1734).

''The garb of religion is the best cloak for power'' (William Hazlitt, *Political Essays*, 1819).

"Religion is the sign of the oppressed creature. . . . It is the opiate of the people" (Karl Marx, *Early Writings*, 1844).

"The more of himself man attributes to God the less he has left in himself . . . in religion the spontaneous activity of human fantasy, of the human brain and heart, reacts independently as an alien activity of gods or devils upon the individual" (Karl Marx, *Economic and Philosophic Manuscripts*, 1844).

"The growth of religious ideas is environed with such intrinsic difficulties that it may never receive a perfectly satisfactory exposition. Religion deals so largely with the imaginative and emotional nature, and consequently with such uncertain elements of knowledge, that all primitive religions are grotesque and to some extent unintelligible" (Lewis H. Morgan, *Ancient Society*, 1877).

"[Religion] has emphasized the duty of truth-speaking, and has itself been a cause of pious fraud" (Edward Alexander Westermarck, *The Origin and Development of the Moral Ideas*, 1908).

"[Religion] is a unified system of beliefs and practices relative to sacred things; that is to say, things set apart and forbidden—beliefs and practices which unite into one single moral community, called a *church*, all those who adhere to them" (Émile Durkheim, *The Elementary Forms of Religious Life*, 1912).

"All Hindus accept two basic principles: the *samsara* belief in the transmigration of souls and the related *karma* doctrine of compensation. These alone are the truly 'dogmatic' doctrines of all Hinduism. . . . An absolute presupposition of Hindu philosophy after the full development of the *karma* and *samsara* doctrines, was that escape from the wheel of rebirth could be the one and only conceivable function of a 'salvation' " (Max Weber, *The Religion of India*, 1917).

"Magic and religion are found everywhere; but a religious basis for the ordering of life which, consistently followed out, must lead to explicit rationalism is . . . peculiar to western civilization alone" (Max Weber, *General Economic History*, 1920).

"[Religion will redeem society] from ignorance, impoverishment, hate, irrational fear, foolish pride, brutal lusts, vice, crime, and self-will" (Charles Ellwood, *The Reconstruction of Religion*, 1922).

"Individual castes develop quite distinct cults and gods" (Max Weber, *Economy and Society*, 1922, posthumously).

"None of these mass religions of Asia . . . provided the motives of orientations for a rationalized ethical patterning of the creaturely world in accordance with divine commandments. Rather, they all accepted the world as eternally given, and so the best of all possible worlds. The only choice open to the sages, who possessed the highest type of piety, was whether to accommodate themselves to the Tao, the impersonal order of the world and the only thing specifically divine, or to save themselves from the inexorable chain of causality by passing into the only eternal being, the dreamless sleep of Nirvana" (Max Weber, *The Sociology of Religion*, 1922, posthumously).

"[Religion is] the great means of promoting faith, hope, and love in human society" (Charles Ellwood, *Christianity and Social Science*, 1923).

"His theory [E. Tylor's animism and nature worship] is avowedly a psychological interpretation pure and simple, but inasmuch as it not only explains the empirical observations, but operates exclusively with facts like death, dreams and visions, all of which demonstrably exercise a strong influence on the minds of primitive men, it must be conceded to have a high degree of probability. I, for one, certainly have never encountered any rival hypothesis that could be considered a serious competitor" (Robert Lowie, *Primitive Religion*, 1924).

"As to the acts which usually would be regarded as religious rather than magical—ceremonies at birth or marriage, rites of death and mourning, the worship of ghosts, spirits, or mythical personages—they also have a legal side clearly exemplified in the case of mortuary performances. . . . Every important act of a religious nature is conceived as a moral obligation towards the object, the ghost, spirit, or power worshipped; it also satisfies some emotional craving of the performer; but besides all this it has also as a matter of fact its place in some social scheme" (Bronislaw Malinowski, *Crime and Custom in Savage Society*, 1926).

"Religion is an attempt to get control over the sensory world" (Sigmund Freud, *New Introductory Lectures on Psychoanalysis*, 1933).

"[A universalized, humanitarian religion is] the supreme embodiment of the values of life" (Charles Ellwood, *The World's Need of Christ*, 1940).

"[It is difficult for religion to apply] the virtues of a society based upon neighborly relationships to the world at large . . . where the basic rules are against the spirit of Christianity" (Karl Mannheim, *Diagnosis of Our Time*, 1943).

"God dwells in the heart of every finite creature and leads mankind steadily and steadfastly to universal freedom and perfection" (Radhakamal Mukerjee, *The Dynamics of Morals*, 1950).

"Nuer are not confused, because the difficulties which perplex us do not arise on the level of experience but only when an attempt is made to analyze and systematize Nuer religious thought. Nuer themselves do not feel the need to do this. . . . It is when one tries to relate Nuer religious conceptions to one another by abstract analysis that the difficulties arise" (E. Evans-Pritchard, *Nuer Religion*, 1956).

"Religion is always a patron of the arts, but its taste is by no means impeccable" (Aldous Huxley, *Tomorrow and Tomorrow and Tomorrow*, 1956).

"[Religion is] a system of beliefs about the nature of forces ultimately shaping man's destiny, and . . . practices associated therewith shared by the members of the group" (Gerhard Lenski, *The Religious Factor*, 1961).

"The genius of Christianity is to have proclaimed that the path to the deepest mystery is the path of love—a love which is not confined to men's feelings, but transcends them like the soul of the world" (André Malraux, *Antimemoirs*, 1967).

"For the Cheyenne there is no Hell or punishment of any sort in after-life; no Judgment or Damnation . . . there is no problem of salvation; goodness is to be sought . . . for its own sake and . . . approval of one's fellow man'' (E. Hoebel, *The Cheyennes*, 1978).

''One of the main advantages of drawing on new religious movements for empirical data in a quest for social knowledge is that, unlike most aspects of the generally messy and complicated world of social reality, the movements present us with comparatively neat, clear-cut objects of study'' (Eileen Barker, ed., *New Religious Movements*, 1982).

''[Religion is a] reaction to wonder, to mystery, to grace (all three of which are the different names for the same phenomenon—an experience which renews hope). . . . Sociologists cannot explain in any ultimate sense such experiences'' (Andrew Greeley, *Religion*, 1982).

''For a world in religious turmoil, as ours is, the notion of 'God' must be the center of dialogue'' (Frederick Sontag and M. Bryant, eds., *God*, 1982).

REMARRIAGE

''Dissolution of marriage disrupts a complex integration of role, which requires a corresponding role to be played by someone in the outside world . . . his need for a partner who will play a complementary role and thus render functional a long-standing role of one's own is undoubtedly a strong motivational drive toward remarriage'' (Jessie Bernard, *Remarriage*, 1956).

''The excess of females in the older age brackets means that many widows will never have an opportunity for remarriage'' (Walter McKain, *Retirement Marriage*, 1968).

''Persons who remarry differ in age and socioeconomic characteristics from those who marry for the first time. . . . In 1969 nearly one-fourth of all persons marrying had been married at least once before. . . . As divorce rates rose during the sixties, the tendency for divorced men and women to remarry also increased. Far more divorced than widowed persons are involved in remarriages and the upward trend reflects the trend for the divorced, not the widowed. . . . Although national estimates of remarriages for men and women are close in number, remarriage rates for men are more than 3 times those for women. This is due to differences in the population bases for men and women. Widowed women far outnumber widowed men in the population and there are also more divorced women than divorced men'' (Kristen Williams and Russell Kuhn, *Remarriages*, 1973).

''Within five years of divorce, three-quarters of all divorced people are remarried'' (Lucile Duberman, *The Reconstituted Family*, 1975).

''Because in our society so many people become divorced and remarried—some, perhaps attempting to emulate the dubious example of Southern California movie stars, marrying many different times—some sociologists have termed the emerging American marital system *serial polygamy*'' (Thomas Kando, *Sexual Behavior and Family Life in Transition*, 1978).

''The reasons why breakup by death is best for remarried relationships, while the marriage being the first for one of the partners is worst would seem to include . . . that one whose spouse had died was better able to completely sever past ties, while those who had not been previously married entered a complex life situation unprepared by a former marriage of their own'' (Bert Adams, *The Family*, 1980).

''The lack of pertinent literature about the remarried family population has been noted by both remarried family members and the professionals with whom they work. People in remarried families have commented that . . . there is little to guide them. . . . Many remarried persons spoke of their lack of preparation for living in this kind of family unit'' (Esther Wald, *The Remarried Family*, 1981).

REVOLUTION

''Because I was youthful, I believed that these revolutionists would introduce a new era of justice. I soon realized, however, that by comparison the previous government was a golden age. This conclusion led me to desert the abusive regime in disgust'' (Plato, *Letters*, c. 400 B.C., perhaps spurious).

''Since we are considering what conditions lead to revolutions . . . at first we must ascertain their beginnings and causes generally. They are . . . three in number. . . . We must ascertain how people revolt, and their motives, and thirdly what are the beginnings of political disturbances and internal conflicts. Now the general and main reason why these people favor change in some way is. . . . Some, desiring equality, revolt when they think they have very little, although they are equal to people having more, and others, desiring inequality and superiority, when they believe that, although they are unequal, they have not more but equal or less (and these may be desired justly or unjustly); for, when they are inferior, they revolt in order to be equal, and when they are equal, in order to be greater'' (Aristotle, *Politics*, c. 350 B.C.).

''Revolution is like Saturn; it devours its own children'' (Georg Büchner, *Danton's Death*, 1835).

''The class making a revolution appears from the very start, if only because it is opposed to a *class*, not as a class but as the representative of the whole of society; it appears as the whole mass of society confronting the one ruling class'' (Karl Marx and Friedrich Engels, *The German Ideology*, 1846).

''Of all the instruments of production, the greatest productive power is the revolutionary class itself. The organization of revolutionary elements as a class supposes the existence of all the productive forces which could be engendered in the bosom of the old society'' (Karl Marx, *The Poverty of Philosophy*, 1847).

''Of all the classes that stand face to face with the bourgeoisie today, the proletariat alone is a really revolutionary class. The other classes decay and finally disappear in the face of Modern Industry; the proletariat is its special and essential product. . . . In depicting the most general phases of the development of the proletariat, we traced the more or less veiled civil war, raging within existing society, up to the point where that war breaks out into open revolution, and where the violent overthrow of the bourgeoisie lays the foundation for the sway of the proletariat'' (Karl Marx and Friedrich Engels, *Communist Manifesto*, 1847).

''All history is full of such wonders [as the failure of the French Revolution along the Loire]. It is not always by going from bad to worse that a society falls into revolution. It happens most often that a people, which has supported without complaint, as if they were not felt, the most oppressive laws, violently throws them off as soon as their weight is lightened. The social order destroyed by a revolution is almost always better than that which immediately preceded it, and experience shows that the most dangerous moment for a bad government is generally that in which it sets about reform. Only great genius can save a prince who undertakes to relieve his subjects after a long oppression'' (Alexis Charles Henri Maurice Clérel de Tocqueville, *The Old Regime and the French Revolution*, 1856).

''At a certain stage of development, the material productive forces of society come into conflict with the existing relations of production. . . . Then begins the era of social revolution. . . . No social order is ever destroyed before all the productive forces for which it is sufficient have been developed'' (Karl Marx, *A Contribution to the Critique of Political Economy*, 1859).

''That force [a violent revolution] . . . plays another role . . . in history . . . that, in the words of Marx, it is the midwife of every old society which is pregnant with the new; that it is the instrument with whose aid social movement forces its way through and shatters the dead, fossilised political forms—of this there is not a word in Herr Dühring'' (Friedrich Engels, *Anti-Dühring*, 1878).

''The revolution of the bourgeoisie abolished the estates and their privileges. Bourgeois society knows only *classes*'' (Friedrich Engels, note in Karl Marx, *The Poverty of Philosophy*, 1847; 1885 edition).

''Give us an organization of revolutionaries, and we shall overturn the whole of Russia'' (Nikolai Lenin, *What Is to Be Done*, 1902).

''Revolutions have never lightened the burden of tyranny: they have only shifted it to another shoulder'' (George B. Shaw, *Man and Superman*, 1903).

''What is now happening to Marx's doctrine has, in the course of history, often happened to the doctrines of other revolutionary thinkers and leaders of oppressed classes struggling for emancipation. During the lifetime of great revolutionaries, the oppressing classes have visited relentless persecution on them and received their teaching with the most savage hostility, the most furious hatred, the most ruthless campaign of lies and slanders. After their death, attempts are made to turn them into harmless icons, canonise them, and surround their *names* with a certain halo for the 'consolation' of the oppressed classes and with the object of duping them, while at the same time emasculating and vulgarising the *real essence* of their revolutionary theories and blunting their revolutionary edge . . . every revolution, by shattering the state apparatus, demonstrates to us how the ruling class aims at the restoration of the special bodies of armed men at *its* service, and how the oppressed class tries to create a new organisation of this kind, capable of serving not the exploiters, but the exploited. . . . The replacement of the bourgeois by the proletarian state is impossible without a violent revolution. The abolition of the proletarian state, i.e., of all states, is only possible through 'withering away' " (Nikolai Lenin, *The State and Revolution*, 1917).

"[In Russia] the robbed and oppressed masses—a hundred millions of men and women—moved toward the goal of their long unfulfilled desires like a flow of molten lava that no human force can dam or turn aside. It [the Bolshevik Revolution] was a majestic and appalling social phenomenon—as elemental almost as an earthquake or a tidal wave" (Edward Ross, *The Russian Bolshevik Revolution*, 1921).

"[Revolution is] a change in the behavior of the people on the one hand and their psychology, ideology, beliefs and valuations on the other . . . a change in the biologic composition of population, and of the reproductive and selective processes in the midst . . . the deformation of the social structure of society" (Pitirim Sorokin, *The Sociology of Revolution*, 1925).

"The political mechanism of revolution consists of the transfer of power from one class to another. The forcible overturn is usually accomplished in a brief time. But no historic class lifts itself from a subject position to a position of rulership suddenly in one night, even though a night of revolution. It must already on the eve of the revolution have assumed a very independent attitude towards the official ruling class; moreover, it must have focused upon itself the hopes of intermediate classes and layers, dissatisfied with the existing state of affairs, but not capable of playing an independent role" (Leon Trotsky, *History of the Russian Revolution*, 1932).

"[Revolution] tends to bring innovations into the cultural life of the collectivity" (Florian Znaniecki, *Social Actions*, 1936).

"The successful revolutionary is a statesman, the unsuccessful one a criminal" (Erich Fromm, *Escape from Freedom*, 1941).

"[Revolution undermines democracy, which is based on] orderly patterns of human interaction" (Karl Mannheim, *Freedom, Power, and Democratic Planning*, 1950, posthumously).

"What is it that brings men to attack the established order? . . . the following motives are encountered with particular frequency: *Hatred of an occupying power. . . . Humiliation. . . . Despair. . . . Fear. . . . Oppression. . . . Envy or resentment. . . . Rejection of incompetence*" (Jean Baechler, *Revolutionary Phenomena*, 1970).

"We do not make revolution for our children . . . we make revolution to get pleasure from life for ourselves" (Daniel Cohn-Bendit, *Obsolete Communism*, 1970).

"Revolution [is] ordinarily defined as fundamental sociopolitical change accomplished through violence" (Ted Gurr, *Why Men Rebel*, 1970).

"The purposes of men, especially in a revolution, are so numerous, so varied, and so contradictory that their complex interaction produces results that no one intended or could even foresee" (Gordon Wood in Lawrence Kaplan, ed., *Revolutions*, 1973).

"The social sciences were conceptual orientations and technologies of middle-class strata newly thrust into positions of power by revolution and facing the problem of understanding and consolidating the society that had come into their hands" (Raj Mohan and Don Martindale, eds., *Handbook of Contemporary Developments in World Sociology*, 1975).

"A revolution begins when a government previously under the control of a single sovereign policy becomes the object of effective, competing, mutually exclusive claims on the part of two or more distinct polities; it ends when a single sovereign policy regains control over the government" (Charles Tilly in Fred Greenstein and Nelson Polsby, eds., *Handbook of Political Science*, 1975).

"Social revolutions are set apart from other sorts of conflicts and transformative processes above all by the combination of two coincidences: the coincidence of societal structural change with class upheaval; and the coincidence of political with social transformation" (Theda Skocpol, *States and Social Revolution*, 1979).

RITE OF PASSAGE

"Almost universally initiation rites include a mimic representation of the death and resurrection of the novice. The new life to which he awakes after initiation is one utterly forgetful of the old; a new name, a new language, and new privileges are its natural accompaniments" (H. Webster, *Primitive Secret Societies*, 1908).

"[Rites make society like] a house divided into rooms and corridors" (Charles-Arnold Kurr Van Gennep, *The Rites of Passage*, 1909).

"The boy [among the Andaman Islanders] kneels down and bends forward until his elbows rest on the ground in front. One of the older men . . . makes a series of cuts on the boy's back. Each cut is horizontal, and they are arranged in three vertical rows, each row consisting of from 20 to 30 cuts. When the cutting is finished the boy sits up, with a fire at his back, until the bleeding stops. During the operation and a few hours following it the boy must remain silent . . . covered with leaves the girl must sit in the hut allotted to her, with her legs doubled up beneath her and her arms folded . . . for three days. Early every morning she leaves her hut to bathe for an hour in the sea. At the end of the three days she resumes her life in the village. For a month following she must bathe in the sea every morning" (A. Radcliffe-Brown, *The Andaman Islanders*, 1922).

"Ritual is part of the educative process, a symbolic affirmation of certain social values, and in traditional Swazi [in Southeast Africa] society where specialized formal educational institutions are nonexistent, the age classes serve as the main channels for inculcating the values of loyalty and group morality" (Hilda Kuper, *The Swazi*, 1963).

"Initiation rites are means for the establishment of sexual identity" (Clifford Geertz in M. Banton, ed., *Anthropological Approaches to the Study of Religion*, 1966).

"Rites of passage . . . mark the transition from one status to another within the life cycle" (Frank Vivelo, *Cultural Anthropology Handbook*, 1978).

''Menarcheal ceremonies are more likely to occur in societies in which residential patterns and economic resource base inhibit the formation of fraternal interest groups and among those having weak fraternal interest groups, as measured by the ability to contract and defend explicit bargains through the action of numerous loyal kinsmen'' (Karen and Jeffrey Paige, *The Politics of Reproductive Ritual*, 1981).

ROLE, SOCIAL

''The husband should manage so that he always maintains his authority over his wife. . . . The husband is lord over his wife, because woman originated from man'' (Desiderius Erasmus, *The Institution of Christian Marriage*, 1526).

''When she is born into the world the young American girl finds ideas firmly established; she sees the rules that spring therefrom; she is soon convinced that she cannot for a moment depart from the usages accepted by her contemporaries without immediately putting in danger her peace of mind, her reputation and her very social existence'' (Alexis Charles Henri Maurice Clérel de Tocqueville, *Democracy in America*, 1840).

''Formerly—half a century ago—the women of Lisbon exhibited some characteristics of Circassian harem inmates. They never descended from their carriages, not even to buy a scarf or a soft drink. They concealed and veiled themselves. It was prohibited to look around and smile. Social disgrace hung over a lady who caught a cold during a drive. She had to refrain from sneezing in order not to be regarded as uncouth. Dancing parties were parades of statues and conversations parades of monosyllables. Whenever they knew how to read, they were unable to go beyond the prayer book'' (Victor de Moigénie, *Woman in Portugal*, 1924).

''The fundamental difference between the game and play is that in the latter the child must have the attitudes of all the others involved in that game. The attitudes of the other players which the participant assumes organize into a sort of unit, and it is that organization which controls the response of the individual. . . . Each one of his own acts is determined by his assumption of the action of the others who are playing the game. What he does is controlled by his being everyone else on that team, at least in so far as those attitudes affect his own particular response. We get then an 'other' which is an organization of the attitudes of those involved in the same process. The organized community or social group which gives to the individual his unity of self may be called 'the generalized other.' The attitude of the generalized other is the attitude of the whole community. Thus, for example, in the case of such a social group as a ball team, the team is the generalized other in so far as it enters—as an organized process or social activity—into the experience of any one of the individual members of it. . . . We cannot be ourselves unless we are also members in whom there is a community of attitudes which control the attitudes of all'' (George H. Mead, *Mind, Self, and Society*, 1934, posthumously).

"A *role* represents the dynamic aspect of a status. The individual is socially assigned to a status and occupies it with relation to other statuses. When he puts the rights and duties which constitute the status into effect, he is performing a role. Role and status are quite inseparable, and the distinction between them is of only academic interest" (Ralph Linton, *The Study of Man*, 1936).

"We say that a priest, a lawyer, a politician, a banker . . . performs a specific social role. Furthermore, the concept (with certain variations) has proved applicable not only to individuals who specialize in certain activities but also to individuals as members of certain groups: thus, an American, a Frenchman, a Methodist . . . a member of the family . . . plays a certain social role" (Florian Znaniecki, *The Social Role of the Man of Knowledge*, 1940).

"It is probably no mere historical accident that the word person, in its first meaning, is a mask. It is rather a recognition of the fact that everyone is always and everywhere, more or less consciously, playing a role. . . . It is in these roles that we know each other; it is in these roles that we know ourselves" (Robert Park, *Race and Culture*, 1944).

"It is . . . the securing of the leverage of the infant's motivation to secure the specific rewards of being fed, kept warm, etc. and avoid the corresponding deprivations which constitute the first beginning of his *playing a role* as distinguished from being merely an object of care" (Talcott Parsons, *The Social System*, 1951).

"An individual may affect the embracing of a role in order to conceal a lack of attachment to it, just as he may affect a visible disdain for a role, thrice refusing the kingly crown, in order to defend himself against the psychological dangers of his actual attachment to it. Certainly an individual may be attached to a role and fail to be able to embrace it" (Erving Goffman, *Encounters*, 1961).

"Society provides the script for all the dramatis personae. The individual actors, therefore, need but slip into the roles already assigned to them before the curtain goes up" (Peter Berger, *Invitation to Sociology*, 1970).

"People expect appropriate behaviour from the holder of a particular position. The sum of these expectations is the role" (R. Frankenberg, *Communities in Britain*, 1970).

RURAL SOCIOLOGY

"If a man has taken up a field for cultivation and then has not raised corn on the field, they shall convict him of not having done the necessary work on the field and he shall give corn corresponding to the crops raised by his neighbor to the owner of the field" (Hammurabi, *Code*, c. 1750 B.C.).

"Producing barley and wheat . . . will not make a man entirely wise . . . the same is true of all kinds of farming" (Plato, *Epinomis*, c. 400 B.C., perhaps spurious).

"Agriculture strengthens fortitude considerably" (Aristotle, *Economics*, c. 350 B.C.).

"The central square is the public field, and eight families . . . cultivate in common the public field. And not till the public work is finished, may they presume to attend to their private affairs" (Mencius, *Book of Mencius*, c. 300 B.C.).

"This is the way it is with farming: if you delay one thing, you will delay all of your work" (Cato the Elder, *On Agriculture*, c. 200 B.C.).

"Learning, mechanical arts, work for wages, service, rearing cattle, traffic, agriculture, contentment with little, alms, and receiving interest on money, are the ten modes of subsistence" (Manu, *Laws*, c. 200 B.C.).

"A man who does not possess land is not really a man" (Talmud: Levirate Marriage 63a).

"The farmer . . . can no more live without profit than the labourer without wages. [His] motive for accumulation will diminish with every diminution of profit" (David Ricardo, *Principles of Political Economy and Taxation*, 1817).

"In the total class structure of society the peasants are at the lowest strata" (Friedrich Engels, *The Peasant War in Germany*, 1850).

"The small peasants form a vast mass, the members of which live in similar conditions, but without entering into manifold relations with one another. Their mode of production isolates them from one another, instead of bringing them into mutual intercourse. The isolation is increased by France's bad means of communication and by the poverty of the peasants" (Karl Marx, *The Eighteenth Brumaire of Louis Bonaparte*, 1852).

"The rural village community is frequently identical with a great family or clan but the more alien elements are taken in the more it loses its kinship characteristics" (Ferdinand Tönnies, *Community and Society*, 1887).

"In the rural economy of the most diverse periods . . . agriculture was increasingly exploited in a profit-making manner" (Max Weber, *Economy and Society*, 1922, posthumously).

"A considerable amount of energy is spent on purely aesthetic effects, to make the garden [among the Trobriand Islanders] look clean, showy and dainty. . . . As to the varieties of yam, taro and taytu, they have literally hundreds of names for each of them" (Bronislaw Malinowski, *Coral Gardens and Their Magic*, 1935).

"In choosing the son to remain upon the farm, the [Irish] father has full power of decision. His interest lies in choosing among his sons the one he thinks will carry on most successfully" (C. Arensberg and S. Kimball, *Family and Community in Ireland*, 1940).

"Peasants are definitely rural—yet live in relation to market towns. . . . They constitute part-societies with part-cultures. They lack the isolation, the political autonomy, and the self-sufficiency of tribal populations; but their local units retain much of their old identity, integration, and attachment to soil and cults" (Alfred Kroeber, *Anthropology*, 1948).

"The problem of the elimination of the conflict between town and country, between industry and agriculture, is a well-known problem which both Marx and Engels have posed. The economic basis of this conflict is the exploitation of the countryside by the towns, the expropriation of the peasants and ruining of the majority of the rural population following the course of the development of industry, commerce, and the capitalist system of credit'' (Joseph Stalin, *Economic Problems of Socialism in the USSR*, 1952).

''Just as the various and varying struggles of laborers arose out of, and have always revolved about, the issues of wages, hours, and working conditions, and just as all these struggles combined constitute the American labor movement, so the varying struggles of farmers arose out of, and have always revolved about, the issues of prices, markets and credits, and all these struggles combined constitute the American Farmers' Movement'' (Carl Taylor, *The Farmers' Movement, 1620–1920*, 1953).

''The subject matter of rural sociology is the description and analysis of groups of various kinds as they exist in the rural environment'' (Lowry Nelson, *Rural Sociology*, 1955).

''A peasant is a person who is in effective control of a piece of land to which he has long been attached by ties of traditions and sentiments. The land and he are parts of one thing'' (Robert Redfield, *The Little Community, and Peasant Society and Culture*, 1960).

''Being rural in Greece means living in a village, which is usually a picturesque collection of houses, lanes, gardens, orchards, vineyards, and fields'' (Irwin Sanders, *Rainbow in the Rock*, 1962).

''The history of the prairie west [in Canada] has been one in which the agrarian community attempted to change and reshape the rules of the game with the purpose of developing legislation and institutions which satisfied their needs and interests. . . . But their efforts in this direction have been made difficult, and at times, almost impossible, by the fact that that agrarian community was never a homogeneous group of men and women'' (L. McCroirie in M. Tremblay and W. Anderson, eds., *Rural Canada in Transition*, 1966).

''The peasant torrent is coming so fast in China that every comrade has only three choices—to march at their head and lead them, to trail behind them, gesticulating and criticizing, or to stand in their way and oppose them'' (Mao Tse-tung, *Selected Readings*, 1971).

''The growth of farm cities has been particularly striking since these are now normally visited for the kind of trade which prior to 1940 was done at the nearest little village'' (Carle Zimmerman and Garry Moneo, *The Prairie Community System*, 1971).

''[Soviet farm administration stresses] the strict administrative subordination of the primary production units to the leaders of the various farm subdivisions, and the latter to the collective farm chairman'' (G. Loz, *Management of State Farms and Collective Farms*, 1972).

S

SAMPLE

''It is the sample that we observe, but it is the population which we seek to know'' (George Snedecor and William Cochran, *Statistical Methods*, 1967).

''Institutions and wards vary as individuals do, and where possible, should be sampled or studied as universes. . . . An ideal study might draw a random sample of institutions or a sample stratified by sponsorship, size, or location, and survey the universe of treatment units within each institution'' (M. Lawton and Jacob Cohen in Marcia Guttentag and Elmer Struening, eds., *Handbook of Evaluation Research*, 1975).

''A sample is a smaller representation of a larger whole. The use of sampling allows for more adequate scientific work by making the time of the scientific worker count. . . . The sampling problems may be divided into those that affect (1) the definition of the population, (2) the size of the sample, and (3) the representativeness of the sample. . . . Three methods of sampling are commonly used. These are *random sampling, stratified sampling*, and *judgmental* or '*purposive' sampling*'' (Delbert Miller, *Handbook of Research Design and Social Measurement*, 1977).

''A sample can contain a single element or all but one of the population elements. For practical reasons, such as limited resources and time, or because the population is infinite in size, most research is carried out with samples rather than with populations'' (Roger Kirk, *Introductory Statistics*, 1978).

''Other things being equal, the larger the sample the more confidence we have that sample results . . . will approximate the true figures for the population'' (Ann and Hubert Blalock, *Introduction to Social Research*, 1982).

SCALE

''No scale can really be called a scale unless one can tell from a given attitude that an individual will maintain every attitude falling to the right or to the left of that point'' (Gardner Murphy et al., *Experimental Social Psychology*, 1937).

''The usefulness of an attitude scale depends upon its properties. At minimum, a useful scale must be reliable (yield consistent results) and valid (measure what it is purported to measure). Other characteristics of an attitude scale that often are desirable include equality of units, unidimensionality, and a zero point'' (Marvin Shaw and Jack Wright, *Scales for the Measurement of Attitudes*, 1967).

''The ideas of 'scales of measurement' constitute a useful set of concepts. Behavioral scientists, and very few other scientists, have been concerned with these problems'' (Gene Glass and Julian Stanley, *Statistical Methods in Education and Psychology*, 1970).

''The ranking of people provides a more general approach to the problem of scaling, since it turns out to be equivalent to the ranking of items when all items are dichotomous, and it also includes the case where items have more than two answer categories'' (Louis Guttman in Gary Maranell, ed., *Scaling*, 1974).

''The basic types of scales . . . are: *nominal, ordinal, interval*, and *ratio*. . . . The nominal scale . . . has the most essential property common to all types of scales: dimensionality. Yet it is not really a scale because it lacks the other essential characteristic of measurement, which is calibration. . . . The *ordinal scale* builds logically upon the nominal scale by adding the property of *rank* to that of *dimensionality*. . . . The interval scale adds the property of *distance* to those of *dimensionality* and *rank*. . . . The *ratio scale* adds . . . a point of *natural origin*, known as the zero point on the scale'' (Raymond Gorden, *Unidimensional Scaling of Social Variables*, 1977).

''Scaling techniques play a major role in the construction of instruments for collecting standardized, measurable data. Scales . . . are significant because they provide quantitative measures that are amenable to greater precision, statistical manipulation, and explicit interpretation'' (Delbert Miller, *Handbook of Research Design and Social Measurement*, 1977).

SCIENCE, SOCIOLOGY OF

''Wise men could not make others like themselves, since wisdom is not based on science'' (Plato, *Meno*, c. 400 B.C.).

''There is no such thing as science of entities which are in constant flux'' (Aristotle, *Metaphysics*, c. 350 B.C.).

''Science perfects the intellect'' (Thomas Aquinas, *Summa Theologica*, 1274).

''Why should I submit this noble science and this new philosophy to the judgment of men who have taken oath to follow the opinions of others, to the most senseless corrupters of the arts, to lettered clowns, grammatists, sophists, spouters, and the wrong headed rabble, to be denounced, torn to tatters, and heaped with contumely! To you alone, true philosophers, ingenuous minds, who not only in books but in things themselves look for knowledge, have I dedicated these foundations of magnetic science'' (William Gilbert, *On the Magnet*, 1600).

''Science is the great antidote to the poison of enthusiasm and superstition'' (Adam Smith, *The Wealth of Nations*, 1776).

''Modern industry makes science a productive force distinct from labor and presses it into the service of capital'' (Karl Marx, *Das Kapital*, 1879).

"The principal object of all sciences of life whether individual or social, is to define and explain the normal state and to distinguish it from its opposite. If, however, normality is not given in the things themselves—if it is, on the contrary, a character we may or may not impute to them—this solid footing is lost" (Émile Durkheim, *The Rules of Sociological Method*, 1895).

"An accumulation of facts is no more science than a pile of bricks is a house" (Jules Henri Poincaré, *Science and Hypothesis*, 1902).

"Theology, philosophy, reflection on the ultimate problems of life, were known to the Chinese and Hindu, perhaps even of a depth unreached by the European; but a rational science and in connection with it a rational technology remained unknown to those civilizations" (Max Weber, *General Economic History*, 1920).

"Through science, man will be enabled more and more to master nature and to control his own behavior" (Charles Ellwood, *The Psychology of Human Society*, 1925).

"No art or craft however primitive could have been invented or maintained, no organized form of hunting, fishing, tilling, or search for food could be carried out without the careful observation of natural process and a firm belief in its regularity" (Bronislaw Malinowski, *Magic, Science and Religion*, 1925).

"The multiplicity of points of view, resulting both from the peculiarities of the intellectual traditions of various nations and from those of the individual sciences, is both attractive and fruitful; and there can be no doubt that such a wide problem can only be solved as a result of co-operation between the most diverse disciplines and nationalities" (Karl Mannheim, *Essays on the Sociology of Knowledge*, 1929).

"Nature is the realization of the simplest conceivable mathematical ideas. . . . Experience may suggest the appropriate mathematical concepts, but they most certainly cannot be deduced from it" (Albert Einstein, *The World as I See It*, 1934).

"Each [ideational, idealistic, and sensate stages] has its own mentality; its own system of truth and knowledge; its own philosophy and *Weltanschauung*" (Pitirim Sorokin, *Social and Cultural Dynamics*, 1937).

"Sensate science cannot deal with the intangibles and imponderables in human relations" (Charles Ellwood, *The World's Need of Christ*, 1940).

"Although the interaction between science and society has been a subject of occasional interest to scholars for more than a century, there has been little effort to provide a systematic organization of the facts and ideas which comprise that subject—the sociology of science" (Robert Merton in Bernard Barber, *Science and the Social Order*, 1952).

"Only after successfully accomplishing the mysterious inner act of 'understanding' each system of ideas or values, can one classify them into adequate classes. . . . Otherwise, all observations and statistical operations are doomed to be meaningless, fruitless, and fallacious simulacra of real knowledge" (Pitirim Sorokin, *Fads and Foibles in Modern Sociology*, 1956).

"If we could teach students how science is made, really made rather than as publicly reported, we cannot fail to expose them to the whole scientist by whom it is made, with all his gifts and blindnesses, with all his methods as well" (Alvin Gouldner, *Anti-Minotaur*, 1963).

"Science is a dispassionate mode of analysis which knows nothing of the cult of free individuality" (Don Martindale, ed., *Functionalism in the Social Sciences*, 1965).

"He [Kuhn] has failed to discuss the *aim* of science" (Paul Feyerabend in I. Lakatos and A. Musgrave, eds., *Criticism and the Growth of Knowledge*, 1970).

"The socially patterned interests, motivations, and behavior established in one institutional sphere—say, that of religion and economy—are interdependent with the socially patterned interests, motivations, and behavior obtaining in other institutional spheres—say, that of science" (Robert Merton, *Science, Technology and Society in Seventeenth-Century England*, 1970).

"After a long gestation, the sociology of science has finally emerged as a distinct sociological specialty. Having evolved a cognitive identity in the form of intellectual orientations, paradigms, problematics and tools of inquiry, it has begun to develop a professional identity as well . . . the sociology of science exhibits a strongly self-exemplifying character. . . . Scholars have positive or negative attitudes toward genuinely new facts, depending upon the extent to which the school's system is established: in the initial stages new facts are at least acceptable, but once the system is fully formulated the intellectual commitment of the school precludes a favorable attitude toward novel findings" (Robert Merton, *The Sociology of Science*, 1973).

"There is no law against daydreaming but science must not indulge in it" (Pierre Grassé, *Evolution of Living Organisms*, 1977).

SEGREGATION

"And Joseph said unto his brethren . . . when Pharaoh shall call you, and shall say, What is your occupation? That ye shall say, Thy servants' trade hath been about cattle from our youth even until now, both we, and also our fathers: that ye may dwell in the land of Goshen; for every shepherd is an abomination unto the Egyptians" (Genesis 46:31,33–34).

"A segregated school system produces children who, when they graduate, graduate with crippled minds" (Malcolm X, *Malcolm X Speaks*, 1965).

"On a Cincinnati street in 1830, Dan Rice, a famous white 'blackface' minstrel, saw a ragged little Negro boy singing 'Jump, Jim Crow.' Rice then copied the urchin's lively song-and-dance and for years performed the act to great applause. Gradually, the words 'Jim Crow'—from this song—came to be applied to the legal segregation of Negroes from whites in everyday life. The blackface minstrels, by their stage portrayal, helped to establish the stereotype of Negro inferiority and the desirability of segregation" (Langston Hughes et al., *A Pictorial History of Blackamericans*, 1968).

''Racial segregation would have been not only impossible but unnecessary on the plantations, where the masters maintained absolute authority. In short, rural plantation slavery and formal segregation could not have existed side by side'' (Philip Foner, *History of Black Americans*, 1975).

''Regionally, the South attained the highest degree of racial residential segregation (mean of 90.9), followed by the North-Central states (mean of 87.7), the West (mean 79.3), and the Northeast (mean 79.2). Thus it can be demonstrated that racial segregation in housing is characteristically American, and regional differences are minor. The likelihood is that the rural black who migrates from the South will settle in an urban black slum elsewhere. Likewise, when his children become adults, they too are likely to reside in the black community'' (Alphonso Pinkney, *Black Americans*, 1975).

''In the United States color prejudice has been very strong, discrimination and segregation have prevailed, and a system of color caste has emerged. In Brazil, on the other hand, amalgamation has been the dominant policy and has become firmly fixed in the mores. . . . *Segregation* means the act, process, or state of being separate or set apart. . . . Segregation is an old story to the Jewish people, who have experienced it in all its forms—voluntary and involuntary, social and spatial'' (Brewton Berry and Henry Tischler, *Race and Ethnic Relations*, 1978).

SELF

''He who knows others is learned; he who knows himself is wise'' (Lao-tse, *Teaching of Tao*, c. 550 B.C.).

''If we lack self-knowledge and wisdom, can we ever know our own good and evil?'' (Plato, *First Alcibiades*, c. 400 B.C., spurious).

''When we wish to know ourselves, we will obtain this knowledge by observing our friends'' (Aristotle, *Great Ethics*, c. 350 B.C.).

'' 'Tis in ourselves that we are thus or thus'' (William Shakespeare, *Othello*, 1605).

''Self-reflection is the school of wisdom'' (Baltasar Gracián y Morales, *The Art of Worldly Wisdom*, 1647).

''Bring him into society, and he is immediately provided with a mirror which he wanted before. It is placed in the countenance and behavior of those he lives with. This is the only looking glass by which we can, in some measure, with the eyes of other people, scrutinize the propriety of our own conduct [cf. Cooley's looking-glass self]'' (Adam Smith, *Theory of Moral Sentiments*, 1759).

''Both of the selves here standing in relation to one another constitute *one* identity, *one* light so to speak, since the 'I' is completely universal, *permeates* them absolutely, is *not interrupted by any limit*, and is the *essence common* to *all* men. Yet they are simultaneously *two*, existing rigidly and tenaciously in opposition to one another, each introreflected and absolutely *distinct* from and *impregnable* against the other'' (Georg Wilhelm Friedrich Hegel, *Encyclopedia of Philosophy*, 1817).

''The self is a relation which relates itself to its own self, or it is that in the relation that the relation relates itself to its own self; the self is not the relation but that the relation relates itself to its own self'' (Sören Aabye Kierkegaard, *Fear and Trembling*, 1843).

''[Each person] has as many different social selves as there are distinct *groups* of persons about whose opinion he cares. He generally shows a different side of himself to each of these different groups. Many a youth who is demure enough before his parents and teachers, swears and swaggers like a pirate among his 'tough' young friends'' (William James, *The Principles of Psychology*, 1890).

''[The self consists of] the imagination of our appearance to the other person; the imagination of his judgment of that appearance; and some sort of self-feeling, such as pride or mortification'' (Charles Cooley, *Human Nature and the Social Order*, 1902).

''Recognizing that the self can not appear in consciousness as an 'I,' that it is always an object, i.e., a 'me,' I wish to suggest an answer to the question, What is involved in the self being an object? The first answer may be that an object involves a subject. Stated in other words, that a 'me' is inconceivable without an 'I.' And to this reply must be made that such an 'I' is a presupposition, but never a presentation of conscious experience, for the moment it is presented it has passed into the objective case, presuming, if you like, an 'I' that observes—but an 'I' that can disclose himself only by ceasing to be the subject for whom the object 'me' exists. It is, of course, not the Hegelism of a self that becomes another to himself in which I am interested, but the nature of the self as revealed by introspection and subject to our factual analysis. This analysis does reveal, then, in a memory process an attitude of observing oneself in which both the observer and the observed appear . . . the stuff that goes to make up the 'me' whom the 'I' addresses and whom he observes, is the experience which is induced by this action of the 'I.' If the 'I' speaks, the 'me' hears. If the 'I' strikes, the 'me' feels the blow. . . . The 'I' of introspection is the self which enters into social relations with other selves. It is not the 'I' that is implied in the fact that one presents himself as a 'me.' And the 'me' of introspection is the same 'me' that is the object of the social conduct of others'' (George H. Mead, ''The Social Self,'' 1913, in Robert Brown, ed., *Mental Hygiene*, 1969).

''In the eye of each, if you look for it, you may see an individual spirit, a self, often only partly at home with its fellows'' (Charles Cooley, *Life and the Student*, 1927).

''The self does not consist simply in the bare organization of social attitudes. We may now explicitly raise the question as to the nature of the 'I' which is aware of the social 'me.' I do not mean to raise the metaphysical question of how a person can be both 'I' and 'me,' but to ask for the significance of this distinction from the point of view of conduct itself. Where in conduct does the

'I' come in as over against the 'me'? If one determines what his position is in society and feels himself as having a certain function and privilege, these are all defined with reference to an 'I,' but the 'I' is not a 'me' and cannot become a 'me.' We may have a better self and a worse self, but that again is not the 'I' as over against the 'me,' because they are both selves . . . the 'I' in memory is there as the spokesman of the self of the second, or minute, or day ago. As given, it is a 'me' but it is a 'me' which was the 'I' at the earlier time. If you ask, then, where directly in your own experience the 'I' comes in, the answer is that it comes in as a historical figure. It is what you were a second ago that is the 'I' of the 'me.' It is another 'me' that has to take that role. . . . There is neither 'I' nor 'me' in the conversation of gestures; the whole act is not yet carried out, but the preparation takes place in this field of gesture. . . . The 'I,' then, in this relation of the 'I' and the 'me,' is something that is, so to speak, responding to a social situation which is within the experience of the individual. It is the answer which the individual makes to the attitude which others take toward him when he assumes an attitude toward them'' (George H. Mead, *Mind, Self, and Society*, 1934, posthumously).

''The person is conceived by his circle as an organic and psychological entity who is a 'self,' conscious of his own existence as a body and a soul and aware of how others regard him. If he is to be the kind of person his social circle needs, his 'self' must possess in the opinion of the circle certain qualities, physical and mental, and not possess certain other qualities'' (Florian Znaniecki, *The Social Role of the Man of Knowledge*, 1940).

''In so far as this mask [a person's role] represents the conception we have formed of ourselves—the role we are striving to live up to—this mask is our truer self, the self we would like to be. In the end, our conception of our role becomes second nature and an integral part of our personality. We come into the world as individuals, achieve character, and become persons'' (Robert Park, *Race and Culture*, 1913–1944).

''[Through love and cooperation, man ascends] from the superficial, egoistic, and evanescent self to the deep, altruistic, and universal self'' (Radhakamal Mukerjee, *The Dynamics of Morals*, 1950).

''In introducing the self, Mead's position focuses on how human beings handle and fashion their world, not on disparate responses to imputed factors. . . . One has to get inside of the defining process of the actor in order to understand his action'' (Herbert Blumer, *Symbolic Interactionism*, 1969).

''A frequent objection to the concept of the ego or self is that its perception involves an infinite regress. This criticism arises from a misunderstanding . . . the conscious experiences listed under the categories outer sense and inner sense are perceived by the ego or self. In contrast, the ego or self is experienced, not perceived. Following Kant, we can make the distinction by saying that the self or ego is apperceived'' (John Eccles, ed., *Mind and Brain*, 1982).

SEXUALITY

"He brake down the houses of the sodomites, that were by the house of the Lord" (II Kings 23:7).

"Men's eyes love to pluck the flowers, but turn away from the faded blooms" (Sophocles, *Trachiniae*, c. 412 B.C.).

"I hate the woman who offers herself because she must do so" (Ovid, *The Art of Love*, c. 8).

"Sex relations make the body more relaxed and weaker" (Galen, *Art of Health*, c. 150).

"It is in the union of the bodies that sexual pleasure consists" (Thomas Aquinas, *Summa Theologica*, 1274).

"In the approach to woman as the spoil and handmaid of communal lust, is expressed the infinite degradation in which man exists for himself" (Karl Marx, *Economic and Philosophic Manuscripts*, 1844).

"Christianity gave Eros poison to drink: he did not die of it but degenerated—into vice" (Friedrich Wilhelm Nietzsche, *Beyond Good and Evil*, 1886).

"Sexuality is the lyricism of the masses" (Charles Pierre Baudelaire, *Intimate Journals*, 1887).

"[Among the Arunta] to promote the growth of the breasts of a girl, the men assemble at the *Ungunja*, or men's camp, where they all join in singing long chants, the words of which express an exhortation to the breasts to grow" (Baldwin Spencer and F. Gillen, *The Arunta*, 1927).

"[In Samoa] jealousy, as a widespread social phenomenon, is very rare. . . . Marriages make no violent claim for fidelity. . . . [The Samoans have the] sunniest and easiest attitudes toward sex" (Margaret Mead, *Coming of Age in Samoa*, 1928).

"[Vertical sun theory:] sex thirst is sharpened by the vertical sun" (Edward Ross, *Seventy Years of It*, 1936).

"The sexual embrace can only be compared with music and with prayer" (Havelock Ellis, *On Life and Sex*, 1937).

"God-fearing Middletown is afraid of sex as a force in its midst, afraid it might break loose and run wild, and afraid to recognize too openly that those 'whom God hath joined together' can be mismated" (Robert and Helen Lynd, *Middletown in Transition*, 1937).

"In contrast with the slow tempo of many cultural changes, the trend toward premarital sex experience is proceeding with extraordinary rapidity" (Lewis Terman, *Psychological Factors in Marital Happiness*, 1938).

"Most of the impulses of sexual life are not of a purely erotic nature but arise from alloys of the erotic instinct with components of the destructive instinct" (Sigmund Freud, *An Outline of Psychoanalysis*, 1940).

"Sexual adjustments are not the only problems involved in marriage, and often they are not even the most important factors in marital adjustments. . . .

Nevertheless, sexual maladjustments contribute in perhaps three-quarters of the upper level marriages that end in separation and divorce, and in some smaller percentage of the lower level marriages that break up'' (Alfred Kinsey et al., *Sexual Behavior in the Human Male*, 1948).

''[Greek sexual emancipation was] far more significant for mankind than anything as yet mentioned in the difference between Greek and most subsequent religious thought and practice concerned with the attitude to sex'' (Charles Seltman, *The Twelve Olympians*, 1952).

''[Freud] sees in the sexual instinct the result of a chemically produced tension in the body which is painful and seeks for relief. The aim of the sexual desire is the removal of this painful tension. . . . Sexual desire, in this concept, is an itch, sexual satisfaction the removal of the itch'' (Erich Fromm, *The Art of Loving*, 1955).

''[Among the Basseri of Persia] the only equipment in the [nuptial] tent is the bride's bedding and a clean white cloth for sleeping on. . . . A male relative of the groom stands guard outside the tent; when the marriage has been consummated, he shoots a gun into the air, and the women of the camp greet the news with their high-pitched trilling. Next morning the white sheet is inspected by both families together; if the girl was not a virgin, her husband may divorce her'' (Fredrik Barth, *Nomads of South Persia*, 1961).

''[Mexican] husbands repeatedly express the opinion that sexual relations should be practiced in one form with the wife, and in another with the lover. The most common explanation refers to the fear that the wife could become too interested in sex if she were introduced to the subtleties of its pleasure'' (Rogelio Diaz-Guerrero, *Studies in the Psychology of the Mexican*, 1961).

''Sexual relationships are intimate forms of social relationships'' (John Burt and Linda Brower, *Education for Sexuality*, 1970).

''As we advance from lower primates to humans, the influence of sex hormones decreases, while cerebral control over sex behavior increases. . . . Symbolic stimulation is more prevalent among humans, animals being more genitally oriented. . . . Sexual interest and activity continue throughout the year in man, offspring thus being born in any month'' (Panos Bardis in Harald Niemeyer, ed., *Social Relations Network*, 1980).

''An enormous amount of research from Kinsey onwards has confirmed the reputation of men for seeking multiple partners and impersonal sexual thrills, while women look to exclusive, 'meaningful' relationships with particular men'' (Glenn Wilson, *Love and Instinct*, 1981).

''[It is] customary in Samoa, as [Margaret] Mead quite failed to report, for the virginity of an adolescent daughter, of whatever rank, to be safeguarded by her brothers. . . . [Samoa] is a society predicated on rank, in which female virgins are both highly valued and eagerly sought after'' (Derek Freeman, *Margaret Mead and Samoa*, 1983).

SLAVERY

"If a man buys . . . a slave or slave-girl . . . from a freeman's son or a freeman's slave . . . that man is a thief; he shall be put to death" (Hammurabi, *Code*, c. 1750 B.C.).

"If a man smite his servant, or his maid, with a rod, and he die under his hand; he shall be surely punished" (Exodus 21:20).

"To make a slave of a man is to take half his worth away" (Homer, *Odyssey*, c. 750 B.C.).

"Servants are the most difficult to behave to. If you are familiar with them, they lose their humility. If you maintain a reserve towards them, they are discontented" (Confucius, *Analects*, c. 500 B.C.).

"Slavery means to be abused and bear it" (Euripides, *Hecuba*, c. 425 B.C.).

"We must punish slaves neither in hot blood nor in a manner that will make them angry; and we must not leave them unpunished lest they become self-willed" (Plato, *Laws*, c. 400 B.C.).

"By nature some are free and others are slaves; the lot of slavery for the latter is both advantageous and just . . . the slave is a living instrument" (Aristotle, *Politics*, c. 350 B.C.).

"A wife, a son, and a slave, these three are declared to have no property" (Manu, *Laws*, c. 200 B.C.).

"[A gentile slave] is acquired by purchase, or by document, or by actual service" (Talmud: Sanctification 1:3).

"As a slave, the slave is his master's chattel" (Thomas Aquinas, *Summa Theologica*, 1274).

"Slavery does not lose its disgrace even when the slave is noble" (Baltasar Gracián y Morales, *The Art of Worldly Wisdom*, c. 1647).

"Force created slavery, and the slaves' cowardice perpetuated it" (Jean Jacques Rousseau, *The Social Contract*, 1762).

"Slavery is an economic category as well as any other" (Karl Marx, *The Poverty of Philosophy*, 1847).

"When, instead of devouring their captured enemies, men made slaves of them, the change was a step in advance . . . this slavery, though absolutely bad, was relatively good—was the best thing practicable for the time being" (Herbert Spencer, *The Study of Sociology*, 1873).

"[In Greece and Rome] slavery no longer paid; therefore, it died. But dying slavery left behind its poisonous sting in the disdain for productive labor on the part of free men. This was the dead-end street without a way out in which the Roman world got stuck; slavery was economically impossible; the labor of free men was morally ostracized. The one could no longer be the basic form of social production. The other, that is free labor, could not yet be that basic form. Only a complete revolution could be the possible solution" (Friedrich Engels, *The Origin of the Family, Private Property, and the State*, 1884).

"Those men whose fate is not determined by the chance of using goods or services for themselves on the market, e.g., slaves, are not . . . a class in the technical sense of the term. They are, rather, a status group'' (Max Weber, *Economy and Society*, 1922, posthumously).

''As she [Rome] extended her frontiers to include peoples and cultures in which slavery has been established for centuries, she acquired at once an apparent sanction and a greater desire for slave-labour'' (R. Barrow, *Slavery in the Roman Empire*, 1928).

''Through religious instruction the bondsmen learned that slavery had divine sanction, that insolence was as much an offense against God as against the temporal master. They received the Biblical command that servants should obey their masters, and they heard of the punishments awaiting the disobedient slave in the hereafter. They heard, too, that eternal salvation would be their reward for faithful service'' (Kenneth Stampp, *The Peculiar Institution*, 1956).

''Abolitionists were not simply trying to prevent slave owners from doing the wrong things; they were trying to help slaves achieve a better life'' (Howard Becker, *Outsiders*, 1963).

''The physical separation of the races was the most revolutionary change in relations between whites and Negroes in South Carolina during Reconstruction. Separation had, of course, marked the Negro in slavery; yet the very nature of slavery necessitated a constant, physical intimacy between the races'' (Joel Williamson, *After Slavery*, 1965).

''[In ancient Athens] most bank managers were slaves, as were clerks in public audit departments. Many were shopkeepers, craftsmen and business agents'' (J. Littlejohn, *Social Stratification*, 1972).

''[In the Caribbean] the heritage of slavery set the pattern of mating outside of marriage. The European masters were very willing to take black mistresses as is clear from the large population of mixed bloods'' (G. Mahy in R. Prince and D. Barrier, eds., *Configurations*, 1974).

''Most Confederates did not acknowledge that the South had sinned in the holding of slaves . . . defeat meant no disgrace, no godly judgment . . . upon Southern devotion to the slave institution'' (Bertram Wyatt-Brown, *Southern Honor*, 1982).

SOCIALIZATION

''Socialization is conceived as the development of a social culture or character—a social state of mind—in the individuals who associate . . . the Theory of Socialization [is] the most important part of the Theory of Society'' (Franklin Giddings, *The Theory of Socialization*, 1897).

''If we would understand the life of societies, we must first learn to understand the way in which individuals become moulded by the society into which they are born'' (William McDougall, *An Introduction to Social Psychology*, 1908).

''From the standpoint of the group, we may define [socialization] as the psychic articulation of the individual into the collective activities. From the standpoint of the person, socialization is the participation of the individual in the spirit and purpose, knowledge and methods, decision and action of the group'' (Ernest Burgess, *The Function of Socialization in Social Evolution*, 1916).

''The defining of the situation is begun by the parents in the form of ordering and forbidding, and information is continued by the community by means of gossip, with its praise and blame, and is formally represented by the school, the law, the church'' (William Thomas in H. Jennings et al., *Suggestions of Modern Science Concerning Education*, 1917).

''[Socialization is] the development of the we-feeling in associates and their growth in capacity and will to act together'' (Edward Ross, *Principles of Sociology*, 1920).

''Socialization, when that word is used as a term of appreciation rather than of description, sets up as the goal of social effort a world in which conflict, competition and the externality of individuals, if they do not disappear altogether, will be so diminished that all men may live together as members of one family'' (Robert Park and Ernest Burgess, *Introduction to the Science of Sociology*, 1921).

''Socialization . . . consists of a modification of the original and purely prepotent reflexes through instruction received in the social environment'' (Floyd Allport, *Social Psychology*, 1924).

''If men define situations as real, they are real in their consequences'' (William and Dorothy Thomas, *The Child in America*, 1928).

''Through imitation and language, as also through the whole content of adult thought which exercises pressure on the child's mind as soon as verbal intercourse has become possible, the child begins . . . to be socialized from the end of its first year'' (Jean Piaget, *The Moral Judgment of the Child*, 1932).

''Socialization, like learning, goes on throughout life. The case of the development of the child is only the most dramatic because he has so far to go'' (Talcott Parsons, *The Social System*, 1951).

''[Socialization is] the whole process by which an individual born with behavioral potentialities of enormously wide range, is led to develop actual behavior which is confined within a much narrower range—the range of what is customary and acceptable for him according to the standards of his group'' (I. Child in Gardner Lindzey, ed., *The Handbook of Social Psychology*, 1954).

''At the moment both the substantive and theoretical aspects of socialization and culturalization (if I may coin an admittedly horrid word) acutely need investigation'' (Clyde Kluckhohn, *Culture and Behavior*, 1962).

''No critical, comprehensive examination of the empirical studies in socialization in the German-speaking areas has been undertaken as yet'' (Gerhard Baumert and Heinz Karl, *German Research on Socialization*, 1963).

''Were we still addicted to the more romantic forms of expression we might say that the socialization process is a struggle over domination of the development of a man's personality by three main adversaries: his innate self, the people who raise him and live with him, and the society in which he will participate as an adult member'' (Alex Inkeles in John Clausen, ed., *Socialization and Society*, 1968).

''An important . . . fact about social learning, is that it takes place in a social environment'' (David Goslin, ed., *Handbook of Socialization Theory and Research*, 1969).

''There is considerable utility in extending the concept of 'socialization' to cover *all forms of the transformation of organic materials and extra-social events into socially relevant form*'' (Don Martindale, *American Society*, 1972).

''The Koreans feel most uncomfortable in a situation when they are put into close contact with other egos with whom their egos remain unoverlapped. A great part of their childhood socialization process is taken up by a learning process in which they master the procedures, etiquettes and rules by which they determine with what egos they may overlap and how'' (Hahm Choon in Edward Wright, ed., *Korean Politics in Transition*, 1975).

''Until recently, many students of socialization have not been trained to think about and to conduct their research in transcultural, or universal human, terms'' (Thomas Williams, *Socialization*, 1983).

SOCIETY

''If civil society had been established in order to preserve and increase property . . . then every person's right in the state would be proportionate to his fortune . . . nor was civil society merely established in order that its members might live, but that they might live well. . . . The person who first founded civil society created the greatest benefit. . . . If human society cannot subsist without actions at law, it certainly cannot exist without the infliction of penalties'' (Aristotle, *Politics*, c. 350 B.C.).

''Either companionship or death'' (Talmud: Fast 23a).

''Society is no comfort to one not sociable'' (William Shakespeare, *Cymbeline*, 1610).

''Social order is a sacred right which serves as the foundation for all others'' (Jean Jacques Rousseau, *The Social Contract*, 1762).

''If man is social by nature, he will develop his true nature only in society'' (Karl Marx and Friedrich Engels, *The Holy Family*, 1845).

''Modern bourgeois society is divided into three great classes—capital, landed property, wage labor'' (Karl Marx, *A Contribution to the Critique of Political Economy*, 1859).

''Society itself . . . is the root of property, of the laws based on it and of the inevitable slavery'' (Karl Marx, *Das Kapital*, 1879).

''The state . . . has not existed from all eternity. There have been societies which managed without it, which had no conception of the state and state power. At a certain stage of economic development, which was necessarily bound up with the cleavage of society into classes, the state became a necessity owing to this cleavage. . . . The society that organises production anew on the basis of a free and equal association of the producers will put the whole state machine where it will then belong: in the museum of antiquities, side by side with the spinning wheel and the bronze axe'' (Friedrich Engels, *The Origin of the Family, Private Property, and the State*, 1884).

''In 1847, the pre-history of society, the social organization existing previous to recorded history, was all but unknown. Since then, Haxthausen discovered common ownership of land in Russia, Maurer proved it to be the social foundation from which all Teutonic races started in history, and by and by village communities were found to be, or to have been the primitive form of society everywhere from India to Ireland. The inner organization of this primitive Communistic society was laid bare, in its typical form, by Morgan's crowning discovery of the true nature of the *gens* and its relation to the *tribe*'' (Friedrich Engels in Karl Marx and Friedrich Engels, *Communist Manifesto*, 1847; 1888 edition).

''Society is imitation [a group of people] who display many resemblances, produced either by imitation or by counter-imitation'' (Gabriel Tarde, *The Laws of Imitation*, 1890).

''Society is not alone in its interest in the formation of special groups to regulate their own activity, developing within them what otherwise would become anarchic; but the individual, on his part, finds joy in it, for anarchy is painful to him. He also suffers from pain and disorder produced whenever inter-individual relationships are not submitted to some regulatory influence'' (Émile Durkheim, *The Division of Labor in Society*, 1893).

''Society is not a mere sum of individuals. Rather, the system formed by their association represents a specific reality which has its own characteristics. Of course, nothing collective can be produced if individual consciousnesses are not assumed; but this necessary condition is by itself insufficient. These consciousnesses must be combined in a certain way; social life results from this combination and is, consequently, explained by it. . . . We know that societies are composed of various parts in combination since the nature of the aggregate depends necessarily on the nature and number of the component elements and their mode of combination. These characteristics are evidently what we must take as our basis. Moreover, as they are of the morphological order, one could call the part of sociology which has for its task the constitution and classification of social types, 'social morphology' '' (Émile Durkheim, *The Rules of Sociological Method*, 1895).

''It is not realized that there can be no sociology unless societies exist, and that societies cannot exist if there are only individuals'' (Émile Durkheim, *Suicide*, 1897).

''It may require years to replace a great leader of men, but a stable and efficient society can only be the outcome of centuries of development'' (Karl Pearson, *The Grammar of Science*, 1899).

''[Society is a] relation among personal ideas'' (Charles Cooley, *Human Nature and the Social Order*, 1902).

"Society is the birthplace of the moral consciousness" (Edward Alexander Westermarck, *The Origin and Development of the Moral Ideas*, 1908).

"While race has been relatively stagnant, society has rapidly developed" (Leonard Hobhouse, *Social Evolution and Political Theory*, 1911).

"[Society is] a group of individuals carrying on a collective life by means of mental interactions" (Charles Ellwood, *Sociology in Its Psychological Aspects*, 1913).

"The great society [is primarily controlled by those] who direct enormous social power without attempting to form a social purpose" (Graham Wallas, *The Great Society*, 1914).

"[A society] acquires a structure and qualities which are largely independent of the qualities of the individuals who enter into its composition and take part for a brief time in its life" (William McDougall, *The Group Mind*, 1920).

"Standards are, perhaps, the most important things in society" (Edward Ross, *Principles of Sociology*, 1920).

"Society is the sum of social relations" (Jean Piaget, *The Moral Judgment of the Child*, 1932).

"Society needs a concentration of power, and in the person of the ruling class . . . irresistibly strives to get it" (Leon Trotsky, *History of the Russian Revolution*, 1932).

"[The folk society is] the basis from which all societies develop" (Howard Odum, *Understanding Society*, 1947).

"Each precivilized society was held together by largely undeclared but continually realized ethical conceptions" (Robert Redfield, *The Primitive World and Its Transformations*, 1953).

"[Society is] an organization and accumulation of values . . . an essentially self-directed and active organization that tends toward increased heterogeneity, wholeness, and macroscopic orderliness" (Radhakamal Mukerjee in Baljit Singh, ed., *The Frontiers of Social Science*, 1956).

"It may even be difficult to distinguish adjacent societies from one another, for some primitive societies are not clearly bounded either in territory or in membership in the sense that more advanced societies are" (Talcott Parsons, *Societies*, 1966).

"The mass society has been identified by its critics with such things as depersonalization, the mechanization of social relations, and bureaucratization. . . . However, there is something wrong with the purely negative estimations of the mass society, for no people voluntarily gives up its fundamental values unless it receives what it considers even more fundamental in return" (Don Martindale, *American Society*, 1972).

SOCIOBIOLOGY

"Deep in the cavern of the infant's breast, lurks the father's nature and lives again" (Horace, *Odes*, c. 13 B.C.).

"It is now the accepted opinion, and it may be correct, that men inherited from their beast ancestors psychophysical traits, instincts, and dexterities, or at least predispositions, which give them aid in solving the problems of food supply, sex commerce, and vanity'' (William Sumner, *Folkways*, 1907).

''It is impossible to study the genetics of a behavior. We can study the behavior of *an* organism, the genetics of *a* population, and individual differences in the expression of some behavior by members of *that* population'' (J. Hirsch in M. Manosevitz et al., eds., *Behavior Genetics*, 1969).

''Behavior cannot be biologically inherited but must be developed and elicited under the combined influence of genetic and environmental factors'' (J. Scott in Margaret Mead et al., eds., *Science and the Concept of Race*, 1969).

''There is no single true value of the heritability of a trait. Heritability is not a constant, but a population statistic, and it can vary according to the test used and the particular population tested'' (Arthur Jensen in C. Brace et al., eds., *Race and Intelligence*, 1971).

''In the process of natural selection . . . any device that can insert a higher proportion of certain genes into subsequent generations will come to characterize the species. One class of such devices promotes prolonged individual survival. Another promotes superior mating performance and care of the resulting offspring. As more complex behavior by the organism is added to the genes' techniques for replicating themselves, altruism becomes increasingly prevalent and eventually appears in exaggerated forms'' (Edward Wilson, *Sociobiology*, 1975).

''Humans are not really pair-bonding animals in the sense that parrots, penguins and ducks are. In terms of our natural inclination we are, just as would be expected, rather like other apes—basically polygynous harem-builders with a capacity for forming strong friendships and short-term exclusive sexual liaisons'' (Glenn Wilson, *Love and Instinct*, 1981).

''Behaviors that must be performed correctly the first time, such as escape from predators, are likely to be under somewhat precise genetic control'' (David Barash, *Sociobiology and Behavior*, 1982).

SOCIOLOGY, APPLIED

''Praxis without theory is a blind thing'' (Polybius, *Histories*, 130 B.C.).

''[Applied sociology] does not itself apply sociological principles, it seeks only to show how they may be applied'' (Lester Ward, *Applied Sociology*, 1906).

''The newer tendency to put social science at the service of society, apart from its practical benefits, can yield theoretical advances'' (John Owen, *Sociology in East Pakistan*, 1962).

''In British social policy and administration, we begin with fact-finding and end in moral rhetoric, still lacking those explanatory theories that might show the process as a whole and reveal the relations of the separate problems to one another'' (R. Pinker, *Social Theory and Social Policy*, 1971).

''The sociologist recognizes that he is part of the social process and not outside of it. The advocates of the enlightenment model reject the view that sociological knowledge produces definitive answers on which policy and professional practice can be based. Sociology is but one aspect of the social sciences, and the social sciences themselves but one type of knowledge required for policy'' (Morris Janowitz, *Sociological Models and Social Policy*, 1972).

''When sociology first came to the United States it was akin to a crusade for social improvement. . . . We have in this review used the policy science terminology of the original authors. Wherever they talk of 'policy scientists' the reader could at every point have substituted 'social engineers,' and we have finally decided to talk of 'applied sociologists' '' (Paul Lazarsfeld and Jeffrey Reitz, *An Introduction to Applied Sociology*, 1975).

''Ideas and conceptualizations are useful to give structure and direction to action. But they must eventually rest on pragmatically tested operations for their implementation'' (Leonard Cottrell in Berton Kaplan et al., eds., *Further Explorations in Social Psychiatry*, 1976).

''Research commissioned by government should include a fairly sizeable proportion which is specified in broad terms, is concerned with processes rather than immediate issues, and is the subject of continuing discussion between researchers and those in government—and, for that matter, those outside it who are interested in the policy debate'' (P. Wilmott in M. Cross, ed., *Social Research and Social Policy*, 1980).

''Social policy . . . refers, in a generic sense, to the aims and objectives of social action concerning needs as well as to the structural patterns or arrangements through which needs are met'' (Ramesh Mishra, *Society and Social Policy*, 1981).

''The frontiers of applied sociology are vast and raw, and the wilderness beyond is virtually unknown'' (Marvin Olsen and Michael Micklin, eds., *Handbook of Applied Sociology*, 1981).

'' 'Applied' social science and 'applied' social research are not homogeneous. Social scientists themselves conceive of them in various ways. Policy-makers expect different things from social science, often different in nature'' (Martin Bulmer, *The Uses of Social Research*, 1982).

SOCIOLOGY, COMPARATIVE

''Comparative sociology is not a particular branch of sociology; it is sociology itself'' (Émile Durkheim, *The Rules of Sociological Method*, 1895).

''Attempts . . . to discover essential similarities between actions classified as crimes in all societies at all periods have failed. The reason for this is clear. All prohibitive rules define and classify actions as experienced and evaluated by those who promulgate the rules from the point of view of standards and norms they consider binding. Hence the agents who perform such prohibited actions *ex definitione* do not conform with these standards and norms . . . a classification by itself contains no information as to what the actions really are from the standpoint of the agents themselves'' (Florian Znaniecki, *Cultural Sciences*, 1952).

"It is only by comparative studies that we can become aware of the *absence* of certain historical phases from a society, which is often quite essential to understanding its contemporary shape. . . . A retreat from history makes it impossible . . . to understand precisely the most contemporary features of this one society" (C. W. Mills, *The Sociological Imagination*, 1959).

"Comparative study means more than the statement of the different historical background and of the different geographical conditions of different countries. Institutions promoted by certain background conditions should be appreciated in connection with the social functions they have to fulfill" (Rudolf Schlesinger in Instituto de Ciencias Sociales, *The Province*, 1966).

"The fundamental reason why more attention should be given to comparative research and analysis is that sociological theory has been developed in one rather small corner of the world and may therefore be highly limited as a universal explanatory scheme . . . cross-societal comparative analysis is fundamental to any general sociological or anthropological theory" (Robert Marsh, *Comparative Sociology*, 1967).

"Nearly all the sources of error are country-specific. . . . In one study, it was said that the key-punching errors reflected differences in national character; Germany showed a total absence of random errors in key-punching . . . in Italy the errors were scattered with apparent Latin abandon . . . errors are highly correlated with country, and the cross-country comparisons on which such studies depend must be made warily . . . all the results reported for Finland were incorrect, due to poor communication" (James Coleman in Robert Bierstedt, ed., *A Design for Sociology*, 1969).

"All comparative research dealing with differing civilizations and social environments raises from the outset the problem of distinguishing those factors peculiar to the spontaneous and internal development of the individual from the specific group or cultural factors of the particular society which provides his environment" (Jean Piaget, *Psychology and Epistemology*, 1972).

"Sociology as a transnational discipline continues to be shaped by the individual nation-states of the world" (Raj Mohan and Don Martindale, eds., *Handbook of Contemporary Developments in World Sociology*, 1975).

"[The Soviet Union is a] particular species of industrial society which in many ways is similar to that of advanced western societies but which in other respects has peculiar and unique features" (David Lane, *Politics and Society in the USSR*, 1978).

"A cross-national and generalising approach is necessary to throw light on the nature and development of social policy in particular national contexts" (Ramesh Mishra, *Society and Social Policy*, 1981).

SOCIOLOGY OF SOCIOLOGY

"The high utilitarian motive, focalizing all considerations in the good of man, can have no other effect than to establish as the ultimate science, for the perfection of which all other sciences exist, the science of human life, which takes the form and name of sociology" (Lester Ward, *Dynamic Sociology*, 1883).

''[Sociology is the science of] the processes of reaction resulting from the mutual stimulation of individuals of the same species'' (Émile Waxweiler, *Outline of Sociology*, 1896).

''[Sociology is] destined to open a new way to the science of man'' (Émile Durkheim, *The Elementary Forms of Religious Life*, 1912).

''[Sociology is] a science which aims to understand clearly social behavior and thus give a causal explanation'' (Max Weber, *Economy and Society*, 1922, posthumously).

''Twentieth century sociology . . . no longer proposes to solve: 1. the problem of the fate of mankind; 2. the problem of order and progress; 3. the problem of the conflict between the individual and society; 4. the problem of the opposition between the psychic and the social; 5. the problem of predominant factors; 6. the problem, finally, of sociological laws'' (Georges Davidovitch Gurvitch, *The Actual Vocation of Sociology*, 1950).

''What we read in textbooks and treatises on sociology is very often nothing else than a retrospective collection of new insights which were gained during periods of social unrest. In the work of Saint-Simon and Comte, for instance, the impact of such direct experiences is clearly visible'' (Karl Mannheim, *Essays on Sociology and Social Psychology*, 1953, posthumously).

''Sociology is a pure science, not an applied science'' (Robert Bierstedt, *The Social Order*, 1963).

''Sociology's ontology has been polarized between holism and elementarism; its epistemology has been polarized between positivism—the proposal to use physical science methods in social spheres—and antipositivism. These polarizations have laid the abstract basis for four general theoretical positions in sociology: positivistic holism; positivistic elementarism; antipositivistic holism; and antipositivistic elementarism'' (Don Martindale, ed., *Functionalism in the Social Sciences*, 1965).

''Sociologists with a sense of history have found a growing dissatisfaction with static 'bootstraps' functionalist analyses'' (Jeffrey Stanyer in Instituto de Ciencias Sociales, *The County*, 1966).

''The history of British sociology before 1914--indeed before 1945--is in no sense a success story'' (P. Abrams, *The Origins of British Sociology 1834–1914*, 1968).

''Alpha Kappa Delta was formed to meet a specific need in the Department of Sociology at the University of Southern California. The need was for the advanced students and the faculty to get together on a common basis of sociological inquiry. . . . It was on the foregoing bases that the idea of a sociology honor society of scholars was conceived and developed at the University of Southern California in 1920'' (Emory Bogardus, *A History of Alpha Kappa Delta, Sociology Honor Society*, 1970).

''With the conceptual and theoretical withdrawal and return occasioned by World War II, sociology's preparadigmatic period of adolescence as a science was drawing to an end. A core vocabulary and a common theoretical posture were beginning to emerge. With them sociology seemed finally on the point of moving from the ordering of its own house to cumulative research. With its subject matter conceived in terms of system analysis, sociologists might confidently set out to piece together the functional imperatives that now appeared all about them, nesting one sub-system within another and enveloping all within a dynamic equilibrium'' (Robert Friedrichs, *A Sociology of Sociology*, 1970).

''We sociologists must—at the very least—acquire the ingrained *habit* of viewing our own beliefs as we now view those held by others'' (Alvin Gouldner, *The Coming Crisis in Western Sociology*, 1970).

''Our sociological consciousness has been deficient in failing to appreciate how much of what happens to sociology as it changes and develops is part and parcel of what is happening to the larger world into which we are inextricably interwoven'' (James McKee in Larry and Janice Reynolds, eds., *The Sociology of Sociology*, 1970).

''[In Italy] the number of 'official' sociologists is very small. In such a context the idea of creating an association of radical sociologists can only be a topic for jokes. In reality, the preoccupation with 'sociologists' and 'sociology' as such is somewhat meaningless'' (Vittorio Capecchi in P. Rossi, ed., *Sociological Research and the Role of the Sociologist*, 1972).

''The position of a professional sociologist in society and in the academic world depends on the establishment of sociology as a science and on the social efficiency of sociological researches'' (Andrei Roth, *On Sociology and Sociologists*, 1975).

''Sociology has taught us very little'' (Pierre van den Berghe, *Human Family Systems*, 1979).

''He [Don Martindale] has found himself in reaction to sociological language much of the time, particularly its abstractness, imprecision, its unnecessary jargon and pretentious emptiness. Ever and again he has felt sociologists mislead themselves by their endless reifications and inappropriate figures of speech, though sometimes . . . they achieve unexpected and undesired comic effects'' (Edith Martindale, ed., *The Sound of Academe*, 1979).

''In contemplating, from a cross-cultural standpoint, leading characteristics of American sociology during the last decades, it becomes apparent that alongside its contentious vitality, technical inventiveness, and impressive growth has been a reinforcement of certain characteristics summed up in the [term provincialism], characteristics more to be expected from the fledgling discipline it represented in the years before World War II than from the mature and self-assured profession it now embodies'' (Peter Dodge in Harald Niemeyer, ed., *Social Relations Network*, 1980).

''Sociology . . . is not the creation of one or a few people of genius but an ongoing enterprise of research, study, and teaching'' (Don Martindale, *The Nature and Types of Sociological Theory*, 1981).

SOCIOLOGY, QUALITATIVE

''Some variables cannot be differentiated according to either implied or explicitly stated units. These are designated as qualitatively defined variables. . . . Sex is not variable in terms of numbers of units of sex, but in terms of the categories male and female'' (Pauline Young, *Scientific Social Surveys and Research*, 1966).

''Qualitative sociologists . . . report observations in the natural language at large. They seldom make counts or assign numbers to these observations. In this sense, qualitative sociologists report on the social world much as the daily newspaper does. This simple difference in commitment to notation systems corresponds to vast differences in values, goals, and procedures for doing sociological research'' (Howard Schwartz and Jerry Jacobs, *Qualitative Sociology*, 1979).

SOCIOLOGY, QUANTITATIVE

''Often a single figure says much more than a long discourse'' (Pierre Guillaume Frédéric Le Play, *The European Workers*, 1855).

''Measurement has long been considered a hallmark of science properly practiced, and once a new discipline has developed a mathematical discourse, it has almost immediately laid claim, at least in the language of its most enthusiastic disciples, to the significant status—science!'' (Harry Woolf, ed., *Quantification*, 1961).

''Quantitative sociologists assign numbers to qualitative observations. In this sense, they produce data by counting and 'measuring' things. The things measured can be individual persons, groups, whole societies, speech acts, and so on'' (Howard Schwartz and Jerry Jacobs, *Qualitative Sociology*, 1979).

''An important characteristic of a science as it matures is that its measurement becomes more accurate, and the limitations of the measurement procedures become known'' (Edgar Borgatta in Everett Lee and Harold Goldsmith, eds., *Population Estimates*, 1982).

SOLIDARITY, SOCIAL

''[In *asabiyya* (social solidarity)] cooperation . . . secures both food and weapons, thus fulfilling God's will of preserving the species . . . the weapons with which they defend themselves against wild beasts cannot serve as a restraint, seeing that each man can make equal use of them. . . . The restraint must therefore be constituted by one man, who wields power and authority with a firm hand and thus prevents anyone from attacking anyone else'' (Ibn Khaldun, *Preface*, 1377).

''[Although punishment is] a quite mechanical reaction . . . it does play a useful role . . . its efficacy is justly doubtful and, in any case, mediocre. Its true function is to maintain social cohesion intact, while maintaining its vitality in the common conscience . . . social solidarity . . . taken by itself, does not lend itself to exact observation nor indeed to measurement. . . . We must substitute for this . . . an external index which symbolizes it and study the former in the light of the latter. . . . Even where society relies most completely upon the division of labor, it does not become a jumble of juxtaposed atoms, between which it can establish only external, transient contacts. Rather the members are united by ties which extend deeper and far beyond the short moments during which the exchange is made. . . . There is, above all, an organ upon which we are tending to depend more and more; this is the State. The points at which we are in contact with it multiply as do the occasions when it is entrusted with the duty of reminding us of the sentiment of common solidarity. . . . [In mechanical solidarity] ideas and tendencies common to all members of the society are greater in number and intensity than those which pertain personally to each member. This solidarity can grow only in inverse ratio to personality. . . . It is this solidarity which repressive law expresses, at least whatever there is vital to it. . . . Solidarity which comes from likeness is at its maximum when the collective conscience completely envelops our whole conscience and coincides in all points with it. . . . [Organic solidarity] resembles that which we observe among the higher animals. Each organ, in effect, has its special physiognomy, its autonomy. And, moreover, the unity of the organism is as great as the individuation of the parts is more marked. Because of this analogy, we propose to call this solidarity which is due to the division of labor, organic'' (Émile Durkheim, *The Division of Labor in Society*, 1893).

STATUS, SOCIAL

``Man as a rule submits to the social status in which parents and forebears, or, as it is wont to be expressed, 'God,' has placed him as if it were his lot to bear, even though it be felt as a burden, which, however, is habit and is lightened by the recognition that it cannot be changed'' (Ferdinand Tönnies, *Community and Society*, 1887).

``Estranged castes might stand beside one another with bitter hatred—for the idea that everyone had 'deserved' his own fate did not make the good fortune of the privileged more enjoyable to the underprivileged. So long as *karma* doctrine was unshaken, revolutionary ideas or progressivism were inconceivable. The lowest castes, furthermore, had the most to win through ritual correctness and were least tempted to innovations'' (Max Weber, *The Religion of India*, 1917).

``Family rank, which existed among the Cheyennes as among other Indians, depended on the estimation in which the family was held by the best people. A good family was one that produced brave men and good sensible women, and that possessed more or less property'' (G. Grinnell, *The Cheyenne Indians*, 1923).

``A *status*, in the abstract, is a position in a particular pattern. It is thus quite correct to speak of each individual as having many statuses, since each individual participates in the expression of a number of patterns. However, unless the term is qualified in some way, the *status* of any individual means the sum total of all the statuses which he occupies. It represents his position with relation to the total society. . . . A status, as distinct from the individual who may occupy it, is simply a collection of rights and duties'' (Ralph Linton, *The Study of Man*, 1936).

''Certain Hindu theological ideas such as *samsara, karma*, and *dharma* are woven into the caste system, but it is not known whether awareness of these concepts is universal or confined only to certain sections of the hierarchy. This depends on the degree to which an area is Sanskritized'' (M. Srinivas, *Social Change in Modern India*, 1966).

''A status, then, is a position or a location that a person may occupy. . . . Some of the statuses you occupy are called *ascribed statuses*. These are statuses that you don't have to 'earn.' 'Female' and 'male' are ascribed statuses. . . . Other statuses you occupy are *achieved statuses*, meaning that you have to do something to occupy them. 'College student' is an achieved status'' (Earl Babbie, *Sociology*, 1983).

STEREOTYPE

''We pick out what our culture has already defined for us, and we tend to perceive that which we have picked out in the form stereotyped for us by our culture'' (Walter Lippmann, *Public Opinion*, 1922).

''The very same behavior undergoes complete change of evaluation in its transformation from the in-group Abe Lincoln to the out-group Abe Cohen or Abe Kurokawa. . . . Did Lincoln work far into the night? This testifies that he was industrious, resolute, perseverant, and eager to realize his capacities to the full. Do the out-group Jews or Japanese keep the same hours? This only bears witness to their sweatshop mentality, their ruthless undercutting of American standards, their unfair competitive practices. Is the in-group hero frugal . . . ? Then the out-group villain is stingy'' (Robert Merton, *Social Theory and Social Structure*, 1957).

''When ethnically heterogeneous groups that were autonomous become parts of a national (and international) economy and polity, their group stereotypes tend to become polarized along three dimensions: (1) urbanism, (2) occupation, and (3) political-technological dominance'' (Robert LeVine and Donald Campbell, *Ethnocentrism*, 1972).

''[Stereotypes] are easy ways of explaining things. They take less effort and give an appearance of order without the difficult work that understanding the true order of things demands'' (George Simpson and J. Yinger, *Racial and Cultural Minorities*, 1972).

''A truly prejudiced person, however, will go on making incorrect judgments *even in the face of contrary evidence*. That is because prejudiced people judge others only on the basis of *stereotypes*, or simplified, rigid mental images of what members of a certain group are like. Ethnic and racial stereotypes are mental pictures of people based not on their individual differences but on attitudes or beliefs about their group's shared characteristics. . . . The actual content of stereotypes is thought to derive from the *projection* of one's own sins onto others'' (Lewis Coser et al., *Introduction to Sociology*, 1983).

STRATIFICATION, SOCIAL

''If a man has caused the loss of a patrician's eye, his eye shall one cause to be lost. . . . If a man has caused a poor man to lose his eye, he shall pay one mina of silver'' (Hammurabi, *Code*, c. 1750 B.C.).

''All communities divide themselves into the few and the many. The first are the rich and the well-born, the other the masses of people'' (Alexander Hamilton, *Records of the Federal Convention*, 1797).

''In the earlier epochs of history, we find almost everywhere a complete subdivision of society into different ranks, a manifold gradation of social positions. In ancient Rome, we have: patricians, knights, plebeians, slaves. In the Middle Ages, we have: feudal lords, vassals, guild-burgesses, journeymen, serfs; and within each of these classes there existed, in almost every instance, further gradations'' (Karl Marx and Friedrich Engels, *Communist Manifesto*, 1847).

''The stratification of classes does not appear in its pure form. Middle and intermediate strata even here obliterate lines of demarcation everywhere (although incomparably less in rural districts than in the cities)'' (Karl Marx, *Das Kapital*, 1879).

''The history of the industrialization of many countries shows that one of the fundamental changes in the social structure which takes place with the coming of the modern industrial age is that the rigidly structured strata of the feudal age gradually give way to an open class society'' (C. Ghurye, *Caste and Class in India*, 1952).

''[Stratification] denotes the differential ranking of the human individuals who compose a given social system and their treatment as superior and inferior relative to one another in certain socially important respects'' (Talcott Parsons, *Essays in Sociological Theory, Pure and Applied*, 1954).

''Such evidence as there is seems to show that there is a considerable amount of either ignorance or vague knowledge about the system of stratification'' (Bernard Barber, *Social Stratification*, 1957).

''As societies become more differentiated, a considerable degree of cohesion and consensus is needed at the top'' (Suzanne Keller, *Beyond the Ruling Class*, 1963).

''The main functional necessity explaining the universal presence of stratification is precisely the requirement faced by any society of placing and motivating individuals in the social structure'' (Kingsley Davis and Wilbert Moore in Harland Bentley, ed., *Readings for Fundamentals of Sociology*, 1969).

''[In India] the classical texts described in terms of varna what must surely have been at that time a caste system in embryo'' (Louis Dumont, *Homo Hierarchicus*, 1970).

''[Stratification involves] significant discontinuities in the distribution of goods and services, or of property, rights and obligations'' (J. Littlejohn, *Social Stratification*, 1972).

''Class stratification appears in societies with expanding economies and is a phenomenon peculiar to industrial society'' (Daniel Rossides, *The American Class System*, 1976).

''[In South Africa] the fact that the White-Black racial division corresponds pronouncedly with a have/have-not differential is certainly not conducive to accommodationist policies. This socio-economic cleavage (roughly equivalent to the European class stratification) would be less divisive if it was not for the historical nexus of class and colour'' (Nic Rhoodie, ed., *Conflict Resolution in South Africa*, 1980).

''Most Brazilian families are unable to educate their children adequately and to postpone their entry into the labor market. The early entry of the children of the lower social classes is in itself a strong indicator of social inequality which historically has permeated the Brazilian social system'' (José Pastore, *Inequality and Social Mobility in Brazil*, 1982).

''The variety of statuses is more limited in Greek society'' (Jane Lambiri, *Social Stratification in Greece*, 1983).

''In Japan . . . the bourgeoisie . . . not only binds together the entire system of production, giving it its characteristic forms, but as a result all the various subordinate elements in Japanese society'' (Bob Steven, *Classes in Contemporary Japan*, 1983).

STRUCTURE, SOCIAL

''Function leads structure and structure limits function'' (Albert Eberhard Friedrich Schäffle, *Structure and Life of the Social Body*, 1878).

''The whole structure of Trobriand society is founded on the principle of *legal status*. By this I mean that the claims of chief over commoners, husband over wife, parent over child, and vice versa, are not exercised arbitrarily and one-sidedly, but according to definite rules, and arranged into well-balanced chains of reciprocal services'' (Bronislaw Malinowski, *Crime and Custom in Savage Society*, 1926).

''Certain aspects of the social structure may generate countermores and antisocial behavior precisely because of differential emphases on goals and regulations. In the extreme case, the latter may be so vitiated by the goal-emphasis that the range of behavior is limited only by considerations of technical expediency. The sole significant question then becomes, which available means is most efficient in netting the socially approved value? The technically most feasible procedure, whether legitimate or not, is preferred to the institutionally prescribed conduct. As this process continues, the integration of the society becomes tenuous and anomie ensues'' (Robert Merton, ''Social Structure and Anomie,'' 1938, in Robert Brown, ed., *Mental Hygiene*, 1969).

''Direct observation does reveal to us that . . . human beings are connected by a complex network of social relations. I use the term 'social structure' to denote this network of actually existing relations'' (A. Radcliffe-Brown, *Structure and Function in Primitive Society*, 1952).

"[Social structure refers to] the conditions involved in the interaction of actual human individuals who constitute concrete collectivities with determinate memberships" (Talcott Parsons in Talcott Parsons et al., eds., *Theories of Society*, 1961).

"It is a curious fact that sociology, which advertises itself as the science of society, has discovered only belatedly, and almost with surprise, the dramatic transformations in social structure which have exploded upon the modern world" (Don Martindale, *Institutions, Organizations, and Mass Society*, 1966).

"I consider social structure . . . to be still the social reality itself, or an aspect of it, not the logic behind it; and I consider structural analysis to be no more than a descriptive method, however sophisticated, not a piece of explanation" (S. Nadel, *The Theory of Social Structure*, 1969).

"[Erving] Goffman does not deal with how men seek to change the structures of these organizations or of other social systems, but with how they may adapt to and within them. It is a theory of the secondary adjustments that men make to the overpowering social structures that they feel must be taken as given" (Alvin Gouldner, *The Coming Crisis of Western Sociology*, 1971).

"All of us sociologists are . . . structuralists in the broadest sense of the term . . . not all of us are structuralists unless we mean by the term 'structuralism' merely the interdependence of elements in a larger social system" (Peter Blau in Peter Marsden and Nan Lin, eds., *Social Structure and Network Analysis*, 1982).

"If *social structure* is not the single most important concept in sociology, and in social science more generally, it is certainly one of a very small number of central concepts. The premise that behaviors or actions are interpretable only in relation to the positions of actors in social structure underlies much social scientific inquiry" (Peter Marsden and Nan Lin, eds., *Social Structure and Network Analysis*, 1982).

SUICIDE

"A man must not commit suicide but wait until God calls him" (Plato, *Phaedo*, c. 400 B.C.).

"None of those who commit suicide in order to avoid pain, as many do, may be called brave" (Aristotle, *Eudemian Ethics*, c. 350 B.C.).

"He who saves a man against his will as good as murders him" (Horace, *The Art of Poetry*, 8 B.C.).

"It is better that He should take the soul Who gave it, and let nobody do violence to it himself" (Talmud: Idolatry 18a).

"Everyone belongs to the community . . . therefore, he who kills himself does an injury to the community" (Thomas Aquinas, *Summa Theologica*, 1274).

"Is it sin to rush into the secret house of death ere death dare come to us?" (William Shakespeare, *Antony and Cleopatra*, 1607).

"The man who, in a fit of melancholy, kills himself today, would have wished to live had he waited a week'' (François Marie Arouet de Voltaire, *Philosophical Dictionary*, 1764).

''[Suicides] do not form, as might be thought, a wholly distinct group, an isolated class of monstrous phenomena, unrelated to other forms of conduct, but rather are related to them by a continuous series of intermediate cases. They are merely the exaggerated form of common practices [such as] the daredevil who intentionally toys with death while seeking to avoid it, or the man of apathetic temperament who, having no vital interest in anything, takes no care of health and so imperils it by neglect. Yet these different ways of acting are not radically distinct from true suicide. They result from similar states of mind, since they also entail mortal risks not unknown to the agent, and the prospect of these is no deterrent; the sole difference is a lesser chance of death . . . such facts form a sort of embryonic suicide. . . . The aptitude of Jews for suicide is always less than that of Protestants; in a very general way it is also, though to a lesser degree, lower than that of Catholics . . . if Protestantism is less unfavorable to the development of suicide, it is not because of a different attitude from that of Catholicism. Thus, if both religions have the same precepts with respect to this particular matter, their dissimilar influence on suicide must proceed from one of the more general characteristics differentiating them. The only essential difference between Catholicism and Protestantism is that the second permits free inquiry. . . . This also explains the situation of Judaism. Indeed, the reproach to which the Jews have for so long been exposed by Christianity has created feelings of unusual solidarity among them . . . of all great Protestant countries, England is the one where suicide is least developed . . . the Anglican church is far more powerfully integrated than other Protestant churches . . . propositions: Suicide varies inversely with the degree of integration of religious society. Suicide varies inversely with the degree of integration of domestic society. Suicide varies inversely with the degree of integration of political society . . . suicide varies inversely with the degree of integration of the social groups of which the individual forms a part [egoistic suicide]. . . . In anomic suicide, society's influence is lacking in the basically individual passions, thus leaving them without a check-rein. . . . [In altruistic suicide the motive is self-sacrifice for the group]'' (Émile Durkheim, *Suicide*, 1897).

''There are some neurotics in whom . . . the instinct of self-preservation has actually been reversed. They seem to have nothing in view but self-injury and self-destruction'' (Sigmund Freud, *An Outline of Psychoanalysis*, 1940).

''There is only one truly philosophical problem, namely, suicide'' (Albert Camus, *The Myth of Sisyphus*, 1942).

''It is not the act of suicide that is horrifying, but the extreme unhappiness that must be presumed to have induced it. Death from despair is the one thing that ought to make us shudder'' (Mary Barrington in David Bender, ed., *Problems of Death*, 1974).

''[Suicides] fluctuate cyclically with socioeconomic conditions, wars, revolution and the dominant life patterns of a people'' (Walter Lunden, *The Suicide Cycle*, 1977).

''[Among Cheyennes] only the souls of those who have committed suicide are barred from [the] journey to the Milky Way'' (E. Hoebel, *The Cheyennes*, 1978).

''The difference between the sexes in the propensity to commit suicide changes sign with the spread of divorce throughout the global society'' (Raymond Boudon, *The Crisis in Sociology*, 1980).

''Scholars in many disciplines . . . have long been fascinated by the topic and study of suicide and suicidal behavior. Despite this continuing fascination . . . it remains a very difficult behavior to study'' (David Lester et al., *Suicide*, 1980).

''A special type of suicide is the *Samsonic* form, which is based on revenge against an enemy'' (Panos Bardis, *History of Thanatology*, 1981).

''Many factors known to be related to suicide in general are experiences typical of aging itself. The most significant factor is the loss of a love object by separation or death'' (Georgia Barrow and Patricia Smith, *Aging, the Individual, and Society*, 1983).

''Mental health professionals urge patients not to commit suicide, but reserve for themselves the right to choose death under some extenuating circumstance. Heroism and martyrdom are extolled, but victims of suicide are stigmatized'' (Fred Cutter, *Art and the Wish to Die*, 1983).

''Among modern nations, by and large the richer the country, the *higher* its suicide rate. . . . The Gallup people, however, found that, by and large, the richer the country, the *higher* its quality of life. That is to say, the higher the proportion of its people who told interviewers they felt pleased and satisfied with life. Now suicide is always a rare event—even in Finland, where the rate is so high; even there, only 1 person in 5,000 each year commits suicide'' (Raoul Naroll, *The Moral Order*, 1983).

SYMBOL, SOCIOLOGY OF

''Spoken words are symbols of passions of the soul; written words are symbols of spoken words'' (Aristotle, *On Interpretation*, c. 350 B.C.).

''[Social symbols] supply the stimulus and framework for all our growth'' (Charles Cooley, *Human Nature and the Social Order*, 1902).

''The symbolic process furnishes a most remarkable means of determining group unity, morale, and control. . . . [Meaning derives from] sequential or functionally dependent relationship existing between parts of behavior'' (John Markey, *The Symbolic Process*, 1928).

''To millions of voters the flag is more sacred than the country which flies it, and a written Constitution is more sacred than the rights and liberties it defines and guarantees'' (Franklin Giddings, *The Mighty Medicine*, 1929).

''Behaviorism reduces the problem of meaning to the meaning of symbols.

But for the human agent not only symbols have a meaning, but every datum of his experience in which he is actively interested; every datum stands not only for itself, but for other data which it suggests'' (Florian Znaniecki, *Social Actions*, 1936).

``Symbolism occurs when natural religions are degenerating'' (Julio Caro Baroja, *A Few Spanish Myths*, 1941).

``All human behavior originates in the use of symbols. It was the symbol which transformed our anthropoid ancestors into men and made them human. . . . It is the symbol which transforms an infant of Homo sapiens into a human being; deaf mutes who grow up without the use of symbols are not human beings. All human behavior consists of, or is dependent upon, the use of symbols. Human behavior is symbolic behavior; symbolic behavior is human behavior. The symbol is the universe of humanity. . . . A symbol may be defined as a thing the value or meaning of which is bestowed upon it by those who use it'' (Leslie White, *The Science of Culture*, 1949).

``[A symbol is] a vehicle of communication and regulation of human relations, a pregnant, epitomised expression of meanings and values shared in human life'' (Radhakamal Mukerjee in Baljit Singh, eds., *The Frontiers of Social Science*, 1956).

``The symbol proper is a dynamic and polysymbolic reality, imbued with emotive and conceptual values: in other words, with true life'' (J. Cirlot, *A Dictionary of Symbols*, 1962).

``The greater the interpersonal distance between individuals involved in a communication situation, the more autonomous must be the symbolic vehicles in order to be understood'' (H. Werner and B. Kaplan, *Symbolic Formation*, 1963).

``The appearance of an alternative symbolic universe poses a threat because its very existence demonstrates empirically that one's own universe is less than inevitable'' (Peter Berger and Thomas Luckmann, *The Social Construction of Reality*, 1967).

``We must think of symbolic interaction as forming the very stuff of human personality, character, self, and identity. Only through communication in terms of shared symbols it is possible for each of us to acquire his sense of self, character, and identity'' (Robert Nisbet, *The Social Bond*, 1970).

``Each new evocation brings about a different reconstruction of old representations, weaves new links among them, integrates into the field of symbolism new information brought to it by daily life'' (D. Sperber, *Rethinking Symbolism*, 1975).

``To describe symbolic culture, two criteria are used . . . the semiotic and the axiological . . . symbolic culture can fulfill its important secondary functions only on the condition that it preserves its original character, that its values remain intrinsic . . . sought for their own sake'' (Antonina Kloskowska, *Sociology and Culture*, 1982).

SYSTEM, SOCIAL

''[A social system] which the individual voluntarily helps to realize must acquire gradually in his eyes a much greater importance and desirability than a system which is imposed on him'' (William Thomas and Florian Znaniecki, *The Polish Peasant in Europe and America*, 1920).

''The most fundamental mechanisms of social control are to be found in the normal processes of interaction in an institutionally integrated social system . . . there are points in the social system at which people are exposed to rather special strains. In a good many such cases we find special phenomena which have been interpreted to function at least in part as mechanisms for 'coping' with such strains with a minimum of disruptive consequences for the social system. Two types may be briefly discussed. One is the type of situation where because of uncertainty factors or specially acute adjustment problems there is exposure to what, for the persons concerned, is an unusual strain. In general the field of religion and magic yields many examples of this. . . . A slightly different type of structuring of behavior which is certainly in part significant as a mechanism of control is what may be called the 'secondary institution.' The American youth culture is a good example. Like ritual it has its conspicuous permissive aspect, so much so that it shades over into explicit deviance'' (Talcott Parsons, *The Social System*, 1951).

''When the system is reified and its state of equilibrium is apotheosized and treated as the cause of all events in it (except for dysfunctions), social change from within the system is in principle excluded'' (Don Martindale, *Social Life and Cultural Change*, 1962).

''Whatever presents a lesser degree of organized complexity and is included within the boundaries of the system is called the subsystem. Whatever presents a greater degree of organized complexity and includes within its boundaries a number of systems is called a suprasystem'' (G. and V. Vassiliou, *A Brief Introduction to the Socioeducational Application of Group Techniques*, 1976).

''Social systems evolve on the basis of mutual association and interdependence among people who strive to adapt themselves to the environment and need one another in this respect'' (Alexander Matejko in Harald Niemeyer, ed., *Social Relations Network*, 1980).

''Three value perspectives play a significant role in the design of social system interventions: the empirical-rational, the normative-reeducative, and the power-coercive'' (David Twain, *Creating Change in Social Settings*, 1983).

T

TABOO

"Thou shalt not eat beans" (Pythagoras, *Golden Verses*, c. 500 B.C.).

"The system of sympathetic magic is not merely composed of positive concepts: it comprises a very large number of negative precepts, that is, prohibitions. It tells you not merely what to do, but also what to leave undone. The positive precepts are charms: the negative precepts are taboos. In fact the whole doctrine of taboo, or at all events a large part of it, would seem to be only a special application of sympathetic magic, with its two great laws of similarity and contact" (James George Frazer, *The Golden Bough*, 1890).

"Taboo is a Polynesian word. . . . Taboo is a very primitive prohibition imposed from without (by an authority) and directed against the strongest desires of man" (Sigmund Freud, *Totem and Taboo*, 1912).

"In 1819 the Polynesians of Hawaii at one stroke abolished their religion. . . . They had however seen Europeans repeatedly violate religious prohibitions—taboos—without being even punished by the native gods, and that must have shaken Hawaiian faith. Among the natives, this taboo system had grown very powerful and no doubt was sometimes felt as onerous. Women might not eat certain foods, such as bananas and coconuts. It was absolutely irreligious and shocking for men and women to eat together" (Alfred Kroeber, *Anthropology*, 1948).

"The greater number of taboos are indeed concerned with the various delimitations of our spheres and boundaries" (F. Steiner, *Taboo*, 1956).

"The delineation of the sphere of intimacy includes every degree of rigidity: it may extend from taboos on everything having to do with sex, through the neutralization of every degree and tendency in sexuality, down to complete asceticism" (Carleton Coon and Edward Hunt, eds., *Anthropology A to Z*, 1963).

"[A taboo is an] authoritative commandment that is internalized" (M. Fortes in *1966 Proceedings of the Royal Anthropological Institute*, 1967).

"The concept of taboo was one of the notions fundamental to the boundary mediation model developed in the anthropology of ritual. Taboos, of course, are prohibitions that do not mediate boundaries, but ritually maintain them. They assert the necessity of separation, inhibition, or regulative control in the form of a prohibition'' (Nancy Munn in John Honigmann, ed., *Handbook of Social and Cultural Anthropology*, 1973).

''Eskimos believe that spirits—particularly if displeased—can determine much of a person's fate. Consequently, the Eskimos carry out their daily tasks within a complex system of taboos. This system of taboos is so extensive that some have suggested that the Eskimos have no need for a formal set of laws'' (Carol and Melvin Ember, *Cultural Anthropology*, 1977).

''A taboo is a proscription, a 'don't,' which, usually, carries with it supernatural sanctions. For example, members of the group may be prohibited from eating a certain food or killing a certain animal'' (Frank Vivelo, *Cultural Anthropology Handbook*, 1978).

TELEVISION, SOCIOLOGY OF

''In Brooklyn, New York, a six-year-old son of a policeman asked his father for real bullets because his little sister 'doesn't die for real when I shoot her like they do when Hopalong Cassidy kills 'em.' . . . In Los Angeles, a housemaid caught a seven-year-old boy in the act of sprinkling ground glass into the family's lamb stew. . . . It was purely experimental, having been inspired by curiosity to learn whether it would really work as well as it did on television. . . . In a Boston suburb, a nine-year-old boy reluctantly showed his father a report card heavily decorated with red marks, then proposed one way of getting at the heart of the matter; they could give the teacher a box of poisoned chocolates for Christmas. 'It's easy, Dad, they did it on television' '' (W. Schramm et al., *Television in the Lives of Our Children*, 1961).

''A college athlete was arrested . . . after he had mailed letters threatening to kill the wife of a bank president unless he was paid $5,000 . . . he stated he got his idea from television . . . four young boys desiring a human skull for their club activities, broke into a Jersey City mausoleum, pried open a coffin and took one. They brought the skull to their clubroom where they desecrated it by sticking a lighted candle in it. Astonished police said the club members . . . got the idea from a television horror show'' (United States Senate, *Effects on Young People of Violence and Crime Portrayals on Television*, 1961).

''In Canada, where broadcasting was at first wholly commercial, a coexisting national public-service network was found to be essential'' (Harry Skornia, *Television and Society*, 1965).

''It is reasonable to conclude that a constant diet of violent behavior on television has an adverse effect on human character and attitudes'' (National Commission on the Causes and Prevention of Violence, *Commission Statement on Violence in Television Entertainment Programs*, 1969).

''The mirror analogy [the network excuse that television is 'a mirror of society'] tends to neglect the components of 'will,' or decisions made in advance to cover or not to cover certain types of events. A mirror makes no decisions

. . . television coverage can, however, be controlled by predecisions'' (Edward Epstein, *News from Nowhere*, 1973).

''In almost every case, he [the U.S. president], and he alone, decides. His ability to choose when and how to appear without cost before millions of viewers is completely unmatched by his political or Congressional opponents'' (Newton Minow, *Presidential Television*, 1973).

''Throughout broadcasting history, Presidents have been given air time at their request, and under circumstances of their choosing. . . . All Presidents . . . have been thought to misuse the privilege, exploiting it for partisan political ends'' (Erik Barnouw, *Tube of Plenty*, 1975).

''We devote more man hours per year to television than any other single artifact'' (Ray Brown, ed., *Children and Television*, 1976).

''Television's focus on the relationships between people may be far more important and have far more potential impact on the sexual socialization of children and adults than the portrayal of any one particular nude scene, rape theme, or sexual act'' (E. Roberts and S. Holt in J. Fireman, ed., *The Television Book*, 1977).

''In the last fifteen years, as a result of the spread of television almost everywhere, America has become the most abundantly observed society in history'' (Anthony Smith, *The Politics of Information*, 1978).

''Television violence seems to be capable of affecting viewers of both sexes and varying ages, social classes, ethnicities, personality characteristics, and levels of usual aggressiveness'' (Aimée Dorr and Peter Kovaric in E. Palmer and A. Dorr, eds., *Children and the Faces of Television*, 1980).

''It is actually the newspaper, not television, which has the larger regular news audience. . . . Most political information must be communicated with the spoken and written word. . . . Yet television's pictures dominate the viewers' attention, sometimes even distracting from television's verbal communication. Thus the evening news is less likely than the newspaper to impress upon its audience the messages it communicates'' (Thomas Patterson, *The Mass Media Election*, 1980).

''Television is seen and heard in nearly every American home. These homes include children and adults of all ages, embrace all races and all varieties of philosophic or religious conviction and reach those of every educational background. Television broadcasters must take this pluralistic audience into account in programming their stations'' (National Association of Broadcasters, *The Television Code*, 1981).

''The danger of TV lies not so much in the behavior it produces as in the behavior it prevents'' (Urie Bronfenbrenner in Joan Wilkins, *Breaking the TV Habit*, 1982).

''By the age of 18 a child born today [1982] will have spent more time watching television than in any other single activity besides sleep'' (Robert Liebert et al., *The Early Window*, 1982).

''The use of television in education has consistently lagged behind its use in business and industry'' (Judith Shoemaker in Nick Smith, ed., *Communication Strategies in Evaluation*, 1982).

''Television in modern politics has been as revolutionary as the development of printing in the time of Gutenberg. Once Gutenberg put the Bible in print, and others followed to explain the world to those who could read, neither church nor prince could maintain authority without controlling, or yielding to, the word in print. Television, especially in America, explains the world to those who, if they will not read, can look. . . . There could have been no Carter presidency without television. But he who comes to power by television must be prepared to be destroyed by television. For the men and women of television, however hungry for drama and clash in politics, are compelled to report the larger drama of upheaval, change, and erosions of old faiths'' (Theodore White, *America in Search of Itself*, 1982).

''That's right. We're big. And we're powerful enough to thumb our nose at threats and intimidation from Government. I hope it stays that way'' (Walter Cronkite in Thomas Dye, *Who's Running America*, 1983).

TERRORISM

''He who terrorizes is himself more terrified'' (Claudian, *Panegyric on the Fourth Consulship of Honorius Augustus*, c. 400).

''Let us put our trust in the eternal spirit which destroys and annihilates only because it is the unsearchable and eternally creative source of all life. The passion for destruction is also a creative passion'' (Mikhail Aleksandrovich Bakunin, *Reaction in Germany*, 1846).

''A man who has never killed is a virgin'' (André Malraux, *Man's Fate*, 1933).

''[Terrorism is] a revolutionary, or, sometimes counterrevolutionary ('police terrorism') method by means of which a population is induced to cooperate with revolutionary outlaws by inspiring it with terror. . . . In the twentieth century terrorism has been used chiefly in nationalist revolutions, e.g. . . . by the Algerians against the French. Counter terrorism was a favorite weapon of the Nazis'' (Edward Hyams, *A Dictionary of Modern Revolution*, 1973).

''Trotsky's opposition to individual terrorism did not flow from any pacifistic, moralistic, or ethical aversion to violence under any circumstances, or from reformist illusions about the possibility of peaceful social revolution. Rather it flowed from an understanding of the basic ineffectiveness of individual terrorism as a strategy for social change'' (Will Reissner, ed., *Leon Trotsky*, 1974).

''[Political terrorism] is the systematic use of murder and destruction, and the threat of murder and destruction, in order to terrorise individuals, groups, communities or governments into conceding to the terrorists' political demands'' (Paul Wilkinson, *Terrorism and the Liberal State*, 1977).

''The tactics of terrorism have the sanction of historical usage in the United States. *Revolutionary* terrorism in contemporary America is imitative. Almost without exception the nationalists, radicals, and psychopaths who have perpetrated terrorist acts in the name of revolution in the United States have taken their cues from the international environment. It is revolutionary rhetoric that is alien to America, not the use of violence for political purposes. As a consequence revolutionary terrorism has had little appeal except to marginal groups'' (J. Bell and Ted Gurr in Hugh Graham and Ted Gurr, eds., *Violence in America*, 1979).

''The U.S. government has recently attempted to make the elimination of 'international terrorism' a major policy thrust. . . . One technique adopted to achieve this goal is to fashion national and international agreements that 'terrorism' is a crime'' (Arnold Anderson-Sherman in Harold Pepinsky, ed., *Rethinking Criminology*, 1982).

THANATOLOGY

''Weeping will not bring back a man from the other world . . . no one has ever come back after he has gone there'' (*The Book of the Dead*, c. 2500 B.C.).

''But of the tree of the knowledge of good and evil, thou shalt not eat of it: for in the day that thou eatest thereof thou shalt surely die'' (Genesis 2:17).

''While you do not know life, how can you know about death? '' (Confucius, *Analects*, c. 500 B.C.).

''A wealthy man and a poor man move side by side toward the end of death'' (Pindar, *Odes of Victory*, c. 480 B.C.).

''Who knows if what we call death is life, and what we call life is death?'' (Euripides, *Phrixus*, c. 420 B.C.).

''By avoiding death, men pursue it'' (Democritus, Fragments, c. 400 B.C.).

''Since true philosophers always deal with the practice of dying, to them death is less terrible than to any other men'' (Plato, *Phaedo*, c. 400 B.C.).

''As for the exposure and rearing of children born, let there be a law that no defective infant shall be reared'' (Aristotle, *Politics*, c. 350 B.C.).

''The most horrible of all evils, death, is nothing to us, for when we exist, death is not present; but when death is present, then we are not. So it is not present either for the living or for the dead, since for the former it does not exist, and the latter do not exist'' (Epicurus, *Letter to Menoeceus*, c. 300 B.C.).

''If among the things which man dislikes there were nothing which he disliked more than death, why should he not do everything by which he could avoid danger?'' (Mencius, *Book of Mencius*, c. 300 B.C.).

''It would be natural to mention all the different causes of death, in order that the one real cause of that man's death be mentioned among them'' (Lucretius, *On the Nature of Things*, c. 60 B.C.).

''A dead man, says the law of the Twelve Tables, must not be buried or burned within the city. I believe that the latter is on account of danger of fire. But the addition of the words 'or burned' indicates that a body which is cremated is not considered buried, but only one which is inhumed'' (Cicero, *Laws*, c. 50 B.C.).

''Death is swallowed up in victory. O death, where is thy sting?'' (I Corinthians 15:54–55).

''We do not fear death, but the thought of death'' (Lucius Annaeus Seneca, *Letters*, 63).

''Death is such that, like birth, it is a mystery of nature'' (Marcus Aurelius, *Meditations*, c. 170).

''Ten strong things have been created in the world . . . death, however, is stronger than them all'' (Talmud: The Last Gate 10a).

''The angel of death . . . will gather you, and afterward unto your Lord ye will be returned'' (Koran: Prostration 11).

''Man naturally shrinks from death'' (Thomas Aquinas, *Summa Theologica*, 1274).

''He that hath a will to die by himself fears it not from another'' (William Shakespeare, *Coriolanus*, 1608).

''Men fear death as children fear to go in the dark; and as that natural fear in children is increased with tales, so is the other'' (Francis Bacon, *Essays*, 1625).

''Even Rome cannot grant us a dispensation from death'' (Jean Baptiste Poquelin Molière, *The Scatterbrain*, 1665).

''The human species is the only one which knows that it will die, and it knows this through experience'' (François Marie Arouet de Voltaire, *Philosophical Dictionary*, 1764).

''The fear of death is worse than dying'' (Johann Christoph Friedrich von Schiller, *The Robbers*, 1781).

''The dead do not hear the sound of the funeral bells'' (Denis Diderot, *Rameau's Nephew,* 1823, posthumously).

''Death seems to be a harsh victory of the species over the definite individual and to contradict their unity'' (Karl Marx, *Economic and Philosophic Manuscripts*, 1844).

''Death is like a fisherman who catches fish in his net and leaves them for a while in the water'' (Ivan Sergeevich Turgenev, *On the Eve*, 1860).

''I think the proof of the universal use of fire in regular burials at this period [Trojan War, 1100 B.C.] is conclusive. . . . In the case of notable persons, the combustion was not complete. For not the ashes only, but the bones, were carefully gathered. In the case of Patroclos, they are wrapped in fat, and put in an open cup or bowl . . . until the funeral of Achilles, when with those of Achilles himself, similarly wrapped, and soaked in wine, they are deposited in a golden urn'' (W. Gladstone in Henry Schliemann, *Mycenae*, 1880).

''One should part from life as Odysseus parted from Nausicaa—blessing it rather than in love with it'' (Friedrich Wilhelm Nietzsche, *Beyond Good and Evil*, 1886).

''The fear of death is alien to the child'' (Sigmund Freud, *The Interpretation of Dreams*, 1900).

''It is indeed a sad insight into the human conscience to discover what elaborate precautions were considered necessary in order to avoid the persecutions of the revengeful dead'' (Bertram Puckle, *Funeral Customs*, 1926).

''The final aim of the destructive instinct is to reduce living things to an inorganic state. For this reason we also call it the *death instinct*'' (Sigmund Freud, *An Outline of Psychoanalysis*, 1940).

''Death is never sweet, not even if it is suffered for the highest ideal'' (Erich Fromm, *Escape from Freedom*, 1941).

''In the depth of the anxiety of having to die is the anxiety of being eternally forgotten'' (Paul Tillich, *The Eternal Now*, 1963).

''Death is an exit which they [Vietnamese] not infrequently choose for themselves deliberately, sometimes for motives of honor but sometimes also for surprisingly futile reasons. Life is all the less valued because of the Vietnamese belief in the survival of the individual after death; and continued contact with the family'' (E. Hammer, *Vietnam, Yesterday and Today*, 1966).

''The dying of the elderly is, by and large, the least disturbing. In our society the aged are not especially valued. I once asked a group of about two dozen Cambodian students in their mid-twenties whether, given the necessity for choice, they would save the life of their mother, their wife or their daughter. All responded immediately that they would save their mother'' (Richard Kalish in Leonard Pearson, ed., *Death and Dying*, 1969).

''[The dying person says] No, it cannot be me. . . . Oh yes, it is me, it was not a mistake'' (Elizabeth Kübler-Ross, *On Death and Dying*, 1969).

''Most developmental psychologists believe that the very young child (from birth to about two years) has no understanding of death'' (Robert Kastenbaum and Ruth Aisenberg, *The Psychology of Death*, 1972).

''Grief is mastered, not by ceasing to care for the dead, but by abstracting what was fundamentally important in the relationship and rehabilitating it'' (P. Marris, *Loss and Change*, 1974).

''Death is a biological event, a rite of passage, an inevitability, a natural occurrence, a punishment, extinction, the enforcement of God's will, absurd, separation, reunion, a time for judgment. It is a reasonable excuse for anger, depression, denial, repression, guilt, frustration, relief, absolution of self, increased religiousness. . . . It has one set of meanings for the dying person, another for those who love him, yet another for those responsible for his health care, and still another set of meanings for those involved with funerals, legal documents, insurance, estates and trusts, public health statistics, wars and executions'' (Richard Kalish in R. Binstock and E. Shanas, eds., *Handbook of Aging and the Social Sciences*, 1976).

''Changes in man's attitude toward death either take place very slowly or else occur between long periods of immobility'' (Philippe Ariès, *The Hour of Our Death*, 1977).

''To exorcise the fear of death, we make those who are about to die redundant and irrelevant while they are still alive. By rendering the about-do-die trivial in life, we lessen the fear that death holds for us. If the about-to-die do not matter, we reason, death may be meaningless also, and we need not be afraid of it'' (R. Jones, *The Other Generation*, 1977).

''Greek poets . . . seldom mentioned graves or cemeteries or funeral processions'' (Emily Vermeule, *Aspects of Death in Early Greek Art and Poetry*, 1979).

''Grief, bereavement, and mourning are related terms used in relation to surviving the death of a significant other person, often of a close family member'' (Kathy Charmaz, *The Social Reality of Death*, 1980).

''The science dealing with death is known as *thanatology* (Greek *thanatos*, death, and *logos*, word or science). . . . [A] prevalent attitude throughout history has been that birth control is much less important than death control (except for infanticide and child exposure, human sacrifice, cannibalism, capital punishment, and war) . . . some societies have considered *senilicide*, or *geronticide* (the killing of the aged), perfectly acceptable'' (Panos Bardis, *History of Thanatology*, 1981).

''Belief in some life after death came very early to mankind, as is indicated by the ceremonial burial customs of Neanderthal man. However in our earliest records of beliefs about life after death it was most unpleasant. . . . The idea of a more attractive after-life is a special feature of the Socratic dialogues, being derived from the Orphic mysteries'' (John Eccles, ed., *Mind and Brain*, 1982).

THEORY, SOCIAL

''Theory without praxis is an empty thing'' (Polybius, *Histories*, 130 B.C.).

''Theory, my friend, is grey; but green is the eternal tree of life'' (Johann Wolfgang von Goethe, *Faust*, 1832).

''Hegel makes man the *man of self-consciousness* instead of making self-consciousness the *self-consciousness of man*, i.e., of man living also in a real objective world and determined by that world'' (Karl Marx and Friedrich Engels, *The Holy Family*, 1845).

''These Hegelians understood nothing about anything, but could write about everything. . . . These gentlemen were, in spite of their sufficiency, so conscious of their weakness that they gave big problems the widest berth possible'' (Friedrich Engels, *Ludwig Feuerbach and the Outcome of Classical German Philosophy*, 1886).

''Instead of a serious discussion among conflicting theories that, in their very conflict, demonstrate the intimacy with which they belong together, the commonness of their underlying convictions, and an unswerving belief in a true philosophy, we have a pseudo-reporting and a pseudo-criticizing, a mere semblance of philosophizing seriously with and for one another'' (Edmund Husserl, *Cartesian Meditations*, 1931).

''All empirically verifiable knowledge—even the commonsense knowledge of everyday life—involves implicitly, if not explicitly, systematic theory. . . . The importance of this statement lies in the fact that certain persons who write on social subjects vehemently deny it. They say they state merely facts and let them 'speak for themselves' " (Talcott Parsons, *The Structure of Social Action*, 1937).

"Sociological theory must advance on these interconnected planes: through special theories adequate to limited ranges of social data, and the evolution of a more general conceptual scheme adequate to consolidate groups of special theories" (Robert Merton, *Social Theory and Social Structure*, 1949).

"[Folk sociology is] a theory of the continuum of society developing from the folk culture to the state civilization" (Howard Odum, *American Sociology*, 1951).

"[The master theory of society] fills the gaps between the various islands of theoretical knowledge . . . [it consists of] the human ecological theory, the sociological theory, and the theory of values and symbols" (Radhakamal Mukerjee in Baljit Singh, ed., *The Frontiers of Social Science*, 1956).

"There is not, at the present time, any general body of sociological theory which has been validated or widely accepted" (Tom Bottomore, *Sociology*, 1962).

"The true task for the dialectical method is to demolish *all established and crystallized concepts*. . . . That is why dialectic, in order to be really fruitful, must be essentially *anti-dogmatic*, that is, eliminate every previous philosophical or scientific standpoint" (Georges Davidovitch Gurvitch, *Dialectics and Sociology*, 1962).

"The relation of phenomenology to the social sciences cannot be demonstrated by analyzing concrete problems of sociology or economics" (Alfred Schutz, *Collected Papers*, 1962).

"The most dramatic development in sociological theory since World War II has been the rise of functionalism to a position of dominance" (Don Martindale, ed., *Functionalism in the Social Sciences*, 1965).

"In the rise of different sociological theories, aspects of social reality which were previously obscure were successively explored. Two kinds of mistakes must be avoided if one is to maximize the values of a review of alternative theoretical treatments of social structure: the assumption that only one of the theories is correct, and the assumption that they are all equally correct" (Don Martindale, *Institutions, Organizations, and Mass Society*, 1966).

"For the time being these two great philosophic orientations, the mechanistic and humanistic, exist simultaneously like some species-wide two party system" (Abraham Maslow, *The Psychology of Science*, 1966).

"[A system must perform these functions] (1) the maintenance of the highest 'governing' or controlling patterns of the system; (2) the internal integration of the system; (3) its orientation to the attainment of goals in relation to its environment; (4) its more generalized adaptation to the broad conditions of the environment—e.g., the non-action, physical environment" (Talcott Parsons, *Societies*, 1966).

"The careful reworking of verbal theories is undoubtedly one of the most challenging tasks confronting us" (Hubert Blalock, *Theory Construction*, 1969).

"The ultimate goal of a Reflexive Sociology is the deepening of the sociologist's own awareness, of who and what he is, in a specific society at any given time, and of how both his social role and his personal praxis affect his work as a sociologist" (Alvin Gouldner, *The Coming Crisis in Western Sociology*, 1970).

"There is a 'macro' dimension to existential phenomenology in relation to sociology, a dimension more developed in European than in American sociology" (Edward Tiryakian in Maurice Natason, ed., *Phenomenology and the Social Sciences*, 1973).

"[Robert Merton's] advocacy of theories of the 'middle-range' quelled a vigorous debate between theoretically and empirically inclined sociologists by reasserting the efficacy of empirically oriented theory and theoretically oriented research" (Jonathan Turner, *The Structure of Sociological Theory*, 1978).

"A sociological theory reflects the social world which is constantly being constructed and reconstructed by people, and also participates in the construction of the social world, by providing knowledge of its qualities and regularities together with directives for changing it" (Piotr Sztompka, *Sociological Dilemmas*, 1979).

"No idea was more widely shared by the creators of sociology than that its task was to develop empirically adequate theories to explain society" (Don Martindale, *The Nature and Types of Sociological Theory*, 1981).

"Functional analysis, while still a strong current, seems to have lost its hegemonic position" (Lewis Coser and Bernard Rosenberg, eds., *Sociological Theory*, 1982).

"The most significant characteristic of historical materialism is that it denies all of our traditionally inherited values such as truth, goodness, beauty, and holiness, by identifying them all as a superstructure derived from productive relations . . . it does not recognize any independent value in truth, goodness, beauty, and holiness" (Masatoshi Matsushita in Professors World Peace Academy of Japan, *Challenging the Future*, 1982).

TIME, SOCIOLOGY OF

"There is a . . . time to every purpose" (Ecclesiastes 3:1).

"The sight of day and night . . . gave us a conception of time. . . . Until the creation of time, all things had been made in the likeness of the original" (Plato, *Timaeus*, c. 400 B.C.).

"It is impossible for time to exist without motion" (Aristotle, *Physics*, c. 350 B.C.).

"Our costliest expenditure is time" (Theophrastus, c. 300 B.C., in Diogenes Laertius, *Lives and Opinions of Eminent Philosophers*, c. 230).

"The sun divides days and nights" (Manu, *Laws*, c. 200 B.C.).

"May the gods blast him who first invented hours and first installed a sundial. . . . When I was a boy, my belly was my only sundial . . . now . . . you don't eat, unless the sun permits it. And the city is full of sundials'' (Plautus, *Boeotian*, c. 200 B.C.).

''Here in the middle of the channel there is an island called Man . . . by exact water measurements, we noticed that the nights were shorter than on the Continent'' (Gaius Julius Caesar, *The Gallic War*, c. 50 B.C.).

''Another Argo will carry chosen heroes; and there will be another war and again a great Achilles will be sent to Troy'' (Vergil, *Eclogues*, c. 37 B.C.).

''Some people would not know they were starving without a clock to remind them'' (Lucius Annaeus Seneca, *On the Briefness of Life*, c. 49).

''All things, from time immemorial, have been uniform and cyclical in their repetition'' (Marcus Aurelius, *Meditations*, c. 170).

''Seeing therefore that God, whose eternity does not alter, created the world and time, how can he be said to have created the world in time, unless you will say that there was something created before the world whose course time follows? . . . The world was made with time and not in time, for that which is made in time is before some time and after some time'' (Saint Augustine, *The City of God*, 426).

''Time is the measure of the movement of natural phenomena'' (Thomas Aquinas, *Summa Theologica*, 1274).

''There's a time for all things'' (William Shakespeare, *The Comedy of Errors*, 1593).

''Absolute, true and mathematical time, of itself, and from its own nature, flows equally without relation to anything external'' (Isaac Newton, *Principia*, 1687).

''As for *Time*, it is the empirically existing Concept itself. . . . Nature is Space, whereas Time *is* History'' (Georg Wilhelm Friedrich Hegel, *Phenomenology of Mind*, 1807).

''When time is correctly defined as infinite succession, it seems plausible to define it also as the present, the past, and the future . . . the eternal is the present as an annulled succession . . . in the eternal there is not to be found any division of the past and the future, because the present is posited as the annulled succession. . . . If one would now employ the instant to define time, and let the instant indicate the purely abstract exclusion of the past and the future, and by the same token of the present also, then the instant precisely is not the present, for that which is purely abstract thinking lies between the past and the future and has no existence at all. . . . The instant is that ambiguous moment in which time and eternity touch one another, thereby positing *the temporal* . . . the temporal seems even more imperfect, and the instant still more significant, than the apparently secure persistence of nature in time. And yet it is exactly the converse, for nature's security is due to the fact that time has no significance for it. Only in the instant does history begin'' (Sören Aabye Kierkegaard, *The Concept of Dread*, 1844).

''Time is everything, man is nothing; he is no more than the carcass of time'' (Karl Marx, *The Poverty of Philosophy*, 1847).

"Time deals gently only with those who take it gently" (Anatole France, *The Crime of Sylvestre Bonnard*, 1881).

"[*Durée* time is] the form which the succession of our conscious state assumes when our ego lets itself *live*, when it refrains from separating its present state from its former states," while spatialized time occurs when "we set our states of consciousness side-by-side in such a way as to perceive them simultaneously, no longer in one another, but alongside; in a word we project time into space, we express duration in terms of extensity, and succession thus takes the form of a continuous line or chain, the parts of which touch without penetrating one another" (Henri Bergson, *Time and Free Will*, 1889).

[Tess] "started on her way up the dark and crooked lane or street not made for hasty progress; a street laid out before inches of land had value, and when one-handed clocks sufficiently subdivided the day" (Thomas Hardy, *Tess of the D'Urbervilles*, 1891).

"The course of life is something temporal; that is what the expression 'course' means. Time is not just a line consisting of parts of equal value, a system of relations, of succession, simultaneity and continuity. If we think of time apart from what fills it, its parts are of equal value. Even the smallest part of this continuum is linear, a succession of parts; nowhere, even in the smallest part, is there anything which 'is.' Concrete time consists rather of the uninterrupted progress of the present, what was present constantly becoming the past and the future becoming the present. The present is the filling of a moment of time with reality. . . . The ship of our life is, as it were, carried along on an overflowing river and the present is always where we live, suffer, strive and remember; in brief, where we experience the fullness of our reality. . . . Because remembering involves recognition everything past is structurally related to a former experience by being a reproduction of it. Future possibilities are also linked to the sequence because of the ranges of potentialities mapped out by it" (Wilhelm Dilthey, *Pattern and Meaning in History*, 1910).

"We perceive time only because we know we have to die. . . . While the 'ahead' includes the notion of a 'before,' neither the 'before' in the 'ahead' nor the 'already' is to be taken in terms of the way time is ordinarily understood. . . . Temporality has different possibilities and different ways of temporalizing itself. . . . Dasein does not come towards itself primarily in its ownmost non-relational potentiality-for Being, but it *awaits this* concernfully *in terms of that which yields or denies the object of its concern*. . . . The inauthentic future has the character of *awaiting*. . . . In contradistinction to the instant of insight as the authentic Present, we call the inauthentic Present 'making *present*.' . . . If *Being*-as-having-been is inauthentic, we call it '*repetition*.' But when one projects oneself inauthentically towards those possibilities which have been drawn from the object of concern in making it present, this is possible only because Dasein has *forgotten* itself in its ownmost *thrown* potentiality-for-Being (Martin Heidegger, *Being and Time*, 1927).

"Subjective time is constituted in absolute, timeless consciousness. . . . Of the interval that has expired we say that we are conscious of it in retentions, specifically, that we are conscious of those parts or phases of the duration, not sharply to be differentiated which lie closest to the actual now-point with diminishing clarity, while those parts lying further back in the past are wholly unclear; we are conscious of them only as empty'' (Edmund Husserl, *The Phenomenology of Internal Time-Consciousness*, 1928).

''The butterfly counts not months but moments, and has time enough'' (Rabindranath Tagore, *Fireflies*, 1928).

''The past is overflow of the present. It is oriented from the present. It is akin on the one side to our escape fancies, those in which we rebuild the world according to our heart's desires, and on the other to the selection of what is significant that must be held and reconstructed, but its decisive character is the pushing back of conditioning continuities of the present'' (George H. Mead in John Coss, ed., *Essays in Honor of John Dewey*, 1929).

''The relation of time, too, which is so hard to describe, is communicated to the ego by the perceptual system'' (Sigmund Freud, *New Introductory Lectures on Psychoanalysis*, 1933).

''The clock, not the steam-engine, is the key machine of the modern industrial age'' (Lewis Mumford, *Technics and Civilization*, 1934).

''The daily timepiece is the cattle clock, the round of pastoral tasks, and the time of day and the passage of time through a day are to a Nuer primarily the succession of these tasks and their relation to one another . . . the Nuer have no expression equivalent to 'time' in our language'' (E. Evans-Pritchard, *The Nuer*, 1940).

''Often in the writings of economists the words 'dynamic' and 'static' are used as nothing more than synonyms for good and bad, realistic and unrealistic, simple and complex. We damn another man's theory by terming it static, and advertise our own by calling it dynamic'' (Paul Samuelson, *Foundations of Economic Analysis*, 1947).

''[Among Algeria's Kabyle peasants prevails] an attitude of submission and of nonchalant indifference to the passage of time which no one dreams of mastering, using up, or saving. . . . Haste is seen as a lack of decorum combined with diabolical ambition'' (Pierre Bourdieu in J. Pitt-Rivers, ed., *Mediterranean Countrymen*, 1963).

''The social sciences have tended to neglect the way the limits and flows of time intersect the persistent and changeful qualities of human enterprises for reasons that are only partly clear'' (Wilbert Moore, *Man, Time, and Society*, 1963).

''Spanish Americans do not regulate their lives by the clock as Anglos do. Both rural and urban people, when asked when they plan to do something, give answers like: 'Right now, about two or four o'clock' '' (J. Pitt-Rivers, ed., *Mediterranean Countrymen*, 1963).

''The question of 'what is time?' is not emotionally neutral. Views held by individual scientists and scholars regarding which domains of knowledge are equipped to deal with this question tend to be dogmatic and often contradictory'' (J. Fraser, ed., *The Voices of Time*, 1966).

''The problem of the genesis of space and time can be discussed meaningfully on two criteria, i.e., the psychological and cultural-historical'' (Jiri Kolaja, *Social System and Time and Space*, 1969).

''In the natural habitat, organismic rhythms are strictly 24 hours in length'' (Frank Brown et al., *The Biological Clock*, 1970).

''Observation of all forms of life demonstrates the remarkable dependence of timing on the actions and the adaptive time changes of plants and animals'' (Eliot Chapple, *Culture and Biological Man*, 1970).

''Time has to be experienced in order to make sense or to become real. . . . For them [African countries], time is simply a composition of events which have occurred, those which are taking place now, and those which are immediately to occur'' (John Mbiti, *African Religions and Philosophies*, 1970).

''By comparing the relative proportions of time allocated to various activities by people in different walks of life, some insight can be gained into differential living conditions, social interest or cultural preferences prevailing in certain parts of society'' (Alexander Szalai in Max Kaplan and Phillip Bosserman, eds., *Technology, Human Values and Leisure*, 1971).

''In J. T. Fraser's (ed.) *Theories of Time*, 26 essays are given but none about time and its meaning in sociology. One reason for this lack is because there are many times (many forms of change) in sociology and one essay could hardly touch the problem. Sociology has more permutations and combinations than other fields and both and all are often operating at the same time'' (Carle Zimmerman, *Sociological Theories of Pitirim Sorokin*, 1973).

''The major characteristics of time for leisure in the decades ahead will be bulk time, and it is to this aspect of time that we must relate ages and social roles'' (Max Kaplan, *Leisure*, 1975).

''Time is not an external 'object.' Although we may commonly use time as a noun in every-day language, we probably would find it more advantageous to consider time as an internal process of judgment rather than a primary object of judgment itself'' (Bernard Gorman and Alden Wessman, eds., *The Personal Experience of Time*, 1977).

''The rate of social change is inversely proportional to the length of the time units emphasized by a given society . . . the value of time is directly proportional to the rate of social change'' (Panos Bardis, *Cronus in the Eternal City*, 1978).

''Horology is concerned with clocks and watches. . . . Though the horological revolution of 1660–1760 has had a considerable influence on the language, themes, and forms of literature, this influence has received virtually no attention from critics'' (Samuel Macey, *Clocks and the Cosmos*, 1980).

''If the concept of time in physics is to be subordinated to that of space, we must somehow circumvent the asymmetry of past and future which characterizes our temporal experience'' (G. Whitrow, *The Natural Philosophy of Time*, 1980).

''We are increasingly detaching ourselves from 'organic and functional periodicity,' which is dictated by nature, and replacing it by 'mechanical periodicity,' which is dictated by the schedule, the calendar, and the clock'' (Eviatar Zerubavel, *Hidden Rhythms*, 1981).

''Jones' Sixth Law: *The amount of time spent by generalists in making technically based decisions is in inverse proportion to the complexity of the subject matter*'' (Barry Jones, *Sleepers, Wake!*, 1982).

''How could research on the clocks that time our sleep and wakefulness, our metabolic, endocrine, and neural functions be so easily ignored?'' (Martin Moore-Ede et al., *The Clocks That Time Us*, 1982).

U

URBAN SOCIOLOGY

''Cities are not happy if they have walls, ships, docks, numbers, or size instead of virtue'' (Plato, *First Alcibiades*, c. 400 B.C., spurious).

''A great city and a populous one are not one and the same thing. . . . A very large city can seldom, if ever, be governed well'' (Aristotle, *Politics*, c. 350 B.C.).

''Divine nature gave us fields, human art built cities'' (Marcus Terentius Varro, *On Agriculture*, c. 50 B.C.).

''The people are the city'' (William Shakespeare, *Coriolanus*, 1608).

''In a great town friends are scattered; so that there is not that fellowship, for the most part, which is in less neighborhoods'' (Francis Bacon, *Essays*, 1625).

''The bourgeoisie has subjected the country to the rule of the towns. It has created enormous cities, has greatly increased the urban population as compared with the rural, and has thus rescued a considerable part of the population from the idiocy of rural life'' (Karl Marx and Friedrich Engels, *Communist Manifesto*, 1847).

''Cities produce wild men, because they produce corrupt men'' (Victor Marie Hugo, *Les Misérables*, 1862).

''*Civitas* and *Urbs*, either of which we translate by the word city, were not synonymous words among the ancients. *Civitas* was the religious and political association of families and tribes; *Urbs* was the place of assembly, the dwelling place, and, above all, the sanctuary of the association'' (Fustel de Coulanges, *The Ancient City*, 1864).

''Civilization has undoubtedly, with its cities, left us a heritage which will take much time and effort to eliminate; but they must and will be eliminated even if this process of elimination will be a laborious one'' (Friedrich Engels, *Anti-Dühring*, 1878).

''Pittsburgh is a smoky, dismal city at her best. At her worst, nothing darker, dingier or more dispiriting can be imagined. . . . It has thirty-five miles of factories in daily operation, twisted up into a compact tangle, all belching smoke, all glowing with fire, all swarming with workmen, all echoing with the clank of machinery'' (Willard Glazier, *Peculiarities of American Cities*, 1884).

"When a community attains a certain size, new needs and purposes manifest themselves. The close association of a large body of people alters even the material conditions of life. The artesian well and cistern must give way to . . . distant springs. . . . The liberty of the individual to do his own sweet pleasure must be curtailed" (Adna Weber, *The Growth of Cities in the Nineteenth Century*, 1899).

"The great glittering cities . . . constitute so many blast furnaces where the talented rise and become incandescent, to be sure, but for all that are incinerated without due replacement" (Edward Ross, *The Foundations of Sociology*, 1905).

"In the medieval city the knights held their tourneys, the guilds their pageants, the people their dances, and the church made festival for its most cherished saints with gay street processions. . . . Only in the modern city have men concluded that it is no longer necessary for the municipality to provide for the insatiable desire for play" (Jane Addams, *The Spirit of Youth and the City Streets*, 1910).

"The city consists simply of a collection of one or more separate dwellings but is a relatively closed settlement. Customarily, though not exclusively, in cities the houses are built closely to each other, often, today, wall to wall. . . . Economically defined, the city is a settlement the inhabitants of which live primarily off trade and commerce rather than agriculture. . . . As a rule the quantitative expansion of the original princely city and its economic importance go hand in hand with an increase in the satisfaction of wants in the market by the princely household and other large urban households attached to that of the prince as courts of vassals or major officials" (Max Weber, *The City*, 1921, posthumously).

"[The city] is something more than a congeries of individual men and of social conveniences—streets, buildings, electrical lights, tramways, and telephones; something more, also, than a mere constellation of institutions and administrative devices—courts, hospitals, schools, police, and civil functionaries. . . . The city is, rather, a state of mind, a body of customs and traditions, and of the organized attitudes and sentiments that inhere in these customs and are transmitted with this tradition. The city is not . . . merely a physical mechanism and an artificial construction" (Robert Park and Ernest Burgess, *The City*, 1925).

"Cities will not be destroyed, but new cities will arise and these cities will be centers of great cultural development, centers not only of big industries but also of the processing of agricultural products, of great developments of all branches of the food industry. This will encourage the cultural growth of the country and will determine a leveling out of living conditions in town and country" (Joseph Stalin, *Economic Problems of Socialism in the USSR*, 1952).

"As to the cities of the Americas, only the most fertile imagination (at the present state of knowledge) can conceive of these as products of diffusion from the Old World" (Gideon Sjoberg, *The Pre-Industrial City*, 1965).

"This increase of urban population [in the United States] is not in the large cities but around them. It is not all over the country but concentrated in about

10 percent of the counties (300 out of more than 3000). Instead of central cities great urban or metropolitan areas (called *Megalopolises*) are being built up'' (Carle Zimmerman in Instituto de Ciencias Sociales, *The County*, 1966).

''The planning of cities is regarded variously as an ivory-tower vision, a practical and necessary program for development, or an undesirable interference with the citizen's freedom to do as he wishes with his own property'' (Ralph Thomlinson, *Urban Structure*, 1969).

''The study of the peripheral poor suburbs [*borgate*] and shantytowns [*baracche*] of Rome is important because it destroys the myth of the city as the expression of naturally harmonious integrated and balanced community'' (Franco Ferracotti, *Rome from the Capital to the Periphery*, 1970).

''The tendency is for small territorial units to be absorbed and stripped of their identities by the larger universe of activities'' (Amos Hawley, *Urban Society*, 1971).

''Don Martindale has called the Chicago school 'urbanism incorporated.' The founder of the firm was Robert Park'' (Collin Bell and Howard Newby, *Community Studies*, 1972).

''[In Poland] the index of urbanization in a small community was closely related to the intensity and level of cultural participation'' (Antonina Kloskowska, *Social Framework of Culture*, 1972).

''[In India] if new employment opportunities are created in the urban areas, the first persons to offer themselves for employment are the marginally employed persons already residing in the urban areas'' (Ashish Bose, *Studies in India's Urbanisation*, 1973).

''Urbanization has a dual meaning . . . it is demographic, referring to the increasing proportion of population in a country or region who reside in cities . . . it has reference to the process whereby people are influenced by the values, behavior, institutions, and material things that are identified as urban in origin and use'' (Noel Gist and Sylvia Fava, *Urban Society*, 1974).

''During the 1960s and the 1970s evidences appeared on every hand of an increasing insecurity of life and property in the nation's towns and cities. Accounts of rioting, burning, and looting in many places, including the national capital, filled edition after edition of the leading newspapers in the United States'' (T. Smith, *Studies of the Great Rural Tap Roots of Urban Poverty in the United States*, 1974).

''Megalopolis ('large city') as a term was first applied by Jean Gottman in his study [*Megalopolis*, 1961] of the urbanized Northeastern Seaboard of the United States. . . . Gottman stresses the economic integration of Megalopolis as the major index of regionalism'' (Delbert Miller, *Leadership and Power in the Bos-Wash Megalopolis*, 1975).

''[In Tokyo] air pollution is so severe that it directly causes scores of deaths each year. Workers in some industries use gas masks while drug stores have machines dispensing oxygen. The level of water pollution was graphically demonstrated when a Tokyo newspaper printed on its front page a photograph that had been developed solely by dipping the negative in a chemically polluted river. Transportation is in similar condition. . . . Tokyo has the worst automobile congestion in the world'' (John Palen, *The Urban World*, 1975).

''Cities that are losing population actually spend more, per capita, in capital investment than cities that are gaining population, due largely to the necessity (and difficulty) of replacing their antiquated capital stock'' (George Peterson in William Gorham and Nathan Glazer, eds., *The Urban Predicament*, 1976).

''Urbanization in twentieth-century America has involved changes that deeply alter social organization'' (David Street et al., *Handbook of Contemporary Urban Life*, 1978).

''The greater the downturn in the national economy, the greater the fiscal difficulties for cities'' (T. Clark and L. Ferguson in Kenneth Newton, ed., *Urban Political Economy*, 1981).

''Increased participation in systems of export and import leads to the growth of central towns'' (Henry Wright, ed., *An Early Town on the Deh Luran Plain*, 1981).

''A sociological approach is not sufficient for understanding cities. Because they are at the center of contemporary life, cities have become an important subject for analysis in virtually every academic field'' (James Spates and John Macionis, *The Sociology of Cities*, 1982).

''For Italians the quintessence of an urban way of life, characterized by a distinct style in residence, speech, clothing, manners, and occupation, is expressed in the term *civiltà*. It signifies the opposite of the rural lifestyle. Throughout most of southern Europe there has been and still is a distinct distaste for the life, and especially the manual work, associated with the country'' (Jeremy Boissevain in Michael Kenny and David Kertzer, eds., *Urban Life in Mediterranean Europe*, 1983).

UTOPIA

''The plowman shall overtake the reaper, and the treader of grapes him that soweth seed; and the mountains shall drop sweet wine . . . they shall build the waste cities, and inhabit them; and they shall plant vineyards, and drink the wine thereof; they shall also make gardens, and eat the fruit of them'' (Amos 9:13–14).

''Atlantis . . . sunk by an earthquake and became an impassable barrier of mud'' (Plato, *Critias*, c. 400 B.C.).

''[The rulers] must have the right kind of education, whatever it is, if they are to possess to the highest degree what will make them gentle to one another and to those they guard . . . their houses and other property provided for them must be such that the guardians will not stop being ideal leaders and will not wrong the other citizens'' (Plato, *Republic*, c. 400 B.C.).

''Yea poverty itself, which only seemed to lack money, if money were gone, it also would decrease and vanish away . . . the unreasonable covetousness of a few hath turned that thing to the utter undoing of your island, in which thing the chief felicity of your realm did consist . . . unless you find a remedy for these enormities, you shall in vain advance yourselves of executing justice upon felons . . . the king ought to take more care for the wealth of his people, than for his own wealth, even as the office and duty of a shepherd is in that he is a shepherd, to feed his sheep rather than himself. . . . For great and horrible punishments be appointed for thieves, whereas much rather provision should have been made, that there were some means, whereby they might get their living, so that no man should be driven to this extreme necessity, first to steal, and then to die'' (Thomas More, *Utopia*, 1516).

''They consider him the more noble and renowned who has dedicated himself to the study of the most arts and knows how to practice them wisely . . . when we raise a son to riches and dignities, and leave an heir to much wealth, we become either ready to grasp at the property of the state . . . or avaricious, crafty, and hypocritical. . . . [In Civitas Solis] men and women are so joined together, that they bring forth the best offspring. Indeed, they laugh at us who exhibit a studious care for our breed of horses and dogs, but neglect the breeding of human beings'' (Tommaso Campanella, *The City of the Sun*, 1623).

''Social salvation [is achieved] by scientific education'' (Francis Bacon, *New Atlantis*, 1627).

''No man can be a politician, except he be first an historian or a traveller; for except he can see what must be, or what may be, he is no politician: Now if he have no knowledge in story, he cannot tell what hath been; and if he hath not been a traveller, he cannot tell what is: but he that neither knoweth what hath been, nor what is; can never tell what must be, or what may be'' (James Harrington, *The Commonwealth of Oceana*, 1656).

''Fantastic pictures of future society, painted at a time when the proletariat is still in a very undeveloped state . . . correspond with the first instinctive yearnings of that class for a general reconstruction of society'' (Karl Marx and Friedrich Engels, *Communist Manifesto*, 1847).

''[Private industry is like] surrendering the functions of political government to kings and nobles for their personal glorification'' (Edward Bellamy, *Looking Backward*, 1887).

''Everyone who has ever built anywhere a 'new heaven' first found the power thereto in his own hell'' (Friedrich Wilhelm Nietzsche, *The Genealogy of Morals*, 1887).

''Ideal society is a drama enacted exclusively in the imagination'' (George Santayana, *The Life of Reason*, 1906).

''[Utopian ideologies imply that] society is capable of improvement and can be made over to realize a rational ideal'' (Joyce Hertzler, *The History of Utopian Thought*, 1923).

''[A utopian idea] seems to be unrealizable only from the point of view of a given social order which is already in existence. . . . [Utopias derive from] ideas and values in which are contained in condensed form the unrealized and the unfulfilled tendencies which represent the need of each age. [The utopian spirit is] incongruous with the state of reality within which it occurs'' (Karl Mannheim, *Ideology and Utopia*, 1929).

''Chief among the factors affecting all Shaker life was the unique relationship existing between brethren and sisters. The application, under the same roof, of the seemingly irreconcilable theories of equality and separation set the movement apart from other communal-religious institutions and aroused, more than any other characteristic of the church, skeptical comment and barbed abuse'' (Edward Andrews, *The People Called Shakers*, 1953).

''The primary issue with which a utopian community must cope in order to have the strength and solidarity to endure is its human organization: how people arrange to do the work that the community needs to survive as a group, and how the group in turn manages to satisfy and involve its members over a long period of time'' (Rosabeth Kanter, *Commitment and Community*, 1972).

''Unlike ideology, utopia has an actual impact on the existing order; it serves as a support for genuine social change'' (Gianni Statera, *Death of a Utopia*, 1975).

''[Utopias] are real. Our current world is only a shadow, intermittently interrupted by the clash and thunder of that reality'' (Martin Krieger, *Advice and Planning*, 1981).

V

VALIDITY

''The earlier statement still holds true today. In other words, in our field we have not achieved the ability to establish clear-cut relationships between concept and empirical item'' (Herbert Blumer in Pauline Young, *Scientific Social Surveys and Research*, 1966).

''The validity of a test, or of any measuring instrument, depends upon the fidelity with which it measures what it purports to measure'' (Henry Garrett, *Statistics in Psychology and Education*, 1966).

''Since scales frequently are constructed to predict outcomes, a scale is considered valid if it in fact successfully predicts'' (Kenneth Eckhardt and M. Ermann, *Social Research Methods*, 1977).

VALUE

''The progress of knowledge about culture demonstrates more and more concretely the *historical relativity* of all human values, including science itself'' (Florian Znaniecki, *Cultural Reality*, 1919).

''[A social value is] any datum having an empirical content accessible to the members of some group and a meaning with regard to which it is or may be an object of activity . . . [it derives from] an attitude acting upon or influenced by some preexisting social value'' (William Thomas and Florian Znaniecki, *The Polish Peasant in Europe and America*, 1920).

''It will be discovered one day that the chief value of social science, far from being academic, is moral'' (Frank Giddings in Robert Bierstedt, ed., *The Making of Society*, 1924).

''[Culture is] an appreciation of values brought about through the accumulation of experience'' (Charles Ellwood, *Cultural Evolution*, 1927).

''[Attitude and value are] two aspects of a single unity or organization'' (Ellsworth Faris in Kimball Young, ed., *Social Attitudes*, 1931).

''I call the *axiological significance* of a value that practical significance which it acquires when it is appreciated positively or negatively with reference to other values as a possible object of activity'' (Florian Znaniecki, *Social Actions*, 1936).

''[Values derive from] a process of conditioning by the influences of the cultural milieu, eventuating in a body of habits'' (William Thomas, *Primitive Behavior*, 1937).

''[A region should be] large enough to comprehend the large number of values specified for applying to the present and to future trends'' (Howard Odum and Harry Moore, *American Regionalism*, 1938).

''[Values] may not be derived by science, and therefore science should have nothing to do with them'' (Robert Lynd, *Knowledge for What?*, 1939).

''Values are values only as calling for attainment or for maintenance—there would be no values in a static world'' (Robert MacIver, *Social Causation*, 1942).

''[The values of cooperation, love, solidarity, and responsibility] can alone supply the sure moral foundation of world reconstruction of the future'' (Radhakamal Mukerjee, *The Social Structure of Values*, 1949).

''It is in terms of values that human behavior and conduct acquire whatever cultural significance they possess'' (John Owen, *Sociology in East Pakistan*, 1962).

''There has been a constant interplay between changing technologies and changing values, both of these being an integral part of the larger process of change in what Teilhard de Chardin calls the 'noosphere' or the totality of images of the world in the minds of the living'' (Kenneth Boulding in Kurt Baier and Nicholas Rescher, eds., *Values and the Future*, 1969).

''What could be more ethically neutral, *wertfrei*, non-hortatory, non-valuative, call it what you will, than the question of how many people fall into which income bracket? Yet the statistics of income distribution can be regarded as highly inflammable'' (Stanislav Andreski, *Social Sciences as Sorcery*, 1972).

''In the human kingdom values pertain to the very order of existence'' (Ludwig Grünberg, *Axiology and the Human Condition*, 1972).

''The *Kamigata* culture is characterized by the merchant's emphasis on self-profit, calculation and self-assertion, in contrast to the samurai's stress on status, appearance and conformity, which characterizes Tokyo'' (Mamoru Iga in T. L. Smith and Man Das, eds., *Sociocultural Change Since 1950*, 1978).

''In contemporary affluent societies, the lack of balance between cultural and moral values on the one hand and technological achievements on the other—the latter being mostly aimed at improving the material aspects of human life—represents a virtual 'hubris' against the universal natural laws'' (Xenophon Zolotas, *Economic Growth and Declining Social Welfare*, 1981).

VARIABLE

''To derive a means of estimating the score of a person on one variable (which we shall denote by Y) from a different variable (X), we must know how X and Y are related. The variable we wish to estimate is called the *dependent variable* (Y), and the variable that will be used to estimate it is the *independent variable*

(X)'' (Gene Glass and Julian Stanley, *Statistical Methods in Education and Psychology*, 1970).

''A variable is *discrete* if its range can assume only a finite number of values or an infinite number of values that is countable. . . . Family size is an example of a variable with a finite range . . . a variable is *continuous* if its range is uncountably infinite. . . . Examples of continuous variables are temperature . . . length of fish . . . and speed of cars'' (Roger Kirk, *Introductory Statistics*, 1978).

''Variables . . . are logical groupings of attributes. . . . *Social class* would be a variable composed of a set of attributes such as *upper class, middle class, lower class*, or some similar set of divisions'' (Earl Babbie, *The Practice of Social Research*, 1979).

VIOLENCE

''God hates violence'' (Euripides, *Helen*, 412 B.C.).

''Shall we say that a wealthy man's violence is just and that of a poor man unjust?'' (Plato, *Statesman*, c. 400 B.C.).

''In all cases of violence . . . he [the judge] must not examine the competence of witnesses too strictly'' (Manu, *Laws*, c. 200 B.C.).

''He who attains power through violence does not truly become master or lord'' (Thomas Aquinas, *The Sentences of Peter Lombard*, c. 1250).

''Wherever a people has grown savage in arms so that human laws have no longer any place among it, the only powerful means of reducing it is religion'' (Giovanni Battista Vico, *A New Science*, 1744).

''As a part of a mob, however, he [the individual] becomes conscious of the power he shares with others, and it is sufficient to suggest ideas of pillage, murder, or violence to him to yield immediately to temptation'' (Gustave Le Bon, *The Crowd*, 1895).

''The conception of the general strike, engendered by the practice of violent strikes, admits the conception of an irrevocable overthrow. There is something in this which will appear more and more terrifying as violence takes a greater place in the mind of the proletariat. But, in undertaking a serious, formidable, and sublime work, Socialists raise themselves above our frivolous society and make themselves worthy of pointing out new roads to the world'' (Georges Sorel, *Reflections on Violence*, 1908).

''It is better to be violent, if there is violence in our hearts, than to put on the cloak of non-violence to cover impotence'' (Mohandas Gandhi, *Non-Violence in Peace and War*, 1948).

''Man is a predator whose natural instinct is to kill'' (Robert Ardrey, *African Genesis*, 1961).

''During the crises that follow assassinations and riots, the speculation about violence reaches feverish proportions. Violence becomes the monomania of the press, the core substance of politics, the mainstay of the cocktail party, and the obsession of the public. Violence is promiscuously viewed, and it is seen everywhere. Historically, it becomes the theme of evolution; psychologically, the corollary of human nature; educationally, the enemy of learning; socially, the wrong road to change'' (Hans Toch, *Violent Men*, 1969).

''Physical punishment by parents does not inhibit violence and most likely encourages it. It both frustrates the child and gives him a model to imitate and learn from'' (Frederick Ilfeld in D. Daniels et al., eds., *Violence and the Struggle for Existence*, 1970).

''Most American violence . . . has been unleashed against abolitionists, Catholics, radicals, workers and labor organizers, Negroes, Orientals, and other ethnic or racial or ideological minorities, and has been used ostensibly to protect the American, the Southern, the white Protestant, or simply the established middle-class way of life and morals'' (Richard Hofstadter and Michael Wallace, eds., *American Violence*, 1971).

''Tread on a dog's foot or tail and it will probably threaten if not actually attack you. Pinch a mouse's tail and it will bite you . . . pain is a precipitant or trigger for aggressive behaviour in mammals'' (John Gunn, *Violence*, 1973).

''Conspirators, madmen, and social outcasts have played some small dramatic parts in American violence, but to give them larger credit or blame is a fundamental misunderstanding of the real social and political meanings of the history of violence in America'' (Hugh Graham and Ted Gurr, eds., *Violence in America*, 1979).

''Physical violence against children is more prevalent among the lower socioeducational classes'' (Panos Bardis in George Kourvetaris and Betty Dobratz, eds., *Political Sociology*, 1980).

''The number of wives who threw things at their husbands is almost twice as large as the number of husbands who threw things at their wives. The rate of kicking and hitting with an object is also higher for wives than for husbands'' (Murray Straus et al., *Behind Closed Doors*, 1980).

W

WAR

"To lead an instructed people to war, is to throw them away" (Confucius, *Analects*, c. 500 B.C.).

"War is the father of all things" (Heraclitus, *On Nature*, c. 500 B.C.).

"Citizens must practice war while they are at peace, not in time of war" (Plato, *Laws*, c. 400 B.C.).

"The art of war is a part of the art of acquisition" (Aristotle, *Politics*, c. 350 B.C.).

"To employ an uninstructed people in war may be said to be destroying the people" (Mencius, *Book of Mencius*, c. 300 B.C.).

"A king who, while he protects his people, is defied by foes . . . must not shrink from battle" (Manu, *Laws*, c. 200 B.C.).

"From whence come wars and fighting among you? come they not hence, even of your lusts that war in your members?" (James 4:1).

"They make a desert and then call it peace" (Publius Cornelius Tacitus, *Life of Agricola*, c. 98).

"Shall it be held lawful to make an occupation of the sword, when the Lord proclaims that he who uses the sword shall perish by the sword?" (Tertullian, *On the Military Crown*, 211).

"The sword comes into the world for the delay of justice" (Talmud: Chapters of the Fathers 5:11).

"Fight in the way of Allah against those who fight against you, but begin not hostilities" (Koran: The Cow 190).

"It is legal to use stratagems in just wars" (Thomas Aquinas, *Summa Theologica*, 1274).

"The most disadvantageous peace is better than the most just war" (Desiderius Erasmus, *Proverbs*, 1500).

"War is just when it is necessary" (Niccolò Machiavelli, *The Prince*, 1513).

"O war, thou son of hell" (William Shakespeare, *II Henry VI*, 1591).

"A just fear of an imminent danger, though there be no blow given, is a lawful cause of war" (Francis Bacon, *Essays*, 1625).

"I observed everywhere in Christendom a lawlessness in warfare of which even barbarous nations would be ashamed. Nations would rush to arms on the slightest pretext or even without cause at all. And arms once taken up, there would be an end to all respect for law, whether human or divine, as though a fury had been let loose with general license for all manner of crime . . . if a man is menaced by a present force so that his life is in inevitable danger, then he must not only attack but even destroy his aggressor . . . private war may, in some cases, be lawful'' (Hugo Grotius, *On the Law of War and Peace*, 1625).

''War is nothing but a duel on a larger scale'' (Karl von Clausewitz, *On War*, 1834, posthumously).

''In all cases of conquest three things are possible. The conquering people subjugates the conquered under its own mode of production (e.g., the English in Ireland in this century and partly in India); or it leaves the old mode intact and contents itself with a tribute (Turks and Romans); or reciprocal interaction takes place, whereby something new, a synthesis arises (the Germanic conquest in part)'' (Karl Marx, *Pre-capitalist Economic Formations*, 1858).

''You say it is the good cause which sanctifies war? I say to you: it is the good war which sanctifies every cause. War and courage have done more great things than compassion'' (Friedrich Wilhelm Nietzsche, *Thus Spake Zarathustra*, 1885).

''Warfare, the great primary coöperation, is usually the mother of discipline'' (Edward Ross, *Social Control*, 1901).

''[Defensive armaments lead to] suspicion, fear and counter-arming in other nations [but a unilaterally disarming nation] runs the risk of being thwarted or beaten'' (Edward Ross, *The Social Trend*, 1922).

''The international commercial war can be done away with; the internecine capitalistic competition can be got rid of; and last, but not least, the class struggle between capital and labor can be avoided. Thus the root of war will be forever exterminated'' (Sun Yat-sen, *The International Development of China*, 1922).

''Anything that encourages the growth of emotional ties between men must operate against war'' (Sigmund Freud, *Why War?*, 1933).

''[There is destructive social change] in being 'prepared' to loose upon one another the most frightful agencies of mass murder'' (Edward Ross, *Seventy Years of It*, 1936).

''The history of the nations active in international politics shows them continuously preparing for, actively involved in, or recovering from organized violence in the form of war'' (Hans Morgenthau, *Politics Among Nations*, 1948).

''Outright war is itself too unambivalent, too undiscriminating a device to be an appropriate means for effecting a mere change of regime in another country'' (George Kennan, *Russia and the West Under Lenin and Stalin*, 1961).

''It is hardly possible to imagine that in the atomic era war could be used as an instrument of justice'' (John XXIII, *Peace on Earth*, 1963).

''In the broadest sense war is a *violent contact* of *distinct* but *similar* entities . . . a narrower definition is needed. For this purpose war will be considered the *legal condition* which *equally* permits two or more *hostile groups* to carry on a *conflict* by *armed* force'' (Quincy Wright, *A Study of War*, 1965).

''Enmity is the innate response of an organism to any and all members of its own species'' (Robert Ardrey, *The Territorial Imperative*, 1966).

''One of the most important reforms in the sphere of defense took place in 104 B.C., when Marius abolished the property criterion required for volunteers, and divided the Roman legion into 10 cohorts. Each of these cohorts consisted of 600 soldiers, the cavalry coming mainly from other lands. Caesar's victories in Gaul were facilitated by this legion, which was also responsible for the creation of the Empire'' (Panos Bardis in Instituto de Ciencias Sociales, *The Province*, 1966).

''Anthropologists, at least, have failed so far to put the results of their 'war research' to work in eliminating war'' (Martina Nettleship et al., eds., *War, Its Causes and Correlates*, 1975).

''The bases for superiority over the enemy are laid in peacetime in the process of developing the economy, modernizing the military doctrine, initiating and perfecting the elements composing the armed forces by equipping them with [superior] weapons and other technology, through mililtary training, etc.'' (*Soviet Military Encyclopedia,* 1980).

WIDOWHOOD

''If brethren dwell together, and one of them die, and have no child, the wife of the dead shall not marry without unto a stranger: her husband's brother shall go in unto her, and take her to him to wife'' (Deuteronomy 25:5).

''She [the widow] must never even mention the name of another man after her husband has died'' (Manu, *Laws*, 200 B.C.).

''The wife is bound by the law as long as her husband liveth; but if her husband be dead, she is at liberty to be married to whom she will'' (I Corinthians 7:39).

''In the case of those of you who are about to die and leave behind them wives, they should bequeath unto their wives a provision for the year without turning them out'' (Koran: The Cow 240).

''Widowhood is secondary continence'' (Thomas Aquinas, *Summa Theologica*, 1274).

''If we can find someone to blame or some explanation that will enable death to be evaded, then we have a chance of controlling things'' (C. Parkes, *Bereavement*, 1972).

''[Grief] is the expression of a profound conflict between contradictory impulses—to consolidate all that is still valuable and important in the past, and to preserve it from loss; and at the same time to re-establish a meaningful pattern of relationships, in which the loss is accepted'' (P. Marris, *Loss and Change*, 1974).

''Widowhood is often assumed to be a problem of the elderly. However . . . we did not consider that adjusting to widowhood need necessarily be linked to the problem of old age. . . . The effect of the father's death on children still at home is both a consequence of and a contributing factor to a widow's problem of adjustment'' (Cécile Strugnell, *Adjustment to Widowhood and Some Related Problems*, 1974).

''Part of the depression and despair that come to the widow in America has its roots in our strange denial of death'' (James Peterson and Michael Briley, *Widows and Widowhood*, 1977).

''The circumstances in which people are widowed vary from the totally unexpected to the predictable. But once the event has occurred it is clearly labelled so it is a crisis which society can identify. Services and help can be mobilized'' (Ann Bowling and Ann Cartwright, *Life After a Death*, 1982).

WORK, SOCIAL

''[Welfare] may mean anything from the most elevated conception of human character and destiny to the baths, refectories, and recreation grounds that figure so prominently in what is known as 'welfare work' '' (J. Hobson, *Wealth and Life*, 1929).

''The caseworkers of today should be prepared to become later the secretary of a state social welfare board or the secretary of a council of social agencies'' (Edith Abbott, *Social Welfare and Professional Education*, 1931).

''Social workers who are entirely without training in administration . . . are given important executive responsibilities'' (Elwood Street in *Social Work Year Book, 1933*, 1933).

''When the representatives of nine states met in New York on May 20, 1874, the first committee appointed was that on uniformity of statistics, a subject on which committees are still meeting'' (Arlien Johnson in *Proceedings of the National Conference of Social Work, 1946*, 1947).

''While both medical and psychiatric social work function within medicine, psychiatric social work and psychiatry seem to be largely within the same framework, whereas medical social work and medicine (in spite of overlapping in the social area) seem to be operating in different frameworks'' (Harriett Bartlett, *Social Work Practice in the Health Field*, 1961).

''Social administration has begun to develop a body of knowledge and a related set of concepts and principles. . . . In doing so, it has borrowed heavily from different disciplines in the social sciences and now faces the task of refining, extending and adapting insights, perspectives and methods so as to further our understanding of the roles and functions of social services'' (Richard Titmuss, *Commitment to Welfare*, 1968).

''A majority of social service functionaries are simply not technically qualified for the demands their positions exert'' (John Sutherland, *Managing Social Service Systems*, 1977).

''[Knowledge] must lead to action which is researchable with outcome demonstrated as effective. Change may be brought about in two ways: (a) by altering the client's behavior or manners of responding, feelings and conditions, or all of these, and (b) by altering any of the social systems or the environment in which the client functions'' (Carel Germain, ed., *Social Work Practice*, 1979).

''When an industrial society reaches an advanced stage of affluence, the rate of increase in social welfare drops below the rate of economic growth and tends ultimately to become negative'' (Xenophon Zolotas, *Economic Growth and Declining Social Welfare*, 1981).

''No one is really happy with the nation's welfare system—not the working taxpayers who must support it, not the social work professionals who must administer it, and certainly not the poor who must live under it'' (Diana DiNitto and Thomas Dye, *Social Welfare*, 1983).

''Of all fields of practice in which social workers help their clients with psychological problems, the field of health and mental health is the largest'' (Rosalind Miller and Helen Rehr, eds., *Social Work Issues in Health Care*, 1983).

''Social work pioneers of the nineteenth and twentieth centuries emphasized the need for meaningful social welfare administration, both within agencies and within communities, but they were slow to move ahead'' (Rex Skidmore, *Social Work Administration*, 1983).

WORLD, THIRD

''The country that is more developed industrially only shows, to the less developed, the image of its own future'' (Karl Marx, *Das Kapital*, 1879).

''[In China] the renaissance of a quarter of the human family is occurring before our eyes'' (Edward Ross, *The Changing Chinese*, 1911).

''The Mexican hides behind a variety of masks, but he tears them away during a fiesta or a time of grief or suffering, just as the nation has cast off all the forms that were stifling it. However, we have not yet found a way of reconciling liberty with order, the word with the act'' (Octavio Paz, *The Labyrinth of Solitude*, 1961).

''You, who are so liberal and so humane, who have such an exaggerated adoration of culture that it verges on affectation, you pretend to forget that you own colonies and that in them men are massacred in your name'' (Jean-Paul Sartre in Frantz Fanon, *The Wretched of the Earth*, 1961).

''Even the most eloquent agricultural extension expert cannot explain the advantage of growing two grains of wheat . . . if the peasant knows full well that both will go inevitably to his landlord'' (John K. Galbraith, *Economic Development in Perspective*, 1962).

''The Korean is suspicious of all moves that seem to hamper his drive for uniting his country and living in peace'' (Louise Yim, *My Forty-Year Fight for Korea*, 1967).

''[In the Third World, reforms must break] up inequalitarian and rigid economic and social stratifications. In agriculture, land reform stands out as the crucial issue. Birth control must be spread among the masses of people. A fundamental redirection of education and a vigorous adult education campaign are needed. Corruption must be stamped out'' (Gunnar Myrdal, *The Challenge of World Poverty*, 1970).

''Mexico and Taiwan have shown that even countries with limited production can, if they use suitable methods, feed their own people'' (Carle Zimmerman and Richard DuWors, eds., *Sociology of Underdevelopment*, 1970).

''Traditional economies are those where economic activity is embedded within a ritualistic and religious framework. All contemporary primitive peoples and many underdeveloped economies are basically of this type. Economic life is circular with no progress or change'' (Irving Horowitz, *Three Worlds of Development*, 1972).

''What is completely new about the present world situation is that the real incomes of almost the whole populations of some countries have been raised far above subsistence, while those of other countries remain at or near that level'' (J. Goldthorpe, *The Sociology of the Third World*, 1975).

''In developing and more or less traditionally oriented societies, females are likely to be more conservative than males are, as status ascription is ordinarily more prevalent among the former'' (Panos Bardis in T. Smith and Man Das, eds., *Sociocultural Change Since 1950*, 1978).

''The United Nations became the major forum and battleground in which the developing countries denounced current injustices'' (U Thant, *View from the UN*, 1978).

''[In Gopalpur, India] some villages in the region have lost nearly half of their population to the booming industries of the big city'' (Alan Beals, *Gopalpur*, 1980).

''Multinational corporations accompany higher income inequality and do not make for greater, but for less economic growth over the long run. And income inequality, quite apart from the presence of multinational corporations, results in slower economic growth for the majority of less developed countries'' (Volker Bornschier, *Multinational Monopolies*, 1980).

''Africa is not the poorest of the regions of the world but it is technically the most retarded . . . though Africa is the most centrally located continent, it is the most peripheral'' (Ali Mazrui, *The African Condition*, 1980).

''Economic growth has not only proved futile, in its inability to secure greater prosperity for already advanced industrial societies, but has also failed to eradicate poverty in the Third World. The gap between rich and poor nations has in fact widened after World War II'' (Xenophon Zolotas, *Economic Growth and Declining Social Welfare*, 1981).

''The hardships and suffering . . . have made our nation [Korea] capable of enduring just about any circumstance in the world. It has fostered in us the power for national development'' (Paik Chull, ed., *Korea*, 1982).

''There is an urgent need for [developing] countries to reassess their politics, industrial and otherwise, and to search for new paths to development'' (Alexander King in Günter Friedrichs and Adam Schaff, eds., *Microelectronics and Society*, 1982).

SELECTED BIBLIOGRAPHY

Abrahamsson, Bengt. *Military Professionalization and Political Power*. Beverly Hills, Calif.: Sage, 1972.

Abrams, Philip. *Historical Sociology*. Ithaca, N.Y.: Cornell University Press, 1982.

Ackerknecht, Erwin. *A Short History of Medicine*. Rev. ed. Baltimore, Md.: Johns Hopkins University Press, 1982.

Adams, Frank. *The Birth and Development of the Geological Sciences*. New York: Dover, 1954.

Adelson, Joseph, ed. *Handbook of Adolescent Psychology*. New York: Wiley, 1980.

Adorno, Theodor. *Introduction to the Sociology of Music*. New York: Seabury, 1976.

Alexander, S. *Space, Time, and Deity*. New York: Dover, 1966.

Ananson, Peter. *American Government*. Cambridge, Mass.: Winthrop, 1981.

Ariès, Philippe. *Centuries of Childhood*. New York: Vintage Books, 1962.

———. *L'Homme Devant la Mort*. Paris: Seuil, 1977.

Babbie, Earl. *The Practice of Social Research*. 2d ed. Belmont, Calif.: Wadsworth, 1979.

Babin, Claude. *Elements of Palaeontology*. New York: Wiley, 1980.

Baechler, Jean. *Revolution*. New York: Harper and Row, 1975.

Baker, Jeffrey, and Garland Allen. *The Study of Biology*. 4th ed. Reading, Mass.: Addison-Wesley, 1982.

Ballantine, Jeanne. *The Sociology of Education*. Englewood Cliffs, N.J.: Prentice-Hall, 1983.

Barash, David. *Sociobiology and Behavior*, 2d ed. New York: Elsevier, 1982.

Bardis, Panos. *Encyclopedia of Campus Unrest*. Jericho, N.Y.: Exposition Press, 1971.

———. *The Family in Changing Civilizations*. 2d ed. Simon and Schuster, 1969.

———. *Global Marriage and Family Customs*. Lexington, Mass.: Ginn, 1983.

———. *History of Thanatology*. Washington, D.C.: University Press of America, 1981.

———. *History of the Family*. Lexington, Mass.: Xerox Corporation, 1975.

Baring-Gould, S. *Strange Survivals*. London: Methuen, 1892.

Barnes, Harry. *A History of Historical Writing*. 2d rev. ed. New York: Dover, 1963.

———. *An Intellectual and Cultural History of the Western World*. 3d ed. New York: Dover, 1965.

———, ed. *An Introduction to the History of Sociology*. Chicago: University of Chicago Press, 1948.

Barnett, S. *Modern Ethology*. New York: Oxford University Press, 1981.

Bass, Bernard. *Stogdill's Handbook of Leadership*. Rev. ed. New York: Free Press, 1981.

Becker, Howard, and Harry Barnes. *Social Thought from Lore to Science*. 3d ed. New York: Dover, 1961.

Bell, E. *Men of Mathematics*. New York: Simon and Schuster, 1962.

Bellack, Alan, et al., eds. *International Handbook of Behavior Modification and Therapy*. New York: Plenum, 1982.

Berelson, Bernard, et al., eds. *Family Planning and Population Programs*. Chicago: University of Chicago Press, 1966.

———, and Gary Steiner. *Human Behavior*. New York: Harcourt, Brace, and World, 1964.

Bergin, Allen, and Sol Garfield, eds. *Handbook of Psychotherapy and Behavior Change*. New York: Wiley, 1971.

Berry, Brewton, and Henry Tischler. *Race and Ethnic Relations*. 4th ed. Boston: Houghton Mifflin, 1978.

Binstock, Robert, and Ethel Shanas, eds. *Handbook of Aging and the Social Sciences*. New York: Van Nostrand Reinhold, 1976.

Birren, James, and K. Schaie, eds. *Handbook of the Psychology of Aging*. New York: Van Nostrand Reinhold, 1977.

Black, Cyril, ed. *Comparative Modernization*. New York: Free Press, 1976.

Blalock, Ann and Hubert. *Introduction to Social Research*. 2d ed. Englewood Cliffs, N.J.: Prentice-Hall, 1982.

Blalock, Hubert. *Social Statistics*. Rev. ed. New York: McGraw-Hill, 1979.

Bogardus, Emory. *The Development of Social Thought*. 4th ed. New York: Longmans, Green, 1961.

Bond, F. *An Introduction to Journalism*. New York: Macmillan, 1964.

Borgatta, Edgar, and William Lambert, eds. *Handbook of Personality Theory and Research*. Chicago: Rand McNally, 1968.

Boring, Edwin. *A History of Experimental Psychology*. 2d ed. New York: Appleton-Century-Crofts, 1957.

Bottomore, Tom, ed. *Sociology*. Beverly Hills, Calif.: Sage, 1982.

———, and Robert Nisbet, eds. *A History of Sociological Analysis*. New York: Basic Books, 1978.

Briffault, Robert, and Bronislaw Malinowski. *Marriage*. Boston: Porter Sargent, 1956.

Brockett, Oscar. *History of the Theatre*. Boston: Allyn and Bacon, 1968.

Brown, Ray, ed. *Children and Television*. Beverly Hills, Calif.: Sage, 1976.

Bullough, Vern. *Sexual Variance in Society and History*. New York: Wiley, 1976.

Bunbury, E. *A History of Ancient Geography*. New York: Dover, 1959.

Burr, Wesley, et al., eds. *Contemporary Theories About the Family*. New York: Free Press, 1979.

Bury, J. *The Ancient Greek Historians*. New York: Dover, 1958.

Cahnman, Werner, and Alvin Boskoff, eds. *Sociology and History*. New York: Free Press, 1964.

Cattell, Raymond, and Ralph Dreger, eds. *Handbook of Modern Personality Theory*. New York: Wiley, 1977.

———, and Frank Warburton. *Objective Personality and Motivation Tests*. Urbana, Ill.: University of Illinois Press, 1967.

Chapman, Antony, and Hugh Foot, eds. *Humour and Laughter*. New York: Wiley, 1976.

Christensen, Harold, ed. *Handbook of Marriage and the Family*. Chicago: Rand McNally, 1964.

Christian, Harry, ed. *The Sociology of Journalism and the Press*. University of Keele, England: 1980.

Christian, Paul. *The History and Practice of Magic*. New York: Citadel, 1963.

Chun, Ki-Taek, et al. *Measures for Psychological Assessment*. Ann Arbor, Mich.: University of Michigan, 1974.

Clarke, Ann and A., eds. *Mental Deficiency*. 3d ed. New York: Free Press, 1974.

Coffey, William. *Geography*, New York: Methuen, 1981.

Cohen, Morris, and I. Drabkin. *A Source Book in Greek Science*. Cambridge, Mass.: Harvard University Press, 1958.

Compton, Beulah. *Introduction to Social Welfare and Social Work*. Homewood, Ill.: Dorsey, 1980.

Corsini, Raymond, ed. *Handbook of Innovative Psychotherapies*. New York: Wiley, 1981.

Coser, Lewis. *Masters of Sociological Thought*. 2d ed. New York: Harcourt Brace Jovanovich, 1977.

———, and Bernard Rosenberg, eds. *Sociological Theory*. 5th ed. New York: Macmillan, 1982.

Cox, Marian. *An Introduction to Folk-Lore*. London: Nutt, 1904.

Cranach, M. von, et al., eds. *Human Ethology*. New York: Cambridge University Press, 1979.

Crombie, A. *Medieval and Early Modern Science*. Garden City, N.Y.: Doubleday, 1959.

Das, Man, and Panos Bardis, eds. *The Family in Asia*. Winchester, Mass.: Allen and Unwin, 1979.

Davis, Gary. *Educational Psychology*. Reading, Mass.: Addison-Wesley, 1983.

Day, Alan, and Henry Degenhardt, eds. *Political Parties of the World*. Detroit: Gale, 1980.

Dellquest, Augustus. *These Names of Ours*. New York: Crowell, 1938.

DeMause, Lloyd, ed. *The Story of Childhood*. New York: Psychohistory Press, 1974.

Diamond, Solomon, ed. *The Roots of Psychology*. New York: Basic Books, 1974.

Dobler, Lavinia. *Customs and Holidays Around the World*. New York: Fleet, 1962.

Dobzhansky, Theodosius, et al. *Evolution*. San Francisco: Freeman, 1977.

Doob, Leonard. *The Pursuit of Peace*. Westport, Conn.: Greenwood Press, 1981.

Dougall, Lucy. *War and Peace in Literature*. Chicago: World Without War Publications, 1982.

Dubin, Robert, ed. *Handbook of Work, Organization, and Society*. Chicago: Rand McNally, 1976.

———. *Theory Building*. Rev. ed. New York: Free Press, 1978.

Dulles, Foster. *A History of Recreation*. New York: Appleton-Century-Crofts, 1965.

Dunnette, Marvin, ed. *Handbook of Industrial and Organizational Psychology*. Chicago: Rand McNally, 1976.

Dunning, William. *A History of Political Theories*. New York: Macmillan, 1902.

Durant, Will. *The Story of Philosophy*. New York: Time, 1962.

Eckhardt, Kenneth, and M. Ermann. *Social Research Methods*. New York: Random House, 1977.

Edmunds, Palmer. *Law and Civilization*. Washington: Public Affairs Press, 1959.

Ehrenwald, Jan, ed. *The History of Psychotherapy*. New York: Aronson, 1976.

Eitzen, D., and George Sage. *Sociology of American Sport*. 2d ed. Dubuque, Iowa: Brown, 1982.

Eliade, Mircea. *Histoire des Croyances et des Idées Religieuses*. Paris: Payot, 1976.

Eliot, Alexander. *Myths*. New York: McGraw-Hill, 1976.

English, O., and Stuart Finch. *Introduction to Psychiatry*. New York: Norton, 1964.

Escarpit, Robert. *Sociology of Literature*. Painesville, Ohio: Lake Erie College, 1965.

Etzioni, Amitai. *A Comparative Analysis of Complex Organizations*. Rev. ed. New York: Free Press, 1975.

———, and Eva Etzioni-Halevy, eds. *Social Change*. 2d ed. New York: Basic Books, 1973.

Evan, William, ed. *The Sociology of Law*. New York: Free Press, 1980.

Evans-Pritchard, Edward. *A History of Anthropological Thought*. New York: Basic Books, 1981.

Eysenck, H., ed. *Handbook of Abnormal Psychology*. 2d ed. San Diego, Calif.: Knapp, 1973.

Falkener, Edward. *Games Ancient and Oriental*. New York: Dover, 1961.

Fararo, Thomas. *Mathematical Sociology*. New York: Wiley, 1973.

Faris, Robert, ed. *Handbook of Modern Sociology*. Chicago: Rand McNally, 1964.

Flake-Hobson, Carol, et al. *Childhood Development and Relationships*. Reading, Mass.: Addison-Wesley, 1983.

Foley, Helene, ed. *Reflections of Women in Antiquity*. New York: Gordon and Breach, 1981.

Fowles, Jib, ed. *Handbook of Futures Research*. Westport, Conn.: Greenwood Press, 1978.

Fraser, J. *Of Time, Passion, and Knowledge*. New York: Braziller, 1975.

———. *Time as Conflict*. Basel, Switzerland: Birkhäuser Verlag, 1978.

———, ed. *The Voices of Time*. New York: Braziller, 1966.

———, et al., eds. *The Study of Time*. New York: Springer-Verlag, 1972.

Freeman, Howard, et al., eds. *Handbook of Medical Sociology*. 3d ed. Englewood Cliffs, N.J.: Prentice-Hall, 1979.

Friedrichs, Robert. *A Sociology of Sociology*. New York: Free Press, 1970.

Fuller, B. *A History of Philosophy*. 3d ed. New York: Holt, Rinehart, and Winston, 1960.

Gabor, Dennis. *Innovations*. London: Oxford University Press, 1970.

Gage, N., ed. *Handbook of Research on Teaching*. Chicago: Rand McNally, 1963.

Gardet, L., et al. *Cultures and Time*. Paris: Unesco, 1976.

Gardner, Eldon. *History of Biology*. 3d ed. Minneapolis, Minn.: Burgess, 1972.

Garrett, Henry. *Statistics*. 6th ed. London: Longmans, 1966.

Gazzaniga, Michael, and Colin Blakemore, eds. *Handbook of Psychobiology*. New York: Academic Press, 1975.

Gibbs, Jack. *Sociological Theory Construction*. Hinsdale, Ill.: Dryden, 1972.

Gilfillan, S. *The Sociology of Invention*. Cambridge, Mass.: M.I.T. Press, 1963.

Glaser, Daniel, ed. *Handbook of Criminology*. Chicago: Rand McNally, 1974.

Goldenson, Robert, ed. *Disability and Rehabilitation Handbook*. New York: McGraw-Hill, 1978.

Goldthorpe, J. *The Sociology of the Third World*. New York: Cambridge University Press, 1977.

Gomme, Alice. *The Traditional Games of England, Scotland, and Ireland*. New York: Dover, 1964.

Goslin, David, ed. *Handbook of Socialization Theory and Research*. Chicago: Rand McNally, 1969.

Gottlieb, David. *The Emergence of Youth Societies*. New York: Free Press, 1966.

Grant, Edward, ed. *A Source Book in Medieval Science*. Cambridge, Mass.: Harvard University Press, 1974.
Grau, Joseph, ed. *Criminal and Civil Investigation Handbook*. New York: McGraw-Hill, 1981.
Gray, Peter, ed. *The Encyclopedia of the Biological Sciences*. 2d ed. New York: Van Nostrand Reinhold, 1970.
Gruner, Charles. *Understanding Laughter*. Chicago: Nelson-Hall, 1978.
Grzimek, Bernhard, ed. *Grzimek's Encyclopedia of Ecology*. New York: Van Nostrand Reinhold, 1976.
———, ed. *Grzimek's Encyclopedia of Evolution*. New York: Van Nostrand Reinhold, 1976.
Guilford, J. *The Nature of Human Intelligence*. New York: McGraw-Hill, 1967.
Gunn, John. *Violence*. New York: Praeger, 1973.
Gunnell, John. *Political Philosophy and Time*. Middletown, Conn.: Wesleyan University Press, 1968.
Gurvitch, Georges. *The Spectrum of Social Time*. Dordrecht, Holland: Reidel, 1964.
Guthrie, W. *A History of Greek Philosophy*. Cambridge, England: University Press, 1967.
Hackwood, Frederick. *Good Cheer*. London: Unwin, 1911.
Hage, Jerald. *Techniques and Problems of Theory Construction in Sociology*. New York: Wiley, 1972.
Haley, Andrew. *Space Law and Government*. New York: Appleton-Century-Crofts, 1963.
Hall, Richard. *Occupations and the Social Structure*. 2d ed. Englewood Cliffs, N.J.: Prentice-Hall, 1975.
Hamilton, Gordon. *Theory and Practice of Social Case Work*. 2d ed. New York: Columbia University Press, 1964.
Hancock, Betsy. *School Social Work*. Englewood Cliffs, N.J.: Prentice-Hall, 1982.
Hangen, Eva. *Symbols*. Wichita, Kans.: McCormick-Armstrong, 1962.
Hardon, John. *Religions of the World*. Westminster, Md.: Newman, 1965.
Hare, A. *Handbook of Small Group Research*. 2d ed. New York: Free Press, 1976.
Harms, Ernest, and Paul Schreiber, eds. *Handbook of Counseling Techniques*. New York: Macmillan, 1963.
Harper, Howard. *Days and Customs of All Faiths*. New York: Fleet, 1957.
Harris, C. *Evolution*. Albany, N.Y.: State University of New York Press, 1981.
Haskell, Martin, and Lewis Yablonsky. *Juvenile Delinquency*. 2d ed. Chicago: Rand McNally, 1978.
Hawkes, Jacquetta, ed. *Atlas of Ancient Archaeology*. New York: McGraw-Hill, 1974.
Hawley, Amos. *Human Ecology*. New York: Ronald Press, 1950.
Hayden, Donald, and E. Alworth, eds. *Classics in Semantics*. New York: Philosophical Library, 1965.
Hecker, Melvin. *Ethnic America 1970–1977*. Dobbs Ferry, N.Y.: Oceana, 1979.
Hergenhahn, B. *An Introduction to Theories of Learning*. 2d ed. Englewood Cliffs, N.J.: Prentice-Hall, 1982.
Hernstein, Richard, and Edwin Boring, eds. *A Source Book in the History of Psychology*. Cambridge, Mass.: Harvard University Press, 1968.
Hertzler, Joyce. *Laughter*. New York: Exposition Press, 1970.
———. *A Sociology of Language*. New York: Random House, 1965.
Hessel, Alfred. *A History of Libraries*. New Brunswick, N.J.: Scarecrow Press, 1955.

Heyden, A. van der, and H. Scullard, eds. *Atlas of the Classical World*. London: Nelson, 1963.

Higham, Charles. *The Art of the American Film*. Garden City, N.Y.: Doubleday, 1974.

Hinkle, Roscoe. *Founding Theory of American Sociology 1881–1915*. Boston: Routledge and Kegan Paul, 1980.

Hockett, Charles. *A Course in Modern Linguistics*. New York: Macmillan, 1964.

Holman, Robert. *Poverty*. New York: St. Martin's, 1978.

Honigmann, John, ed. *Handbook of Social and Cultural Anthropology*. Chicago: Rand McNally, 1973.

Horowitz, Irving. *Philosophy, Science and the Sociology of Knowledge*. Springfield, Ill.: Thomas, 1961.

———. *Three Worlds of Development*. 2d ed. New York: Oxford University Press, 1972.

Horton, Paul, and Gerald Leslie. *The Sociology of Social Problems*. 6th ed. Englewood Cliffs, N.J.: Prentice-Hall, 1978.

Howard, George. *A History of Matrimonial Institutions*. New York: Humanities Press, 1964.

Howard, Ronald. *A Social History of American Family Sociology, 1865–1940*. Westport, Conn.: Greenwood Press, 1981.

Iggers, Georg, and Harold Parker, eds. *International Handbook of Historical Studies*. Westport, Conn.: Greenwood Press, 1979.

Inkeles, Alex. *Exploring Individual Modernity*. New York: Columbia University Press, 1983.

Janson, H. *History of Art*. 2d ed. New York: Prentice-Hall, 1977.

Jarvie, I. *Movies and Society*, New York: Basic Books, 1970.

Johnson, Doyle. *Sociological Theory*. New York: Wiley, 1981.

Kalisch, Beatrice. *Child Abuse and Neglect*. Westport, Conn.: Greenwood Press, 1978.

Kanner, Leo. *Child Psychiatry*. 3d ed. Springfield, Ill.: Thomas, 1966.

Kaplan, Max. *Leisure*. New York: Wiley, 1975.

Kennedy, G. *Paleoanthropology*. New York: McGraw-Hill, 1980.

Kephart, William. *Extraordinary Groups*. 2d ed. New York: St. Martin's, 1982.

———. *The Family, Society, and the Individual*. 4th ed. Boston: Houghton Mifflin, 1977.

Kess, Joseph. *Psycholinguistics*. New York: Academic Press, 1976.

Kim, Young. *World Religions*. New York: Golden Gate, 1976.

Kirk, G. *Myth*. Berkeley, Calif.: University of California Press, 1970.

Klein, D. *A History of Scientific Psychology*. New York: Basic Books, 1970.

Kneale, William and Martha. *The Development of Logic*. Oxford, England: Clarendon, 1962.

Köhler, Carl. *A History of Costume*. New York: Dover, 1963.

Kolaja, Jiri. *Social System and Time and Space*. Pittsburgh, Penn.: Duquesne University Press, 1969.

Konopka, Gisela. *Social Group Work*. 3d ed. Englewood Cliffs, N.J.: Prentice-Hall, 1983.

Kourvetaris, George, and Betty Dobratz, eds. *Political Sociology*. New Brusnwick, N.J.: Transaction, 1980.

Kroeber, Alfred. *Anthropology*. New York: Harcourt, Brace, and World, 1948.

Kruskal, William, and Judith Tanur, eds. *International Encyclopedia of Statistics*. New York: Free Press, 1978.

Lang, Kurt. *Military Institutions and the Sociology of War*. Beverly Hills, Calif.: Sage, 1972.

Laurenson, Diana, and Alan Swingewood. *The Sociology of Literature*. New York: Schocken, 1972.

Lehner, Ernst. *Symbols, Signs, and Signets*. New York: Dover, 1969.

Leiter, Kenneth. *A Primer on Ethnomethodology*. New York: Oxford University Press, 1980.

Leslie, Gerald. *The Family in Social Context*. 5th ed. New York: Oxford University Press, 1982.

Lewis, Wyndham. *Time and Western Man*. Boston: Beacon Press, 1957.

Lindberg, David, ed. *Science in the Middle Ages*. Chicago: University of Chicago Press, 1978.

Lindzey, Gardner, and Elliot Aronson, eds. *The Handbook of Social Psychology*. 2d ed. Reading, Mass.: Addison-Wesley, 1968.

Little, Roger, ed. *Handbook of Military Institutions*. Beverly Hills, Calif.: Sage, 1971.

London, Harvey, and John Exner, eds. *Dimensions of Personality*. New York: Wiley, 1978.

Loomis, Charles and Zona. *Modern Social Theories*. 2d ed. Princeton, N.J.: Van Nostrand, 1965.

Lowry, Nelson. *Rural Sociology*. 2d ed. New York: American Book Company, 1955.

Lyon, Quinter. *The Great Religions*. New York: Odyssey, 1957.

Macey, Samuel. *Clocks and the Cosmos*. Hamden, Conn.: Archon Books, 1980.

MacKenzie, Donald. *The Migration of Symbols*. New York: Knopf, 1926.

Malitz, J. *Introduction to Mathematical Logic*. New York: Springer-Verlag, 1979.

Mangen, David, and Warren Peterson, eds. *Research Instruments in Social Gerontology*. Minneapolis, Minn.: University of Minnesota Press, 1982.

March, James, ed. *Handbook of Organizations*. Chicago: Rand McNally, 1965.

Marcson, Simon, ed. *Automation, Alienation, and Anomie*. New York: Harper and Row, 1970.

Marsh, Robert. *Comparative Sociology*. New York: Harcourt, Brace and World, 1967.

Marti-Ibañez, Felix, ed. *The Epic of Medicine*. New York: Potter, 1962.

Martindale, Don. *The Nature and Types of Sociological Theory*. 2d ed. Boston: Houghton Mifflin, 1981.

Mascia, Carmin. *A History of Philosophy*. Paterson, N.J.: St. Anthony Guild, 1964.

May, Earl. *The Circus from Rome to Ringling*. New York: Dover, 1963.

Mechanic, David. *Medical Sociology*. 2d ed. New York: Free Press, 1978.

Mendoza, Manuel, and Vince Napoli. *Systems of Society*. 3d ed. Lexington, Mass.: Heath, 1982.

Merton, Robert. *The Sociology of Science*. Chicago: University of Chicago Press, 1973.

———, et al., eds. *Reader in Bureaucracy*, New York: Free Press, 1952.

Meyer, Jerome. *Great Inventions*. New York: Pocket Books, 1962.

Miller, Delbert. *Handbook of Research Design and Social Measurement*. 3d ed. New York: McKay, 1977.

———, and William Form. *Industrial Sociology*. 3d ed. New York: Harper and Row, 1980.

Mitchell, G. *A Hundred Years of Sociology*. Chicago: Aldine, 1968.

Mohan, Raj, and Don Martindale. *Handbook of Contemporary Sociology*. Westport, Conn.: Greenwood Press, 1975.

Moore, Wilbert. *Man, Time, and Society*. New York: Wiley, 1963.

Morris, Charles. *Psychology*. 4th ed. Englewood Cliffs, N.J.: Prentice-Hall, 1982.

Murcott, Anne, ed. *The Sociology of Food and Eating*. Hampshire, England: Gower, 1983.

Murdock, George. *Atlas of World Cultures*. Pittsburgh, Penn.: University of Pittsburgh Press, 1981.

———. *Ethnographic Atlas*. Pittsburgh, Penn.: University of Pittsburgh Press, 1967.

Nagler, A. *A Source Book in Theatrical History*. New York: Dover, 1959.

Neel, Ann. *Theories of Psychology*. Rev. ed. New York: Schenkman, 1977.

Nelson, Brian. *Western Political Thought*. Englewood Cliffs, N.J.: Prentice-Hall, 1982.

Nettleship, Martin, et al., eds. *War, Its Causes and Correlates*. The Hague: Mouton, 1975.

Newman, William, ed. *The Social Meanings of Religion*. Chicago: Rand McNally, 1974.

Nickell, Paulena, et al. *Management in Family Living*. 5th ed. New York: Wiley, 1976.

Nicoll, Allardyce. *The Development of the Theatre*. 4th ed. New York: Harcourt, Brace, 1957.

Nie, Norman, et al. *Statistical Package for the Social Sciences*. 2d ed. New York: McGraw-Hill, 1975.

Nisbet, Robert. *History of the Idea of Progress*. New York: Basic Books, 1980.

Noyes, John. *History of American Socialisms*. New York: Dover, 1966.

Nye, F., and Felix Berardo, eds. *Emerging Conceptual Frameworks in Family Analysis*. New York: Praeger, 1981.

Ogburn, William. *Social Change*. New York: Dell, 1966.

Olsen, Marvin, and Michael Micklin, eds. *Handbook of Applied Sociology*. New York: Praeger, 1981.

Orcutt, James. *Analyzing Deviance*. Homewood, Ill.: Dorsey, 1983.

Orum, Anthony. *Introduction to Political Sociology*. 2d ed. Englewood Cliffs, N.J.: Prentice-Hall, 1983.

Osborn, Richard, et al. *Organization Theory*. New York: Wiley, 1980.

Osofsky, Joy, ed. *Handbook of Infant Development*. New York: Wiley, 1979.

Peñalosa, Fernando. *Introduction to the Sociology of Language*. Rowley, Mass.: Newbury House, 1981.

Peters, R., ed. *Brett's History of Psychology*. Cambridge, Mass.: M.I.T. Press, 1965.

Petersen, William. *Population*. 3d ed. New York: Macmillan, 1975.

Piddington, Ralph. *The Psychology of Laughter*. New York: Gamut, 1963.

Plott, John. *Global History of Philosophy*. Delhi, India: Motilal Banarsidass, 1963.

Pool, Ithiel, and Wilbur Schramm, eds. *Handbook of Communication*. Chicago: Rand McNally, 1973.

Priestley, J. *Man and Time*. New York: Crescent Books, 1964.

Rabb, Theodore, and Robert Rotberg, eds. *The Family in History*. New York: Harper and Row, 1971.

Rapaport, David, et al. *Diagnostic Psychological Testing*. Rev. ed. New York: International Universities Press, 1968.

Raynor, Henry. *Music and Society*. New York: Taplinger, 1976.

———. *A Social History of Music*. New York: Taplinger, 1978.

Redéi, George. *Genetics*. New York: Macmillan, 1982.

Renshon, Stanley, ed. *Handbook of Political Socialization*. New York: Free Press, 1977.

Rhodes, Colbert, and Clyde Vedder. *An Introduction to Thanatology*. Springfield, Ill.: Thomas, 1983.

Ritzer, George. *Sociological Theory*. New York: Knopf, 1983.

Roach, Mary, and Joanne Eicher, eds. *Dress, Adornment, and the Social Order*. New York: Wiley, 1965.

Roback, A. *History of Psychology and Psychiatry*. 2d ed. New York: Citadel, 1964.

Roberts, Ron, and Robert Kloss. *Social Movements*. 2d ed. St. Louis, Mo.: Mosby, 1979.

Roberts, Vera. *On Stage*. New York: Harper and Row, 1962.

Robins, R. *A Short History of Linguistics*. Bloomington, Ind.: Indiana University Press, 1968.

Rosenberg, Morris, and Ralph Turner, eds. *Social Psychology*. New York: Basic Books, 1981.

Rossi, Nick, and Sadie Rafferty. *Music Through the Ages*. Washington, D.C.: University Press of America, 1981.

Rossides, Daniel. *The American Class System*. Boston: Houghton Mifflin, 1976.

———, *The History and Nature of Sociological Theory*. Boston: Houghton Mifflin, 1978.

Roucek, Joseph, ed. *Social Control for the 1980s*. Westport, Conn.: Greenwood Press, 1978.

Runes, Dagobert, ed. *Classics in Logic*. New York: Philosophical Library, 1962.

———, ed. *Treasury of World Philosophy*. Paterson, N.J.: Littlefield, Adams, 1959.

———, ed. *Treasury of World Science*. Paterson, N.J.: Littlefield, Adams, 1962.

Sahakian, William, ed. *History of Psychology*. Itasca, Ill.: Peacock, 1968.

Samuelson, Paul. *Economics*. 3d ed. New York: McGraw-Hill, 1976.

Sanders, Irwin. *Rural Society*. Englewood Cliffs, N.J.: Prentice-Hall, 1977.

Sarton, George. *A History of Science*. New York: Wiley, 1964.

Schudson, Michael. *Discovering the News*. New York: Basic Books, 1978.

Schwartz, Richard, and Jerome Skolnick, eds. *Society and the Legal Order*. New York: Basic Books, 1970.

Scott, Mel. *American City Planning Since 1890*. Berkeley, Calif.: University of California Press, 1969.

Sellin, J. *Slavery and the Penal System*. New York: Elsevier, 1976.

Shaw, Marvin. *Group Dynamics*. New York: McGraw-Hill, 1976.

———, and Philip Costanzo. *Theories of Social Psychology*. New York: McGraw-Hill, 1970.

Shinn, Ronald. *Culture and School*. Scranton, Penn.: International Textbook Company, 1972.

Siegman, Aron, and Stanley Feldstein, eds. *Nonverbal Behavior and Communication*. Hillsdale, N.J.: Lawrence Erlbaum, 1978.

Skornia, Harry. *Television and Society*. New York: McGraw-Hill, 1965.

Slotkin, J., ed. *Readings in Early Anthropology*. Chicago: Aldine, 1965.

Smelser, Neil. *The Sociology of Economic Life*. Englewood Cliffs, N.J.: Prentice-Hall, 1963.

———, and R. Warner. *Sociological Theory*. Morristown, N.J.: General Learning Press, 1976.

Smigel, Erwin, ed. *Handbook on the Study of Social Problems*. Chicago: Rand McNally, 1971.

Soper, Edmund. *The Religions of Mankind*. 3d ed. New York: Abingdon, 1951.
Sorell, Walter. *The Dance Through the Ages*. New York: Grosset and Dunlap, 1967.
Sorokin, Pitirim. *Contemporary Sociological Theories*. New York: Harper and Row, 1964.
———. *Modern Historical and Social Philosophies*. New York: Dover, 1963.
———. *Sociological Theories of Today*. New York: Harper and Row, 1966.
Spates, James, and John Macionis. *The Sociology of Cities*. New York: St. Martin's, 1982.
Spiegel, Henry. *The Growth of Economic Thought*. Englewood Cliffs, N.J.: Prentice-Hall, 1971.
Stahl, William. *Roman Science*. Madison, Wis.: University of Wisconsin Press, 1962.
Stamatis, Evangelos. *Philogelos*. Athens: Karydi-Siaphaka, 1970.
Stark, W. *The Sociology of Knowledge*. London: Routledge and Kegan Paul, 1967.
Stineman, Esther. *Women's Studies*. Littleton, Colo.: Libraries Unlimited, 1979.
Strasser, Hermann, and Susan Randall. *An Introduction to Theories of Social Change*. London: Routledge and Kegan Paul, 1981.
Straus, Murray, and Bruce Brown. *Family Measurement Techniques*. Rev. ed. Minneapolis, Minn.: University of Minnesota Press, 1978.
Strauss, Leo, and Joseph Cropsey, eds. *History of Political Philosophy*. 2d ed. Chicago: Rand McNally, 1972.
Street, David. *Handbook of Contemporary Urban Life*. San Francisco: Jossey-Bass, 1978.
Struening, Elmer, and Marcia Guttentag, eds. *Handbook of Evaluation Research*. Beverly Hills, Calif.: Sage, 1975.
Stubbe, Hans. *History of Genetics*. Cambridge, Mass.: M.I.T. Press, 1972.
Summers, Montague. *The History of Witchcraft and Demonology*. New Hyde Park, N.Y.: University Books, 1965.
Sutherland, Edwin, and Donald Cressey. *Criminology*. 10th ed. Philadelphia: Lippincott, 1978.
Sweetland, Richard, and Daniel Keyser, eds. *Tests*. Kansas City, Mo.: Test Corporation of America, 1983.
Szacki, Jerzy. *History of Sociological Thought*. Westport, Conn.: Greenwood Press, 1979.
Taton, René, ed. *History of Science*. New York: Basic Books, 1963.
Timasheff, Nicholas. *Sociological Theory*. 3d ed. New York: Random House, 1967.
Trattner, Walter. *From Poor Law to Welfare State*. 2d ed. New York: Free Press, 1979.
Travers, Robert, ed. *Second Handbook of Research on Teaching*. Chicago: Rand McNally, 1973.
Triandis, Harry, and Wiliam Lambert, eds. *Handbook of Cross-Cultural Psychology*. Boston: Allyn and Bacon, 1980.
Turner, Jonathan. *The Structure of Sociological Theory*. 3d ed. Homewood, Ill.: Dorsey, 1982.
Turner, Ralph, and Lewis Killian. *Collective Behavior*. 2d ed. Englewood Cliffs, N.J.: Prentice-Hall, 1972.
Turner, William. *History of Philosophy*. Boston: Ginn, 1957.
Ulich, Robert. *History of Educational Thought*. Rev. ed. New York: American Book Company, 1968.
Ullmann, Stephen. *Semantics*. New York: Barnes and Noble, 1964.
United States Department of Commerce. *Social Indicators 1976*. Washington, D.C.: 1977.

Urlin, Ethel. *A Short History of Marriage*. London: Rider, 1913.
Usher, Abbott. *A History of Mechanical Inventions*. Boston: Beacon Press, 1959.
Vagts, Alfred. *A History of Militarism*. Rev. ed. New York: Free Press, 1967.
Wagner, Leopold. *Manners, Customs, and Observances*. London: Heinemann, 1894.
———. *Names and Their Meaning*. 3d ed. Detroit: Gale, 1968.
Walsh, William. *Curiosities of Popular Customs*. Philadelphia: Lippincott, 1898.
Ward, Russell. *The Aging Experience*. 2d ed. New York: Harper and Row, 1984.
Warren, Roland. *The Community in America*. 3d ed. Chicago: Rand McNally, 1978.
Warshay, Leon. *The Current State of Sociological Theory*. New York: McKay, 1975.
Watson, Robert. *The Great Psychologists from Aristotle to Freud*. Philadelphia: Lippincott, 1963.
Wells, Alan. *Social Institutions*. New York: Basic Books, 1970.
Whelan, Christopher. *Sociological Approaches to Law*. New York: St. Martin's Press, 1981.
Whitehouse, David and Ruth. *Archaeological Atlas of the World*. San Francisco: Freeman, 1975.
Whitrow, G. *The Natural Philosophy of Time*. 2d ed. Oxford, England: Clarendon, 1980.
Whittick, Arnold. *Symbols, Signs, and Their Meaning*. London: Hill, 1960.
Wigmore, John. *A Panorama of the World's Legal Systems*. Washington, D.C.: Washington Law Book Company, 1928.
Williams, L., and Henry Steffens. *The History of Science in Western Civilization*. Washington, D.C.: University Press of America, 1977.
Williams, Thomas. *Socialization*. Englewood Cliffs, N.J.: Prentice-Hall, 1983.
Wilson, Edward. *Sociobiology*. Cambridge, Mass.: Harvard University Press, 1975.
Wilson, John. *Religion in American Society*. Englewood Cliffs, N.J.: Prentice-Hall, 1978.
Wilson, Robert, ed. *The Arts in Society*. New York: Prentice-Hall, 1964.
Wolman, Benjamin, ed. *Handbook of Clinical Psychology*. New York: McGraw-Hill, 1965.
———, ed. *Handbook of General Psychology*. Englewood Cliffs, N.J.: Prentice-Hall, 1973.
———, ed. *Handbook of Parapsychology*. New York: Van Nostrand Reinhold, 1977.
Wormser, René. *The Story of the Law*. New York: Simon and Schuster, 1962.
Wright, Quincy. *A Study of War*. 2d ed. Chicago: University of Chicago Press, 1965.
Yinger, J. *Countercultures*. New York: Free Press, 1982.
Young, Pauline. *Scientific Social Surveys and Research*. 4th ed. Englewood Cliffs, N.J.: Prentice-Hall, 1966.
Zampaglione, Gerardo. *L'Idea della Pace nel Mondo Antico*. Turin, Italy: Eri-Edizioni Rai, 1967.
Zimmerman, Carle, and Richard DuWors, eds. *Sociology of Underdevelopment*. Montreal: Copp Clark, 1970.
Zusne, Leonard. *Names in the History of Psychology*. New York: Wiley, 1975.

NAME INDEX

SUBJECT INDEX

Italicized page numbers indicate the location of the main entry headings in the text. *See* references to names refer to entries in the Name Index.

About the Author

PANOS BARDIS is Professor of Sociology at the University of Toledo, Ohio. Currently the Editor and Book Review Editor of the *International Social Science Review* and the *International Journal on World Peace*, he has written and edited numerous books, articles, and papers for a wide range of professional publications.